THE BOOK
of
ENGLISH
MAGIC

Also by Philip Carr-Gomm

Sacred Places
What do Druids Believe?
Druid Mysteries
The Druid Way
The Elements of the Druid Tradition
Druidcraft – The Magic of Wicca & Druidry
In the Grove of the Druids
The Druid Animal Oracle (co-author)
The Druid Plant Oracle (co-author)
The DruidCraft Tarot (co-author)
La Force des Celtes (co-author)
The Book of Druidry (editor)
The Druid Renaissance (editor)

Also by Richard Heygate

Endangered Species (co-author)

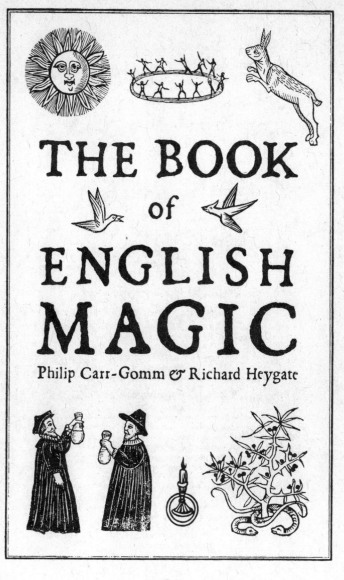

THE BOOK

of

ENGLISH

MAGIC

Philip Carr-Gomm & Richard Heygate

THE OVERLOOK PRESS
New York, NY

This paperback edition first published in the United States in 2012 by
The Overlook Press, Peter Mayer Publishers, Inc.
141 Wooster Street
New York, NY 10012
www.overlookpress.com
For bulk and special orders, please contact sales@overlookny.com

Cataloging-in-Publication Data is available from the Library of Congress

Typesetting by Servis Filmsetting Ltd, Stockport, Cheshire
Manufactured in the United States of America

4 6 8 10 9 7 5 3
ISBN 978-1-4683-0069-7

To all the magicians of England, who have allowed us to understand, and sometimes experience, the extraordinary 'other' world in which they live.

∾ Contents ∾

⁓ Preface ⁓

The Book of English Magic explores the curious and little-known fact that, of all the countries in the world, England has the richest history of magical lore and practice.

English authors such as J.R.R. Tolkien, C.S. Lewis, Terry Pratchett, Susanna Clarke, Philip Pullman and J.K. Rowling dominate the world of magic in fiction, but while children accept the magical world without reservation, most adults are not only sceptical of its place in modern society but are ignorant of the part magic and magicians have played in English history.

From the earliest times, England has acted as home to generations of eccentrics and scholars who have researched and explored every conceivable kind of occult art. *The Book of English Magic* surveys England's magical past from the moment the first humans inhabited her shores to our present-day fascination with all things magical. Here, historical explorations and biographies of leading figures are combined with suggestions for sites to visit and experiments to perform that will allow you to begin experiencing for yourself the world of magic and enchantment that has intrigued generations of seekers. In the following pages you will also meet many of England's leading magicians and hear directly from them how and why they practise their art.

In *The Book of English Magic*, an extraordinary parallel world is revealed in which secret societies still practise ritual magic, our ancient landscape yields up its hidden powers, and the lost magical origins of centuries of tradition and folklore are revealed.

Key

1. Mooted site of Camelot
2. Arthur's Chair
3. Pendragon Castle
4. The Cumbrian Round Table
5. Greymoor Hill
6. Bewcastle Cross
7. Bede's World
8. Mother Shipton's Cave
9. Pendle Hill
10. Cresswell Crags
11. Biddulph Moor
12. Church of St Chad
13. Kinver Edge rock houses
14. Royston Cave
15. Witches cottage, Brickett Wood
16. Mother Ludlam's Cave
17. Co-Masonry temples
18. Garway
19. Golden Valley
20. Meon Hill
21. Shell Grotto
22. Barge Inn
23. White Horse of Uffington & Dragon Hill
24. Wayland's Smithy
25. Rollright Stones
26. Sulgrave Manor
27. St John's College, Cambrige – university of Dee & Nichols
28. Rufus Stone, New Forest
29. Kingly Vale
30. Long Man of Wilmington
31. Silbury Hill
32. West Kennet Long Barrow
33. Wilton House
34. Cadbury Castle
35. Cerne Abbas Giant
36. Exeter Castle
37. Witchcraft Museum, Boscastle
38. Merry Maidens
39. Steyning
40. Nine Maidens
41. Grimes Graves
42. The Devil's Arrows
43. Rudston Monolith
44. Old Bewick
45. Chislehurst Caves

A Magical Map of England

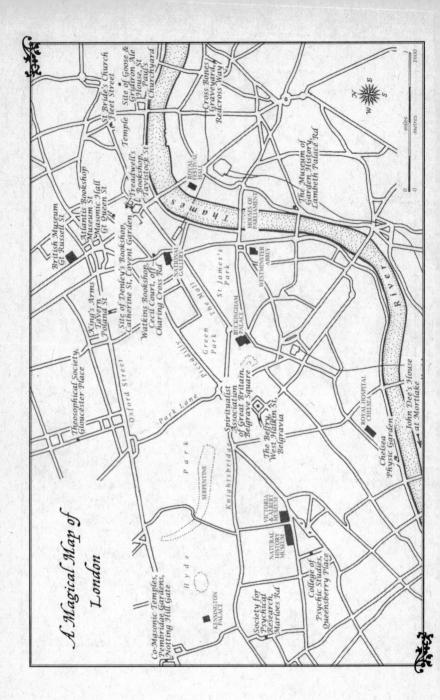

A Magical Map of London

Co-Masonic Temples, Pembridge Gardens, Notting Hill Gate

Theosophical Society, Gloucester Place

British Museum, Gt Russell St

Atlantis Bookshop, Museum St

Masonic Hall, Gt Queen St

King's Arms Tavern, Poland St

Site of Denley's Bookshop, Catherine St, Covent Garden

Watkins Bookshop, Cecil Court, off Charing Cross Rd

St Bride's Church, Fleet Street

Site of Goose & Gridiron Ale House, St Paul's Churchyard

Cross Bones Graveyard, Redcross Way

The Temple

Treadwell's Bookshop, Tavistock St

Thames

NATIONAL GALLERY

ROYAL FESTIVAL HALL

HOUSES OF PARLIAMENT

The Museum of Garden History, Lambeth Palace Rd

Oxford Street

Park Lane

Piccadilly

Green Park

St James's Park

The Mall

BUCKINGHAM PALACE

WESTMINSTER ABBEY

RIVER

Hyde Park

SERPENTINE

Knightsbridge

Spiritualist Association of Great Britain, Belgrave Square

The Belfry, West Halkin St, Belgravia

ROYAL HOSPITAL CHELSEA

John Dee's House at Mortlake

KENNINGTON PALACE

Society for Psychical Research, Marloes Rd

NATURAL HISTORY MUSEUM

VICTORIA & ALBERT MUSEUM

College of Psychic Studies, Queensberry Place

Chelsea Physic Garden

N
W E
S

miles
metres
0   1600

At the present day, Britannia is still fascinated by magic, and performs its rites with much ceremony . . .

PLINY, *HISTORIA NATURALIS*, XXX, 13

INTRODUCTION

Magick is a faculty of wonderful virtue, full of most high mysteries, containing the most profound contemplation of most secret things ...

HENRY CORNELIUS AGRIPPA, *THREE BOOKS OF OCCULT PHILOSOPHY*, (FROM THE FIRST ENGLISH TRANSLATION, 1651)

Every country has its magic: in its wild places, in its history, and in the traditions of its healers and mystics. The lands that border England have a special magic – Wales and Scotland are brimming with tales of wizards and seers – but this book focuses on the country that has grown, by design or quirk of fate, into the world's richest storehouse of magical lore: England.

Our story begins in a bookshop. Treadwell's in London's Covent Garden is everything a bookshop should be – warm, inviting, comfortable – and yet most people hurry past it, because it specialises in a subject they don't believe in: magic.

Magic is fun for children, and for the child in all of us, but it belongs to the world of fantasy books and films, and Treadwell's doesn't stock these – it's not a place for children. And it's not a place for people interested in conjuring and stage magic. Treadwell's is a specialist bookshop for the practising occultist and wizard.

A century ago Edward Bulwer-Lytton began his Victorian occult novel *Zanoni* in just such a shop: 'It is possible that among my readers there may be a few not unacquainted with an old-book shop, existing some years since in the neighbourhood of Covent Garden . . . there, perhaps, throughout all Europe, the curious might discover the most notable collection, ever amassed by an enthusiast, of the works of alchemist, cabalist, and astrologer.'

Bulwer-Lytton was a prolific novelist, a contemporary and close friend of Charles Dickens, and the owner of Knebworth House in Hertfordshire, which is now open to the public. Today you can walk through his sitting room and library, and imagine his gaunt figure studying astrology beside the fire, with a long pipe of opium in one hand. And just like the hero in *Zanoni*, who discovers a doorway to the world of magic in a bookshop in Covent Garden, you can walk into Treadwell's to begin a journey of exploration into the hidden world of magic – its history and its power to stir the imagination.

Lord Edward Bulwer-Lytton (1803–1873), novelist, playwright, poet, politician and member of the Rosicrucian Society in England (Societas Rosicruciana in Anglia). Bulwer-Lytton's fictional bookshop was based on London's most important occult bookshop, run by John Denley in Catherine Street, Covent Garden.

The best place to start finding out about magic is not Cairo or Calcutta, Paris or Prague, but London. Just as the English language has grown to become the dominant world language in science, diplomacy and commerce, so fate and history have decreed that England, and in particular its capital, has over the centuries become the most important repository and breeding-ground of the magical arts in all the world.

Here in ancient times the Druids cast their spells before Caesar's armies ever crossed the Thames. Here Dr John Dee, astrologer to Queen Elizabeth I, amassed a vast library of occult books and consulted angels through his magic mirror of obsidian. Here robed magicians of the Hermetic Order of the Golden Dawn invoked the gods, and naked witches danced – as they dance still – in suburban sitting rooms.

It was in London that the mediums of the Spiritualist Association of Great Britain in Belgrave Square began exploring the mysteries of life after death, and where, in nearby West Halkin Street, between the two world wars, the novelist and mystic Dion Fortune performed her Rites of Isis before invited guests.

The tradition continues. The owner of Treadwell's, Dr Christina Oakley-Harrington, is steeped in a knowledge of magic, and is well aware of London's significance in its history. An American, she was first drawn to London because she had a strong feeling for the Elizabethan period, 'when every street corner in London would have a practising astrologer, and one could almost breathe the magic in the air!'

She is also conscious of the role a bookshop can play in the life of an individual. When someone goes into a bookshop, they are standing at a series of gateways into other worlds – each book can pull them into a different universe. Open one and they are spirited to South America; open another and they enter the world of astrophysics. Sitting at the desk every day, and often in the evenings too, Christina acts as gatekeeper, steering her customers expertly in the direction she believes will be the most helpful. 'Going into an occult bookshop is a magical experience in its own right,' she explains. 'In most cities in the world there is probably an occult bookshop. Visitors start by wandering aimlessly around, perhaps afraid to speak to the person behind the till, not realising that this is all part of their initiatory experience. And then they pick up a book, or ask a question – and before they know it they are set on a magical path.'

Treadwell's stocks plenty of second-hand books, which Virginia Woolf called 'Wild Books, Homeless Books', because, explains Christina, 'they have already had a journey, so they have extra energy in them from where they have been before, and they're looking for a home'. Christina likes being part of this tradition. 'When a new customer asks me to recommend a book I ask them a few general questions to find out where they are starting from. Then I suggest that they shouldn't feel rushed, but should just allow the books on the shelves to "speak" to them. There are usually lots of chairs and sofas in occult bookshops, so that the books can draw you in and fire your imagination.'

❧

The story of magic in England begins as the very first humans start to populate the land, seeking solace and healing in the powers of nature. As layer after layer of magical knowledge and practice build upon each other across the centuries, the story becomes more complex and colourful, the cast of characters ever wider, as we reach the modern era, when more people practise magic in England than at any other time in her history.

If you scratch the surface of our so-called 'normal' world you will soon discover witches and wizards, Druids and alchemists, astrologers and mystics in abundance, leading normal and yet also very unusual lives – here in England in the twenty-first century.

Their world, and the story of the different kinds of magic they practise, is all around us – written in the land, in ancient monuments, in old city streets, in museums and in the stories of those who have dared to practise the old arts, often risking their own lives. And yet few people are aware of the fact that England just happens to have acquired over the centuries the most varied, most extraordinary magical history of all the countries on earth.

The purpose of this book is to explore this history and the magic that is still practised here today. Moving through time, each chapter surveys the scene, and suggests places to visit and things to do that will help you discover and experience the essence of each of the kinds of magic being explored. In creating this book we've interviewed over fifty contemporary magicians and many of these are presented here, along with explorations of magical fiction, biography and autobiography, and comprehensive resource guides, so that – if you choose – you can delve deeper into this strange and fascinating world.

Who should read this book, you may ask? The answer is simple: anyone with an open mind who seeks adventure . . .

∽ What is Magic? ∾

Magic, madam, is like wine and, if you are not used to it,
it will make you drunk.

SUSANNA CLARKE, THE LADIES OF GRACE ADIEU

In the seventeenth century Sir Walter Raleigh wrote that 'The art of magic is the art of worshipping God'. Three hundred years later the infamous magician Aleister Crowley reintroduced the archaic 'k' into his spelling of magic and defined it as 'the Science and Art of causing Change to occur in conformity with Will'. Later he said, 'Magick is the Science of understanding oneself and one's conditions. It is the Art of applying that understanding in action.'

Dion Fortune, who started her own magical lodge in 1922,

The Fraternity of the Inner Light, revised his definition to that of 'causing changes in consciousness at will'.

The Cheltenham magician W.G. Gray was more specific, and held quite a different opinion to Raleigh, when he wrote in 1969 that magic is: 'Man's most determined effort to establish an actual working relationship through himself between his Inner and Outer states of being. By magic, Man shows that he is not content to be simply a pawn in the Great Game, but wants to play on his own account. Man the meddler becomes Man the Magician, and so learns the rules the hard way, for magic is concerned with Doing, while mysticism is concerned with Being'.

CHAPTER ONE

ANCIENT ROOTS AND MAGIC WANDS

Caves and the Hidden Treasure of the Land

She is not any common Earth
Water or wood or air,
But Merlin's Isle of Gramarye,
Where you and I will fare.

RUDYARD KIPLING, *PUCK OF POOK'S HILL*

The image of the magician is exciting and tantalising, and familiar to us all. Think of Merlin or Gandalf and we think of excitement, mystery and adventure. But what do we feel or even know about real magicians, not of the stage variety, but those figures who throughout history have practised the kind of magic that for centuries was a forbidden art?

Secretly we would all probably like to know a magician, or even be one. And – extraordinary as it may seem – there has never been a greater opportunity to fulfil either of these ambitions, since there are now more practising wizards in England than at any other time in her history. Some will see this as an example of the triumph of irrationalism, others as evidence of a rebirth in an understanding of the world that is only now being touched upon by the most advanced physicists and cosmologists.

A magician can be a philosopher or a fraud, a master of illusion or a dedicated seeker of the Truth. In the image of the magus we see the scientist and the artist, the sage and seer, the superhuman figure who can protect us and the imposter who, like the Wizard of Oz, stands behind a curtain wielding not a magic wand but simply a megaphone. Part of the journey towards an understanding of magic involves untangling these contradictory images – of learning to distinguish between the charlatan and the genius, that sometimes exist within the same person.

But what exactly is magic and what inspired our ancestors to begin its practice? Magic begins in darkness – the darkness of the earth, the sky and the body – and an awareness of it is born with light. Seeing green shoots appearing out of the dark soil, the sun, moon and stars rising and setting in the sky, babies emerging from the womb, fire leaping up in the midst of a cold night, were all primal experiences that awakened that sense of awe and wonder that lies at the heart of the magical experience.

From the moment the ice-sheets melted and the first tribes began to colonise this small spot of earth, magic was born in England. And, fittingly for a birth, it emerged initially from caves.

Robin Hood cave, Cresswell Crags.

In the centre of the country, on the border between Derbyshire and Nottinghamshire, five caves at Cresswell Crags show us that 45,000 years ago some of the first colonisers of the primeval landscape of England inhabited caves. The evidence of paintings in these caves, dated to 12,000 years ago, shows that by then they were being decorated, and used for magical ceremonies.

The most famous caverns of this kind are at Lascaux in France, where vast figures of animals are painted on the walls, together with a half-man, half-beast, known as the 'shaman'. An even older cave has now been found in France at Chauvet, with even more spectacular images, and further south in Spain the Altamira caves are just as inspiring. But now, with new dating techniques and the ability to analyse rock surfaces more accurately, scientists have discovered that the caves at Cresswell Crags were also painted with scenes of people and animals. Due to our colder, wetter weather, however, all that remains are some images of deer and four nested, elongated shapes, which might depict birds but which are believed by scholars to be highly stylised naked women, with large, projecting buttocks and knees curved in a ritual dance. Their legs can no longer be seen, which is why the image is now known as 'The Legless Ladies of Cresswell Crags'.[1]

In a cave you are as if in a womb, safe in the darkness of the earth's belly. And it was almost certainly in caves that the very first magical rites were conducted, with initiates emerging into the light of dawn or beneath the panoply of stars, having undergone various ordeals and preparations for their next phase of life.

Freemasons' Hall, headquarters of the United Grand Lodge of England.

Much of magical practice today is still influenced by this earliest of activities. If you come to Covent Garden late in the afternoon, you will notice in Great Queen Street, just around the corner from Treadwell's bookshop, a peculiar phenomenon. The cafés and pubs are filled with men dressed in sober black suits, all carrying small cases, like piccolo players biding their time before the evening's performance at the Royal Opera House. Inside these cases are an apron, white gloves and often a magic wand. These men are Freemasons waiting for their Lodge meeting at Freemasons' Hall. At these meetings they will practise rites, developed in the seventeenth century, that carry echoes of these earliest of magical practices. They will be blindfolded to produce the experience of darkness, and they will use wands, in an echo of the very first magic wands ever found in the world – in the Paviland cave in Wales, where broken mammoth tusks, unearthed beside an ochre-coloured skeleton, are thought to have been deliberately snapped in recognition of the life that had ended.

Away from London, in the countryside once more, we can see that magic has escaped from its cavernous origins and is written everywhere in the land around us. England is strewn with standing stones and stone circles, holy wells, barrows and strange mounds known as 'toots' or 'tumps'. These flat-topped hills are artificial and, like their cousins the rounded barrows, were built around 5,000 years ago. The largest of their kind is Silbury Hill in Wiltshire, but there are other similar, less well-known mounds found all over the countryside – from Mutlow in Cambridgeshire and Ludlow in Shropshire, to Lewes in Sussex.

Silbury Hill, Wiltshire.

Despite the sprawling towns and ugly mass of roads that blight the landscape, you can still walk on pathways that are thousands of years old and that run from one ancient magical site to another. Pulling into a lay-by on the A420 in Oxfordshire, you can immediately join the well-worn Ridgeway and walk to Wayland's Smithy (*right*) – a great barrow filled with stories of ghosts and

Read about this Period in Fiction

Green Man, Henry Treece (The Bodley Head, 1968)
Ancient beliefs based in the cycles of the land underpin
the story of the Barley Queen, the Green Man and the
often brutal magical practices involved in fertility and
kingship.

Mythago Wood, Robert Holdstock (Gollancz, 2007)
Within an ancient wood with a living spirit, magical
reality holds sway and mythagos, archetypes, monsters
and folk heroes constantly re-enact their legends, bringing
danger and magic to the family who live on its edge.

magic – before walking on until you stand above the White Horse
of Uffington, looking down on to yet another flat-topped artificial
mound: Dragon Hill.

These places are intimately
connected with England's
magical history. Over the centuries, the earliest primal traditions of magic in this land
– the remains of which can
be seen in cave and standing
stone, tump and stone circle
– have been enriched and
developed as a result of immi-
gration, conquest and impor-
tation. Each of these places has
its own stories and customs,
which often link one site with

The White Horse of Uffington.

another, or are set within the same sacred landscape. So, up on the Ridgeway, if you leave a silver coin at the entrance of Wayland's Smithy, your horse will be shod by a ghostly blacksmith; and if you travel on to the great white horse a mile along the track and make a wish beside its eye, it is said it will come true.

✍ Finding the Mythic Landscape ✍

Walking these old tracks can provide both clue and starting point for an exploration of magic. To begin this study we do not need to worry about arcane formulae and complicated rituals. Marcel Proust got to the heart of the matter when he said: 'The real magic

of discovery lies not in seeking new landscapes, but in having new eyes.'

It is as if there is another world just waiting to be discovered if only we can learn to see in a new way. Up until the seventeenth century most people in England took little notice of the prehistoric monuments that littered the land. Viewing them as a nuisance, they often dismantled them to clear fields or to provide building materials. Even so, folklore and stories lingered around many of them, such as the Rollright Stones in Oxfordshire, which were said to be uncountable.

When antiquarians such as John Aubrey and William Stukeley began to survey these old monuments in the seventeenth and early eighteenth centuries, and suggested they were the temples of the Druids, it dawned upon the intelligentsia that they inhabited a landscape of sacred sites.

JOHN AUBREY, 1626–1697

John Aubrey, famous for *Brief Lives*, his collection of colourful and gossipy biographies, was an antiquary and writer, born in Wiltshire and educated at Trinity College, Oxford.

In 1648, when only twenty-two, he came across the great stones at Avebury while hunting with friends who believed the stones were natural formations in the landscape. Aubrey, however, saw them as the remains of a great prehistoric temple of the Druids. He began to explore the countryside, discovering and writing about many of the magical places that have now become familiar landmarks, such as Stonehenge and Wayland's Smithy. In 1663, he became a member of the Royal Society and accompanied King Charles II to Avebury, recounting: 'His

Majesty commanded me to dig at the bottom of the stones . . . to try if I could find any human bones; but I did not do it.' The fifty-six post-holes at Stonehenge were named 'Aubrey Holes' in his honour by archaeologists in the 1920s.

Monumenta Britannica, his great survey of the ancient monuments of Britain, which he originally titled *Templa Druidum* or *Temples of the Druids*, was published only in 1981 and was edited in Lyme Regis by John Fowles, author of the novel *The Magus*.

WILLIAM STUKELEY, 1687–1765

William Stukeley is known as the 'founding father' of archaeology. Born in Lincolnshire, he attended Corpus Christi College, Cambridge, and studied medicine at St Thomas's Hospital in London. In 1717, he became a Fellow of the Royal Society and in 1721 was initiated into Freemasonry at the Salutation Tavern in Tavistock Street, Covent Garden, just a few doors from the current Treadwell's bookshop.

Inspired by Aubrey's work, Stukeley believed that the prehistoric landscape of Britain had been laid out in a sacred pattern by the ancient Druids. This pattern involved great serpent-forms, which he discerned in the stone circles and earthworks he surveyed. Linking these to local tales of dragons and dragon-slayers, he named the sites 'Templa Dracontia' – dragon temples. His theories were revealed in his book, *Stonehenge, a Temple Restored to the British Druids*, published in 1740, and *Abury, a Temple of the British Druids*, published three years later.

Stukeley was fascinated by Pythagoreanism, Neoplatonism, and the Egyptian Mysteries, as well as Druidism. His friends called him 'The Druid', and after he had met Augusta, Princess of Wales, the mother of the future George III, he wrote to her as 'Veleda, Archdruidess of Kew'. He created a Druid temple in his garden, laying it out as a sacred landscape, with an apple tree covered with mistletoe at the centre of concentric circles of hazels and evergreens. Beside an altar he built a tumulus, and when his wife miscarried they ritually buried the foetus on the camomile lawn they had planted in front of the altar. After an earlier miscarriage, a friend had written to Stukeley, urging him to 'assemble the sacred college of druids'. Unfortunately no further references to this mysterious group have been found.[2]

In 1730 he was ordained as vicar of All Saints Church in Stamford in Lincolnshire, and died in London on 3 March 1765.[3]

✎ Ley Lines ✎

Imagine a fairy chain stretched from mountain peak to mountain peak, as far as the eye could reach . . .

ALFRED WATKINS, *THE OLD STRAIGHT TRACK* (1925)

Three centuries after Aubrey and Stukeley, Alfred Watkins, a landscape photographer in Herefordshire, noticed that ancient sites seemed to be aligned with others near by.

His idea was that our ancestors built and used prominent features in the landscape as navigation points. These features included prehistoric standing stones and stone circles, barrows and mounds, hill forts and earthworks, ancient moats, old pre-Reformation churches, old crossroads and fords, prominent hilltops and fragments of old, straight tracks.

Watkins went on to suggest that the lines connecting these ancient sites represented old trackways or routes that were followed in prehistoric times for the purposes of trade or religious rites, and in 1921 he coined the term 'ley lines' to describe these alignments. Watkins founded the Old Straight Track Club to encourage ley hunting, and members spent their weekends looking for traces of these ancient trails.

The old track was no mean achievement in surveying and engineering. Road-making was not part of its scheme, for the attitude seems to have been: 'Mother earth is good enough for you to walk or ride on, and we will pave a way through the streams, soft places, and ponds; our chief job is to point the way.' This the old ley-men did magnificently.

ALFRED WATKINS, *THE OLD STRAIGHT TRACK*

*Members of the Old Straight Track Club having a picnic
in the 1930s. A bearded Watkins walks towards the
camera.*

ALFRED WATKINS, 1855–1935

Famous for his concept of ley lines, Alfred Watkins, a Fellow of the Royal Photographic Society, was also a keen amateur archaeologist and antiquarian.

Alfred Watkins spent his long life in the city of Hereford, working first for his father's brewery and flour mill. His passion for photography led him to invent an exposure meter, which he manufactured in a room at the mill. The Watkins Meter Company was formed to sell them at a guinea each. He invented and produced more photographic equipment, and published two manuals on photography. In 1910 he was made a Fellow of the Royal Photographic Society. While at the mill he also formulated a new flour blend for making brown bread, known as the Vagos or 'Wandering Maiden' loaf, from the Roman name for the River Wye.

Watkins was a man of many enthusiasms. A keen bee-keeper, he gave public talks to promote the Liberal Party, and often lectured with slide shows at the Woolhope Naturalists' Field Club. A keen archaeologist and antiquarian, the idea of ley lines came to him one day in June 1921 when he had finished his work for the day. The weather was fine, and as he looked at his map for somewhere interesting to explore he noticed that several ancient sites fell into a straight line that passed over prominent hilltops.

He spent the rest of his life researching leys and his book, *The Old Straight Track*, has remained in print ever since its publication in 1925. You can see an exhibition on his work at the Hereford City Museum. His collection of books and negatives is housed in the city library, where you can also buy prints of his photographs.

Members of the Old Straight Track Club at Old Sarum,
July 1934.

Watkins attributed no magical power to leys, but while he and his friends pored over maps and drove out to ancient sites, other groups believed the lines were in fact magical – that they represented lines of subtle energy that travelled along the land. According to this theory, prehistoric people were more sensitive to the existence of these lines, and therefore erected their single standing stones or built their circles to channel the energy of these lines, in order to use it for their own purposes – perhaps for healing, for radiating fertility to the land and for worshipping the gods.

The occultist Dion Fortune suggested in her 1936 novel, *The Goat Foot God*, that leys marked 'lines of force' between 'power centres'. Here her heroine is telling her lover how to find a ley and what it could be used for. In the exercise that follows you will find detailed instructions on how to do this yourself.

'Look at this map. You see Avebury? That was the centre of the old sun-worship . . . Put the edge of the ruler on it and revolve it slowly. Where is it now?'

'One end's on Cornwall and the other to the north of London.'

'Can you see Tintagel?'

'Yes, it's just north of my ruler.'

'Then bring the ruler onto Tintagel. That's the western power-centre. Now draw a line right across the map to Avebury.' Hugh ran the pencil down the ruler.

'Now project your line to St. Albans. Is that straight?'

'Dead straight. It's one line.'

'St Albans is the eastern power centre. Now take St Albans Head in Dorset and lay your ruler from there to Lindisfarne, off the Northumberland coast. Does that pass through Avebury?'

'Yes.'

'Lindisfarne is the northern power-centre. So you see, if you take a line through Avebury from either Lindisfarne or Tintagel, you end up at St Albans. Odd isn't it?'

Fortune goes on to explain that Alban was Britain's first saint, but that the early saints were originally pagan gods whose roles were taken over by historical figures, and that these gods can still be called upon for help along one of these magical lines of power.

Subsequent writers built on this idea. By the 1960s the vision was clearly in place and was best articulated by John Michell, author of the 1969 best-seller *View Over Atlantis*, in which he presented a picture of Britain criss-crossed with lines of force, like the dragon-lines of China used by Masters of the Chinese art of geomancy, Feng Shui. He claimed that it was possible to tap into these dragon lines to develop powers of telepathy and to produce altered states of consciousness.

JOHN MICHELL, 1933–

John Michell lives in Notting Hill, holding impromptu salons in the cafés of Portobello Road. Educated at Eton and Trinity College, Cambridge, he has written over a dozen books and contributed for over a decade to *The Oldie* magazine.

Continuing in the great tradition of Aubrey and Stukeley, Michell has captivated the readers of his books on the sacred landscape of Britain.

In 1969, his *View Over Atlantis* became a cult classic, popularising the notion that Britain was covered with lines of magical earth-energy that our ancestors understood, but which we have forgotten.

Blending Alfred Watkins' ideas about the 'Old Straight Track' with cabbalistic numerology, sacred geometry and theories drawn from the Chinese geomancy of Feng Shui, *View Over Atlantis* suggests that Stonehenge and the other great prehistoric monuments of the English landscape are laid out in accordance with sacred geometry to fulfil a magical purpose: bringing harmony to the land.

Many centuries ago, one of the names for Britain was 'Merlin's Isle' and legends recount that Stonehenge was built by the wizard Merlin, the great blocks of stone being moved into position by his

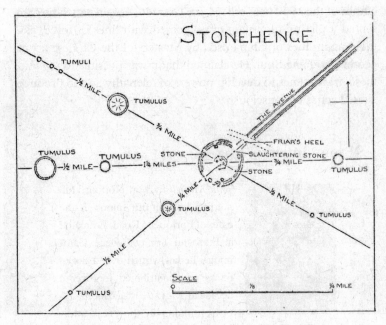

Ley lines intersecting at Stonehenge, from Watkins' The Old Straight Track, *1925*

magic powers without the aid of human engineering. Michell's vision of a Britain covered in a network of power-lines allows us to imagine Merlin using these lines like invisible shipping lanes to convey the bluestones from their quarry in the Preseli mountains of Wales to their destination on Salisbury Plain.[4]

⊙ *How to Hunt for Ley Lines*

It is a most intriguing and fascinating hobby. In these days when rambling over hill and dale is such a popular amusement, there should be countless opportunities for young people to discover markstones and other reminders of by-gone days, and to trace out possible alignments from them on the maps when they return home.

MARK CULLING CARR-GOMM,
THE STRAIGHT TRACK CLUB (1938)

Does a ley line run through your house or garden? Do perhaps several cross there or elsewhere in your neighbourhood? There's only one way to find out: ley hunting!

Equipment Needed

- 2 maps covering the area under investigation: one, 1:50,000 scale, of the general area; and one, 1:25,000 scale, covering the ley area
- a straight edge at least 2 feet long
- a sharp 'H' grade pencil
- a map pin
- a compass
- binoculars and a camera

To find a ley you will need to do some fieldwork and mapwork at the very least, and ideally you should also follow this up with research into local history and folklore.

All these activities are perfect for the winter: when it's raining you can be indoors, with a map spread out on the kitchen table, or inside your local library, poring over books on local folklore and history. When it's clear and sunny you can be exploring old footpaths, following hunches and looking for unusual features in the landscape, which is much easier in the winter when the leaves are off the trees.

MAPWORK

Start with the 1:50,000 scale Ordinance Survey map. Lay this out on a flat surface and, taking a straight edge at least 2 feet long, move it around on the map in a relaxed way. As Paul Devereux and Ian Thomson say in *The Ley Hunter's Companion*: 'Move it slowly, follow a whim, let the eye be caught, be prepared to be surprised.' If you spot at least four sites in alignment you may be on to something.

What sort of sites should you be looking for? Alfred Watkins suggested the following features, which are listed in order of importance:

1. Ancient mounds, whether called tumulus, tump, barrow, cairn or some other name.
2. Ancient unworked stones, not those marked 'boundary stone'.
3. Moats and islands in ponds and lakelets.
4. Traditional or holy wells.
5. Beacon points.
6. Crossroads with place names and ancient wayside crosses.
7. Churches of ancient foundation and hermitages.
8. Ancient castles and old 'castle' place names.

If you can't locate any alignment, try this method: draw a small circle with a pencil around any ancient monument, such as a tumulus, standing stone or stone circle. Stick a map pin in one of these and, using your straight edge, rotate this around to see whether it aligns with at least three other ringed points, so that a total of at least four features are connected. If it aligns with only two other points, you may still be on to something, especially if a stretch of straight road or track is also aligned.

With a bit of luck you might be on the scent of a ley! Take a sharp 'H' pencil and draw in the line between the points. If you've sharpened your pencil well the line will be about ½₈th of an inch wide, which will represent a width of about 11 yards on the ground. Watkins believed leys were about half that width.

Now draw in the same alignment on the larger-scale map, the 1:25,000 one. This will be the map you will use in your fieldwork, although if your ley crosses two maps you will need to take great care in plotting it. *The Ley Hunter's Companion* or another detailed guide will explain how to do this.

FIELDWORK

Once your mapwork is complete, it's time for the wellington boots, because you are going to try to walk the ley you have plotted. For this you'll need your map or maps, a compass and a pair of binoculars. Motorways, private land or rivers might well bar the way, and if you don't feel like swimming or trespassing you will have to content yourself with following the ley only intermittently. Even so, you should be able to walk at least part of the alignment and visit most or all of its marker points.

Apart from the sheer pleasure of exploring the countryside, you may also be able to add further points, such as old marker stones, which are not noted on the map. As you walk along the alignment or stand at each marker point, look to see whether you can spot any other features that could be markers, and make a photographic record of the route. Use your binoculars to help you. The perceptions of our ancestors, who were finely attuned to the world of nature, were probably better than our own.

This detective work is not easy. As Watkins points out in *The Old Straight Track*: 'ancient tracks and roads have disappeared (and most of the barrows and mark stones) wherever the plough touches.' But every so often traces of an old path or marker stone will be discovered in this way. And although ley hunting can be undertaken at any time of the year, in the winter the undergrowth will have died back, so that you are more likely to spot a significant-looking old stone hiding under foliage. As you walk the ley, remember to respect the Countryside Code: closing gates, avoiding walking on crops and asking permission to cross land if there is no right of way.

For a ley hunter, local people – particularly the elderly – can be mines of information. Devereux and Thomson recount how they asked a septuagenarian in a remote village the location of an elusive stone, without mentioning the subject of leys: 'Not only did he know the stone's whereabouts, he also volunteered the information that it stood in line with another old stone and an ancient cross miles away!'

Some leys were probably old funeral tracks. According to the Society of Ley Hunters, 'Walking the old paths can be a revelation. Old references to a paved funeral path can be confirmed by finding the old cobbles underfoot. Some old routes are named, some sections may have been unused for years.'[5]

THE FINAL PHASE: RESEARCH WORK

Once you've done your mapwork and fieldwork, it's time to build up the 'story' of your ley. The local studies section in your library is a good place to start. There will probably be no references to leys as such, but you will find plenty of leads for hunting down sites in books on local history and folklore. In particular, look at the old tithe maps that were drawn up at the time of the Enclosure Acts, between 1750 and 1860, which may give you the names of old tracks that have now disappeared. Research work can be invaluable when you have a ley with just a few points. If your research suggests that others existed but have since succumbed to tarmac, concrete or the plough, you can add them to the line.

If you happen to live in a city or town, tracing leys on the ground and on maps will be that much harder, and this research work will be vital. You might even have to start first with researching your area before you move on to mapwork and fieldwork.

It's important to know, however, that just as you can go trout fishing in a pond nicely stocked with plenty of hungry trout, rather than in a river, so you could also take the lazy route to ley hunting and follow one that has already been detected. Guides to these can be found in the books listed at the end of this chapter. You can even buy a map and plot out an already identified ley to get practice before hunting your own.

❧

Today, when people talk about ley lines, they may be using Watkins' original definition: referring to alignments that have been traced between ancient monuments and landscape features for navigation purposes, or they may be referring to alignments that convey special 'earth energy', which may or may not also have been ancient trackways.

The idea that there is a hidden network of energy lines across the earth, like the acupuncture meridians that flow through our bodies, fired the imagination of the burgeoning New Age movement, and dowsers in particular became keen on detecting leys with dowsing.

❧ Dowsing ❧

Dowsing is another way of attempting to map these lines of force. It is the art of divining things that are hidden, such as water sources, oil or mineral reserves, even treasure. Most dowsers also believe that lines of energy run through the earth, and that often sacred places, such as churches and stone circles, have been built where these lines cross and the energy is stronger.

Dowsing is one of the most fundamental magical skills still practised in Britain today. By dowsing we are attempting to tune into the 'hidden treasure' that lies beneath the earth.

Here Peter Taylor, one of the most expert dowsers working today, describes how he became interested in dowsing and how he finds magic in his everyday world.

A Dowser's Story – PETER TAYLOR

Peter Taylor is in his late sixties and lives in Mold, North Wales. He worked for Pilkington's, the glass makers, until his mid-forties, when he became interested in dowsing. Self-taught, he is now a registered expert for the British Society of Dowsers and has an international clientele ranging from ordinary individuals to major oil and gas companies. Peter is a deeply religious man, with an extraordinary dowsing ability.

I first got interested in dowsing when we had a big problem with water flow at our local fishing club on the River Allen. On TV, I had seen dowsing expert Roy Talbot show how he worked with a combination of map dowsing, site visits and drilling to find new springs and I asked permission from the landowner to experiment. My first attempt was a disaster. I picked up a false trail – what we call a 'reaction line' – to the new water, rather than the actual flow, and when we dug a big hole we found nothing.

I soon learnt the right procedure and served my apprenticeship working for an environmental improvement agency. I found over fifty new springs covering a wide area of the river and its tributaries, as well as helping create a new wildfowl lake from scratch. Although still working full time, I was beginning to get a local reputation for finding water and solving drainage problems on some of the big estates, so I thought I'd try to build a full-time career. I began to advertise locally – but the results were not what I expected . . .

The first evening, I got a call from a man who asked whether I could dowse for future movements in the FTSE 100. I thought I'd give it a try and, for the first time in my life, read the financial pages. I dowsed and got an answer that predicted the next day's trading. It must have been spot on, because the next day my client was back on the phone. Once again my dowsing worked and for the rest of the week I came up with accurate beginning and ending values every day. I was beginning to get a bad feeling about the whole business – dowsing purely for unearned wealth somehow didn't feel right to me – but my client told me that he hadn't been betting on my predictions, just checking me out. The next week, he said, he would try the scheme for real.

I was still nervous, but he offered me a stake in any profit and promised he would not come back at me for any losses. The first evening the phone went mad. None of my predictions had come true, and my client and his partner were well down. By the end of the week, it was a disaster: they had lost a huge sum of money and one of the two had actually been wiped out financially. For me, there was worse in store. I was to be punished. The next time I tried dowsing, nothing worked. L rods, V rods and pendulums: all refused to move. It was to be a full eighteen months before I got the gift back. Quite a lesson, I can tell you.

When my dowsing ability came back, I joined the British Society of Dowsers and, as my dowsing improved, I got better at asking myself the questions 'May I? Can I? Should I?' which I had ignored on the FTSE project. My first big job came from a soft drinks company in Wrexham, and with it an understanding of the sorts of problems you get on big projects. We needed a deep bore-hole, at least 45 metres down, to avoid contamination from the surface. I dowsed a good source of water at 57 metres, but what I did not know was that there was a thick layer of marl on the way down, which confused my estimate, and it proved to be nearly 148 metres to the bottom of the source of water. Thank goodness the company had enough confidence in me to drill deeper, because the water we found was very good quality and they still take 25,000 litres an hour – day in, day out.

In the 1990s, I began to realise that I could never make a full-time living as a dowser just searching for water, so I decided to try oil and gas. I got my son to hide a large bag of oil in a field and located it accurately, so I knew it was possible. This gave me the confidence to approach the large oil companies, and one of them asked me to do a demonstration. They showed me a map of Italy and asked me what I could find in a given area. I found nothing and told them so. Without saying whether I was right or wrong, they then presented me with a seismic graph of the North Sea. I found two shallow oilfields and another, massive one, going down to 10,000 feet, of oil and gas. The same night, they announced a huge find exactly where I had predicted.

Much of my work is now in the oil and gas industry. I found a big field in Colombia in South America, although I was told that my findings could not be made public, because the company did not want its shareholders to know they were using dowsers, which was very disappointing. I have also had success with gold mining – often my accuracy is to within 6 feet or less – and have started a voluntary scheme to find clean village water in western Zambia, which has uncovered many new wells.

Most recently, I have started 'psychic' dowsing. I was working for a local builder who told me the story of a worker who always felt ill when he worked on a particular machine. I dowsed the area and found a rock, which was a source of bad energy. The builder buried the rock in the deepest hole he could find, and the worker recovered. These problems of bad energy seem especially to affect children and I now advise on 'geopathic stress', which causes sensitive people to sleep badly, become irritable and suffer from all sorts of minor ailments. I have even learnt how to turn bad energy into good, and I guess you could say that that is in itself magic.

☉ *How to Dowse*

TOOLS

You will need three sorts of tools to begin your dowsing: an angle rod (or two), a V rod and a pendulum. You can make all these yourself or buy them over the internet.

An **angle rod** is the easiest to make. A light and sensitive version can be made from a wire coathanger. You can use one or two, depending on what you feel works best for you.

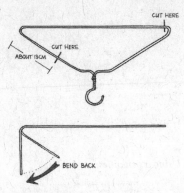

*Making an angle rod from
a wire coathanger.*

A **V rod**, which is the dowsing tool that is most familiar, can be cut from any young tree; a hazel is preferred by the purist. Most dowsers use a newly cut branch, as it will be more supple.

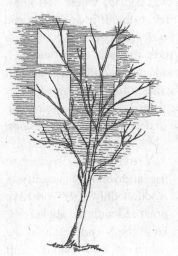

*Where to locate a V rod
on a young tree.*

A **pendulum** can be made from almost anything – a bit of pointed plastic, or even a ring, attached to about 6 inches of cotton thread with a shirt button on the end by which to hold it. Crystal or wooden dowsing pendulums can also be bought from New Age shops or from the British Society of Dowsers' website: www. britishdowsers.org

Using a pendulum.

GETTING STARTED

Angle rods are the easiest to begin with. Hold one or both rods lightly in the fist, with the rods pointing directly forward. Fix your mind on flowing water and walk over a place where you know an underground stream or water main to be. If it works, the rod or rods will suddenly turn about 90 degrees, seemingly of their own accord. If you are using two rods, they will cross over each other and end up pointing to either side of you rather than straight ahead. As you experiment, try fixing these questions firmly in your mind: 'Where does the water come from?' 'Where is it going to?' By doing this you may soon be able to detect the water's direction of flow as well as its source.

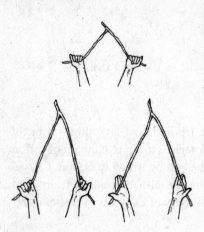

V rods can be trickier to use, and you may get a strong reaction only after you have practised with the angle rods. Hold the V rod lightly in the palms of both hands, with the V facing upwards, and then 'wake it up' by twisting both handles to the outside to put tension on the rod. Walk forward, pointing the rod in front of you. Again, use a known source of underground water as a test. When you reach the source, the stick will point either up or down (reactions vary according to individuals). Try 'asking' the rod how deep the water is. Start with 1 foot deep and then count clearly in your mind until you get a reaction. If you are using a mains water supply to test yourself, you can check how accurate your reading is.

Once you have mastered the angle and V rods, it is time to start to work with pendulums, which are the most interesting dowsing tool of all. Hold the pendulum string lightly between the thumb and forefinger of your writing hand, clear your mind and ask, 'What will the pendulum do if it wants to indicate a positive reaction?' You will find that the pendulum wavers about a bit, but should then settle into a circular or diagonal path. Again, this will be different for each person. Let the pendulum swing for a bit until it steadies, then ask for the negative reaction, which will be different. You are now ready to dowse – but always remember to 'ask permission' before you start each new subject. If the pendulum gives a negative reaction, do not continue.

The most interesting use of pendulums, and the hardest for sceptics to accept, is map dowsing, but you may well find out that it really works for you. On a flat table spread out a large-scale map, or even a drawing. Hold a pointed object, like a pen or knitting needle, in one hand and the pendulum in the other. Start at the bottom of the page, fix your mind on the object you are looking for, such as the site of a well or spring, and ask the pendulum to tell you where it is. It helps if you can visualise clearly what you are looking for, including the place it might be. Follow the swing of the pendulum with the pointer until it gives you a reaction. To check your reading, start again from another side of the page – and then cross-check your findings with an expert.

As you gain experience you will find you can pinpoint many things but, as with any magical endeavour, never dowse something that does not feel right – especially for anything involving significant personal gain. For some reason, this interferes with dowsing skills and you will end up with a confusing or just plain wrong result. Give the National Lottery a miss, or you will be disappointed!

❧ Going Deeper ❧

Ley hunting includes contact with the old shrines of the earth spirit and thus provides a course of initiation in its most natural and lasting form.

JOHN MICHELL, INTRODUCTION TO *THE LEY HUNTER'S MANUAL*

You might want to go ley hunting because you love the countryside and its history, and because you want to discover the old straight tracks that were used in ancient times. But you might equally be interested in tracing these lines because you believe they convey a magical energy. Some people believe that simply by walking along ley lines they are helping to stimulate the flow of earth-currents, their footsteps acting like the fingertips of a masseur or even an acupuncturist, working along the meridians of their client's body to stimulate the flow of the life force. Walking the leys then becomes an act of pilgrimage.

Combine the art of ley hunting with the skill of dowsing and you have another way to research leys – in the field and on maps – and another way, too, to begin exploring the hidden treasures of the countryside. And if you are keen on astronomy or astrology, you can start to look at the orientations of the leys you have uncovered. Are they perhaps pointing to solstice or equinox sunrises or sunsets, to distant stars or constellations, and, if so, what does that signify?

If the earth is covered in a web of subtle energies, what happens if you walk the threads of this web with a heightened awareness and sensitivity – pausing at 'nodes' where threads cross to meditate or open yourself to inspiration? The aboriginals of Australia have remembered all their old stories and customs related to their ancient places. The stories are linked together and are known as songlines. As aboriginals walk from place to place they can recount the tales associated with each hill and cleft in the rock, each watering hole and cluster of trees. In England we used to be able to do that too, although now only fragments of the tales remain. But enough does remain, and can be reclaimed, to make it possible for us in this modern age to walk the songlines here once again.

✐ Traps for the Sorcerer's Apprentice ✐

The idea of a web of lines in the human body and on the ground is prevalent in magical traditions in many cultures. It can offer one explanation as to why we feel good in some places and not in others – and why we sleep well in certain houses and not in others. The electromagnetic field of the earth varies from place to place and it can affect our feelings, so there can be any number of other reasons why a particular place feels good or bad. Wonderful or awful things may have happened there, for example. Stradivarius used to hang his violins in his bedroom after he had made them, and some say that this was his great secret: since he was a passionate and loving husband, the instruments somehow absorbed the vibrations of love and ecstasy generated so often in that small room. In contrast, where awful crimes have been committed people tend to feel uncomfortable.

It has been suggested that ley lines have particular electromagnetic properties and when flying saucers were seen in numbers, during the 1960s, over the English countryside, some writers suggested that they might have been using ley lines both for navigation and as a power grid – sucking the energy in the ley network straight into their engines to power their craft.

In the 1980s, sightings of flying saucers tailed off but were soon replaced by something just as odd: crop circles, which continue to appear every year in the fields of southern England, particularly in the triangle of land between Avebury, Wantage and Devizes, where a high density of prehistoric monuments and UFO sightings also coincide. Mysteriously, it seems as if there is a correlation between these phenomena and ley lines. Some crop circles were undoubtedly produced by hoaxers, but others are harder to explain away, and whatever their origin we can say that they are now an intrinsic part of England's magical landscape – bringing a fresh crop of mystery to the countryside every summer.

As yet there is no real proof that leys affect us or even exist. Scientists point out that there are so many ancient sites in Britain that it is possible to connect many of the lines purely on the basis of chance. But there is plenty of evidence of the deliberate alignment of individual sites to celestial phenomena. In Carnac in France we see the extraordinary sight of hundreds of standing stones aligned in rows, and in Peru the Nazca lines stretch across the desert in alignment for miles.

The most sensible approach to ley lines and to dowsing seems to lie in being open-minded and unattached to any particular theory. The idea of a web of energy needs to inspire us, not trap us in a spider's web of attachment to a theory that may prove to be unfounded. Ultimately, the purpose of magic is to free our potential, not bind us to ideas.

HAMISH MILLER

After a career first in the Army and then as an engineer with GEC, Hamish Miller started a furniture business in Sussex, only to see the economic downturn of the early 1980s destroy everything he had built up. He then moved to Cornwall, where he became a successful black-smith and sculptor. Introduced to dowsing and the concept of ley lines by John Michell and Colin Bloy, Miller is the author of three books, the first of which, The Sun and the Serpent *about the discovery of the energies underlying the 'St Michael line', has become a cult success. He lives with his second wife Ba Miller, herself an accomplished dowser, in Cornwall.*

From the age of six, I wanted to be a blacksmith, and it has taken me nearly fifty years to realise this dream. Working creatively with fire, air, earth, water and spirit, roots you in reality but instils a desire to answer deeper spiritual questions, as the old Alchemists found out.

All this might seem pretty far fetched for a down-to-earth blacksmith, but I have been privileged to have had some extraordinary personal experiences that have given me glimpses of a body of ancient knowledge, which may well pre-date the Druids and go back to the days when Stonehenge was built.

One of the first of these occurred when I became intrigued by an old stone, which was propped in the doorway of the church in Steyning, Sussex, where my furniture factory was located. Every time I passed the stone, I was tempted to touch it and, each time felt a jolt of energy and meaning. One day I took my courage in my hands and hugged the stone across the full length of my body. Suddenly I had the sensation that I was flying with no limit to time and space. It was a vivid experience almost impossible to describe, but so real that 25 years later I can still remember it distinctly.

The stone is carved deeply with what I believe are runic and

The Steyning 'Flying' Stone.

other markings and dates from the Anglo-Saxon era, when Shamans used flying to visit the other worlds as part of their every day practices, before Christianity drove them underground.

The Steyning Stone shows 3 runes – the classic '3 Norns' reading used for divination or spell casting. The big rune around the outside is 'Perth', representing mystery. It shows that despite fate, you have a choice in anything you do. The top, smaller rune is 'Ingwaz', or harmony, which describes a spiritual path and how important it is not to get diverted by dreams. The 'here and now' is what matters. The bottom rune is 'Gebo', forgiveness. It shows that the Gods are offering you a gift, which you can accept or refuse, but must give something in return. Taking the three together, you have a spiritual question about whether or not to take a hand in your fate and seek the help of the gods. The sword with the hilt portrayed as two horns is the traditional representation of Odin's sword. Odin is the God of Journeying to other worlds. The runes are depicted as if carved onto the blade of a sword, which is how they would have been used by the Saxons. The carving around the sword blade is clearly a gateway, and this is, I believe, its purpose. It is a pagan altar for worshipping, ritual and journeying – in particular, 'flying' to other worlds. I had not been dreaming. The ancient magicians had been there before me!

My long years of work with the St Michael line were inspired by John Michell's belief that a major ley line sweeps from Land's End to the Norfolk coast, through Glastonbury and other standing stones and monuments and passing many churches named after St Michael.

To dowse the St Michael line, I made my own angle-iron dowsing rods at my forge. They are heavy to counteract any muscle movements that might influence the result. Although my first attempts at proving John Michell's theory did follow the Michael route, the path twisted and turned along the way often by 90 degrees or more. At places of high energy like Avebury, for instance, the lines would almost describe a full circle.

My first major discovery was that, in fact, there are two lines not one, representing male and female energy. The second one,

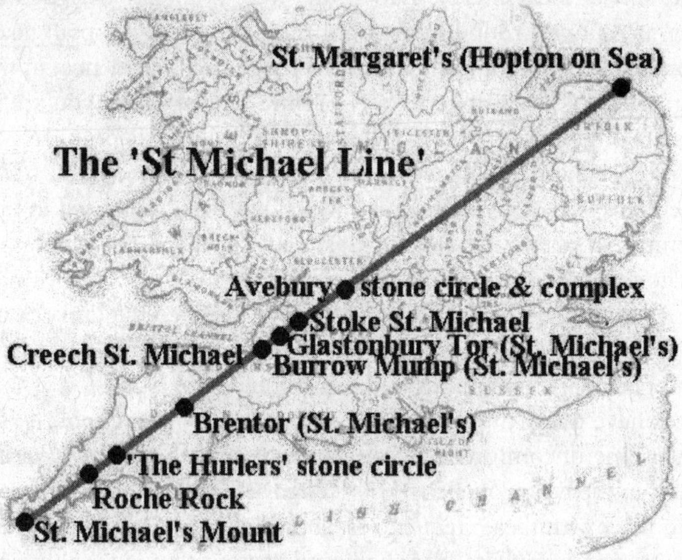

The 'St Michael Line'

St. Margaret's (Hopton on Sea)

Avebury stone circle & complex
Stoke St. Michael
Creech St. Michael Glastonbury Tor (St. Michael's)
Burrow Mump (St. Michael's)
Brentor (St. Michael's)
'The Hurlers' stone circle
Roche Rock
St. Michael's Mount

St Michael Line

I call the 'Mary' line. The lines coil and turn about each other, much like mating snakes, which inspired the title of my first book, *The Sun and the Serpent*. Serpents and dragons are symbols of great power in England, and myths, such as St George killing the dragon, a part of local history.

Places where the two lines cross appear to have the strongest energy. I found I could dowse quite extraordinary patterns around such spots, patterns which, in some way, were replicated in the crop circle phenomenon of the 1980s. I have always maintained that it would be impossible for people to fake the more complex circles with a plank, as cynics have suggested and in fact I found I could detect the fakes through dowsing. Some crop circles seemed linked to the energy spots I was discovering next to ancient monuments, springs and other 'sacred' sites as well as places where the two lines of energy cross.

The ancient art of making labyrinths plays a part in harnessing this sort of local energy. Labyrinths were originally designed so that if you walk round in the right frame of mind, the path takes you across different energies in exactly the right sequence, in the right way. When you get into the centre of a labyrinth you are in a state of grace and open to all sorts of new ideas. People seeking spiritual enlightenment would use the most famous examples, like the one at Chartres Cathedral – which has been replicated in this country in places like Benton Castle in Wales – as an alternative to going on a pilgrimage to Jerusalem.

As my experience as a dowser grew, I uncovered a darker side to this magic. There are 'black' ley lines that seem to cause illness and personal unhappiness to those in their path. I have learnt that lines have many different frequencies, some of them being good and some uncomfortable. You can tune into these subtle variations in the way a musician will recognise a musical chord. If you can react with these frequencies, showing 'intent' to change, you can re-program them from being unpleasant to good – although one such experience came close to wiping me out. I was standing in a small lane, willing the 'black' line that passed through it to change, when I felt an express train of black energy rushing towards me. For a moment I felt out of my body and in the air; then my one desire was to get away across water, which I believed might act as a barrier to the lines. It wasn't until I gunned the car down the road and over a bridge that I began to feel better.

My wife Ba and I extended our researches into energy lines to

other countries, in particular South Africa and New Zealand and returned from our trips more than ever determined to understand the paths of communication that the indigenous people we met found so easy. One of our most interesting experiments was in the creation of an earth sculpture in our garden, based on the ancient Egyptian 'Seed of Life' (*see below left*), one of the most ancient symbols of creation, the building block of the universe.

The strangest experience came after we held a small ceremony around the Seed at a recent eclipse. A new energy line had appeared at the moment the sun started to reappear, which met the existing one right at the heart of our Seed: something which we had never imagined to be possible.

We have moved a long way beyond such basic questions as 'Does Dowsing Work' and today Ba and I are researching the 'light orbs' which appear around energy spots and are clearly visible using digital photography. I also struggle for new insights as I work at my 'Spiritual' forge. I have looked at many other types of magic, but it is the old varieties used by the indigenous people with their closeness to nature that I believe hold the secrets we need.

Things to Do

There are many ways in which you can begin to explore the magic of England on your own, with your family, or in the company of like-minded people.

- Join a group such as the Society of Ley Hunters (www.leyhunter.com), the Gatekeeper Trust (www.gatekeeper.org.uk), RILKO – the Research into Lost Knowledge Organisation (www.members.aol.com/rilko), or the Antiquarian Society (www.theantiquariansociety.com).

- Go ley hunting and walk the old tracks, learning the folklore and stories of the old places.

❧ Learn dowsing. The British Society of Dowsers (www.britishdowsers.org) offers courses for beginners and advanced practitioners, and holds an annual conference.

❧ In the crop-circle season seek out a crop circle – perhaps try to dowse it for underground water. You could also try to work out whether it is on a ley line.

❧ Buy the Ordnance Survey map *The Ancient Monuments of Britain*, or rock star Julian Cope's magnificent book *The Modern Antiquarian: A Pre-Millennial Odyssey Through Megalithic Britain* (Thorsons, 1998), and start to explore and dowse some of these sites.

❧ As well as stone circles, barrows and tumps – not to mention the hundreds of stone monuments that can be seen, include in your visits holy wells, old churches and ancient yew trees.

To visit holy wells, see Jeremy Hart, *English Holy Wells* and Janet Bord, *Holy Wells in Britain: A Guide* (Heart of Albion Press, 2008); to explore old churches, see whether you can find an old copy of *The Observer's Book of Old English Churches* by Lawrence Elmore Jones (1965). Although now out of print, copies of this guide can often be bought in second-hand bookshops.

In England there are groves of ancient yew trees, sacred to the Druids, that are over 3,000 years old, which are well worth visiting. See the gazetteer at www.ancient-yew.org or read Fred Hageneder, *The Yew: A History* (The History Press, 2007).

❧ Use the internet to 'fly' to some of the sights. Try looking on Google Earth at the chalk hill figures of the White Horse of Uffington, the Cerne Abbas Giant in Dorset and the Long Man of Wilmington in Sussex – the views are amazing.

❧ Visit Cresswell Crags to walk in the gorge, visit the Museum and Education Centre, take a tour of Robin Hood Cave, and view the rock art in the Church Hole Cave. See www.creswell-crags.org.uk

❧ Visit the Barge Inn, Pewsey in Wiltshire, and mingle with crop-circle enthusiasts or go one step further and attend a ley hunters or crop circle convention.

The Mecca for crop-circle enthusiasts – the Barge Inn, Pewsey, near the Vale of the White Horse, in Wiltshire, where circle hunters gather and pictures of famous crop circles adorn the walls.

⤙ Resources ⤚

⊙ *The Ancient Landscape*

BOOKS

Atlas of Magical Britain, Janet and Colin Bord (Bracken, 1993)

Ancient Britain, James Dyer (Guild, 1990)

A Guide to Occult Britain – The Quest for Magic in Pagan Britain, John Wilcock (Sphere, 1977)

Landscape of Memory, Living Folklore in England, Jerry Bird (Green Magic, 2009)

◉ *Ley Hunting*

BOOKS

The Ley Hunter's Companion, Paul Devereux and Ian Thomson (Thames & Hudson, 1979)

The Ley Hunter's Manual: A Guide to Early Tracks, Alfred Watkins (Aquarian, 1989)

Leys: Secret Spirit Paths in Ancient Britain, D.P. Sullivan (Wooden Books, 2004)

Quicksilver Heritage – The Mystic Ley: Their Heritage of Ancient Wisdom, Paul Screeton (Thorsons, 1974)

WEBSITES

The Society of Ley Hunters: www.leyhunter.com

◉ *Dowsing*

BOOKS

The Definitive Wee Book on Dowsing: A Journey Beyond our Five Senses, Hamish Miller (Penwith, 2002)

Dowsing for Health and Vitality: Tuning into the Earth's Energy for Personal Development and Wellbeing, Patrick MacManaway (Lorenz, 2001)

The Sun and the Serpent, Hamish Miller and Paul Broadhurst (Mythos, 2003)

WEBSITES

The British Society of Dowsers: www.britishdowsers.org

CHAPTER TWO

THE MAGICIANS ORGANISE THEMSELVES

The World of the Ancient Druid

You are about to enter a world in which people and animals talk to each other and take on each other's shapes, in which trees communicate through their own language, a language which you can learn to speak and read. It is a world of visions, spirit guides, journeys into other worlds, ancestral teachers, past lives, and gods who are at once ancient and ever young; such is the world of the Druid.

PHILIP SHALLCRASS, *DRUIDRY*

Magic began in caves and under the stars, in our ancestors' awe of the forces of nature all around them. The play of light and darkness – of the cave's depths and of the brightness of the dawn sun as it struck the cave's opening – was the primal experience that fashioned the very earliest practice of magic.

This dynamic relationship between light and dark was seen too in the canopy of the heavens, and along with magic was born a growing belief in the power of the moon and stars to influence life on earth. From around 3500 BC tribal people living in Britain began erecting stone monuments that linked earth and sky: giant standing stones that stretched towards the heavens, built perhaps to channel the fertilising forces of the sky into the earth; stone circles, often oriented to the rising or the setting of the sun, the moon or certain stars, such as Arcturus, and some of which acted like astronomical calculators to predict eclipses and solstices; conical mounds that were probably places of harvest offering; and barrows for housing the dead and perhaps for initiating the living too, in imitation of those first temples – the caves. All were connected by a system of trackways to lead pilgrims and to channel trade from one site to another.

For at least 2,500 years our ancestors lived in this world, walking the old tracks to ceremonial sites to bury their dead and to observe the solstices, building great stone monuments with engineering skills we find hard to imitate even today – until everything changed and no more stones were erected.

Like the sculptors of the great Easter Island statues who ceased almost overnight due to some ecological disaster, the megalith builders of Britain were overcome by a dramatic change in the climate. Starting in 850 BC, this resulted in the abandonment of settlements all over Western Europe as temperatures dropped. Warfare ensued and little evidence remains of religious and magical activity in these lands for the following five hundred years.

Illustration based upon Aylett Samuel's History of Ancient Britain, *1676*

As climate conditions improved and peace returned, it seems that religious activity gradually became increasingly sophisticated as magicians, priests and priestesses began to organise themselves. From the accounts of classical writers such as Julius Caesar and Diodorus Siculus, we learn that by the first century BC Britain had developed into the centre for a religion led by a group of people known as 'Druidae' – the Druids. Caesar first came across them in France, in the area known as Gaul. In his *Gallic Wars*, he wrote: 'These Druids, at a certain time of the year, meet within the borders of the Carnutes, whose territory is reckoned as the centre of all Gaul, and sit in conclave in a consecrated spot.' The great gathering he refers to occurred once a year by a holy well, probably the one now found in the crypt of Chartres Cathedral, which, like so many Christian churches, was deliberately built on top of a pagan site.

Caesar goes on to comment: 'It is believed that their [the Druids'] rule of life was discovered in Britain and transferred hence to Gaul; and today those who would study the subject more accurately journey, as a rule, to Britain to learn it.'[1]

It seems that, to 'study the subject more accurately', Druid students not only from Gaul, but from Ireland too, crossed the sea to England. In the most famous epic of Irish mythology, *The Tain Bo Cuailnge*, or *The Cattle Raid of Cooley*, we learn of a powerful female

Druid: Fidelma. In the tale, Queen Medb of Connacht is about to engage her armies in battle with the King of Ulster. She consults Fidelma, asking her whether she possesses the 'Light of Foresight' – in other words whether she can see into the future. Fidelma predicts the queen's defeat, confirming that she is indeed a seer, having just returned from 'learning verse and vision in Albion'.[2]

Some writers say that the Druids were divided into three classes: Bards, Ovates and Druids.

Bards were trained in the magic of sound, using the power of words and music to spellbind their listeners. They were the story-tellers and the genealogists of the tribe whose prodigious memories were trained to retain long lists of ancestors, and hundreds of stories of their heroic deeds. After twelve years of training they were expected to be proficient in the 'four arts of poetry', and to know by heart 120 orations and 350 complete stories.

The Ovates were the prophets, seers and healers. They were trained in tree, herb and animal lore and were taught how to divine the future from observing the flight of birds or the shapes of clouds, using a magical skill known as 'neldoracht'.

The Druids were the elite of the three groups, who acted as advisers to kings and queens, were teachers of nobility, and were the judges and ritualists who supervised the great ceremonies that occurred at key moments in the year such as the solstices.[3]

To get a feel for what the Druids were like, imagine you are in a forest clearing somewhere in England at the time Caesar was writing – about 50 BC – perhaps on Salisbury Plain with the great stones of Stonehenge standing on the horizon, just visible through the trees. Even at this time Stonehenge was already over two thousand years old, built in another age by a people long gone.

The stars are starting to appear in the sky and you turn to the blazing fire as the Bard begins his tale. He tells a story of a magical battle between two heroes, in which good triumphs over evil and the virtues of bravery, plain-speaking and honour are upheld. His story over, a flagon of mead is passed amongst the company, until an Ovate stands and draws everyone's attention to the stars, which

A The Stones call'd Corfitones, 12 Tonn Weight
   24 foot high, 7 broad, and 16 round
B The Stones call'd Coronette, of 6 or 7 Tonn
C The place where Mens bones are dug
   up .

J. Kip Sculp.

now shine brightly overhead. As he talks a little of the star lore he learnt from his old teacher, a string of dark clouds passes across the moon. A woman, seated in the shadows, begins to utter a prediction, based upon her reading of the clouds and all turn to her, since she is the Chief Druid of their clan.

We will never know how accurate such an imagined scene might be, but each of its elements is based upon historical sources. Classical writers and the old Irish and Breton stories record that women were Druids as well as men. We know, too, that star lore, divination and storytelling were all key components of the ancient Druidism that probably formed the spiritual heart of much of the early tribal life of Britain. And we also know that mead was drunk in those times.

Such a scene may seem light years away from the world we live in now, but for modern followers of Druidry as a magical path, it would feel very familiar. All over England (and, indeed, all over the world now), small groups of people who call themselves Druids come together and camp out in the countryside, light bonfires and follow what they call the 'Old Ways'. They tell stories and make music by the fire, discuss star, animal and plant lore, and practise methods of divination. Surveys show that just as many women attend these gatherings as men. In this way time seems to have come full circle, although there are now probably more practising Druids in Britain today – about six thousand – than there ever were in the past. There are another 50,000 or so people who, although they would not call themselves Druids, have adopted many of the ideas of modern Druidism, and incorporate them into their lives in their own way.[4]

How has it come about that the ancient Druids, and the little we know about them, have inspired so many people today? The

Read about this Period in Fiction

The Power of the Serpent, Peter Valentine (Futura, 1987)
The second in the trilogy *The Seedbearers*, it takes as its premise a belief widely held amongst occultists that an occult elite fleeing the destruction of Atlantis settled in England.

Druids battle a corrupt and perverted priesthood, aided by Egyptian priests. The story incorporates initiation rituals, the theories of stone circle design, the building of Stonehenge and its deliberate partial destruction by the Druids.

modern renaissance of interest in the Druids began in London in the seventeenth century. As the Enlightenment made possible the open discussion of religion, and as the antiquarians John Aubrey and William Stukeley (see Chapter 1) began discussing their theories on the origins of the megaliths found all over Britain, the intelligentsia began to question the received wisdom concerning their pre-Christian forebears. When references in classical texts to the Druids were translated and published, a picture began to emerge of wise sages who were philosophers, judges and teachers. Far from being savages, these elders were revealed as principled leaders of men. As a result intellectuals began to see our ancestors as equals to the Greek philosophers and the Old Testament prophets.

⤫ The Druid Revival ⤬

By the late eighteenth century there was sufficient interest in the Druids as symbols of Britain's glorious past for a group to decide to form a working man's version of the Freemasons, taking the image of the Druid as its inspiration. In 1781, Henry Hurle founded the Ancient Order of Druids at the King's Arms Tavern in London's Poland Street. Set up to provide mutual support for its members, it offered social gatherings in groups known as 'lodges', and a type of ceremonial similar to those of other fraternal societies, where a Bible was placed on a lectern at each meeting, and discussion of religion was prohibited. Most lodges were open only to males, although later some 'Ladies' Lodges' were established.

These lodges proliferated first throughout England, then dispersed abroad to most corners of the British Empire and to parts of Europe. In 1908 the young Winston Churchill was initiated into the Order and, by 1933, incredibly, over one and a half million members called themselves Druids. The lodges produced engraved certificates, rings and even porcelain tea sets, which can still sometimes be found in antique shops or are dusted down as ancestral heirlooms.

Even though the Druid was used as a symbol of the wise philosopher, most members of the Ancient Order considered themselves Christian, and the Order's main purposes were charitable and social. If your grandfather was a Druid, he might have owned a Druid tea set and a certificate, but he was almost certainly not a magician. In the days before the introduction of the National Health Service or insurance cover, illness or bereavement often resulted in families falling into poverty. On these occasions, fraternal organisations such as the Druids and the Freemasons provided financial aid to members' families.

Although much reduced in numbers, Fraternal Druids still exist. Wearing regalia such as badges and blazers, they hold social and fund-raising meetings, which include a simple ritual inspired by the ancient Druids.

Winston Churchill became a Fraternal Druid. Here he is being initiated into the 'Albion Lodge' of the Ancient Order of Druids at Blenheim Palace in August 1908. Note the false beards surrounding young Winston.

✦ The Druid as Poet and Bard ✦

In addition to the 'Fraternal Druid', the eighteenth century saw the development of another kind of Druid: 'The Cultural Druid'. In 1792 on London's Primrose Hill – not far from the home of William Blake, the visionary poet and painter who was fascinated by Druidry – a Welsh stonemason named Iolo

Morganwg, who was working in the capital, assembled a group of friends and held a 'Gorsedd', or gathering, of Bards and Druids.

WILLIAM BLAKE, 1757–1827

> *All things Begin and End in Albion's Ancient Druid Rocky Shore.*
>
> WILLIAM BLAKE, *JERUSALEM*, 1804

The visionary poet and artist William Blake believed that the Druids originated in England and journeyed across the world with missionary zeal to establish the sacred groves of their 'one true religion'. Some writers claim that Blake was a practising Druid. This now seems unlikely, but he was deeply influenced by the idea that his native country was once the original Holy Land, writing his famous poem 'Jerusalem' to echo the idea that Jesus had once walked 'upon England's mountains green'.

Blake was undoubtedly influenced by the legend that Jesus had travelled to Glastonbury as a boy with his uncle, Joseph of Arimathea. In more recent times, the writer Gordon Strachan has suggested in his book, *Jesus the Master Builder: Druid Mysteries and the Dawn of Christianity* (Floris, 1998), that Jesus may have returned to the West Country as an adult during his 'silent years' to train with the Druids.

On Midsummer's Evening Iolo took a handful of pebbles out of his pocket and formed an instant stone circle around the company of his friends. Together they performed a ceremony that he said was ancient, but which was probably distilled from memories culled from his study of old Welsh texts that had been steeped in the fertile cauldron of his own laudanum-laced mind. A few decades later, however, Iolo's ceremony was adopted by the Welsh National Eisteddfod, a gathering with genuine roots in the ancient Bardic and Druidic past of Wales. At the Ivy Bush Inn in Carmarthen in 1819, the first eisteddfod was held, complete with Iolo's Druid ceremony, and the era of modern 'Cultural Druidism' was born.

Cultural Druids are members of the Welsh or Cornish Gorseddau, or associations, which hold arts festivals, known as eisteddfodau, to promote the Welsh or Cornish language. Like Fraternal Druids, they consider their role to be purely symbolic, and are often devout Christians who wish to distance themselves from anything that might be perceived as occult or pagan. In the last few years references to Druids in their websites and literature have been changed to focus more on their Bardic rather than their Druidic origins.

Until recently the eisteddfod was patronised by the royal family, and was known as the Royal National Welsh Eisteddfod. Honorary Cultural Druids have included the late Queen Mother,

The future King George VI and Queen Elizabeth,
then Duke and Duchess of York, in druidic robes at
the National Eisteddfod of Wales in Swansea.

whose Bardic name was Betsi o Efrog, and Dr Rowan Williams, the Archbishop of Canterbury.

⁓ Druidism as a Spiritual and ⁓ Magical Pursuit

It was not until the twentieth century that the Druids began to appear in England again in their original guise: as magicians. The ancient Druids were known as priests of the Celts, and although many traces of Celtic history can be found in England, most of the information about them and their lore comes from Wales, Ireland, Scotland and Brittany. For this reason you would expect a revival of interest in the Druids to emerge from one of these great strongholds of Celtic culture, but in reality England, and London in particular, is the location for the appearance of all three kinds of Druids in the last three hundred years. The Fraternal Druid movement was born in a Soho pub; the Cultural Druid movement first began on Primrose Hill; and the Spiritual Druid movement emerged in Clapham, and at Stonehenge, at the end of the First World War.

⚶ GEORGE WATSON MACGREGOR REID, ?1850–1946

George Watson MacGregor Reid was a highly eccentric character, prone to exaggeration and passionate enthusiasms. An ardent socialist all his life, he campaigned for dockers' rights in New York, before returning to England to promote the ideas of natural health, fairer distribution of wealth and the freedom to worship at Stonehenge. Acquainted with key members of the Hermetic Order of the Golden

Dawn, including Aleister Crowley and MacGregor
Mathers (see Chapter 11), he founded the first order of
Druids in the modern era to adopt Druidism as a spiritual path. He also promoted the Universalist Church,
which merged with the Unitarians in the 1950s. Towards
the end of his life he ran a holiday camp in Blackboys in
Sussex.

In the early years of the twentieth century, a charismatic and
pugnacious resident of Clapham, George Watson MacGregor
Reid, founded the British Nature Cure Association to promote
vegetarianism, outdoor living, natural medicine and wholesome food. He also became fascinated by religion and magic,
founding a group known as 'The Universal Bond of the Sons of
Men'. At first this group combined a number of interests in an
exotic mix: esoteric Christianity, Druidism, Cabbala, Buddhism,
Zoroastrianism and mystical Islam. They began holding ceremonies at Stonehenge, and championed a number of political
causes, including that of the Bab – the man who inspired the
Baha'i religion and was publicly executed in Iran in 1850 – and
the Senussi people of the Libyan desert, who were under threat
from the British and the Italians. MacGregor Reid claimed the
headquarters of his Universal Bond were in Senussi-land, in the
area of the Libyan desert immortalised in the film *The English
Patient*.

By 1918 the Universal Bond had become the Ancient Druid
Order, and a new type of Druidism for the modern era was born.
Although it contained elements of Cultural and Fraternal Druidry,
its main focus was religious and spiritual. An eccentric radical,
MacGregor Reid was interested in the indigenous spirituality of
Britain as well as in the universal themes of all religions, and over
the following decades this type of Druidry outstripped in popular-
ity the other two approaches.

After MacGregor Reid's death in 1946, three Druid leaders
emerged of particular note in the largely unknown history of

English Druidism, and all were Londoners: Thomas Maughan, Ross Nichols and Vera Chapman.

Thomas Lackenby Maughan, who became Chief of the Ancient Druid Order in 1964, was the main catalyst, along with a colleague John DaMonte, in the training of lay homoeopaths in England. Until his initiative, only qualified GPs could become homoeopaths. Maughan changed all that and was noted for his sometimes miraculous gifts of healing.

ROSS NICHOLS, 1902–1975

After reading history at Cambridge and working as a journalist and teacher, Ross Nichols became the principal of 'Jimmy's', a 'crammer' in West London, which tutored Winston Churchill.

In 1949 he became assistant editor of *The Occult Observer* and in 1952 edited and published Paul Christian's *The History and Practice of Magic* in two volumes. In 1954 he joined the Ancient Druid Order and a decade later founded the Order of Bards, Ovates and Druids, now one of the world's largest magical groups.

Ross Nichols, the Chief of the Order of Bards, Ovates and Druids, radiating peace to one of the cardinal directions in a Druid spring equinox ceremony on London's Parliament Hill in 1967.

Ross Nichols was fascinated by magic and was acquainted with most of London's occult intelligentsia, including Aleister Crowley, Idries Shah and Gerald Gardner. He injected a passion for Celtic mythology and seasonal celebrations into modern Druidism. He was aided in this work by fellow Druid Vera Chapman, founder of the Tolkien Society and one of the first women to matriculate from Oxford University.

Magic in London. The two central figures, Vera Chapman, founder of the Tolkien Society, and Ross Nichols, Chief of the Order of Bards, Ovates and Druids, swear on 'Excalibur' during a spring equinox ceremony on Parliament Hill in 1967: 'Whilst this sword is unsheathed, we promise that England our home and mother shall be illuminated by the swords of our spirits and that to the true spirit of England we shall ever be true.'

The kind of Druidism developed by MacGregor Reid, Maughan, Nichols and Chapman between 1918 and the early 1970s was inspired by the classical accounts of the ancient Druids, by Celtic mythology and folklore, and eventually by *The White Goddess*,

Robert Graves's work on Ogham, which has become known as the tree language of the Druids. In addition, like most modern magical groups, it was inevitably influenced by the Freemasons and the Hermetic Order of the Golden Dawn, which we will explore in Chapters 9 and 10.

Spiritual Druidry is now considered a valid spiritual and magical path in its own right. Some adherents now combine their Druidry with another approach such as Christianity, Buddhism, Wicca or Taoism. Many consider themselves Pagan or Pantheistic, but not all by any means. Most Druids belong to a group, or 'Order', but others prefer to practise alone and consider themselves 'solitary' or 'hedge' Druids.

Like its cousin, modern witchcraft or Wicca, Spiritual Druidry developed a threefold initiation system. Drawing on the accumulated magical heritage of what has come to be known as the Western Mystery Tradition, it developed ceremonial forms that include casting a magic circle, consecrating that circle with fire and water, and invoking the blessings of the four elements and the cardinal directions.

A Druid initiation from Lewis Spence's The Mysteries of Britain, *1929.*

The most distinctive feature of this kind of Druidry is that it combines this magical style of ritual with a simple form of nature reverence and an underlying philosophy that is essentially magical. And, incredibly, it often does all this in public. Unlike most magical groups, which insist on secrecy, Druids celebrate the seasons in their homes, in parks, and at old stone circles at the solstices, equinoxes and

Druid ceremony at Stonehenge from
The Mysteries of Britain.

old quarter-days. Today, in England, anyone can witness a magical ceremony being performed, as the Druids say, 'in the eye of the sun'.

Today's Druids also practise more private rites and follow techniques of shamanic journeying in inner worlds, communicating with plants and animals, ancestral spirits and spiritual guides. As the natural world becomes increasingly threatened, more and more people are turning to the inspiration of the very earliest of forms of spirituality, believing, perhaps rightly, that the oldest magic is the best.

A Modern Druid – ADRIAN

Adrian grew up on an estate in Bristol. His father was a pub landlord. When he was twenty-one, an undiagnosed heart disease made Adrian so ill that even his surgeon thought he had little chance of survival. During the operation he had a vivid near-death experience, which, he feels, created a strong sensitivity to the spiritual and started him on a quest that eventually led him to learning modern-day Druidry, as practised by the Order of Bards, Ovates and Druids. Now a full-time counsellor to those with drug and alcohol abuse problems, he lives in a converted garage, next to a small stone circle that he built himself. It is very comfortable, filled with pagan paraphernalia and a huge library of books.

Ever since I was a small child, I felt disconnected from what everyone else found normal. I didn't enjoy rowdiness in the playground like all the other kids, but felt a deep connection to nature. There was a stretch of woodland behind our house, where I spent a lot of time, rushing through the long grass with a butterfly net, or fishing for sticklebacks in tiny streams. When I was seven or eight, I found a copse of hawthorn and blackberry, hollowed out into the shape of a bell, where I felt secure. I could sit quietly and listen to the birds. It was a very happy time.

As I grew up I started to look for ways of satisfying my increasing spirituality. My parents were not religious, but I told them that I wanted to join a church properly, so found a deeply sincere, 'happy clappy' one, which first suited my enthusiasm. I soon fell out with the pastor when I told him that I thought God was a woman. At that time, one of my friends was a Hindu, and I had become captivated with the little altars, the incense and all the iconography of what he and his family did together. None of this seemed to be reflected in the churches I tried attending.

Later, I became more involved with my father's pub, which led me to becoming a heavy drinker and very much a party animal, but all this had to stop when an undiagnosed heart disease nearly killed me. Whilst I was being operated on, I had an extraordinary near-death experience. I knew that my chances of survival were tiny, and had come to accept that I might well die young. As the surgeon began to operate on me I felt myself floating above the operating table, linked to my real body by a pencil-thin shaft of light. I was absolutely certain that if this was severed I would be dead, but the sense of peace was so strong that I felt it would be best if I died now. Suddenly I knew I had to be back in my body. Something kept on telling me that it was not my time and I had work to do. When I came round, I was able to tell one of the doctors the details of the conversations they had been having over my body, which astonished and excited them.

After the operation, I experienced a dramatic intensification of many of my senses. Colours were sharper and I could read people's feelings with great accuracy. I started trying to make some sense of this new life. I tried everything from New Age groups to hallucinogenic mushrooms, and eventually found my way to a local spiritualist church. To my astonishment, the medium leading the meeting began to choke and gasp, then asked what terrible things had happened to my body. I told her about the operation.

'You poor dear,' she said. 'You have been through a lot. But, you know, you are at a crossroads. You can use your gifts for healing, or just carry on drifting through life. You should know that you have a spirit guide to help you. I see him as a family member, who died in the war and seems to be wearing a strange uniform with a "pillbox" style cap. You must know that if you take the wrong path now, it will be very bad for you.' The woman then surprised me even further by telling me that she had played a part in my healing.

Being sceptical about the woman's predictions, I spoke to my grandmother who described my guide: her younger brother, a ship's stoker, who had been torpedoed and drowned during the war. Even more amazingly, it turned out that my friend's family had prayed for me to recover in exactly the same spiritualist church that the medium had belonged to, so she had indeed helped me.

The incident inspired me to resume my spiritual quest, and I tried every group I could find. Each attempt left me dissatisfied, until one day the word 'Druid' suggested to me it should be followed up. At that time there was nowhere to ask and only stuffy old books to read but shortly afterwards a customer in the grocery shop I was running at the time brought in a magazine called *Prediction*. I tossed it on to a table, where it fell open at a tiny advertisement for courses in Druidry. As it turned out, this was the very first correspondence course of modern Druidry, offered by the Order of Bards, Ovates and Druids. I sent off for it and it appealed to me immediately, especially with its love of nature, its creatures and the land. The teaching was not dictatorial or evangelical in any way. I found the lessons were inspirational and could be practically applied to my daily life, filling it with the spiritual meaning that I was looking for.

At the same time, I started exploring stone circles, and I found a local one – Stanton Drew – that gave me a strong, personal sense of history and past lives. I began to find the sacred sites that appealed to me most, although, oddly, I never liked Stonehenge, despite its association with Druidry. As I found the quieter places I liked, I tried out simple ceremonies, which called on the Ancestors. Some of these were truly extraordinary and fulfilling, especially as I began to help other people find their own connection to the energy of such places.

It takes quite a leap of faith to take part in a Druid ceremony, which is aimed at creating an altered state of consciousness. Sometimes I ask myself why I am standing in a field in the middle of the night, covered in sheep shit, but, for me, the spiritual experience of connection to a sacred place is truly extraordinary. It feels like coming home. I once helped to facilitate a ceremony for a big group of pagans and non-pagans at the stones of Stanton Drew. Each person held a candle, yet despite their standing in the midst of a strong gale, by some miracle every candle stayed alight. The experience left even me lost for words.

There is a danger in using this power, though, and learning the skills of personal protection is important if you want to move to a deeper level of magic. We still don't really know what the original Druids did and how they used the power they found in nature. The main writings about early Druidry all came from the Romans, who had conquered them and were therefore hopelessly biased. We do know that the ancient Britons had a natural spirituality, which recognised that there was something greater than themselves, but we know almost nothing of how they accessed this. We modern Druids have had to work from scratch in many cases, using the natural power of the sacred places and the little historical information that has come down to us, weaving the magic together – experimenting and venturing into new areas of experience.

When I first joined the local group of the Order of Bards, Ovates and Druids fourteen years ago, I found they were really open and friendly. On the night of my first meeting they had a piper playing to welcome us into the sacred circle. For a moment I could see two strange Druids standing on either side of me, who pulled back their hoods to reveal themselves as my father and my best friend, both dead. Their nods of approval and the look in their eyes affirmed that I had come home to a spiritual framework that would continue to hold and inspire me for years to come.

Working magical rituals is incredibly powerful. One of the most striking experiences I've ever had using this kind of magic involved trying to sell my grocery shop. After years of working there, I had had enough of it, but could not sell it to anyone. Finally I decided to try magic. I arrived there early one morning and performed a Druid ceremony, which began with casting a circle amongst the cabbages and cauliflowers, sprinkling the circle with water from the sacred island of Iona in Scotland and burning sage as an incense. I then opened my heart and begged the spirits to set me free. The ritual done, I cleared up and got on with the day. Lo and behold, the following morning at 6 a.m., I arrived at the fruit market to purchase the day's produce and was accosted by a salesman who had just been made redundant. He told me he wanted to buy a grocery shop, and I offered him mine. Ten days later the contracts were signed and I stood in the shop for the last time. Magic or coincidence? I believe it was magic. I was finally free – and it felt fantastic.

✑ The Tree-Language of the Druids ✑

Ogam (Old Irish) or Ogham (Modern Irish), said to be the secret language of the Druids, is the earliest written record of the Irish language. It emerged in about the fourth century AD as a script of twenty letters, and a century later a further five were added. These were supposedly based on twenty-five woodland plants, mostly trees, an important element in Druid lore.

Inscriptions in Ogham, usually made on hard surfaces like stone, wood and metal, have been found mainly on stone monuments, and on some personal or ritual items such as jewellery and chalices. In the old tales it is said that Ogham was carved on wooden rods or staves, but no example of these has survived.

The script was used for divination, to encode messages and to record ownership. Right up until at least the eighteenth century it was also used as a memory device to help Bards remember stories and poems.

Each of the twenty-five letters is associated with a number of different items and concepts, including letters of the alphabet. As the largest group of letters with an identifiable theme is that of trees, Ogham has gained the reputation of being a 'tree-language of the Druids' or 'the Druid tree alphabet'. Robert Graves's grandfather undertook a major study of the alphabet, but it was Robert Graves himself who made Ogham famous when he published his study of poetic myth, *The White Goddess*, in 1948.

You can use Ogham as a mnemonic to help you learn lists, for divination, or to encode messages. To learn about its use in divination will take some time and you will need either to study books such as those listed at the end of the chapter, or to take a distance-learning course offered by groups such as the Order of Bards, Ovates and Druids.

However, learning how to encode a message in Ogham is easy. Draw a vertical line and then just transpose letters into Ogham strokes. As you can see from the table opposite, certain letters are missing. Your message must be free of the letters J, K, P, W, X, Y, Z or you will have to develop your own convention for them, perhaps using the five combination letters at the end of the alphabet to stand for the letters you need.

Ogham is ideal for carving. You could create a treasure hunt in the garden or in the woods with staves carved with clues stuck in the ground in key places.

The following table shows the Ogham signs and the letters that they correspond to, together with the names of the trees they represent and the Divinatory Meanings given to them by John Matthews and Will Worthington in their book and card set, *The Green Man Tree Oracle* (Connections, 2003).

	Letter	Irish name	Tree
	B	beith	birch
	L	luis	rowan
	F	fearn	alder
	S	saille	willow
	N	nuinn	ash
	H	huathe	hawthorn
	D	duir	oak
	T	tinne	holly
	C	coll	hazel
	Q	quert	apple
	M	muinn	vine
	G	gort	ivy
	NG	ngetal	broom/fern
	STR	straif	blackthorn
	R	ruis	elder
	A	ailm	fir/pine
	O	onn	gorse
	U	ur	heather
	E	edhadh	aspen
	I	ido	yew
	EA	ebhadh	aspen
	OI	oir	spindle
	UI	uileand	honeysuckle
	IO	iphin	gooseberry
	(AE)	phagos	beech

ᔆ Druid Tree Lore ᔆ

The term 'Druid' has been translated as 'magician' or 'forest sage', but originally it probably meant 'strong seer' or 'wise person of the oak'. Classical authors recount how Druids worshipped in sacred groves and ritually cut mistletoe from the boughs of oak trees.

The image of the Druid as a lover of trees grew over the centuries, and today the modern Druid is a staunch defender of trees under threat from development and deforestation.

Each of the three groups of Druids, the Bards, Ovates and Druids, is symbolised by a tree.

The birch tree, known as *Beith* in the tree-language of Ogham, is known as the pioneer tree. Traditionally it was used to make babies' cradles and is the first tree to plant if you wish to forest virgin land. For this reason, when used in divination it signifies birth and new beginnings, as well as a clearing out of the old to make way for the new. Switches of birch are used in saunas, and also in Druid sweat-house ceremonies, to help cleanse the body of impurities; traditionally, criminals were 'cleansed' of their misdeeds by being 'birched'. Maypoles are traditionally made from birch trunks and symbolise the Bard who weaves their magic with word and song.

The yew tree, called *Ioho* in Ogham, is the tree of eternity and of reincarnation – a central doctrine of the Druids. We associate yews with death since they are a familiar sight in graveyards, and the dark green spikes of this evergreen are deadly poisonous (the word toxic derives from *taxus*, the Latin for yew), but for Druids they represent the eternal process of renewal, which includes both death and rebirth. Yews seem to have discovered the secret of renewing themselves; the oldest yews in England are probably over four thousand years old and can be found in Crowhurst in Surrey, in Tisbury in Wiltshire, and at Linton in Herefordshire. The yew's powers of renewal make it the symbol of the Ovates whose main concern is with healing.

The oak tree, *Duir* in Ogham, is the symbol of the Druid. It signifies strength, solidity, continuity of tradition and endurance. Although not as long-lived as the yew, the oak often lives for over five hundred years, and frequently stood at the hub of a village as a symbol of its age and continuity. The oak was thus a tree that acted as a gathering-place for the populace – a remnant of the tradition that Druids taught under the oak tree. Edward the Confessor, for instance, renewed the City of London's charter and swore his oath upon the Bible at what became known as 'Gospel Oak' in Highgate.

✒ Druid Herb Lore ✒

Classical scholars describe how, for magical and healing purposes, the ancient Druids used mistletoe, vervain, and two other plants that they called 'samolus' and 'selago', which were probably fir club moss and water pimpernel. Recent research has added to the list of plants they are likely to have used, and today Druids use herbs to decorate their homes and sanctuaries, and to make incenses, elixirs and magical baths, believing that plants offer ways of healing body and soul.

Meadowsweet has been associated with indigenous spiritual practice in Britain for thousands of years. It was considered sacred in the pre-Druidic period of the Bronze Age when its flowers were offered as floral tributes at burial sites. In medieval times it was used to flavour mead and was given in posies to bridal couples. It was also strewn on the ground to perfume the air with its sweet scent, rather like marzipan, with hints of honey and musk. Modern Druids consider it the perfect herb and flower to use for all rites of passage – marriages, funerals, coming-of-age, and magical initiation. The flowers are used to scent ritual clothing, or are used in an infused oil for ritual anointing.

Mistletoe was ritually gathered by Druids from oaks on the sixth day of the new moon, according to the Roman writer Pliny. It was considered a magical cure for many ailments and became known as 'all-heal', even though it is in fact toxic. Recent research, however, suggests that the plant stimulates the immune system and contains cancer-fighting ingredients. Mistletoe is traditionally associated with fertility: we kiss under the mistletoe at Christmas, and in some parts of England in earlier days a woman who wanted to conceive would tie a sprig around her wrist or waist. In modern Druid practice, mistletoe is used at the winter solstice, with sprigs being distributed to all present as tokens of good luck and fertility in its widest sense for the coming New Year.

Woad is a plant that produces a blue dye. In his *Gallic Wars*, Caesar tells us that British warriors painted themselves blue before riding into battle. The paint they used was most likely woad, since it helps to contract the blood vessels and is therefore good for staunching wounds. By the Middle Ages, woad cultivation was so developed that woad guilds grew up across Europe, and 'woad barons' controlled its lucrative trade. In the sixteenth century, indigo began to be imported from the tropics, and the use of woad as the main source of blue dye began to decline, although it was not until the 1930s that British police and air force uniforms were no longer dyed with it, and the last two woad mills in the country closed down.

Scientists have now found that the plant has powerful cancer-fighting properties, producing large amounts of glucobrassicin, more than sixty times the amount found in broccoli, which is already known for its potential to reduce tumours. It is now produced commercially for home dyeing and painting, and modern-day Druids use it to dye their robes.

∾ Druid Animal Lore ∾

All indigenous shamanic cultures throughout the world regard animals as sacred and believe they convey healing and messages through their appearance in dreams and trance. British and Celtic folklore is full of stories about animals and their qualities, and much of this lore probably arose out of the shamanic experiences of the early inhabitants of these isles, in particular the Druids and, later, the Anglo-Saxon sorcerers whose world is explored in the following chapter. On encountering animals in the wild, as well as in trance states, these early magicians translated their experiences into songs and stories, which, travelling through the generations, became embedded in folklore.

The salmon is notable for the way it returns, jumping upstream, to the place of its birth to spawn and die. In ancient folklore, the salmon  was the oldest and wisest of creatures, symbolising the wisdom and inspiration sought by the Druids. To find wisdom we too need to 'jump upstream': to go against the prevailing current of superficial interests and trends, to journey in consciousness back to our beginnings, recapitulating our lives and 'remembering ourselves' again.

The bear was revered in Britain and throughout Europe from the earliest of times. Its great strength and ferocity was both feared and admired, and early heroes were described as bears as a mark of respect. The name Arthur derives from the Celtic word for bear – 'Art' – and in Welwyn in Hertfordshire an Iron Age chieftain, whose  burial was unearthed, was found wearing a bearskin. Bear's teeth were considered potent charms and ancient bear amulets made out of jet have been found in Yorkshire. For contemporary Druids, the bear symbolises our potential to marry our inner strength with our intuition, so we can be sensitive without becoming weak.

The stag has been seen as a creature of great power for thousands of years in England. Every year at rutting time in September, the Abbots Bromley Horn Dancers in Staffordshire perform a stag dance with antlered headdresses, and there is evidence that such dances were being performed over 9,500 years ago at Star Carr in Yorkshire, where a number of stag skulls, complete with antlers, have been found with hollowed-out insides and holes cut to make them easy to wear. Such was the prevalence of similar activities throughout Britain that in the seventh century St Augustine issued strict instructions that no one must indulge in 'that most filthy habit of dressing up as a stag'. For Druids today the stag is connected with fertility, sexuality and new beginnings.

C.S. LEWIS, 1898–1963

Almost every era of magic in England has inspired a writer of fiction. C.S. Lewis loved Celtic myth and legend, whilst his friend J.R.R. Tolkien was fascinated by the Anglo-Saxon period. T.H. White told tales of England's most famous wizard, Merlin. Terry Pratchett writes about witches, Susanna Clarke about nineteenth-century magicians. Yet none of these famous writers has actually practised magic themselves – in the sense of joining covens or magical orders, of conducting occult rites or magical ceremonies. Despite this, their careers prove them to be extremely successful magicians, since they have accomplished one of the great goals of magic: to re-enchant the world, to make us experience life as exciting and mysterious, to fill us with wonder.

C.S. Lewis was born and brought up in Northern Ireland where he had a difficult childhood. His father remained a distant figure for him, his mother died when he was ten years old, and the headmaster of the boarding school he later called 'Belsen' ended up in an insane asylum. At the age of thirteen he moved to England and at first hated the country. Although he was raised a Christian, by the age of fifteen he lost his faith and became interested in mythology – particularly Celtic – and the occult. He loved the work of the mystic poet W.B. Yeats, who was a practising magician in the Hermetic Order of the Golden Dawn, and met him twice. He regained his belief only when he was thirty-three, remaining a deeply committed Christian until his death.

As a boy he fell in love with the Beatrix Potter books. He and his brother created an imaginary world called 'Boxen', peopled with animals that thought and talked like humans. The world of Boxen never left him, and later, in his most successful books, *The Narnia Chronicles*, animals that talk are central to the story. By the time he wrote these, he was a Christian, and he uses the *Chronicles* allegorically to convey his faith. Aslan the lion, for example, who sacrifices himself to save the children of the tale, symbolises Christ.

Despite his turning away from the world of the occult and pagan mythology, we can see their influence on his work, whether or not Lewis was conscious of this. His depiction of the 'Other-world' of Narnia, and of the way the children travel there, is reminiscent of shamanic journeying, a technique that may well have been used by the ancient Druids and Anglo-Saxon wizards, and which is used by modern-day practitioners such as Caitlin Matthews and Brian Bates, who feature in this and the following chapter. As Caitlin Matthews explains, in shamanic journeys it is important to find animals in the Other-world who can guide and counsel you, and this is a central theme in the Narnia stories. Perhaps it is no coincidence that a white stag, a powerful pagan and magical symbol, appears at the beginning and the end of the children's visit to Narnia in *The Lion, the Witch and the Wardrobe*.

C.S. Lewis once wrote: 'Nature is not the only thing that exists. There is "another world" and that is where we come from.' He returned to that world on 22 November 1963 when he died in Oxford – on the same day that Aldous Huxley died and John F. Kennedy was assassinated.

*The Eagle and Child pub in Oxford. It was here that C.S. Lewis and
J.R.R. Tolkien formed an informal literary club they called 'The Inklings'.
Before lunch on weekdays, they and others would meet here, and in other
pubs, to read out excerpts from their latest writing and to discuss literature
– particularly of the fantasy genre. The Inklings met between the 1930s
and 1960s, and its members included Tolkien's son Christopher, Charles
Williams and Lord David Cecil. There is now a display of memorabilia in
a corner of the pub.*

The Druid as Shaman – CAITLIN MATTHEWS

*Caitlin Matthews lives in Oxford with her husband John, who is one
of the foremost experts on the 'Matter of Britain' – the Arthurian and
Grail mysteries. Caitlin first encountered the Druids when she met
Ross Nichols as a young woman. She now holds the Order of Bards,
Ovates and Druids Mount Haemus Award for Druid scholarship.*

*Caitlin's special area of expertise lies in teaching people the art of
'journeying' – a shamanic technique that many people believe was
employed by the Druids and the Anglo-Saxon wizards who followed
in their wake. Journeying involves entering into a trance state through
the use of drumming and visualisation, to explore the 'inner world' or
'Otherworld'.*

An expert in contemporary and Celtic shamanism, Caitlin has taught many people how to journey in her courses and in the shamanic practice that she runs from her home. Her book, Singing the Soul Back Home, *has become a standard text on the subject. In the interview below she gives an insight into the preliminaries of shamanic journeying.*

Shamanism pre-dates organised religion by several thousand years. It is the servant of all religions, and a variety of cultural forms of shamanism are still found on every continent, which use healing  methods that would have been understood and practised by our ancestors. We could say that it's a co-operative method of finding healing and balance by consulting known and loved allies and spirits.

Certain fears often arise when people consider shamanism, but practitioners today are clear about the ethics of their craft. The distinction between shamanism and sorcery is quite clear: a shaman co-operates with the spirit world; a sorcerer tries to manipulate it. The mistake is to go looking for power through shamanistic techniques. Using power for selfish ends destroys our authority with the spirit world. To speak of possessing power is as stupid as saying you own the air in your lungs.

Whilst indigenous shamans may use powerful, mind-altering substances, these are not necessary for successful journeying. Western society has a recreational rather than a sacred understanding of drugs that is unhelpful and actively dangerous when people do not understand dosage levels and have no practical experience of the Other-world.

Shamanism requires discipline, order and groundedness; no one should practise it while in an unclear or confused condition. Journeying is the basis of shamanic work, but not everyone who can journey is necessarily a shaman. That requires a special calling, which most people would wish to avoid; following a code of ethical responsibility, accessibility to clients and a setting aside of one's personal preferences is a hard way to live.

The Other-world has three dimensions: Upper, Middle and Lower. The Middle World is familiar and like a mirror image of our own; the Lower World is the place of the ancestors and inherited knowledge. It is not the Underworld or 'Hell' by which Christianity used to demonise the practice of early magic, but is the place of natural power. The Upper World is the world of enlightenment, overviews and the beauty of vision. Everyone wants to go straight there first, but you need to start in the Lower World, to meet beings who will act as your guides and to get a grounding in how journeying works. But before you can start, you need a gateway and a specific issue or question to give purpose and direction to your journey. Journeying is not aimless.

A gateway is something that you can visualise, which will help you gain entry to the Other-world. It will usually be some familiar spot that exists in nature, perhaps a favourite place from your childhood. A Lower World gateway may be a hole, a tunnel, a well, a spring – something that goes down. An Upper World gateway may be a tree, a mountain, a path – something that goes up. Both need to feel familiar and comfortable.

To support your journeying and enable your soul to travel to locations and meet allies, one uses drumming or some other monotonic sound or rhythm. The trick is to attend to and travel upon the overtones of the drum, which create the wave on which the soul travels. You can even use a specially made drumming CD for this, and most provide a call-back signal to remind you to return to your gateway and finish the journey.

Once you are immersed in the sound wave, imagine yourself leaving part of your soul in the here and now and take the rest of your soul with you as you go down and down through your gateway until you emerge into a place that has ground, landscape and sky. You won't know in advance what this will look like and, just like arriving in a foreign country for the first time, it can be a bit disconcerting, so you need to be met and introduced to this new world – hence the need for inner 'guides' or 'allies'.

Your first aim should be to meet your power animal: a spirit animal that may be very familiar to you, since it will have been with you all your life, although you have not realised it. You might already be aware of other spirits and allies, or you may become acquainted with them as you learn to journey. Connection to your animal or guide is absolutely critical to the art of journeying. It is like plugging into an electric socket, making the right connection to the spirit world, and when you find the right one – and you should always carefully discern that you have met an ally by questioning and monitoring your own responses – you will get a sense of excitement. You and your animal may communicate by words, perhaps by images or even with heart-to-heart communication. All of us are different and these methods of communication are instinctive, but modern life has persuaded most of us to drown them out. Keep your animal with you at all times.

With your animal to guide you, you can journey to the Lower World. If you are uncertain where to go, let your animal decide for you. Always ask: 'Show me how', 'Teach me how': the more dynamic the verb, the better the journey. In the journey, be aware of moving, rather than sitting and waiting. Stay with your animal at all times. Journeying is active, whilst meditation is passive. When you get the call-back signal, come back through the gateway and then ground yourself by saying something like: 'I am back now.' Bring your animal back with you, dance with it, speak with it, let it feel and smell your world – make it a true friend. You might feel reluctant, at first, but gradually you and your ally will meld! Trust is built up over many journeys and consultations with each of our allies.

ᴈ Things to Do ᴇ

Ever since their own time, the Druids have acted as potent stimulants to the creative mind, every age dreaming them anew, and often in two or three markedly different ways at once. An age of British society, in particular, which fails to work creatively with the image of them is one which is hardly doing justice to its own inheritance, and may easily be suspected of a poverty of imagination.

RONALD HUTTON, *THE REBIRTH OF DRUIDRY*

❋ Attend a traditional Bardic Celebration this summer. In Cornwall, the Gorseth Kernow ('Kernow' is the ancient name for Cornwall) is known as the 'Open Gorseth'. Members of the Gorseth wear traditional robes and perform a ceremony in which new Bards are admitted, and competition prizes and major awards are presented. It is performed, weather permitting, in the open, at various points across Cornwall, and the public is encouraged to attend. For details see their website: www.gorsethkernow.org.uk

A similar celebration in Wales, known as the eisteddfod, is a much bigger affair, and is held over a week at a different location each year. Imagine the atmosphere of an agricultural show with stalls and exhibits, a caravan park and campsite, combined with the excitement and variety of an arts festival, then add the pageantry of robed Bards and Druids performing ceremonies and awarding prizes, and you come close to the spirit of the eisteddfod. For details see www.eisteddfod.org.uk

❋ See Druids at work – and a magical ritual in the open air. The best time to do this is at one of their eight festival times (featured in Chapter 12):

Druid Festivals

The Winter Solstice – 21/22 December
Imbolc – 1 February
The Spring Equinox – 20/21/22 March
Beltane – 1 May
Summer Solstice – 21/22 June
Lughnasadh – 1 August
Autumn Equinox – 20/21/22 September
Samhain – 1 November

Many Druid groups hold their celebrations in public places and welcome visitors. Check dates and times because festivals may be held on the nearest weekend, rather than on the actual day. All eight celebrations are regularly held at the stone circle in Avebury, Wiltshire, at the Long Man of Wilmington in East Sussex, at Stanton Drew in Somerset, and at Castlerigg stone circle in Cumbria, amongst other places. See the events listings at the Order of Bards, Ovates and Druids' website, www.druidry. org, and the Druid Network's website at www. druidnetwork.org

If you attend one of these celebrations you are likely to experience a colourful event that will include magical ritual, music, dance and perhaps a pagan marriage, known as a handfasting, or a child's naming ceremony. After the event participants will probably resort to a nearby tavern, such as the Red Lion in Avebury or the Giant's Rest in Wilmington (which proudly bears a framed certificate on its wall declaring it 'The most Druid-Friendly pub in Sussex').

❈ Visit Druid pubs. A dedicated researcher into the
history of Druidry, or simply the curious, might
want to visit some or all of the pubs named after the
Druids. Thankfully they are sufficiently far apart from
each other to prevent a Druid pub crawl ever catching on.

Only one town has two Druid pubs in it: Brighton in
Sussex, which boasts The Druid's Head and The Druid's
Arms. Otherwise the pubs are conveniently sprinkled
across the land at irregular intervals. Another Druid's
Head is in Herne Bay, Kent. Matlock in Derbyshire has
The Druid Inn, Nottingham The Druid's Tavern, and
in Bradford, West Yorkshire, there is a pub called simply
The Druids. The most popular name for a Druid pub,
however, is The Druid's Arms, which is found not only
in Brighton, but in Portsmouth in Hampshire, at Stanton
Drew in Somerset, at Doncaster in south Yorkshire, at
Halifax and Keighley in West Yorkshire, at Oldham in
Lancashire, and at Penrith in Cumbria.

The most historic Druid pub is The King's Arms in
Poland Street, Soho, London. It was here that the first
Druid fraternal society, the Ancient Order of Druids,
held its inaugural meeting on 28 November 1781.
A plaque on the wall commemorates the occasion.
Visitors should be aware that the fraternal influence has
intensified and it is now a gay pub.

❈ Spend an evening in. Try tuning in to 'Druidcast – the
podcast of the Order of Bards, Ovates and Druids'.
Each programme combines a lively mix of music and
interviews, which will give you a good feel for the way
Druidry is practised in Britain in the modern era. You
can hear episodes or download them to your iPod from
iTunes or from www.druidry.org

❈ Spend an evening out. Try mingling with 25,000 other
people at dawn at Stonehenge on the summer solstice.

Somewhere in the middle of the stones you might find Druids performing a ceremony, and the sun just might appear between the stones at the appointed hour, making all the effort worthwhile. For details, see www.english-heritage.org.uk

❀ Go camping. If you like the idea of camping out under the stars, and hearing about Druid lore around a bonfire, try visiting a Druid camp. For details, see www.druidry.org or www.druidnetwork.org

❀ Try writing in Ogham. Send a secret message to your kids or a love letter in Ogham ... Somehow you'll have to let the recipient 'discover' the alphabet or they won't be able to decipher it! Set up an Ogham treasure hunt and leave clues written in Ogham.

❀ Learn Druid lore and magic by post. The Order of Bards, Ovates and Druids will send you monthly packages of lessons, including CDs. Write to OBOD, PO Box 1333, Lewes, East Sussex BN7 1HB, or telephone 01273 470888. The email address is office@druidry.org, and the website is www.druidry.org

↜ Resources ↝

BOOKS

The Druid Animal Oracle, Philip Carr-Gomm and Stephanie Carr-Gomm (Connections, 1994)

Druid Mysteries: Ancient Wisdom for the 21st Century, Philip Carr-Gomm (Rider, 2002)

The Druid Plant Oracle, Philip and Stephanie Carr-Gomm (Connections, 2008)

The Druid Way: A Shamanic Journey Through an Ancient Landscape, Philip Carr-Gomm (Thoth Books, 2006)

What Do Druids Believe? Philip Carr-Gomm (Granta, 2006)
Natural Druidry, Kristoffer Hughes (Thoth Books, 2007)
Living Druidry, Emma Restall Orr (Piatkus, 2004)

BOOKS ON THE HISTORY OF THE DRUIDS
The Druids, Ronald Hutton (Hambledon Continuum, 2007)

BOOKS ON THE USE OF OGHAM AND OGHAM DIVINATION SETS
The Celtic Tree Oracle, Liz and Colin Murray (Rider, 1989)
Celtic Wisdom Sticks, Caitlin Matthews (Connections, 2001)
The Green Man Tree Oracle: Ancient Wisdom from the Greenwood, John
    Matthews and Will Worthington (Connections, 2003)
*Ogam: How to Read, Create and Shape your Destiny through the Celtic
    Oracle*, Paul Rhys Mountfort (Rider, 2001)

WEBSITES
The Druid Network at www.druidnetwork.org
The Order of Bards, Ovates and Druids at www.druidry.org
The British Druid Order at www.druidry.co.uk

CHAPTER THREE

STAR-CUNNING AND WYRD-CRAFT

The World of the Anglo-Saxon Sorcerer

*Against a dwarf one must take seven small holy
wafers, such as one makes holy communion with,
and write these names on each wafer: Maximian,
Malchus, John, Martimian, Dionysus,
Constantine, Searfion. Then again the charm . . .
one must sing, first in the left ear, then in the right
ear, then upon the top of the man's head. And
then go to a maiden and let her hang it around his
neck, and do so for three days; it will speedily be
better for the patient.*

'CHARM AGAINST A DWARF OR A FEVER', BL MS
HARLEIAN COLLECTION 585 (C.1000 AD)

Every generation builds upon the bones and ashes of its pre-decessors. As the Roman occupation of Britain came to an end, a new era was ushered in that has come to be known as the Dark Ages, but it was out of the fertile soil of this so-called dark-ness that a new kind of magic emerged. This is the magic familiar to us all, thanks to the work of J.R.R. Tolkien and his trilogy, *The Lord of the Rings.*

The world created by Tolkien is magical, exciting and terrify-ing – but it is not simply a world of fantasy created out of thin air. Tolkien drew his inspiration from history, from the mythology and world-view of the Anglo-Saxons, who believed in the exist-ence of elves and orcs, demons, dwarves and goblins. They forged swords with magical names and carved rings with runes of power. And they battled against the forces of evil with the help of wizards and sorcerers.

Evil stalked the earth in the guise of illness, plague, poverty and warfare. And it was the magician who acted as priest and doctor – as the hero-figure who would do battle with these forces with spells, charms and rituals to chase away the spirits that caused these maledictions.

By exploring the world of the Anglo-Saxon sorcerer – of the skills they used to help their communities – we can get closer to understanding what it is that makes Tolkien's wizard Gandalf so evocative for us, and why some people today still practise Anglo-Saxon magic.

◈ The Coming of the Anglo-Saxons ◈
and the Creation of England

The fifth century was a time of turmoil, as the Roman Empire collapsed and Britain was abandoned by its colonial rulers. The old world – of pagan worship and the Druids – went into decline as the new faith of Christianity began to challenge the old ways. The steady press of migrations from northern Europe, which the Romans had attempted to prevent, not only with their appointment of a 'Count of the Saxon Shore' to police the southern and eastern coasts of Britain but by building fortresses along the east coast, now became a tide. But it was out of all this turmoil that the people known as 'the English', and the country known as 'England', emerged.

England takes its name from the Angles, a Germanic tribe who arrived here in the fifth century, alongside the Saxons and Jutes from Germany and Scandinavia who began settling in the east and the south. With their arrival a new kind of magical and religious practice appeared on these shores, epitomised in the world of the Anglo-Saxon wizard.

This period of change between the old order and the new is illustrated in the legend of Merlin, first recounted in the twelfth century by Geoffrey of Monmouth in his *History of the Kings of Britain* when the evil King Vortigern asks the young wizard Merlin why the fortress in Snowdonia that he is building to defend himself from the Saxons keeps falling down. Merlin, using his visionary powers, tells him that two dragons, one white and one red, are fighting in a subterranean pool beneath the site chosen for the castle. The white dragon represents the Saxons, the red the Britons. Merlin prophesies that Vortigern will be slain and that the Saxons will almost triumph, only to be beaten back by a new king – Arthur, champion of the Britons.

We will explore the world of Arthur and his wizard Merlin more closely in the next chapter. History did not conform to myth, however, and whilst the Saxons failed to penetrate all of Britain, they succeeded, along with the Jutes and Angles, in settling much of England, in the process changing the nature of the culture and the language that has come to be known as English. It was during these 'Dark Ages' – the period roughly between the fifth and ninth centuries – that the English identity as a nation was created, with the kingdoms of England uniting for the first time as one country under one king in 828.

Merlin and Nimue *by Gustav Doré.*
The story of England's most famous magician was set in the
fifth century, when Britain was in turmoil following the collapse
of Roman rule. Merlin ensured that Arthur succeeded to the
throne to repel the Saxons, and master-minded the Grail Quest.
Some writers believe that Merlin was based on a real historical
figure, Ambrosius Aurelius.

It was this period, formed as the heathen world of the Anglo-Saxon interacted with the part-Christian, part-Druid or pagan world of the Celts and the Romano-British, that so inspired the young Tolkien as he studied Old English at Oxford University. 'Middle Earth' was a term used by the Anglo-Saxons to describe the everyday world that exists between the Upper World, or Heaven, and the Underworld, or Hell, and it became Tolkien's life's work to create a mythology for England, as he once put it, by creating his history of Middle Earth, in *The Lord of the Rings* and other writings.

Although Tolkien's work is fiction, it is inspired by, and is based upon, historical material, most of it Anglo-Saxon. Gandalf is the wizard Merlin reborn for the modern age, and just as England has evolved to become the world's leading storehouse of magical traditions, so it has become the world's greatest source of magical fiction, with writers such as J.K.Rowling, Terry Pratchett and Susanna Clarke being only the most recent in a line of writers that might seem to stretch from Tolkien's day, but which is really rooted much further back in the times of Geoffrey of Monmouth, and the earlier tales of the ancient bards.

J.R.R. TOLKIEN, 1892–1973

J.R.R. Tolkien's and C.S. Lewis's evocation of worlds steeped in magic marked the beginning of an era in which many English writers have excelled in presenting fictional or fantasy worlds peopled by magicians.

Tolkien's genius was born out of a painful early life in the West Midlands. His mother died when he was four, his father when he was twelve. He and his brother, as destitute orphans, were boarded out and taken under the wing of a Catholic priest. From an early age Tolkien was fascinated by languages, inventing his own and mastering not only the classics, but a number of other languages, including Gothic and Finnish.

At the age of sixteen he found friendship in Edith, a girl three years his elder. Three years later the priest forbade them from meeting or even corresponding until Tolkien was twenty-one. While he was at Oxford University his fascination for the Anglo-Saxon period intensified. It was a couplet from Cynewulf's poem

'Crist', which ran: 'Hail, Earendel, brightest of angels, over Middle Earth sent to men', that inspired his creation of the imaginary world that would form the setting for most of his writing.

During the First World War, at the age of twenty-four, he married Edith, and was then sent to France where he contracted trench fever. Most of his childhood friends were killed in the war. On returning to England he worked first as Reader in English Language at the University of Leeds. In 1925 he was appointed Professor of Anglo-Saxon at Oxford, where his scholarly study, 'Beowulf: the Monsters and the Critics', became highly influential. He became a founder member of 'The Inklings', a group of authors that included his close friend C.S. Lewis, who met regularly for conversation and to share their work (see Chapter 2).

He and Edith were both Catholics, and had four children, for whom Tolkien wrote stories about a world peopled with hobbits, elves, dwarves and magicians. It was these stories that would one day become the most widely read works of fiction in the world – *The Hobbit* and *The Lord of the Rings*. His son Christopher has worked tirelessly to edit his father's unpublished writings, presenting much of this in a twelve-volume collection entitled *The History of Middle Earth*.

Tolkien's lifelong love of Anglo-Saxon Old English can be seen in his remark that he would like to speak nothing but Old Mercian – a dialect of Old English.

The Middle Earth of England has truly enchanted the world, and yet so little remains today from that period of the Dark Ages, partly because the Anglo-Saxons chose to build in wood rather than stone, but mainly because Henry VIII's Dissolution of the Monasteries resulted in the loss of all but a handful of literary works from that era. Even so, from these manuscripts, such as

'The Exeter Book of Riddles', the story of Beowulf, and the collection of magico-medical texts known as the 'Lacnunga', we can piece together the world of the Anglo-Saxons, and in particular the world of their sorcerers.

We can also turn to the few existing artefacts to help us build a picture of what life was like then. We know that runes, an alphabet that came originally from Scandinavia but which developed its own variant in England, were used here for five hundred years, and they can still be seen on the Bewcastle Cross in Cumbria, on the Northumbrian Franks Casket, and on a few other remains, such as rings and swords.

The most spectacular finds from the Anglo-Saxon period are their ship burials, which they carried out long before those of the Vikings, who only began raiding or migrating to Britain much later, in the eighth century. Clearly, the idea that after death the soul must

The seventh-century Northumbrian Franks Casket.

travel across a river or sea is rooted deep in the human psyche. The Greeks wrote of the River Styx, and the ancient Egyptians also buried a ship, which was probably a funerary barge, beside the Great Pyramid at Giza. Three Anglo-Saxon ship burials have been unearthed in England, all in East Anglia: one in Norfolk, at Caister-on-Sea, and two in Suffolk: at Snape Common near Aldeburgh, and at Sutton Hoo, which has yielded the greatest amount of treasure, now on view at the British Museum.

Apart from these few artefacts and a handful of manuscripts, Anglo-Saxon culture lies closest to us in the most familiar of ways – the old gods speaking to us through the names of towns and villages and days of the week. Four are named after Saxon gods: Tuesday after the god Tiw, Wednesday after Woden, Thursday after Thunor or Thor, and Friday after the goddess Frig or Freya. And as Anglo-Saxon scholar Stephen Pollington says: 'All our hardiest words – mother, father, land, earth, tree, field, sky, love, hate, live, die, eat, drink, sleep, wake – are Anglo-Saxon words.'[1]

To get a feeling for this period, you can visit the old burial site of Sutton Hoo or the reconstructed village of West Stow near Bury St Edmunds, but there are other more intimate, less popular places where a hint of the old Saxon magic still clings to earth, tree and stone. The Saxons left almost no buildings from the pagan period before AD 700 – in fact, they refused to live in the comfortable villas of the departed Romano-British – but place names give us a clue to their settlements. Names ending in '-orm', for example, suggest that they were the dwelling places of dragons, as well as Saxons. They believed dragons were like huge worms with long, scaly and slimy bodies, short legs, or none at all, and usually no wings. They killed with their poisonous breath, rather than with fire, and guarded treasure, objects of power and secrets. Tales such as the well-known 'Lambton Worm' from Northumbria may well have originated in Saxon times.

A typical village with a Saxon history is Steyning in West Sussex. Now a quiet rural backwater of thatched cottages and a few shops, it was once a busy port where King Alfred's father was buried and where Cuthman, the Saxon saint, was said to have founded a church. A local museum displays the history of the village, and in the church is a stone carved with patterns that may well be runes (see p. 39).

✒ Unearthing the Magic ✑

To capture a real sense of the magic of those times, imagine that the Roman governor and his Count of the Saxon Shore have abandoned their fortresses and villas, and returned to Rome with most of their troops. There are less than a million people on this island and, although much of the forest has already been felled, there are still great swathes of ancient woodland. One such is the 2,500 square miles of the Anderida forest in southern England, which stretches from the Rother in Kent to East Meon in Hampshire, bounded to north and south by the Downs. Bears, boars and wolves still find shelter in these wild places and although Christianity reached Britain during the Roman occupation, its hold on the populace is still tenuous.

Pope Gregory's letter to Abbot Mellitus on his departure for England, dated 17 June 601, advises him:

When (by God's help) you come to our most reverend brother, Bishop Augustine [in Kent], I want you to tell him how earnestly I have been pondering over the affairs of the English: I have come to the conclusion that the temples of the idols in England should not on any account be destroyed. Augustine must smash the idols, but the temples themselves should be sprinkled with holy water and altars set up in them in which relics are to be enclosed. For we ought to take advantage of well-built temples by purifying them from devil-worship and dedicating them to the service of the true God. In this way, I hope the people (seeing their temples are not destroyed) will leave their idolatry and yet continue to frequent the places as formerly, so coming to know and revere the true God. And since the sacrifice of many oxen to devils is their custom, some other rite ought to be solemnized in its place such as a Day of Dedication or Festivals for the holy martyrs whose relics are there enshrined. On such high days the people might well build themselves shelters of boughs round about the churches that were once temples and celebrate the occasion with pious feasting. They must no more sacrifice animals to the Devil, but they may kill them for food to the glory of God while giving thanks for his bounty as the provider of all gifts.[2]

From the time of the collapse of Roman rule it took at least five generations for Christianity to truly take hold in England, and it was not until the Synod of Whitby, in Yorkshire, in the seventh century that all of England could be called Christian – at least in name. Prior to that, the English were for the most part pagan and, as we can see from the Pope's letter, they had to be enticed away from the worship of the old gods, which he called 'devils', towards a worship of the 'One True God'. Other Church writings help to complete the picture of a people who, in Anglo-Saxon regions, worshipped divinities such as Woden, Thunor, Tiw and Frig.

Many of the magical practices and beliefs of the Anglo-Saxons were identical to those practised by the earlier inhabitants of the land, the Celts and the Romano-British. In addition to a number of gods, they believed in nature spirits – elves, demons and fairies. Swords were given names and were believed to have their own innate power. Like the Druids, Anglo-Saxons worshipped in sacred groves and revered springs, casting precious objects into bogs and holy wells as offerings. Like those of the Celts, their rites involved the sacrifice of animals and followed the turning wheel of the year. Key moments of the farming cycle, such as lambing, sowing and harvesting, were celebrated with feasting and ritual.

As papal bulls record, the Church deliberately took over these special times as well as the holy places of these pagans, so that the people could still enjoy their festivities but within the new faith. In this way the winter solstice was gradually forgotten as Christmas replaced it; the spring equinox was transformed into Easter; the old Celtic rite of Imbolc, which marked the first lambing, was replaced by Candlemas, and so on.

Even so, despite their attempts at dominion over the old sacred times and places, the Church was unable to suppress the magic that was still being practised, and the Anglo-Saxon texts can be read as records of a world in transition, in which pagan rites and customs are mingled with Christian devotion, until, from the seventh century onwards, their pagan origins were gradually forgotten by the majority of the populace.

᭣ Anglo-Saxon Magic ᭣

Our best insight into the world of the Anglo-Saxon wizard comes from the 'Lacnunga', a collection of medical and magical texts from the tenth and eleventh centuries. To combat illness or crop failure, the effects of malevolent witchcraft or the work of thieves, Anglo-Saxons turned to their local wise person or wizard (a word that derives from the Middle English *wys* meaning wise). The 'Lacnunga' shows how this wizard used incantations, prayers, herbs, charms and ritual acts to encourage healing, and to repel harmful magic or evil spirits, which were often described as elves. In addition, Dr Brian Bates, the foremost authority on Anglo-Saxon magic, believes they also used techniques, which we now term shamanic, such as dancing or the ingestion of certain plants or mushrooms, to enter into a trance-like state to receive guidance and healing.

Two examples from the 'Lacnunga', the Nine Herbs Charm and the Land Ceremonies Charm, show how herb lore, star lore and probably rune lore were used in these times to give healing and promote the fertility of the land.

⊙ *The Nine Herbs Charm*

'The Nine Herbs Charm' was used to treat wounds and nine different poisons or infections. It begins powerfully and mysteriously, addressing each of the nine herbs directly:

> These nine stand in opposition against nine poisons.
> Recall, mugwort, what you declared,
> what you established, at the Great Council.
> 'Unique' you are called, most senior of herbs.
> You prevail against three and against thirty,
> you prevail against poison and against infection,
> you prevail against the harmful one that travels throughout the land.[3]

The other herbs of the charm are then spoken to, and their virtues listed: Plantain (known as 'waybread'), lamb's cress, attorlape (thought to be cockspur grass or betony), camomile, wergulu (which may be nettle), chervil, fennel and crab apple.

Once all nine herbs are invoked and praised, instructions are given on how to prepare and administer them. The practitioner is told to sing the charm three times as each ingredient is ground to a powder and mixed with soap and apple juice. They should then 'prepare a paste of water and of ashes, take fennel, boil it with the paste and wash it with a beaten egg when you apply the salve'. Before applying it, however, the healer should sing the charm into the patient's mouth, into both their ears and over their wound.

Although this bit of magic may seem like pure superstition, we now know that each of these herbs offers specific pharmacological benefits, and that even if singing over the ingredients and the patient exerts only a placebo effect, this in itself can be 'magical' in its capacity for healing.

In common with magical practice across the world and down the centuries, the moment that a plant was picked was considered of great significance. Anglo-Saxon herbalists were deeply versed in star lore, or star-cunning as it was often called, when cunning meant 'knowing' rather than 'wily'. The 'Lacnunga', for example, tells us that mulberry should be picked 'when to all men the moon is seventeen nights old, after the meeting of the sun, ere the rising of the moon'. Periwinkle, on the other hand, should be plucked 'when the moon is nine nights old, and eleven nights, and thirteen nights, and thirty nights, and when it is one night old'.[4]

⊙ *The Land Ceremonies Charm*

The magical power of the elements of nature – of sun and moon, of earth and water – is most strongly conveyed in the 'Lacnunga' in a ritual designed to improve the fertility of the fields. Known as 'The Land Ceremonies Charm', the rite is clearly pagan, although it includes Christian symbolism.

The practitioner is told to dig up, 'at night before daybreak', four sods of earth from the four sides of the land that is to be blessed, and then to take 'oil and honey and yeast and milk of all the cattle that are on the land, and part of every tree growing on the land, except hard trees, and part of every well-known herb, except burdock only, and pour moonglow dew [or holy water, depending on your translation] on them, and then let it drip three times on the bottom of the sods'.[5]

In the manuscript, which was written by Christian scribes, whoever is performing the rite is then urged to say, 'Grow, and multiply and fill the Earth,' followed by the Lord's Prayer repeated a number of times. The sods must then be taken into a church so that a priest can sing four masses over them. Dr Brian Bates believes that the mass is a later substitution, and that 'in the original ceremony it is likely that the sods would be taken to a sacred site, a forest sanctuary or stone circle, where they could be placed so that the first rays of the sun would strike upon the grass, and incantations would be sung rather than a mass.'[6]

As if this were not enough, more magic had to be performed. The 'Lacnunga' tells us that 'four aspen tokens of Christ' (i.e. crosses) should have the names Matthew, Mark, Luke and John written on their arms, and that a cross should be laid in each of the four holes created when the sods were dug up. Once the sods are laid on top of them, the word 'Grow!' should be repeated nine times, followed by the Lord's Prayer, also repeated nine times.

Bates believes that this is a distortion of the original magical act: the carving of rune messages designed to attract fertility on aspen rune-staves. These would then 'surround and criss-cross the field with magical powers'.

What an extraordinary ritual! But the magic was not over. The magician – for whoever was practising this rite was clearly practising magic, whatever the Christian gloss – was instructed to turn east, bow nine times and say a prayer, which in its Christian form calls upon God's grace to make the crops grow, and which in its pagan form finishes by asking that the 'swelling crops be wakened for our worldly need; that the fielded earth be filled, and the green fields made beautiful'.

Then, after turning around three times clockwise, the magician prostrated himself on the ground, 'chanting for the fields to be green for the benefit of the owner of the land and all those who were subject to him', according to Dr Bates, or reciting the Litany and the Sanctus, the Magnificat, and the Lord's Prayer, according to the usual interpretation of the 'Lacnunga'.

The plough and the land were then blessed. Frankincense, fennel, 'hallowed paste and hallowed salt' were rubbed into the plough. Finally, seed was put 'in the body of the plough' as a charm was recited that began: 'Erce, Erce, Erce, Mother of Earth, may the Almighty, the eternal Lord, grant you fields growing and thriving . . .'

The first furrow was then ploughed while prayers were said, and a loaf made with milk and holy water was laid in it, completing this long and remarkable ritual.

✑ Charms and Spells ✑

The magical treatment for sickness in many cultures involves the use of healing herbs, combined with the power of prayer and song. All over the world from the earliest of times practitioners would say prayers and chant over their medicines and their patients as they administered their remedies. Anglo-Saxon medicine followed the same pattern. Elves were often seen as the bearers of disease, whose poisons could be expelled with charms and spells that combined the power of plants and prayer.

Here are the instructions for administering a charm against 'water-elf disease', thought to be possibly chickenpox or measles, recorded in the tenth century:

> If someone is suffering from water-elf-disease then the nails of
> his hands are discoloured and the eyes watery and he prefers
> to look down [i.e. avoid light]. Prepare this for his
> medicine: boarthroat [aarline thistle], cassock, the tuber
> of iris, yew-berry, lupin, elecampane, the heads of
> marshmallow, water-mint, dill, lily, attorlothe [probably
> betony], pennyroyal, horehound, dock, elder, centaury,
> wormwood, strawberry leaves, comfrey. Steep in ale, add holy
> water and sing this charm over it thrice:
>
> > I inside have inscribed the best of war-bandages,
> > so wounds shall not burn nor burst,
> > nor spread, nor multiply, nor throb,
> > nor wound grow, nor injury deepen,
> > but to him I myself proffer a cup of healing;
> > let it not pain you any more than earth hurts earth.
>
> Then sing this many times: 'Let earth reduce you with all her
> might and power.' These charms one can sing over the
> wound.[7]

By the time Anglo-Saxon charms were written down, their original pagan origins had become fused with Christian elements. Many of the charms are short formulae in Latin, sometimes combined with misunderstood words in Greek, Irish or Hebrew. The instructions given with the longer charms show how various elements were combined to produce a magical effect: the Anglo-Saxon healer would chant, sometimes in gibberish, sometimes adding spittle to his medicine and blowing on the patient's wounds. A priest might be asked to bless the remedy, and holy water was often added to it.

A romantic view of the Anglo-Saxon shaman might see him as a sorcerer wielding supernatural powers, but the historical record suggests that many practices were redolent with superstition, like this tenth-century charm for curing a sick horse:

> If a horse be shot with illness, take a knife whose hilt is of yellow horn of the ox, and let there be three iron nails in it. Then inscribe on the front of the head of the horse the sign of Christ [i.e. the cross], so that it bleeds; then inscribe the sign of Christ on the spine and on such limbs as you can get to. Then take the left ear, and pierce it, keeping silence. This also you shall do: take a wand, hit the horse on the back, and it shall be well again. And write on the horn of the knife these words: Blessed be all the work of the Lord of Lords. If it is a question of elves in this case, this may well help.[8]

Modern-day magician and author Nigel Pennick claims that a tradition of magic containing elements of its Anglo-Saxon roots is still practised in East Anglia. He believes it can also be found in Norfolk, Suffolk, Cambridgeshire, in the southern Lincolnshire Fens, Huntingdonshire and Essex – all areas colonised by the Anglo-Saxons. He calls this kind of magic 'The Nameless Art', whose spells and rites some practitioners have recorded in their own personal 'grimoires', which they call their 'Little Black Book' or 'Secret Granary'. Filled with fascinating information on folk-lore and magical practice, Pennick's *Secrets of East Anglian Magic* may well contain elements of traditions that have descended from Anglo-Saxon times, such as this recipe for making a 'Lucky Hand' charm:

> The Lucky Hand is an amulet made from bracken. To make one, we uproot the fern on Midsummer Eve. Then, using our magic knife, we cut away all but five of the fronds, leaving the image of a hand with hooked fingers. Next, to preserve it, we dry and harden it in the smoke of the Midsummer bonfire, whose purifying fumes will endow it with the desired magic virtues. Then the Lucky Hand can be kept in the house as protection against all kinds of bad luck and ill fortune.

The Shaman – PETER AZIZ

Pete Aziz has developed his shamanistic skills over more than 25 years by visiting other similar cultures, amongst them the Pueblo Indians of the Amazonian jungle, the Kahuna shamans of Hawaii and the Voodoo priests of Haiti. The author of two books, Working with Tree Spirits in Shamanic Healing *and* Spiritual Allies in the Plant Kingdom, *he now concentrates on healing, teaching shamanism to a select few and fighting what he sees as a global campaign against natural healing.*

From a very early age I knew that I had psychic powers, but it was not until the age of eight when my grandmother began my magical education that I started getting serious. She was a village witch in her native Hungary and her speciality was 'Dragon Magic', which had originally come from Egypt, where worship of dragons and crocodiles was once common. As Egypt was invaded by new cultures, the skills, as so often with magic, went underground then moved first to Hungary and then, with my grandmother, to England, which has its own deep magical roots in the dragon world: King Arthur's family name was Pendragon.

My grandmother did not believe in complex rituals. Instead, she taught me how to communicate with nature spirits through their secret languages. The dragon language, for instance, has 108 runic symbols and is the same throughout the world. It cannot be taught through books; its power lies in the sound itself.

After this I went on to learn astral projection – the ability to come out of the body, which is the basis of shamanism – and healing techniques. Such skills are natural to most people, but each individual will develop them differently. The most important thing to realise is that if you don't try them out you will never discover anything. Magic is about constant practice and learning, not listening to gurus or reading books.

Ancestor reverence is another path to finding wisdom for yourself. You must feed your ancestors to give them strength and attract them into your worlds. My grandmother – now dead – is still a huge help to me, and I prepare traditional Hungarian food – Goulash or Apple Strudel for example – for her which I serve on a special altar. When you are cooking for your ancestors remember to leave out the salt, or it will drive them away.

As I began to be familiar with this new world, I started experimenting with healing. I learnt that illness stems from both physical and emotional causes. Emotional causes might be anger, frustration or a feeling of loss of power. Such negative energies build up at a number of pressure points in your body, and can lead to specific illnesses. Physical healing can address the symptoms but not always the causes. A more permanent solution can involve identifying the emotional problems at source with help from the spirit world.

My grandmother also passed on her herbal knowledge. She believed that when a plant has been through certain challenges in the way it has grown, then the strength and knowledge gained by overcoming these experiences can be transferred to humans. Herbs can be used physically (by carrying them with you) or invoked mentally by talking their language. For example, marjoram will respond to a deep rumbling noise in the throat. More dangerous plants, such as belladonna (which can make the eyes of a beautiful woman shine, or be used as a powerful poison) respond to a short, shrill sound – rather like a mosquito flying past your ear at night. I believe in the existence of 'Aka' cords (originally a Hawaiian notion), which bind us to events in our past lives that have diminished us personally. These represent a constant draining of power. Once you understand this, you can cut the cords, using spirit helpers like dragons, then restore the lost power by invoking the spirit of a herb such as marjoram.

Healing ability is also closely linked to the power of the shaman. Books such as Michael Harner's *The Way of the Shaman* describe in simple terms the techniques of shamanic journeying, and you can test out your own abilities by experimenting with visualisation and astral projection.

Trees are great helpers of those who want to learn journeying. Find two or three trees you feel are 'compatible' and sit with each until they become extremely familiar on both visual and spiritual levels. If you have any dowsing ability you can feel the five levels of a tree's aura, the last being under the bark. Sit quietly by the trunk and visualise yourself 'rooted' within the earth, with only your top half above ground. Imagine the strength you get from your roots. As you become aware of this, the tree becomes aware of you and you will find the aura opens, becomes more embracing. Later, when you meditate quietly in a dark room, you will be able to travel to each of the trees in your mind and use it as a stepping stone to other places and worlds.

Each tree is a doorway between worlds and has a specific place it will take you to. As you pass down through its roots you will find a mirror image of your tree growing upside down in other worlds. As you enter this world, at first it seems very familiar. The first task is to find your 'power animal'. In my first journey I found myself turning into a snake; I felt the vibration in my jaw and the new sense of awareness that it gave me. The snake is now both my power animal and a permanent part of me.

Once you have made contact with your animal, then it is time to explore your new world. I found caves, then forests, lakes and mountains, which proved to be my stepping-stones. Soon I was able to move to the deeper underworld and much of my work nowadays is spent in going deeper and deeper into this darkness. It is here that you will find the most powerful allies. While an amateur journeyer will seek a simple visualisation experience, a true shaman will force himself to go deeper and deeper into the spirit world and gain power. It is not something for the faint-hearted.

Journeying of this type was a strong part of old English culture, especially for the Anglo-saxons. In very old churchyards, you can still see the ancient yew trees used for journeying and so called 'Holy Springs', once used for initiation.

My own path of development as a shaman has taken me to many places to learn from indigenous peoples. I have spent time with the Pueblo Indians in New Mexico, who taught me how sounds could be used in healing, and in Hawaii, where the local shamans, the Kahuna, heal through the use of body pressure to flow energy into the affected area. I've also travelled to the Peruvian jungle where I learnt about Ayahuasca, the natural mind-altering drug used by the native people there to enhance their shamanic journeying.

With this knowledge, I felt drawn to explore the spirits of England, which have been neglected since the Druids and the Anglo-Saxons and driven underground by Christianity. Modern day historians tend to underestimate the huge power that the ancient magicians had, but the old groups knew that only by being very secret would they survive. You can also still find a few dedicated people with the old knowledge in England. I learnt a lot from the fourteenth 'Dusty Miller' who comes from a long line of spirit shamans and lives in Kent. Given the huge investment of time and energy needed to become a real shaman, I wonder if there will be a fifteenth. To be a shaman you must be prepared to face all sorts of frightening experiences. In my time, I have been eaten by a dragon and swallowed by a huge snake, but I am coming to believe that there are worse forces at work in our own world as legislation works to suppress natural cures in favour of pharmaceutical drugs. There are fascinating and powerful elements of the old magic still here if you care to search, but sometimes I feel that we shamans are fighting a battle for the future of the world and I wonder how long we can survive.

⤞ The Web of Wyrd ⤝

What we call Wyrd is really the work of God about which
He is busy every day.

KING ALFRED THE GREAT, 888[9]

A basic premise of the magical world-view is that most people go through life oblivious of the magic that is all around them, like the Muggles of J.K. Rowling's Harry Potter stories. Learning magic involves developing a curiosity about the world – particularly about nature and about history – so that its secrets can be revealed in all their wonder. Like an alchemist finding gold, Tolkien discovered in the Dark Ages a treasure trove of material that revealed the romantic and evocative power of the English imagination of that age, with its rune-masters and warlocks, dragons, elves and orcs, land wights and hedge-riders.

Whilst all this could be dismissed as fantasy, Brian Bates and other writers on the runes and magic of that age have shown us that much of the magical knowledge of this era can be rescued from obscurity and used once more. When Dr Bates teaches budding actors at RADA or students on his university courses in shamanism, he encourages them to experiment with shape-shifting into the form of animals and spirit-journeying into the Other-world, using the power of their imagination. But the most important insight he provides on his courses and in his books is into the 'web of Wyrd'.

> ### Read about this Period in Fiction
>
> *The Way of Wyrd*, Brian Bates (Arrow Books, 1983)
> This book burst upon the modern pagan world,
> re-establishing Saxon magic in its rightful place after a
> period of neglect.
>
> An Anglo-Saxon sorcerer inducts a Christian scribe into
> the pagan magical mindset, via experiences of a multi-
> layered world of ceremony and ritual shared with spirits
> and elves, where every event in the natural world might
> be either a messenger or a threat.

'Wyrd' is an Anglo-Saxon term usually translated as 'fate' or 'destiny'. It occurs nine times in *Beowulf*, for example. But Wyrd literally means 'that which has turned' or 'that which has become', and it suggests the idea, confirmed now by physics, that everything in the universe is in a state of change. In the 'web of Wyrd' everything is connected as if in a giant, three-dimensional spider's web. The magician is someone who understands this and knows how to influence the web as well as how to benefit from being a part of it.

This idea is familiar to us now from the science of ecology and Gaia theory, but it was an idea that was grasped intuitively by magicians and shamans thousands of years ago, and it forms the basis of magical practice the world over.

It is perhaps best expressed in the following words by the script-writer Ted Perry in his 1972 film about ecology, *Home*, which were later mistakenly attributed to the Native American Indian, Chief Seattle: 'Whatever befalls the earth befalls the sons and daughters of the earth. We did not weave the web of life; we are merely a strand in it. Whatever we do to the web, we do to ourselves.'

If our reading of Anglo-Saxon magical practice is correct, then this very modern understanding was also shared by their sorcerers and healers.

Professor BRIAN BATES

Professor Bates is former Chairman of Psychology and Head of the Shaman Research Project at the University of Sussex and the world's foremost authority on Anglo-Saxon magic.

For a thousand years or more, the world of the Anglo-Saxon wizard was all but forgotten until J.R.R. Tolkien succeeded in reawakening this magic for generations to come, but it took a psychologist in Sussex with an interest in mysticism to popularise the idea that this magic could actually be used in the modern world. By the middle of the twentieth century, individual writers and practitioners, as well as a scattering of small groups, had already discovered Anglo-Saxon magic and the power of the runes, but it was Brian Bates's book The Way of Wyrd *that made these ideas widely accessible. Published in 1983, it tells the story, based on historical research, of a Christian missionary who meets an Anglo-Saxon wizard who instructs him in the magical lore of plants, runes, fate and the life force until he finally journeys to the spirit world on a quest to encounter the true nature of his own soul.*

Bates based his story on the 'Lacnunga', a manuscript of magic and medicine. He explained how the idea for the book came to him: 'I discovered the key when I found a reference to an obscure ancient text preserved in the vaults of the British Library. It was written in England about one thousand years ago, but reckoned by historians to reflect oral traditions stemming from many centuries earlier. That manuscript is a handbook of healing remedies, sacred ceremonies, and spiritual secrets of an indigenous shaman of ancient England.'

In the twenty-five years following the publication of The Way of Wyrd, *described as England's version of writings by Carlos Castaneda, Bates has explored this material in two subsequent books, and through establishing the first experiential course on shamanism at an English higher education institution – Sussex University. Exeter and Kent Universities now offer courses in related fields: the history of magic, divination and esotericism, but only Bates's course has so far included attempts to deal with the living experience of magic and shamanism, when the arts being studied are actually practised. In addition to teaching and lecturing widely on the subject, Professor Bates is currently the Research Director of the Christensen Foundation project on recovering the nature-based knowledge of ancient England.*

We are used to thinking that the ancient Celtic culture was magical in practice and mythology, but many people seem to think that the Anglo-Saxons were just a bunch of clodhoppers who never had the glamour of the Celts, with their jewellery, poetry, legends and Druids. On the contrary, I want to try to encourage people to rethink the cultural history of England in such a way that it includes an appreciation of the Anglo-Saxon contribution, and in particular their magic, which I believe we can bring back into our daily lives.

I started exploring the Anglo-Saxon world of magic by trying to re-create ancient Saxon ceremonies, but somehow this did not feel right in a modern world, so I began again where all magic must start: with the imagination. I experimented with a set of workshops for actors at the Royal Academy of Dramatic Art, showing them how they could use techniques drawn from my understanding of Anglo-Saxon shamanism, to broaden their acting skills and deepen their powers of imagination. The workshops that I run today have been very much influenced by my work at RADA and are very theatrical. For example, we explore people's individual life 'destiny', which is the real meaning of the Anglo-Saxon word *wyrd*, by building a 'ship of destiny' in the workshop. Following meditation, writing and talking about the direction of their lives, people pin to the mast paper messages characterising their direction in life, then act out their life intention with a voyage.

Nowadays it is easy to get lost in the tedium of everyday routine and to lose a sense of purpose. My aim is to recapture the flow of life, the excitement, the sense of adventure. We have to learn to tack into the life forces, the storms and currents all around us.

My book, *The Way of Wyrd*, emerged from these and other experiences. I started off by writing the book as non-fiction, based around the 'Lacnunga', the ancient book of Saxon healing. But it soon became clear to me that to convey the richness of the magic it would be better to write the research as a story, in which the reader could use their imagination to identify with the experiences of training as a wizard in ancient England. I therefore wrote the book based around the journey of a historical character, a young monk sent to the pagan 'wilderness' of the South Saxons (now the county of Sussex), which was one of the very last areas of the country to convert to Christianity. Through his adventures with a Saxon wizard, I could express for the reader the insights of *wyrd*, or ancient English magic. It took six years to research and write the book, some of which was written up on the Downs behind Lewes, sometimes at night.

Since the novel was published, I've been lucky enough to be invited to become involved in all sorts of exciting projects, the latest one being dedicated to preserving the integrity of tribal communities around the world. I'm very aware of how much magical knowledge has been lost from the Western world. England especially has lost its sense of community with the decline of big families and village life, and, perhaps as a result, the passing on of magical lore has declined as well. The development of science has encouraged people to rely on it for all aspects of life, even those for which it is not especially suitable, and it has squeezed out those aspects that are difficult to research within the usual scientific parameters and which we now call magic. The Church's hostility towards magic has been another factor, especially since the Reformation. People nowadays will happily read Harry Potter, but are wary of the real stuff.

The success of *The Way of Wyrd* made me realise what a split view of magic we have today in the West. Having read the book, hundreds of people wrote to me, describing remarkable or 'beyond science' experiences they had had, which they wanted to share with me. About half of them said that the experiences were exciting, joyful and revelatory, and seemed similar to some of the stories in the book. The other half said that, until they read the book, they felt that they should keep secret the experiences they were having, for fear that others would disapprove – family, church, friends and so on. The book had made them feel they could talk about these things for the first time.

It was then that I realised that the experiences described in all of these letters were very similar. The difference was whether the people felt it was acceptable or taboo to have, and talk about, such experiences. This seems to reflect a long process of the driving underground, through disapproval by various establishment interests, of people's interest in and experience of events that fall outside the boundaries of social approval and that therefore are beyond control.

In general, this is how experiencing English magic can fill people's lives with imagination, creativity, and enchantment. It challenges perceptions that have become too fixed, too automatic, and are therefore limiting the options people think they have, while encouraging them to see their lives afresh, and to live them in a way that more fully expresses their hopes and dreams.

Having done my workshops, or worked with me individually, people often tell me what has happened as a result of seeing their lives magically. I aim to help them to move their thinking from the analytical cortex of the brain, which is appropriate for some but not all of the issues we face in life, and instead encourage them to think from their intuition, and see issues imbued with images and stories, rather than simply as cause-and-effect narratives.

For example, one participant recognised, through this different way of doing things, that she was not expressing her own creativity in her working life. She was doing what was safe and taking no risks. But once she got a sense of her own destiny, and an understanding of her real potential, she was able to retrain and move from an office job that had outlived its place in her life and become a psychotherapist. She was elated by this change, for her new career was more challenging and made her feel fulfilled.

Another told me how he had come to see the level of stress that he had placed on himself by always thinking of his mistakes in life, and how he had let people down. A more magical view takes a broader perspective on how things happen to us. Whilst taking individual responsibility for what we do, we also realise that in any one event there are a myriad of influences working at the same time. Often we find that if we use intuition, imagination, or imaging, rather than thinking in words, trusting our bodily feelings to guide us as well as our brains, and finding our place in the wider world, we are empowered to solve our issues without feeling guilty or put-upon. The person telling me this story was amazed and delighted to find that his life experience could be seen from a fresh perspective, and as a result his physical health improved, he lost weight, and his social life thrived!

As I say in my book *The Real Middle Earth*, our understanding of magic seems to be coming back after a thousand years, for people in the helping professions and in business are fascinated to hear how to use these techniques of imagination, and to open themselves to more flexible ways of using knowledge in their work and lives.

In teaching this work, I tend not to try to teach people as if it were 'new knowledge', but rather to try to help them discover it in themselves. We have always known about magic and this knowledge has always been inside us, but it is blocked from our consciousness by all sorts of taboos, perceptions and dogma. Once people are aware that they already have this resource of knowledge, the floodgates open and they are able to think and act in all sorts of more empowered ways than before.

My research into Anglo-Saxon magic has shown me that in days long ago we knew more about the various ways the mind works than we do now. Recovering this knowledge will help us in all areas of our lives. For example, there is remarkable research into the effects of rhythmic percussion sound (for example, drumming) on the way that our imagination streams and uses information that we have stored subconsciously. All shamanic societies seem to have used some version of rhythmic sound to induce altered states of mind, from which we can think more creatively and have extraordinary insights that do not occur to us in our usual mode of everyday thinking, and this is a process that involves no drugs at all. The Anglo-Saxons used the metaphor of a journey to engage with their own enlightenment, as in, for example, the quest of the hero Beowulf to rid the world of the monster Grendel. This sort of applied imagination is a natural resource that is at the heart of magic, and it is just waiting for us to use it in our lives today.

✧ Runes and How to Use Them ✧

A man shall utter wisdom, write runes, sing songs, earn praise, expound glory, be diligent daily.

ANGLO-SAXON MAXIMS, I (C. 1000)

Runes are the letters of an alphabet that evolved in pre-Christian times in Scandinavia and Germany, which developed their own form in England with the arrival of the Anglo-Saxons.

'Rune' is an Old English word meaning 'mystery, secrecy, and hidden knowledge' that derives from the Old Norse word *runa*. The runic alphabet used in England was known as the Futhorc, and was used for writing and for magical purposes. Runes carved on talismans, swords or rings could act as charms to protect their owner and ward off evil, and runes cast in lots could be read for signs and omens.

The earliest evidence of runes being used in England comes from the inscriptions on fifth-century cremation urns found in Norfolk and Lincolnshire, which show that Futhorc was used for at least half a millennium before falling into disuse soon after the Norman Conquest in 1066.

The ninth-century Thames scramasax knife-blade, recovered from the Thames at Battersea, London. It shows twenty-eight Futhorc runes. Futhorc is a variant of 'Futhark', spelt from the first six runes of the alphabet.

Whilst runes were used for practical everyday purposes – carved on sticks and carried as messages, or inscribed on property to affirm ownership – they were also used for magic, and a mastery of runes was clearly one of the most important skills an Anglo-Saxon wizard could possess. Old English literature reveals numerous terms that show the significance of this mysterious alphabet: *runlic*, rune-like, meant mysterious, occult; *runian*, to rune, meant to whisper or tell secrets; *runcraeftig*, rune-skilled, meant skilled in mysteries and the occult; *runcofa*, rune-chest, meant chamber of secrets or innermost thoughts; and *runwita*, rune-knower, meant counsellor or adviser.

Winston Churchill remained unimpressed by runes and wrote in his *A History of the English-Speaking Peoples*: 'The people had lost entirely the art of writing. Some miserable runic scribblings were the only means by which they could convey their thoughts to one another at a distance. Barbarism reigned in its rags . . .'

Runnymede, the spot by the River Thames where the Magna Carta was signed in 1215, may have derived its name either from an Anglo-Saxon-cum-Norman derivation, from *rynel* and *mé* meaning a wet meadow, or more interestingly from *rune-mede*, meaning a place where runes were cast and counsel taken, which would make it a fitting place to be associated with one of the founding documents of the English nation.

⟡ Runes as Charms and Spells ⟡

*Runes were used to ward off strife and care, to charm
away sickness and disease, to blunt the foeman's sword, to
break fetters that bind, to still the storms, to ward off the
attacks of demons, to make the dead to speak, to win the
love of a maid, and to turn away love that is not desired.*

DONALD A. MACKENZIE, *TEUTONIC
MYTH AND LEGEND*

Runes were used as charms or spells to attract luck or ward off
evil, to encourage healing and invoke protection. The old texts
refer to many of these uses when they speak of victory runes,
birth runes, health runes, speech runes, thought runes, fertility
runes, love runes, battle runes, weather runes and ale runes. This
last rune may refer to inscriptions on drinking horns to ensure the
wholesomeness of the ale in them, or it may refer to a mysterious
word, *alu*, which occurs often in runic inscriptions and seems to
be a protective formula.

Historians differ in their interpretations of many inscriptions.
An antler inscribed with runes from the ninth century that was discovered at Brandon in Suffolk may have the charm, 'Grow thou,
by means of the wild beast!' carved upon it, or the more prosaic
interpretation: '[this] grew on a wild animal.'

Runes play a significant part in Tolkien's work. The cover
of the first edition of *The Hobbit*, drawn by Tolkien and published in 1937, included a border of runes, which looked magical
but when translated simply read: '*The
Hobbit or There and Back Again*, being the
record of a year's journey made by Bilbo
Baggins; compiled from his memoirs by
J.R.R. Tolkien and published by George
Allen & Unwin.'

The idea of a ring carved with runes that
exerts a magical power and binds people

The Kingmoor ring.

to the bidding of its master, which was so central to his next book, *The Lord of The Rings*, may well have come from Tolkien's knowledge of the Kingmoor ring that was unearthed in 1817 at Greymoor Hill, Kingmoor, near Carlisle in 1817. The other candidate for its inspiration – the all-powerful ring of Wagner's Ring Cycle – was specifically dismissed by Tolkien when he said: 'Both rings were round', and there the resemblance ceased.' A ring similar to the Kingmoor ring was found on Bramham Moor, West Yorkshire, and both are inscribed with a charm against fever and leprosy.

Tolkien's runes, embedded as they were in his evocative world of Middle Earth, remained uncontaminated by the Nazis' use of them as insignia for their SS and for certain Panzer divisions. For a long time after the war many scholars steered clear of runes because of these associations, which had developed as a result of the Nazis' perversion of Norse and Anglo-Saxon mythology. However, by the 1980s books began to appear that showed readers how to use the runes as a divination system, attempts that were criticised by academics since they involved less than rigorous scholarship, and included creative additions and adaptations. Creators of the new divination systems argued that if a magical technique is to be meaningful to modern people, it must grow and change.

The most widely distributed of these new systems is *The Book of Runes* by Ralph Blum, which has sold over a million copies, each of which includes a bag of clay tablets painted with runes and produced in China. Blum openly admits that he divined the sequence of runes and their interpretation intuitively as he worked through the night of a summer solstice with rune stones given to him by a woman who lived in Redhill in Surrey. One by one he took each stone in his hand and meditated on its meaning, writing down what came to him. When the 'flow dwindled', as he put it, he turned to the Chinese divinatory system, the I Ching, for insights. As a result, critics point out that the most popular runic system in use today is one that depicts the runes in a sequence that never existed historically, and with interpretations that come mainly from Blum's inspiration and from China, rather than from their lands of origin.

If you would like to try your hand at working with runes, rune teachers recommend using an approach that draws its inspiration from the runes themselves in their original historical context.

Bob Oswald, in Buckinghamshire, who has been studying the runes for over fifty years, makes hand-crafted rune sets, under the name of 'Oswald the Rune Maker'. Bob is an example of a twenty-first-century magician, someone working with an ancient magical system in a way that is adapted to the modern era. As the author of *Discovering Runes*, he has developed a set of inter-pretations for the Futhorc that draws upon ideas suggested in the Anglo-Saxon *Rune Poem*, which probably dates from the tenth century and may have been written in Winchester. The poem has twenty-nine stanzas, each beginning with a rune whose meaning is then clarified in the rest of the stanza. As an example, the first rune of the Futhorc is 'Feoh', which means 'wealth', and the first verse of the *Rune Poem* runs:

> Wealth is a comfort to all men;
> yet must every man bestow it freely,
> if he wish to gain honour in the sight of the Lord.[10]

From this clue, rune-masters, such as Bob Oswald, and rune-mistresses, such as Freya Aswynn and Diana Paxson, derive interpretations based upon ideas of wealth and generosity. When the rune falls upside down, a reverse interpretation is suggested.

⊙ *How to Cast Runes*

To become an apprentice rune-caster, first buy a set of runes or draw the symbols on a series of cards, paint them on to stones, or carve them on to sticks or wooden discs. If pyrography appeals, wood-burning equipment can be obtained from a craft shop or online, and the runes can be burnt on to a set of discs about an inch in diameter, cut from a single branch.

It is tempting to use the runes to try to peer into the future, but they should be used instead to gain insights into questions that are troubling you or that need some clarification. A calm, clear mind is needed for this work, and an attitude of reverence too. This is important, whether you believe that your subconscious will pick the right rune or that 'Higher Forces' will guide your choice. If you undertake rune casting when you are upset or confused, you will probably find it hard to make sense of the reading.

Find a quiet place without distraction, then relax as much as possible and focus clearly on the question to be asked. Try to make it as simple as possible. Place the discs, cards, sticks or stones in a bag, then, holding your question firmly in your mind, swirl the runes around gently with your hand, and just allow one to fall naturally into your fingers. Sense with your intuition whether it is the right one to draw and, if it is, take it out and lay it down in front of you.

From the chart opposite you will see some of the meanings given by rune experts such as Oswald, Aswynn and Paxson, showing the Old English names for the runes, followed by the Anglo-Friesian/Germanic names that are more commonly used. Fuller interpretations can be found in the resources listed.

ᚠ   FEOH (FEHU) – reward, wealth, nourishment

ᚢ   UR (URUZ) – physical or mental health, virility, manhood, fertility, womanhood

ᚦ   THORN (THURISAZ) – magical power, the forces of chaos or evil, temptation, a warning

ᚩ   OS (ANSUZ) – knowledge, the mouth, wisdom, communication, a message

ᚱ   RAD (RAIDO) – a journey, an arrival, a departure, a union or a reunion

ᚲ   KEN (KAUNO) – heat, light, enlightenment

ᚷ   GYFU (GEBO) – love, partnership, forgiveness, gift, talent, skill, ability

ᚹ   WYN (WUNJO) – happiness, light, emotional satisfaction

ᚻ   HAEGL (HAGALAZ) – weather, damaging natural forces, disruption, interference

ᚾ   NYD (NAUDIZ) – need, want, craving, demand, deprivation, compulsion, desire

ᛁ   IS (ISA) – ice, cold, freezing, stagnation, lack of emotion

ᛄ   GER (JERA) – harvest, fertility, fruition

ᛇ   EOH (IHWAZ) – magic, deflection, prevention, weapon

ᛈ   PEORTH (PERTH) – mystery, chance, gamble, pot luck, science, technology

ᛉ   EOLH (ALGIZ) – opportunity for growth, rapid development, protection, safe refuge

ᛋ   SIGIL (SOWILO) – wholeness, energy, light, discovery, disclosure

ᛏ   TIR (TIWAZ) – courage, compassion, battles, legislation

ᛒ   BEORC (BERKANAN) – growth, fertility, rebirth, new life, a new broom, physical beauty or stature

ᛗ   EH (EHWAZ) – horse, steed, mount, momentum, speed

ᛗ   MAN (MANNAZ) – mankind, humanity, the self,
inner being or soul, manhood, womanhood

ᛚ   LAGU (LAGUZ) – water, sea, ocean, river, lake,
cleansing, tide

ᛝ   ING (INGWAZ) – harmony, approval, unity,
agreement, love, peace

ᛟ   ODAL (OTHILA) – home, homeland, hearth,
family, inheritance, estate, possessions

ᛞ   DAEG (DAGAZ) – day, daylight, dawn, breakthrough, radical change

It may take a while to develop your interpretations from
the few key-words given for each rune, but divination techniques are supposed to be acquired over time and with effort,
so that the apprentice gradually develops a familiarity with each
symbol.

'Spreads' of a number of runes can be used, details of which
can be found in the books listed in the Resources section, but
first try using a simple three-rune technique when trying to gain
insight into a specific situation. Ask first for a rune that will
throw light on the issue as it is at the moment, then pick a rune
for insights into the situation as you would like it to be, and
finally pick a rune that may give some ideas on how you can
help move the situation from its present condition to the one
desired.

ᖇ Going Deeper ᖆ

Runes are also magic symbols, each possessing its own
esoteric power that may be evoked and directed to
accomplish ritual purposes. The occult power of each rune
can express itself as a basic force, as an intelligent spirit, or
as an astral environment.

DONALD TYSON, *RUNE MAGIC*

In ritual magic, runes can be used as sigils – magical signs – to attract or repel certain conditions. Some writers even suggest holding the body in positions that mimic the runes to attract their qualities.

Rune magicians believe that combining two or more runes into one glyph can create a symbol that will attract specific energies or conditions to the person who carries the symbol, perhaps as a talisman or even as a tattoo. These glyphs are known as 'bind runes' and should be created in a magical way while concentrating on the objective.

Bind runes are used to attract love, financial success, harmony, protection and health, and form part of the advanced magic of a rune wizard. Beginners would do well to avoid using bind runes, especially being tattooed with them!

ᚱᚩ Traps for the Sorcerer's Apprentice ᚩᚱ

The subject of runes has, unfortunately, the potential to upset the unwary or sensitive student. Simply researching the subject on the internet will quickly lead you to quarrelling magicians, white supremacists, enthusiasts of the 'dark arts' and the usual run-of-the-mill fortune-tellers wanting their palms stroked with silver.

Magicians have as much propensity for squabbling as any other group, but with the added edge that some lay claim to occult powers that they may use to support their arguments. Runic quarrels are less dramatic and can be read about through the medium of Amazon.com reviews. Look for those with one star and enjoy the arguments!

The Nazis perverted Nordic and Saxon mythology, harnessing it to further their aims of racial supremacy, and their use of the runes has made them attractive to white supremacist groups and neo-Nazi sympathisers. As you research the subject, you simply need to be aware of this fact and remain alert to any hidden agenda that may be present.

Some writers about runes are interested in the 'dark arts' and following a few links on a search engine can lead you to websites that promote vampirism and other unpleasant activities. It is better to be forewarned, rather than stumbling upon these unsettling figures by accident, and there is something to be said for consciously facing these issues at the start of one's explorations, on the principle that it is best to 'know one's enemy'. If you agree with this idea, the internet can provide you with a quick overview of the territory. If you are of a sensitive disposition, avoid this research.

Far easier to cope with are commercial sites that promise you instant success with their 'rune spells' or fortune-telling. Rune expert Peter Taylor advises students not to use the runes for fortune-telling, but instead for gaining self-knowledge and uncovering their life purpose. He writes: 'If you come to the realisation that you have forgotten the reason for your presence on Earth, the Runes can be used to restore that memory.'

The Rune Maker – BOB OSWALD

Bob Oswald, now in his sixties, is an expert in making runes by traditional means. Appropriately enough, he started his working life as a door-to-door vacuum salesman for the Speedy Goblin Company in Ireland. A variety of jobs followed, from bus conductor to holiday courier, before he eventually settled into a career as an engineer.

His interest in runes is lifelong, but he did not begin making rune sets to sell until 1997. In the early years it was just a hobby, but from 2003 onwards he was making enough to keep a succession of ancient cars on the road, maintain himself in beer and contribute useful amounts to the household budget.

My fascination with runes started when I was a boy. I was walking along Hadrian's Wall with my father and we stopped at a little church in Bewcastle. In the churchyard there is an old stone cross with strange inscriptions carved into the sides, still clearly readable. I asked Dad about them, but he could not explain them and suggested we asked my aunt, who was known in the family as a 'wise woman' – no one in those days dared mention the word 'witch'.

She was extraordinary: small and bright as a sparrow, with flaming-red hair. Although she could not read or write, she knew everything about runes: how to make them, how to 'consecrate' them, then use them for divining, spell-casting and protection against evil. She claimed to be able to trace her ancestry back forty-two generations, which I guess would be a direct link to Anglo-Saxon times, and she taught me everything I still practise today.

To make runes, you need to find the right wood. Ash is best and this is supposed to be what the Norse god Odin used. Some people say you should ask the tree's permission first, but I don't believe that. I use broken branches or off-cuts. I cut discs of wood about a quarter-inch thick evenly from the branch, and then burn the rune symbols on to the discs before varnishing them. But the most important art is the consecration.

You need to find a place of sacred energy in a wood to do that magic, a spot where two energy lines cross. If you are no good at dowsing, like me, you should hire an expert. I used a local witch. The procedure is important and you should stick to it exactly. First bury the runes for nine days (nine was a sacred number for the Anglo-Saxons), then dig them up, ideally on a moonlit night, and consecrate them. You must be in the right frame of mind to make the ceremony work, and I always do it alone. You use a wand, which I call a 'gander', to call on the gods from the four elements of fire, water, earth and air, using a repetitive incantation that my aunt taught me. Then blow a little air on to each rune and the job's done.

In my experience, runes work over 80 per cent of the time if you cast them seriously. Your attitude is everything. I believe they act as a focal point between your subconscious mind and what I call the 'spiritual ether', which can be whatever you think is out there: the spirits of the dead perhaps, or even gods and fairies.

The runes can be used to give you insights into any decision that faces you, however simple. I know some people don't like to use rune-casting for peering into the future, but I find it can be uncannily accurate, as long as you are prepared to do a little work of interpretation, as you'll see from the story of this rune-cast I did for my daughter a few months ago.

She had just finished her MA and was wondering whether to go for a PhD. She first asked whether she would be accepted for the course and drew three runes. She got Os (knowledge), Ger (success) and Daeg (new beginnings). I interpreted this as 'Yes' because the fact that she drew Os, referring to her past, indicated that her knowledge was sufficient; the fact that she drew Ger for success referred to the present, which I thought meant she would be accepted, and finally she drew Daeg (a new start), which represented the future. This last I thought must mean she would embark on the PhD course. As it turned out, I was wrong about that.

She was also worried about whether she would get a grant, so we did a single rune-cast and got Feoh reversed, meaning 'lack of wealth'. I then had to revise my opinion about Daeg in the first result and suggested it meant she would have to find some form of employment if she wanted to continue her studies.

As it happened, she went to the PhD interview and was accepted for the course right away. She applied for a grant but two weeks later her application was turned down. She had just about decided to look for a job when her MA course tutor told her about a teacher training course becoming available with a grant. The meaning of the Daeg (new beginnings) rune in the first session then became clear. Sure enough, she was accepted for the teacher training course, the grant for that course was approved, and she will be starting the course in January. The new beginning predicted by Daeg is about to take place.

But as well as using the runes to get an idea of what might happen in the future, you can also use them as amulets to attract a certain outcome. I often make 'bind runes', which are several runes combined into one symbol, which my customers can then carry around for some specific need. Often it's something simple, like losing weight or getting richer, but you do need to put in some effort to make them work – there is no such thing as a free lunch in the rune world! Then there are runes to ward off spells or personal attacks, the best of which is Eolh, the rune of self-interest and protection.

Your runes can turn out to be your best friends, but always treat them with care and respect. You won't regret it.

❧ Things to Do ❧

❋ Gaze at the Kingmoor ring that inspired Tolkien in London's British Museum, or see a replica of the ring at Tullie House Museum in Carlisle. There are other Anglo-Saxon artefacts at the British Museum, such as the Franks Casket, made in the seventh century in Northumbria out of walrus ivory, and carved with Anglo-Saxon runes and images depicting the story of Wayland the Smithy. The Sutton Hoo treasure is also on exhibit at the British Museum, and can be viewed online at www.britishmuseum.org

❋ Visit the reconstructed Anglo-Saxon village at West Stow, near Bury St Edmunds in Suffolk, where the chance discovery of fragments of pottery led to the excavation of the remains of an entire Anglo-Saxon village that had been covered with a sand dune since the thirteenth century. See www.oldcity.org.uk/ stowfriends

❋ Visit Sutton Hoo near Woodbridge in Suffolk. Owned by the National Trust, Sutton Hoo is one of Britain's most important and atmospheric archaeological sites. Here in this burial ground of the Anglo-Saxon kings of East Anglia, priceless royal treasures were discovered in a huge ship grave.

❧ Join an Anglo-Saxon 'living history' or re-enactment society. Thousands of people enjoy this activity, which can include all the family. See www.regia.org

❧ Cast runes at Runnymede. Brian Bates in *The Real Middle Earth* gives an evocative account of his visit to the ancient 'Ankerwyke' yew, an hour's walk from the village of Wraysbury in Berkshire. Within sight of 'Rune-Mede', the tree is over two thousand years old and the Magna Carta may have been signed beneath it.

❧ Visit the Kinver Edge cave-homes near Stourbridge in Worcestershire, which informed Tolkien's vision of hobbit-holes. On a wooded escarpment in a remnant of the old Mercian forest, you can walk inside the last troglodyte dwellings in Britain, which were inhabited until the 1950s. Carved out of soft sandstone, the 'Holy Austin' caves were a hermitage until the Restoration, and are now owned by the National Trust.

❧ See the *Exeter Book of Riddles* in Exeter Castle.

❧ Create a set of runes, cast runes to gain insight, and send cryptic runic messages to friends and family.

❧ Immerse yourself in a day of lectures and explorations of the Anglo-Saxon period, organised by Dr Sam Newton and Wuffing Education, and located in the historic Tranmer House overlooking the burial mounds of Sutton Hoo. See www.wuffings.co.uk

❧ Visit Bede's World in Jarrow, Northumberland. In AD 731, the Venerable Bede completed his *Ecclesiastical History of the English People*, a book that is our primary source for understanding the beginnings of the English people and the history of the Anglo-Saxon period. It is the first work of history in which the AD dating system is used. An Anglo-Saxon farm and herb garden have been re-created on the site of an Anglo-Saxon monastery, and there is also a museum dedicated to Bede's life. See www.bedesworld.co.uk

✌ Resources ✌

◉ *Anglo-Saxon Magic*

BOOKS

Aspects of Anglo-Saxon Magic, Bill Griffiths (Anglo-Saxon Books, 2003)
Looking for the Lost Gods of England, Kathleen Herbert (Anglo-Saxon Books, 1994)
The Lost Gods of England, Brian Branston (Thames & Hudson, 1957)
The Real Middle-Earth: Magic and Mystery in the Dark Ages, Brian Bates (Sidgwick & Jackson, 2002)
Secrets of East Anglian Magic, Nigel Pennick (Robert Hale, 1995)
The Way of Wyrd, Brian Bates (Arrow Books, 1983)
The Wisdom of the Wyrd, Brian Bates (Rider, 1996)
Leechcraft: Early English Charms, Plantlore and Healing, Stephen Pollington (Anglo-Saxon Books, 2001)

WEBSITES

The website of Professor Brian Bates: www.wayofwyrd.com
There is a comprehensive site on Anglo-Saxon heathenism at: www.englishheathenism.homestead.com

◉ *Runes*

BOOKS

Complete Illustrated Guide to Runes, Nigel Pennick (Element Books, 1999)
Discovering Runes, Bob Oswald (Bookmart, 2008)
Northern Mysteries and Magick: Runes, Gods and Feminine Powers, Freya Aswynn (Llewellyn Publications, 1998)

Rudiments of Runelore, Stephen Pollington (Anglo-Saxon Books, 1995)
Taking up the Runes: A Complete Guide to Using Runes in Spells, Rituals, Divination, and Magic, Diana L. Paxson (Weiser, 2005)

WEBSITES
For Oswald the Runemaker, see www.runemaker.com
For the runic journey, see www.tarahill.com
For Runes, alphabet of mystery, see www.sunnyway.com/runes

CHAPTER FOUR

THE MATTER OF BRITAIN

Merlin, King Arthur and the Search for the Holy Grail

A damsel shall be sent from the city of the forest of Canute, to administer a cure. Once she has practised her oracular arts, she shall dry up the noxious fountains by breathing upon them. Afterwards, as soon as she shall refresh herself with the wholesome liquor, she shall bear in her right hand the wood of Caledon, and in her left the buttressed forts of London.

GEOFFREY OF MONMOUTH, *THE PROPHECIES OF MERLIN* (TWELFTH CENTURY)

Everyone has heard of Merlin, Britain's most famous wizard, but few people know that an extraordinary series of prophecies about the fate of the world were written in his name.

In the medieval era, Geoffrey of Monmouth's book, *The Prophecies of Merlin*, offered a series of statements, sometimes cryptic, sometimes straightforward, about the fate of their country to puzzled but enthusiastic readers, anxious to discover what the future might hold. Prophecies such as 'There shall be a miserable desolation of the kingdom, and the threshing floors shall become again forests' most probably refer to the incursions of the Danes in the ninth century, for example. Many of the statements follow a threefold pattern reminiscent of the wisdom-sayings of the Welsh Bards and Druids, known as triads, and Merlin specialist R.J. Stewart is convinced that the prophecies have predicted events centuries ahead of their time, including the union of England and Scotland, the Industrial Revolution, and the discovery of North Sea oil.[1]

Seership – being able to see beyond the veil of time – is one of the prime characteristics of a magician. She or he has intimations of the future denied to ordinary mortals, and it is for this reason magicians have traditionally been so closely allied to tribal chiefs and kings and queens. A leader is in charge of armies and the country, but a magician is able to see the fate of those armies and that people, and can ward off potential catastrophe by warning their leader in time.

Echoes of this primal relationship between chieftain and magician are still found today when the tabloids reveal that the wives of leaders, such as Cherie Blair, Hillary Clinton and Nancy Reagan, have been consulting astrologers or New Age gurus.

In Russia, the mystic Rasputin held sway over the Tsar and his family, and in Britain during the Second World War a group of occultists, including the astrologer Stuart Watkins, the founder of Watkins' esoteric bookshop in London's Cecil Court, allegedly advised Winston Churchill.

The archetypal wizard, acting as adviser to a leader of the people, is Merlin. But who was this figure in reality? He may have been an actual historical figure, Merddyn Wyllt (Merlin the Wild), who came either from Scotland or from Wales in the sixth or seventh centuries. Equally, he may be a purely mythical figure who emerged as far back as the fifth century, during the period when Christianity began to triumph over the pagan cults of Britain, and in which the realm of England began to coalesce out of the minor kingdoms of the Anglo-Saxons and the Britons.

In legend, Merlin was born of a human mother and an Other-worldly father. His story succeeded in bridging the worlds of paganism and Christianity when it was immortalised by Geoffrey of Monmouth, the twelfth-century chronicler of mythical history, in his two books, *The Prophecies of Merlin* and *The Life of Merlin*, and when he also wrote about the wizard in his monumental work *The History of the Kings of Britain*.

Geoffrey probably picked up the stories of Merlin from two sources: the work of a ninth-century monk, Nennius, and the ancient oral tradition of the Bards of his native Wales. According to Bardic tradition, one of the purposes of magic is to provide creative inspiration, and from this point of view Geoffrey of Monmouth succeeded in performing one of the most effective magical acts of all time. His books became some of the great medieval best-sellers and probably provided the impetus for the development of the whole phenomenon of the 'Matter of Britain', a term used to describe the tales of King Arthur and his knights, and their quest for the Holy Grail.

The seeds sown by Geofffrey of Monmouth have proved extremely fertile. Over the years, thousands of works of fiction and of non-fiction have been supplemented by films, plays, television programmes and even musicals about Merlin, Arthur and the Grail. And behind this array of creative outpourings and obsessions stands the lone figure of Merlin, the archetypal wizard who masterminded the birth and rearing of King Arthur, who acted as his Druid, advising him from the shadows during his reign. Indeed, it was Merlin who was responsible for the creation of the Round Table and, ultimately, for the knights' quest for the Holy Grail.

THE ARTHURIAN LEGENDS

Somewhere in Britain, high in the mountains, the body of King Arthur, clothed in armour and wearing his crown, lies in a state of suspended animation in a hidden cave. When his people need him, he will awaken from his sleep and lead them once again to fulfil their destiny. Some say the cave is in Scotland, others in Wales; others still claim that Arthur sleeps at Alderley Edge in Cheshire or at Sewingshield Crags in Northumberland.

This powerful image of the hero-king who will return to save his people is found in legends all over the world. King Menelik of Abyssinia, for instance, is said to sleep on the Roof of Africa – within Mount Kilimanjaro, ready to awaken and restore the land to its former glory. The same idea is expressed in Christianity in the hope of the Second Coming.

There are many versions of the Arthurian legend, but the basic story remains the same. Arthur was the illegitimate child of Igraine, the wife of Gorlois of Cornwall, and the king of Britain, Uther Pendragon. Their union was masterminded by Merlin, who ensured that Arthur was raised in secret until the time came for him to claim the throne. Arthur was recognised as the rightful king when he was the only contender to succeed in withdrawing a sword embedded in stone. Another sword, Excalibur, was given to Arthur by a mysterious Lady of the Lake.

Advised by Merlin, Arthur was a wise and magnanimous ruler, who gathered around him the knights of the Round Table at his court at Camelot. His fate was sealed, however, when his sister, the sorceress Morgan le Fay, encouraged his estranged son (or, in some tales, nephew) Mordred to seize the throne. At the Battle of Camlann, before Arthur killed him, Mordred delivered a fatal blow, and Arthur's body was carried away on a barge to Avalon.

Read about this Period in Fiction

The 'Matter of Britain' is the chief area where historical romantic fiction crosses with occult fiction, so the reader is urged to be discerning. The following classics might be regarded as representative of Arthurian fiction.

The Once and Future King, T.H. White (Collins, 1958) The book is in four parts: *The Sword in the Stone*, *The Queen of Air and Darkness*, *The Ill-Made Knight*, and *The Candle in the Wind*, beginning at Arthur's childhood and continuing through his life until just before the final battle. This is the Arthur story in a medieval setting, but brought up to date by the freshness of the writing style and modern allusions. The theme of the first book is that of Arthur learning the lessons of kingship by changing into fish, animals and birds. The light-hearted style gradually becomes more sombre as the story progresses.

The Merlin Quartet, Mary Stewart The four volumes are: *The Crystal Cave* (William Morrow, 1970) *The Hollow Hills* (Hodder & Stoughton, 1973) *The Last Enchantment* (G.K. Hall & Company, 1979) *The Wicked Day* (Ballantine Books, 1983)

Merlin is the narrator both of his own history and, from his meeting with the exiled Ambrosius and Uther, of the story of Arthur. Magic is a potent force, which dictates the action throughout, and Merlin is an awesome and human figure, often compelled to make harsh human choices in the service of his destiny.

Mists of Avalon, Marion Zimmer Bradley (Michael Joseph, 1983)
The Arthurian myth is told here from the women's perspective, first through the story of Igraine, and later concentrating on Morgaine, Arthur's sister, and her training as a priestess on the Isle of Avalon, presided over by the Lady of the Lake.

War in Heaven, Charles Williams (Faber, 1930)
The Holy Grail is discovered in a country church, occasioning a struggle for its possession between the forces of darkness and of light, in the persons of a group of occultists and their black magic rituals, and a parish priest.

T.H. WHITE, 1906–1964

T.H. White was born in India, but on his parents' return to England he attended Cheltenham College, and Queens' College, Cambridge, where he wrote a thesis on Thomas Malory's *Le Morte d'Arthur*. He then taught at Stowe School and wrote *England Have My Bones*, an autobiographical account of a year spent living in the country. With the success of this book he decided to dedicate himself to writing, which suited his reclusive nature.

He lived a simple life in a small cottage, where he taught himself falconry and looked after an unusual collection of pets. Tall, with a powerful beard, he must have been an eccentric character. One story relates how his cottage was visited by a Jehovah's Witness collecting for their church. 'I am Jehovah!' roared White. 'How much have we made?'

He soon started work on the series of books about Arthur that would make his name. The first, *The Sword in the Stone*, told of Arthur's boyhood as an apprentice to Merlin, which includes the famous sequence where Arthur is shown how to shape-shift into different animals. White's genius in this, and the three Arthurian novels that followed, was to forget any attempt at historical cohesion. Just as the Arthurian legends combine many disparate elements from different contexts, so White showed – as the critic Martin Turner wrote – 'a rampant imaginative disregard for any kind of historicity', creating 'a firework display of deliberate anachronisms'. In this way, for example, White quite happily introduces Robin Hood into his story.

During the Second World War, White became a conscientious objector and moved to Ireland, where he continued writing, then to Alderney in the Channel Islands. Driven by many personal demons, he was never a happy man, but his imagination and creativity were so enormous that they live on, long after his death.

His other books include *The Age of Scandal*, a witty description of eccentric, eighteenth-century characters, such as Squire Mitton who set light to his nightshirt to cure himself of the hiccups, and *The Goshawk*, a beautifully written account of his experience training a hawk for falconry. But it is his *The Once and Future King*, a sequence of four novels, for which White will be most remembered, particularly since the musical *Camelot* and the Walt Disney film *The Sword in the Stone* were based upon these books.

ᴥ 'The Matter of Britain' and ᴥ the Story of the Grail

The modern world tends to think of the Holy Grail as a priceless chalice, the cup used by Christ at the Last Supper, sought after through constant danger by the likes of Indiana Jones. The truth, however, is much more ancient and much more interesting. The

Grail and its companion icon, the sword or spear, have served as magical images since pagan times, and today, over two thousand years later, they are still used in the rituals of ceremonial magicians, witches and Druids. Over time, they have been pursued as symbols of spiritual and magical power – as mythical objects of romantic and religious adoration – and as real artefacts, at the centre of the extraordinary stories of those who have searched for and found them, including the mysterious Knights Templar.

The search for the Grail has become an obsession for some people – Hitler included – and just like the cunning-folk's search for treasure, which we shall explore in Chapter 8, or the alchemists' search for gold, which we will explore in Chapter 6, lives have been ruined, and fortunes spent, in seeking its elusive magic.

Modern experts on the Grail, such as John Matthews in his book, *The Grail Seeker's Companion*, point to ancient myths involving magical vessels that may be the primal sources of the Grail symbol, such as the 'Cauldron of Annwn', which had the power to restore the dead to life again. The very early Welsh text, the *Preiddeu Annwn*, tells how King Arthur set sail with three shiploads of warriors to find this vessel in the Underworld.

When understood in this way, the Grail emerges first as a pagan symbol, embraced by the Celts and Druids amongst others. As a symbol of the Mother Goddess it is ideal as it represents both womb and breast. By the medieval era this vessel of nourishment and rebirth was transferred from Goddess to God, and became the chalice that was used by Christ at the Last Supper, which later caught drops of his blood when on the cross. In recent years writers have attempted to return the Grail to the Goddess once more. For example, the authors of *The Holy Blood and the Holy Grail* suggest that it should actually be understood as the womb of Mary, which carried the bloodline of Jesus, an idea also found in Dan Brown's novel *The Da Vinci Code*.

The Christian Grail was first mentioned in medieval France, when Celts fleeing the Saxon invasion arrived in Brittany and Gaul, bringing with them their stories of 'The Matter of Britain'. Inspired by these tales, Chrétien de Troyes wrote *The Story of the*

Grail in about 1180, although he left it unfinished at his death. Unlike Chrétien's earlier works, which dealt with the adventures of famous knights such as Lancelot, *The Story of the Grail* is not so much a romance as a psychological tale of the changes occurring in a knight's character as he encounters a number of adventures and mysteries whilst on his quest. This was a modern notion indeed for those times.

Perceval, the central character in *The Story of the Grail*, is described as a simple soul whose mother has kept him away from the world, until he meets two strange knights in the forest who take him to King Arthur's court. After various mishaps, he is eventually knighted and sets off on his adventures. Having rescued a fair maiden, he reaches a magnificent castle where he finds a handsome older nobleman reclining on a bed. The man apologises for his weakness but makes Perceval welcome, even giving him a splendid sword, 'with a pommel of the finest Gold from Arabia and a scabbard woven from gold thread from Venice'.

While the two of them are talking, a servant enters the room carrying a white spear, from the tip of which runs a drop of blood. The spear is quickly followed by a procession led by a girl, 'fair and comely and beautifully adorned', who is carrying a 'golden Grail, set with many precious stones' and is surrounded by a light as brilliant 'as the stars or the moon when the sun rises'. Another girl follows her with a silver dish from which is served a delicious meal, while the Grail passes mysteriously back and forth in front of the diners. Next morning, Perceval rises to discover the castle empty, and his horse saddled and ready to go. Fresh in his mind as he leaves the castle are the mystery of the Grail, the wounded lord, whom he comes to know as 'The Fisher King', and the bleeding spear.

The rest of the story mostly concerns Perceval's realisation that he has lost a golden opportunity to uncover the meaning behind the strange scene in the castle of the Fisher King, and the purpose of the Spear and the Grail. After many years of wandering, he meets an old hermit who tells him that his sins prevented him from understanding what he had seen in the castle, and that he must now be reconciled with God and lead a righteous life. The story continues with tales of another knight, Sir Gawain, and we meet Perceval no more.

Over the next thirty years, a number of other medieval writers attempted to complete Chrétien's story, elaborating the original with new quests and adventures, but leaving the central symbolism intact. It took another writer, Robert de Boron, to explain the history and purpose of the Grail itself. From him we learn that the Grail was the vessel that Christ used at the Last Supper, which was given first to Pontius Pilate, then to Joseph of Arimathea, and that it was in the Grail that Christ's blood was collected as his body was washed after it was taken down from the cross. The spear now reappears as the one carried by Longinus, the Roman soldier who pierced Christ's side during the crucifixion.

These two sets of stories hold the essential imagery of the Grail, a strange mixture of knightly adventure and deep religious significance. Over the years that followed, the story was extended and embellished by many other hands, most notably by the thirteenth-century Bavarian knight, Wolfram von Eschenbach, in his book *Parzival*. In this, he introduced some provenance for the symbolism – namely a mysterious poet called Kyot, who in his turn  had the tale from 'Flegetanis the Heathen', a Muslim astronomer. It was later taken up by Sir Thomas Malory in his great Arthurian work, *Le Morte d'Arthur*, completed in 1470. More recently, Wagner made use of the story in his last opera, *Parsifal*, which is based on the search for the Grail.

This great spread of tales, which strike deeply into their readers' and listeners' imagination, span most of the last millennium, but leave one question unanswered: did the Grail and the Spear of Destiny ever really exist as material objects or were they simply features of legend? Strangely, in medieval times, when religious relics formed much of the power-base of the Church, very few claimed possession of a physical grail or spear. The Church even maintained a curious detachment from the Grail story, tacitly recognising that it existed, but not embedding it in mainstream religious doctrine.

In the old stories, the Grail appears in different guises. Chrétien's tale speaks of both a golden vessel, encrusted with precious stones, and a silver dish, which could have held a large fish. Wolfram von Eschenbach describes the Grail in a completely different way, as a 'stone whose essence is most pure', which is named 'lapsit exillis', by virtue of which a mysterious bird – the phoenix – is able to die and be born again. Malory confuses the picture even further by referring to the Grail as the 'Sankgreall', derived from the French *sang real*, or 'royal blood', which has suggested to some that the Grail is a bloodline, rather than a physical object.

Dish, chalice, stone, bloodline: what could be more confusing and yet also more tantalising? Perhaps this explains the success of books such as *The Holy Blood and the Holy Grail* and *The Da Vinci Code*. The search for the Grail offers all the excitement of a detective story with the added ingredients of magical and religious symbolism. Remember the last scene in the film *Indiana Jones and the Last Crusade*, when the greedy Nazi drinks from the elaborate cup, which destroys him? A Grail quest combines high hopes, few tangible clues and the frisson of potential danger. It is easy to see why some people believe that the quest itself, rather than any physical object, may be the ultimate spiritual goal, representing the true nature of the Grail.

✍ The Grail Quest and ✍ the Knights Templar

The history of the search for the Grail is filled with an extraordinary catalogue of adventures undertaken by those who have fallen under its spell. Knights Templar, Nazis and treasure hunters have all played their part.

The first and only reported sighting of the Grail and the Spear comes from Palestine in the seventh century. The Gaulish monk Arculf journeyed there and described what he saw to Adamnan, the abbot of the island monastery of Iona, who reproduced this story in his three-volume account of Arculf's travels, *De Locis Sanctis*:

> Between the basilica of Golgotha and the Martyrium, there is
> a chapel in which lies the chalice of the Lord, which he himself
> blessed with his own hand and gave to the apostles whilst
> reclining with them at Supper the day before he suffered. The
> chalice is silver, has the measure of a Gaulish pint and has two
> handles fashioned on either side . . . After the resurrection, the
> Lord drank wine from this same chalice, according to the supping
> with the apostles [sic]. The holy Arculf saw it, and through an
> opening of the perforated lid of the reliquary where it reposes, he
> touched it with his own hand that he had kissed. All the people of
> the city flock to it with great veneration. Arculf saw the soldier's
> lance as well, with which he pierced the side of the Lord when
> he was hanging on the cross. This lance is in the porch of the
> Basilica of Constantine.

The story of the Grail then moves on several centuries to the Knights Templar, a monastic order of knights founded in around 1119 to protect Christian pilgrims to the Holy Land. The order

began as a group of warrior-monks sworn to poverty and was originally quartered in the captured Al-Aqsa mosque, built over the original Temple of Solomon in Jerusalem. According to some scholars, Wolfram von Eschenbach may have thought that the Templars were the guardians of the Grail, based on his writing in *Parzival* that 'the Grail is housed in a Temple and its keepers are called Templeisen'.

Whatever their role, the Templars rapidly became immensely wealthy, with property and land stretching from the Holy Land right across Europe. They developed one of the earliest banking systems, and were absolved by papal dispensation from obeying local laws. They wielded immense power and wealth for nearly two centuries, but their luck turned when King Philip IV of France applied pressure on the Pope to disband the Order. On Friday, 13 October 1307, Philip ordered the arrest of all the French Templars. Many were tortured and burnt at the stake, while the Order was disbanded and its assets seized.

In evidence given at the Templar trials in Paris in 1307, a sergeant, John of Chalons, maintained that the Templar Preceptor in France had been tipped off about his imminent arrest and had escaped with eighteen galleys, carrying the Templar Treasure – possibly to Scotland. Some Templar historians believe that, as a result of this, the Grail ended up in Rosslyn Chapel, seven miles outside Edinburgh. Enthusiasts suggest that it might even be hidden in one of the church's pillars, but the evidence they cite is flawed and no historian takes this idea seriously.

A more plausible destination for the Templar fleet is offered by Michael Baigent and Richard Leigh in their book, *The Temple and the Lodge*, citing in support of their theory a series of carved gravestones in Jura and Argyll that show ships, a large, iron-bound box and Freemasonic symbols. It is quite possible that the surviving Templars were enthusiastically welcomed by the Scots, and actually helped Robert the Bruce win the Battle of Bannockburn where a hundred knights, dressed in white, were said to have appeared at a crucial time in the battle to comprehensively defeat the English. Similar stories of white knights appearing at crucial times during battles can be found in Switzerland, where it was believed Templar knights also fled as the Order was persecuted.

In reality the fate of the Templars varied according to their location. In Portugal, the Order simply changed its name to the Order of Christ and continues to exist, although in a diluted form as an 'Order of Merit' rather than as a religious order. Some of the Templars – and certainly much of their wealth – became absorbed into another order, the Knights Hospitallers, and other aspects of their traditions and symbols emerge later in certain orders of the Freemasons.

But did the Templars somehow manage to retain their magical practices and their most sacred symbols in secret? Is it possible that the Grail and the Spear were taken to England, bringing the central symbols of the Grail story to rest in the heartland of Arthurian Romance? Tales abound of the Grail being brought to these shores – the most famous being that of Joseph of Arimathea who, accompanied by eleven missionaries, is said to have travelled to Glastonbury after the crucifixion, bearing the Holy Grail.

❧ Arthur, Guinevere and the Grail ❧

Glastonbury's association with 'The Matter of Britain' was consolidated in the twelfth century. In 1184, fire destroyed much of Glastonbury Abbey, which had taken 120 years to build. Six years

later the abbey monks announced that they had discovered the burial place of King Arthur and Guinevere, his queen. Digging to a depth of 16 feet, they had discovered the hollowed-out trunk of an oak tree, in which lay two skeletons, and upon a slab of stone covering this primitive coffin they had found a cross of lead bearing the inscription: *Hic jacet sepultus inclitus rex Arthurus in insula Avalonia* ('Here lies interred the famous King Arthur on the Isle of Avalon'). Most scholars believe the discovery was faked to ensure that pilgrims would return to the abbey and the town, which since the fire had lost a major source of revenue.

As a result of the find, Glastonbury soon became a major site of pilgrimage, and when the remains of Arthur and Guinevere were reburied at the foot of the high altar in 1278, King Edward I and Queen Eleanor attended the service.

More than the abbey's now-dubious reputation as the last resting place of King Arthur, it is as a home of the Grail that the town has developed a reputation for being one of the most significant sacred sites in the country. Some believe the Grail lies buried to this day beneath Chalice Hill, which rises beside the rugged outcrop known as Glastonbury Tor.

In 1906 a grain merchant from Bristol, Wellesley Tudor Pole, claimed that two sisters, on the promptings of a dream of his,

had found a greenish-blue, saucer-shaped dish with a repeating pattern of flower-like shapes in a spring just outside Glastonbury. As one of them wrote: 'It was with a deep feeling of reverence and awed feeling of responsibility that I realised the Vessel we had brought to light was the Holy Graal. I wondered many times why such an event should have come into my life, feeling a keen sense of unworthiness to be called as one of the custodians of this Sacred Relic.'[2]

Bronze ' Glastonbury Bowl', now in Taunton Museum.

Tudor Pole retrieved the dish, and there was great excitement when it was dated by experts to the time of Christ. For a while the newspapers announced that the Grail had been found. Later dating to the medieval era overturned these findings, but the dish is still revered as a sacred object and is held by the guardians of Chalice Well, which nestles between the Tor and Chalice Hill.

Despite numerous conspiracy theories that seek to link the Grail

Chalice Well, Glastonbury.

mystery to arcane religious groups such as the almost certainly bogus Priory of Sion, none of the contenders for the title of the 'true holy Grail' has been found to be historically genuine. Even though historians tell us that they cannot have been used in the Holy Land at the time of Christ, some of the 'Grails' have developed a reputation for miraculous powers. Those who have held the dish now kept at Chalice Well in Glastonbury often report an intense sense of peace and holiness emanating from it.

Another 'Grail', known as the 'Nanteos Cup', also originates from Glastonbury and was used to offer healing for over four centuries. The plain bowl, made of ancient olive wood, was smuggled out of Glastonbury Abbey when Henry VIII's commissioners came to strip the abbey of its treasures in 1539 during the Dissolution of the Monasteries. Seven monks escaped with the bowl to Strata Florida Abbey in Cardiganshire, and then gave it to Lord Powell for safe keeping. It remained in the Powell family's home at Nanteos in Wales for four hundred years, with pilgrims coming from far and wide to drink water from it in the hope of a cure. It is said that Richard Wagner came to see it before he wrote his Grail opera, *Parsifal*, as did Alfred Tennyson, author of the remarkable Arthurian poem cycle *Idylls of the King*. The cup is now thought to have been made in the fourteenth century.

There are many intriguing stories that might lead us to the discovery of a Grail. In a small cottage in Templecombe in Somerset, for example, during the Second World War, Mrs Mollie Drew discovered a strange and impressive painting of a man's face, which has been carbon-dated to AD 1280. Some have suggested that the 'Templecombe Head' is a depiction of Christ's face as seen on the Turin Shroud. Since there was an important Templar preceptory in the village, the painting was almost certainly a Templar treasure, hidden for safety and surviving intact for over seven hundred years. Have some of the other treasures survived in this way, hidden from the world in humble cottages? Does the Grail itself exist amongst a jumble of family possessions on a farmhouse shelf?

✺ The Chalice and the Blade in ✺ Practical Magic

While some have sought the Grail and the Spear of Destiny as treasures or relics, others have chosen to seek and work with them in other ways: in the worlds of symbol, imagination, magical ritual and even the landscape itself. Cup and lance, chalice and blade, the Holy Grail and Arthur's sword Excalibur, all represent the two forces that, when united, bring life into being. The chalice symbolises the feminine, the Goddess, the vulva or womb; the blade symbolises the masculine, the God, the phallus. In the East the terms used to describe these two forces are yin and yang.

Some magicians believe these forces flow in ley lines across the earth. The St Michael and St Mary lines mentioned in Chapter 1 are often cited as examples of a masculine and feminine line that weave together across southern England. There are others who believe that the 'true Grail' is indeed physical, as well as spiritual, but that it exists not fashioned in gold or silver but within the very earth herself. The land, they believe, has energy centres – known as chakras in Eastern terminology – and that there are various 'grails' or 'heart centres' across the planet, whose function is to radiate an atmosphere of love and harmony to the surrounding area.

According to Peter Dawkins, one of the pioneers of this under-standing of the grail, Kingston-upon-Thames just outside London is the heart chakra of a 'grail line' of energy centres that runs from the Golfe du Lion on the French Mediterranean coast, through London and up to the 'crown chakra' of Ben More Assynt in Scotland. He writes: 'The Grail is particularly associated with the heart and head, and so it is perhaps not by chance that the original source of the Grail legends is in Britain and constitutes the chief part of the British (Celtic) mythology.'[3] Others maintain that Glastonbury itself is a heart chakra, and enthusiasts of these ideas believe that they can accelerate their own spiritual development and planetary evolution by making pilgrimages to these centres and meditating or performing rituals there.

In the version of modern witchcraft called Wicca, which is explored in detail in the next chapter, a chalice and a dagger known as an athame are used as 'working tools' of the craft. When wine is consecrated, the High Priest kneels before the High Priestess, raising the filled chalice towards her. She slowly lowers the blade of the athame into the chalice, saying: 'As the athame is to the male, so the cup is to the female; and con-joined, they bring blessedness.'[4] At other times  the High Priest and High Priestess perform the 'Great Rite': an alchemical or tantric union in which the Priestess's body becomes the grail, the Priest's the athame.

In modern Druidry, the story of Taliesin, which features a pri-mordial grail in the shape of Ceridwen's cauldron, is used as a teaching vehicle for spiritual development. When the Druid initi-ate casts a magic circle about them, they often sense the sacred space created in this way as a grail or vessel in which they can open themselves to receive and radiate inspiration and blessings. In public Druidic ceremonies, a sword is sometimes raised aloft with the cry: 'Behold this sword Excalibur, which rose from the lake of still meditation and was returned to it again. The sword of spirit, of light and truth, is always sharp and always with us, if our lake be stilled.'[5]

JOHN MATTHEWS

John Matthews has been involved in the study of the mysteries of Britain and the Grail myth for forty-five years. His many books include The Encyclopaedia of Celtic Wisdom, The Grail Tarot *and* The Grail: Quest for Eternal Life. *He teaches throughout Europe and America, and lives in Oxford with his wife Caitlín, who is an expert on shamanism.*

The Grail legends are like seeds, with many different manifestations that have appeared in different places all over the world. If you recognise that the whole point is the quest, rather than finding it, the Grail can transform your life.

Everyone thinks of the Grail as a Christian symbol, but the truth is more strange and more magical. The Grail was never accepted formally by the Church, nor was it presented as a holy relic, although everyone in medieval Europe knew about it. The strands woven into the Grail's origin are partly Christian, partly Arthurian legend and partly pagan. You will also find that the cabbala is steeped in Grail images, which were associated with different parts of the cabbalistic diagram, the Tree of Life.

In the twelfth century, when the Grail legend first emerged, the Church was enormously strong and anything that did not fit in with its way of thinking was viewed as heresy. The Grail legends were a wonderful way of conveying many diverse strands of magical thought, such as gnostic beliefs, folk stories, and so forth, without fear of retribution. Once the story of the Grail became attached to the British national myths of King Arthur, this gave it a curious kind of legitimacy and drew the message into a cycle of stories that appealed to everyone. At a time when only the richest people could afford books, the Grail legends were moulded into courtly stories and could be told at that level.

When I started doing shamanic work, in one of my first journeys with a trusted guide I asked how I could find the Grail. He fell about with laughter and said, 'But the Grail is a story!' I realised later that, more than anything else, the Grail is a method of communicating with whatever is out there – call it god or goddess or whatever. It's similar to many other magical philosophies that open the mind to Other-worldly experience and power, such as the cabbala, or even the Tarot, which has Grail symbolism in it in the images of cup, lance, dish and sword.

The most important thing is what the Grail contains, not what it is. It's a gift of the Other-world that the outer world needs. It comes only when needed, and then it goes away. The Grail question is so important: 'Whom does the Grail serve?' It is sought for and found by a hero, like Perceval, who is the best known of those seeking the Grail. Then it goes back to its home and is guarded again until the next seeker comes along. There seems to be a new guardian for each generation.

The Cathars strongly believed the Grail was with them. At the end of the siege of Montségur, one of the leaders of the garrison – probably Trencaval or Roger Mirepois – went out on to the battlements dressed in silver armour. The French army below thought it was the Grail Knight come to help the Cathars and ran away.

Then, there is the story of the Grail being hidden in a cave after the siege. It is difficult to know what the Cathars believed was the physical form of the Grail. My own belief is that it was some sort of book or scroll, maybe an early Gospel, like Matthew, but the story has been so sensationalised that it's hard to know what, if anything, they might have hidden in the cave, or smuggled out.

Then there is an extraordinary story of the 'Wooden Book of Montségur', which was apparently discovered in the foundations of the old castle. It proved to be part of a system of astrology to link past, present and future lives, practised by an Indian magical sect called the Nadis. The enigma is how these pages ended up in Montségur, and why.

Himmler recognised the inherent power in the Grail and, of course, tried to enlist it in the Nazis' plans for world domination. He sent Otto Rahn to look for the Grail, but he failed in his quest and was forced to commit suicide. Otto Skorzeny, Hitler's private pilot, was sent for another try. It is a matter of record that he dispatched a telegram, saying: 'Eureka'. Himmler then ordered a plane to sky-write a Celtic cross over Montségur.

There are further amazing stories of the Nazis sending two German U-boats, U-530 and U-977, to the North Pole, carrying on board seven bronze boxes of artefacts for storage. Some authors have suggested that these may have contained material relevant to the Grail, or even the Grail itself. Two months after the war ended, these subs mysteriously surfaced off the coast of Argentina, where the crews were handed over to the American authorities, who interrogated them at length, and then flew them all back to the United States to be questioned further for almost a year. Even odder, after the war the Americans sent a four-star general with 40,000 men to the North Pole, supposedly to drill for oil. Might they have been looking for the Grail, stashed away in some abandoned submarine pen under the ice?

The stories of those who have searched for the real Grail, and the magical power associated with it, are amazing. I believe that the Templars were sitting on a lot of incredible artefacts towards the end of their time, so the question is: what happened to them?

Despite the fascination of these fantastic stories, my own preference is to search for the Grail in an inner spiritual way, but in any case when it comes to hearing a tale by the fire nothing can beat a good story about the Grail!

Professor ROLAND ROTHERHAM

'Roly' Rotherham, or 'The Doctor' as he prefers to be called, has led an extraordinary life. After a career in a top cavalry regiment, he became a member of the Queen's Household, living at Buckingham Palace. He is now a well-known and highly entertaining writer, speaker and teacher about the Grail, with a professorship in Arthurian and Grail studies. He lives near Lichfield, Staffordshire, and is still a dedicated searcher for the Grail after over forty years.

Although my professorship is in Arthurian and Grail studies, my passion is centred on the bleeding lance, 'The Spear of Destiny'. I have sat in front of the case that holds the Charlemagne spear, which is believed to be one of its two incarnations, and felt cold as if I were in the presence of something totally malevolent. It is pure evil. There is a horrible feeling to it, but I am fascinated by it.

The spear supposedly traces its ancestry back to a prophet at the court of King David. The spearhead was crafted to represent the blood of the chosen people and it became part of the crown regalia for the king, usually being carried by the temple guards. It was the one that was thrown in anger at Saul.

At the time of the crucifixion, the Romans wanted to distance themselves from the act, so handed over responsibility for it to Herod, who was also not keen to be associated with it. Instead he passed the spear to an old soldier by the name of Longinus (some accounts say it was Gaius Cassidus). Longinus, who was extremely short-sighted – he had cataracts – took hold of the spear and thrust it into Jesus's side to end his suffering. The blood that spurted out cured his sight.

The spear's subsequent history is incredible. Because it had performed a deed of mercy, it was imbued with huge power. It became an early Christian artefact and was carried into battle by the Theban legion. Eventually it came to England and was owned by Ethelred, then was transferred to the court of Charlemagne.

It passed through a succession of Holy Roman emperors and is now in the Hofburg Museum in Vienna, where it is known as the spear of Charlemagne.

It has been dated accurately. It seems that the main part comes from the time of Charlemagne; he used it to prove his right to power. There are later additions of silver and gold sheaths. Magnification of the nail in the centre of the spearhead shows that there are traces of other smaller pieces of metal hammered into it, perhaps from another nail. Since the nail is dated to the first century AD, it is rumoured to have been used at Christ's crucifixion.

Just after the First World War, Hitler became absolutely fascinated by the Spear and would sit and stare at it for long periods. Later he said:

> I stood there quietly gazing upon it for several minutes quite
> oblivious to the scene around me. It seemed to carry some
> hidden inner meaning which evaded me, a meaning which I felt
> I inwardly knew yet could not bring to consciousness . . . I felt
> as though I myself had held it before in some earlier century
> of history. That I myself had once claimed it as my talisman of
> power and held the destiny of the world in my hands.[6]

Everyone who has held the spear has committed outrages and blood-letting, and as a result the spear itself has become increasingly powerful. It reached its pinnacle of power when it was in the hands of General Patton at the time when President Truman ordered the bombing of Nagasaki. Patton is supposed to have found it in one of Hitler's bunkers, after Hitler had ordered Himmler to bring it from Schloss Wewelsburg, the headquarters of the SS occult division, as the tide of the war turned against Germany.

There are rumours that the spear in Vienna is only a copy and that the original is in South America, but no one can be sure. If this is true, the likelihood is that the real spear is in the hands of someone obsessed with power.

I have spent a lot of my life looking for the 'Terrestrial Grail' – the actual cup used by Christ at the Last Supper, but I have to admit that, if I found it, I'd put it back and not tell anyone, otherwise I would be responsible for taking away other people's dreams.

The one place that I myself have felt closest to the Grail is in the Basilica of the Holy Blood in Bruges. I can recommend a visit to anyone. This is a very early basilica, with a huge silver monstrance that contains a reliquary of the Holy Blood. Two pillars separate the church from the chapel next door. One pillar has an image of Mary Magdalene holding a green ointment cup, used to dress wounds. The other is much more interesting. It shows Joseph of Arimathea holding a bowl.

Go down the stairs to the ancient basilica and there you will find, carved in the stone above the altar, a pelican, which is a symbol of the crucifixion. In front of it are two plain tombstones, which are without any shadow of doubt early Templar. The grave markers show a Grail on each. To your right is the tomb of Christ, laid out on the sarcophagus, and above him the articles of the Passion.

Look just slightly to one side and you can just see carved in the stone a bowl, with two matching jugs on each side. These are the 'Arimathean Cruets' of blood and water. Right underneath is a spearhead, cut into the living stone by the original Templars, who must have worshipped these images.

In my view, the Templars used the occult as a working tool but paid lip service to Christianity. By virtue of their elitism and massive power, they considered themselves out of reach, which they were. After their Order was dissolved, they disappeared into a secret world. Why make waves? They had got what they needed. Many became pirates and flew the 'Jolly Roger'. The battle flags of the Templar war galleys were black on white and the skull is of course the head of Baphomet. Many of the Order turned to preservation and conservation – not acquisition – and the best way to do that is to keep a low profile. The Freemasons did not emerge until centuries later, and although they continued some of the Templar rituals, I suspect they have forgotten most of the meaning.

I became fascinated with the Grail mysteries when I was very young. At the age of seven I was given a book for Christmas, the first real book that I had ever owned. *The Legends of King Arthur and his Table Round* was not a children's book and it was in grown-up language. I would lie in bed reading it and shiver with excitement. Of all the tales, it was the story of Perceval finding the Grail that got to me – this incredible object, which was all things to all people; this incredible quest, where you lose everything, even your sanity, before you achieve anything. You are stripped back to the bones first.

In ancient Celtic lore, you find references to the 'spear of Lugh'. If you crash the end down on the floor, it sends out lightning bolts, but at the end of each day the spear has to be immersed in a vase of sanctified blood or it goes on a killing spree. In the same way, I believe that the Grail controls the Spear and makes it more benign. If there was no knowledge of evil, you would never see what good is. It is the same with the Grail and the Spear.

Every civilisation has its legends of cups or cauldrons. For example, the Cauldron of Inspiration from the Welsh myth – where Taliesin spills drops from it on his thumb, then receives eternal wisdom – is very indicative of rebirth and of finding your spirit guides, which have become a hugely important part of my own life. The cauldrons and the Grail legend are a way of getting in touch with the next world, by making you believe in something that is pure and beautiful.

Evelyn Waugh has Sebastian ask in *Brideshead Revisited*: 'Is it possible to believe in anything simply because it is beautiful?' My answer is: yes!

◉ *How to Undertake a Grail Quest*

You can attempt to search for the Grail in the physical world, or in the inner world of the soul or imagination. Enthusiasts for the

physical search include those who
use dowsing and psychic or intuitive
promptings, along with historical
research, to pursue their goal, while
enthusiasts of the inner quest use the
power of their imagination to invoke
the Grail as a state of consciousness, or as a gift of blessing or
inspiration. Magicians who adopt this latter approach often see
the Grail as symbolising the true nature of the heart or soul, and
the fluid that flows into and out of this Grail as the state of grace
sought by mystics.

If you would like to try the inner quest, first familiarise yourself
with the Grail stories and their landscape in a way that you can
clearly visualise, and that will kindle the fires of your imagination.
Of primary importance are:

* The 'Forest Sauvage', a vast, tangled tract of woodland
with few paths to guide you. Here you may meet
the 'Questing Beast', or be tempted, like Perceval,
by beautiful girls and ruined castles with ferocious
guardians. Imagine yourself traversing the forest paths,
with all sound shut out by the huge trees, and only the
rustle of wild beasts and your own fear of the unknown
to keep you company.

* The Grail castle, the home of the wounded 'Fisher King'.
Imagine its towers and drawbridge, over which Perceval
canters to be welcomed by the servants. Then visualise the
huge central banqueting room, the Fisher King lying on a
rich sofa, and finally the Grail procession itself.

* The cave of the hermit and the small chapel near by, in
which Perceval at last found his way back to God and
some explanation of his Grail quest. Imagine yourself
sitting with the hermit and sharing his simple meal of
'beets, chervil, lettuces, cress and millet, accompanied by

bread made of barley and oats, washed down with clear spring water'.

* Merlin, the great wizard of English history and Arthur's adviser. Merlin was supposed to be born to a human but sired by a 'succubus', an Other-world sprite, which gave him unearthly powers. Some even claimed that he hailed from Atlantis, where he fled from the great flood, carrying with him many secrets, in company with a priestess who became Arthur's mother, Igraine. He appears in many of the Grail romances, and is a prime mover behind the scenes in arranging which of the knights is selected for the quest and the type of magic they use. The famous 'Round Table' of Camelot is supposed to have been made by Merlin to show the roundness of the world and the firmament. Yet Merlin, as his parentage dictates, is also a shadowy figure, only half of this world, enchanted, as Tennyson wrote, by the fairy Nimue. Imagine him at the heart of the magic wood, dreaming in his hawthorn tower, or appearing suddenly, as he did to Arthur, in the guise of a wondrous youth.

With these images clear in your mind, sit comfortably in a quiet room without light. Let the worries of your life and the familiar things in the room fade away. Slow your breathing and close your eyes. Imagine yourself on a great horse, with hairy fetlocks and huge reddened nostrils, as it sways down a narrow path in the forest. Be aware of the trees and the animals around you, as if the forest itself were a living being. Quicken your senses to imagine danger, adventure and magical discoveries. Whatever image comes next, explore it to the full and allow it to become a stepping-stone in your own personal quest. Allow yourself to enter a reverie, a waking dream, and see where it takes you. After a while, let the real world seep back into your consciousness – the ticking of a clock, the sound of the traffic outside your house.

Open your eyes, stretch and reach for pen and paper to record your experience.

If you would prefer to undertake an outer quest, you can gain tips on how to proceed by exploring the subject of 'psychic questing', discussed each year at the Psychic Questing Conference held in Glastonbury. See www.psychicquesting.com

Psychic questing can, however, sometimes trap the unwary in a fruitless chase after 'signs and omens'. A different but probably more satisfying approach can be found in the work of Peter and Sarah Dawkins, who suggest that the Grail can be found not only in the human heart but also in the subtle energetic landscape of the earth. Finding the Grail then becomes a search not for a physical object, such as a chalice of gold, but instead a pilgrimage to particular heart or Grail centres where the sacred can be found. For details of their work, see www.zoence.co.uk

∽ Things to Do ∾

England is so extraordinarily rich in sites related to Merlin, the Arthurian stories, the Holy Grail and the Knights Templar that spiritual seekers come from all over the world to explore its magical landscape, and are often more impressed and knowledgeable about the sites they visit than the local inhabitants, who tend to take them for granted.

Once you have tasted the mystery and romance of the 'Matter of Britain', perhaps by watching John Boorman's 1981 film *Excalibur* or through reading the stories in one of the numerous collections of early or modern versions, you will probably want to set out on a quest of your own to discover the places associated with them.

Armed with information from internet searches and a good guidebook, such as John Michell's *The Traveller's Guide to Sacred England* (Gothic Image, 2003) or Geoffrey Ashe's *The Traveller's Guide to Arthurian Britain* (Gothic Image, 1997), see which of the locations seems to whisper to your soul or imagination, asking you to pay a visit – to make a pilgrimage.

❀ In search of the Templars, visit the impressive Temple
Church in London, situated between Fleet Street and
the Thames, and made famous by Dan Brown's *The Da
Vinci Code.*

❀ Travel to Lewes in Sussex, where a legend suggests that
the last Grand Master of the Order brought the Grail to
the Templar church in Albion Street, although little trace
now remains of the church.

❀ Visit Templecombe church in Somerset to view the
'Templecombe Head' – possibly a rendition of the head
of Christ from the Turin Shroud, and equally possibly
one example of the Templar treasures that could be
hidden in different locations around the country.

❀ Explore a cave just off the High Street of Royston,
Hertfordshire, that was probably used by Templars
during the times of persecution. Medieval carvings adorn
the cave walls. See www.roystoncave.co.uk

❀ In search of King Arthur, his knights and the Holy
Grail, a visit to Glastonbury is essential. In the abbey
see the sites of Arthur and Guinevere's tombs, then sit
in the abbey grounds, imagining the escape of the seven
monks with the wooden cup that would become the
Nanteos Grail. Climb Wearyall Hill to visit the Holy
Thorn tree, whose ancestor was planted, according to
legend, by Joseph of Arimathea, bringing the Grail to
Glastonbury. Then make your way to Chalice Well
gardens. Here between the Tor and Chalice Hill, drink
the iron-rich water flowing from the well, and pause
a while to tune into the peaceful atmosphere. Some
believe the Grail is hidden in Chalice Hill; others that it
is hidden in a cave beneath the Tor. For a time Tudor
Pole placed his Grail on a shelf in the well-head, and

there are some who believe that the well itself is a living Grail – pouring forth healing waters from the depths of the earth.

To get a feeling for how a cave within the Tor might feel, visit the White Spring in Wellhead Lane beside the gardens. While the water from Chalice Well is red from its iron content, clear water flows from the White Spring and joins the well water in a culvert. Enthusiasts of alchemy point to the symbolism of this union of masculine and feminine symbology in one of the most magical places in England. See www.chalicewell.org.uk and www.whitespring.org.uk

Climb to the summit of the Tor and gaze out upon the landscape. It was here in 1929 that Katherine Maltwood received a revelation that the tales of King Arthur were based on an astrological pattern formed by ancient features of the landscape around Glastonbury. Working with maps and aerial photographs, she identified the figures of a giant zodiac created by streams, tracks and field boundaries. A local astrologer, Jane Walker, organises regular walks around the Glastonbury Zodiac. See www.isleofavalon.co.uk/avalon-zodiacwalks.html

From the Tor you can see a high plateau 11 miles to the south-east, now called Cadbury Castle, but known in the sixteenth century as Camelot. On its summit, the locals believed, stood Arthur's court, and in a cave within the hill the old king still lies sleeping, ready to awaken if his kingdom should ever need him. Archaeological evidence indicates that the hill has been an important site since prehistoric times, and according to the writer John Michell a walk to its summit leads one to the 'centre of the legendary landscape of the quest for the Holy Grail'.

❦ Another site identified as Camelot by early chroniclers lies in Winchester, Hampshire. In the great hall of the castle you can see King Arthur's Round Table, deprived

The Round Table, from a fifteenth-century French manuscript.

of its legs and hanging on a wall – a massive 18 feet in diameter and weighing 1.25 tons. The surface was painted at some time after 1522, dividing the table into twenty-five segments: twenty-four of them for twelve knights and their ladies, and one for the king. King Henry VIII used the table when entertaining the visiting emperor Charles V. The table itself dates from the thirteenth century, recording how Edward I modelled himself on King Arthur and attended the opening of Arthur's tomb in Glastonbury in 1278.

❧ Arthurian sites can be found not only in Hampshire and Somerset, in Cornwall and Cumbria, but also in Wales, Scotland and Brittany too. Sir Thomas Malory's *Le Morte d'Arthur* implies that Camelot was located in Carlisle, and all around the city there are sites with Arthurian associations, such as Arthur's Chair at King's Crags, 6 miles east of Greenhead; and the Cumbrian Round Table, Mayburgh Henge, 1 mile south of Penrith.

Further afield, 40 miles south-east, lies Pendragon
Castle, said to have been built by Arthur's father Uther
Pendragon.

❧ On a rocky windswept headland at Tintagel in Cornwall
stands what is claimed to be Uther Pendragon's castle.
Visit the legendary birthplace of King Arthur and, on the
shore below, enter Merlin's cave.

At all of these places it is worth taking the time to be still and
to tune into the atmosphere of the place. Some magicians believe
that certain spots on earth act as portals or gateways to other
dimensions, and that if you approach them with reverence and
openness, visions or insights will be given to you from the spirit
world. It is possible that some of the sites linked to the 'Matter of
Britain' and the Holy Grail may be such gateways, but it is up to
each seeker to discover for themselves whether this is so.

๑ Resources ๑

BOOKS

Crusade against the Grail, Otto Rahn (Inner Traditions, 2006). Originally
published in German in 1933, this is an account of the struggle
between the Cathars, Templars and the Pope.

The Grail Seekers' Companion, John Matthews and Marian Green (Thoth
Publications, 2003). This provides practical advice on how to start
your quest.

The Holy Grail: The History of a Legend, Richard Barber (Penguin Books,
2005)

Merlin Through the Ages: A Chronological Anthology and Source Book, John
Matthews and R.J. Stewart (ed.), (Cassell, 1995)

*Otto Rahn and the Quest for the Holy Grail: The Amazing Life of the Real
'Indiana Jones'*, Nigel Graddon (Adventures Unlimited Press, 2008)

The Prophetic Vision of Merlin, R.J. Stewart (Thoth, 1991)

The Quest for Merlin, Nikolai Tolstoy (Sceptre, 1988)

*The Secret Tradition in Arthurian Legend: The Magical and Mystical Power
Sources Within the Mysteries of Britain*, Gareth Knight (Aquarian, 1983)
The Templars, Piers Paul Read (Phoenix Press, 2001)
The Temple and the Lodge, Michael Baigent and Richard Leigh (Arrow
Books, 1998). This delves into the mystery of the Templars after their
dissolution and their link to Freemasonry.

WEBSITES

Visit the website of Professor Roland Rotherham at
www.unicorn-dreams.freeserve.co.uk

The website of Grail specialists John and Caitlin Matthews:
www.hallowquest.org.uk

For a distance-learning course in 'Avalonian Magic' and the Grail
mysteries, taught by the author Mara Freeman, see
www.avalonmysteryschool.net

For a beautiful website that explores the grail as symbolic of the
Feminine, see www.magdalene.org

CHAPTER FIVE

SKIN-TURNING AND SPELLCRAFT

The World of Witches and Warlocks

Women who are wont to practise enchantments,
and magicians and witches,
do not allow them to live.

KING ALFRED, NINTH CENTURY

Of all the different kinds of magic ever worked in Britain, witchcraft is undoubtedly the most ubiquitous. Today it is the most commonly practised magic in the country, and you will find covens meeting everywhere, from the tip of Cornwall right up to the Borders and beyond. Go to the Fairfield Halls in Croydon around Hallowe'en and you can mingle with hundreds of witches as they attend workshops, browse bookstalls and dance the night away. Go online and you will discover forums bustling with thousands of contributors discussing every possible aspect of their 'craft' and of magic in general.

This activity is not confined to one gender either: witches are not, nor have they ever been, only women. In the past, male witches were sometimes called warlocks but this is no longer the case.

What exactly is the craft that these men and women practise? How did it evolve? What did witches do in the old days and what do they do now? A story from the time of the Second World War offers a clue . . .

It is 1 August 1940 – Lammas night: the ancient festival originally marking the end of summer. Hitler is threatening to invade Britain, and Churchill has recently warned of the risk that 'all that we have known and cared for' could 'sink into the abyss of a new dark age made more sinister . . . by the lights of a perverted science'. Near the site of the Rufus Stone in the New Forest, where some say King William II was offered as a pagan sacrifice, stands a clearing surrounded by tall trees. One by one, under the pale light of a waning moon, naked figures step into this clearing. Just a little to the south-east of the centre a small bonfire burns. One of the figures walks around the clearing, tracing pentagrams in the air with a dagger at each of the cardinal directions. The smell of incense drifts in the breeze.

The group then joins hands and begins to dance in a circle, faster and faster, chanting in some strange tongue. On and on they dance until they seem to spin in a supernatural whirl, until suddenly they stop. Two of them break hands and walk in opposite directions, pulling their colleagues with them until they stand in one straight line facing the fire. Now they all rush at the fire, shouting: 'You cannot cross the sea! You cannot cross the sea! You cannot come! You cannot come!' They continue to rush and chant until one by one they fall exhausted beside the bonfire. Over the coming days they repeat this ritual three more times. Each time that it reaches its climax and they rush at the fire, they imagine they are shouting at Adolf Hitler – that their message reaches right into his brain.

This magical working was so exhausting that some of the participants reportedly died. It is even said that a sacrifice was needed to make the magic work, and that the oldest and frailest member of the coven deliberately failed to cover his naked body in the protective grease that the witches used to ward off the cold, and that he died of pneumonia soon afterwards.

If the story is true, it describes one of the most significant acts of magic ever performed in England. Gerald Gardner, the moving force in the promotion of witchcraft in the modern era, insisted that he took part in the rite, and that it had been performed by witches before – when invasion was threatened both by Napoleon and by the Spanish Armada.

Gardner was known to fabricate and exaggerate, but we know for certain that other occultists attempted to influence the Nazis through magic. Dion Fortune, whom we shall meet again in Chapter 11, had members of her magical group concentrating their powers together every Sunday to influence the outcome of the war, and the witches of Kent are said to have scattered 'Go Away powder' into the sea, so it seems perfectly possible that a group would perform such a ritual when their country was threatened. However, Cecil Williamson, a former MI6 officer and founder of the Witchcraft Museum in Boscastle, Cornwall, claimed that

Gerald Gardner at the Witchcraft Museum.

Gardner 'borrowed' his story from Williamson's own account of a ritual organised in the Ashdown Forest in Sussex as an elaborate hoax to unnerve Hitler who believed in the powers of the occult. Forty Canadian soldiers, wearing army blankets embroidered with occult symbols, performed a fake ceremony that centred on a dummy of Adolf Hitler. An account of this was then deliberately 'leaked' to Germany.

Even if Gardner's story is untrue, it contains all the elements of a modern witchcraft ritual, in which participants dance in a magic circle that has been cast by a dagger. Witches believe that by dancing and chanting in a circle, they generate a 'cone of power', which they can then direct to achieve a specific end, such as casting a spell, or – as in this story – influencing someone's mind. Many believe that they can generate this 'cone' of magical energy more effectively if they are naked or, as Gerald Gardner called it, 'skyclad' – a term taken from the Jain religion. Magical power is seen as emanating from the body and the natural world, and clothing is said to impair the flow of this energy during a rite.

Other witches work in robes or everyday clothes, while still others prefer to work alone rather than in groups or covens. Since the 1980s many solitary witches have taken to calling themselves 'hedge witches' after a book of the same title by Rae Beth. As with every religion and magical path, there are many different schools of practice, but what they all have in common is their sense of continuity with the past – a belief that they are practising a form of magic that is ancient and that originated in the pre-Christian era. But although modern witchcraft is certainly inspired by the folk magic of our ancestors, it has also been influenced by more recent strands of thought, including Freemasonry, Spiritualism, and medieval High Magic.

✎ Three Kinds of Witches ✎

To understand the story of witchcraft in England we need to look at three different groups of people: those who practised folk magic up until the early part of the twentieth century; those who were accused of being witches during the centuries of persecution; and those who began practising a magic that they termed 'witchcraft' from the middle of the twentieth century.

Some writers have advanced the idea that these three groups of people represent a continuity of tradition that stretches in an unbroken line back into the past. They claim that witchcraft was once a 'secret religion', a survival of pre-Christian nature worship, that held its followers together across the centuries, that was persecuted from the fifteenth to the seventeenth centuries, and that emerged into the light of day with the repeal of the Witchcraft Act in 1951.

However, historians now believe it is highly unlikely that organised groups of people met as witches in covens to pass on

traditional lore and to carry out rituals that had been passed down the generations from time immemorial. It seems more likely that what we think of as the witchcraft of earlier centuries was a type of folk magic practised by individuals, perhaps by members of the same family, in the way that it has been practised throughout time and throughout the world. To stave off illness and starvation, bad weather and harvest failures, people have always turned to the supernatural – using chants and dances, blessings and the 'sympathetic magic' of ritual enactments of success, in an attempt to attract beneficent forces and to repel malign ones. Beliefs and practices of every age – of the Druid and Anglo-Saxon wizards, of every kind of pagan and even Christian practice – were included in this folk magic, which was not termed 'witchcraft' by its practitioners, since it was designed to repel the magic of witches, who were believed to be evil and the cause of misfortune. It was only in the twentieth century that a reversal of meaning occurred, and the term 'witch' started to be used in a positive sense to designate followers of the 'Old Ways' who used folk magic for benign purposes.

The great majority of people who practised the kind of folk magic we might now think of as witchcraft – from pagan times right through the Saxon and medieval ages, into the seventeenth century and beyond – were what would be termed in Africa 'witch doctors'. Witch doctors are not doctors who are witches, but doctors who treat patients who have been attacked by witches. Much of the magic performed in the English countryside was of this kind, and was concerned with protecting livestock, crops and people from the curses and blights of evil forces.

The sort of person who performed this kind of magic was known as the local 'wise woman' or man, and would be called upon to offer charms or herbal remedies, and to cast spells or counter-spells against witchcraft. As Professor Wayne Shumaker says in *The Occult Sciences in the Renaissance*: '[Even] at a time when England was still thinly populated, enough persons in a country village might think they were bewitched to provide full-time work for a "wise-woman".'[1]

By the fifteenth century these 'witch doctors' were often termed 'cunning-folk', who sold remedies, performed healings and protected your property, family and animals – for a fee. We will be looking at them in detail in Chapter 8. To contribute to the confusion surrounding the term 'witch', in the twentieth century (possibly earlier in Devon), some started using the term 'white witches' to describe 'cunning-folk' and to distinguish them from the 'black witches' who caused harm. Whether these 'black witches' believed they were using occult power or whether they were in reality trying to earn a living through a combination of offering healing, begging and extortion is a moot point.

The historian John Swain has suggested that the outbreaks of witchcraft that culminated in one of the most famous witch trials in England, in Pendle, Lancashire in 1612, demonstrate the

extent to which people could make a living through engendering fear: either by posing as a witch, or by accusing or threatening to accuse others of being a witch.[2] We will never know how many people actually worked with magic to harm others, as opposed to using the idea that they had occult powers as a way of scaring people into parting with money. Certainly, human nature being what it is, there will have been people who cursed others, even brewed poison, but by far the greatest amount of magic being practised would have been positive and protective rather than harmful, with the most malicious influence coming instead from quite another quarter – the Church itself.

The obsession of early Christians with the power of evil, with the need for vigilance against Satan and sin, provoked an intense fear of the power of witches as evil sorcerers, which fed into the activities of those who 'fought' witches with spells and folk magic. This is why we see the use of Christ and the cross in many of the early spells of the Anglo-Saxons. (An example of this can be seen in Chapter 3 where a sick horse is cut with a sign of the cross.)

It was not, however, until the sixteenth century that this fear became so intense that, in England, people, mainly women, began to be persecuted as witches and killed. An activity that we might associate with medieval superstition or the Inquisition occurred here much later and was the product not of Catholic but of Protestant zeal.

↶ The Witchfinder General ↷

Even on the Continent the witch hunts began in earnest, not in the Dark Ages but during the time of the High Renaissance in the fifteenth century. They were triggered by Pope Innocent VIII issuing his papal bull in 1484, calling upon secular authorities to aid the Inquisition in exterminating witchcraft. Over the next two centuries or so, it is estimated that between 40,000 and 50,000 people were accused of witchcraft, brutally tortured and killed – mostly in Germany, France and Scotland, where James VI (later King James I of England) wrote a book on the subject, *Demonologie*, and participated in the trial of a witch.

Whereas between 800 and 2,500 so-called witches were burnt at the stake in Scotland, it is estimated that, in England, fewer – between 400 and 500 people – died, needlessly and cruelly, as a result of this lunacy, where death by hanging, rather than by the stake, was the punishment for 'invoking evil spirits and using witchcraft, charms or sorcery'.[3]

Almost half of this death toll was accounted for in the one county of Essex where Matthew Hopkins, a Puritan fanatic, took it upon himself to rid it of witches. Born in Wenham in Suffolk, the son of a minister, Hopkins was a failed lawyer with no qualifications. He began his work in Manningtree in Essex in 1645, when he accused seven women of talking to imps and of attempting to kill him by conjuring up the devil in the shape of a wild bear. Torture was illegal but Hopkins devised ways to prove the women's guilt: confessions were wrung from them by making them stay awake while seated on a stool for days and nights on end in a freezing cell, or, in an astonishing display of illogicality, they were bound and thrown into the river. If the victim drowned and died, she was declared innocent. If she lived, she could have survived only with the aid of the devil, and was promptly hanged.

Soon Hopkins, now with a band of helpers, began holding trials all over Essex. He became known as the 'Witchfinder General' and over the next two years terrorised the local populace. In his trials he focused on specific indicators of guilt – 'witches' teats' – abnormal extra teats which the devil used to suck blood; the 'Devil's mark' which was a patch of skin said to be insensible to pain; the presence of pets, such as cats, who might be 'familiars' – allies that aided the accused in their evil work; and the presence in the house of unguents, clay images or any other 'implements of sorcery'.[4]

Hopkins' reign of terror was not the norm, as Professor Ronald Hutton explains:

In England the accused were tried at county assize sessions, by juries of strangers directed by professional judges, and about 70% were acquitted. Those who died were normally senile, saddled with an unusually bad local reputation, or convinced that they had actually cursed people, with success. The East Anglian bloodbath of 1645–7 occurred because the assize system had collapsed in civil war, leaving a gap into which stepped Hopkins, a nobody from the minor gentry with a personal hatred of witchcraft.[5]

In Sussex, for example, only thirty-three people were ever accused of witchcraft and brought to court, of whom only one was executed.

Of those accused of witchcraft during the sixteenth and seventeenth centuries, 80 per cent were female, and two kinds of women seem to have been particularly targeted. Reginald Scot, in his *Discoverie of Witchcraft*, published in 1584, wrote of 'One sort of such as are said to be witches, are women which be commonly old, lame, bleary-eyed, pale, foul, and full of wrinkles'. Scot was a rare sceptic who saw superstition and paranoia all around him, where every misfortune was blamed not on natural causes, or simply bad luck, but upon that strange, ugly woman who lived further down the lane, alone and in poverty: 'But if all the devils in hell were dead, and all the witches in England burnt or hanged; I warrant you we should not fail to have rain, hail and tempests, as now we have . . . I am also well assured, that if all the old women in the world were witches; and all the priests, conjurers: we should not have a drop of rain, nor a blast of wind the more or the less for them.'[6] But contrary to popular imagination, the old and isolated spinster was the lesser of the two targets. Research now shows that competent, middle-aged and middle-class women were more often picked upon, usually because they had a reputation for a hot temper and a sharp tongue.[7]

Some of those accused may have been 'white witches' – acting as local 'wise women or men', offering herbal remedies or charms against disease or poor crops and, ironically, against the malevolence of 'witches'. If a client or their livestock got worse or died under their care, it is easy to see how they could become figures

of hatred and blame. Others, who will have engaged in no magic whatsoever, were simply casualties of witch-hysteria and sometimes mental illness. None of those accused, historians believe, was a member of an organised cult or sect that practised ritual magic – meeting together in covens to dance naked under a full moon, and to perform rites that were unspeakable, but fascinating to the witch hunters.

After two years of his witch hunts, East Anglians grew tired of Hopkins and villages refused him entry. Legend tells that he himself was accused of witchcraft and was hanged. In reality, he returned to Manningtree and died of consumption in 1647.

Gradually the enthusiasm for killing so-called witches began to wane. The last people definitely hanged for witchcraft in England were Temperance Lloyd, Susanna Edwards and Mary Trembles, at Exeter in 1682. As the eighteenth century dawned, a more enlightened spirit reigned, as we can see from a typical witch trial of the time. In 1712, Jane Wenham, who bore the name of Hopkins' birthplace, was convicted but then pardoned and set free. In 1734, the Witchcraft Act was introduced to target dubious fortune-tellers and fraudulent mediums, rather than any other kind of so-called 'witch'.

Read about this Period in Fiction

High Magic's Aid, Gerald Brosseau Gardner (I-H-O Books, 1999)
Written by the founder of modern witchcraft, it is set in the twelfth century and contains ceremonial magic taken from *The Key of Solomon*; the witchcraft ceremonies conducted by the main character, Morgen, will be recognised by modern Wiccans.

Lancashire Witches: A Romance of Pendle Forest, W. Harrison Ainsworth (Printwise Publications, 1992)

Mist Over Pendle, Robert Neill (Arrow, 1987)
Both these books are based on the true story of the Pendle witches, believed to have been responsible for murder by witchcraft around the Forest of Pendle in 1612.

⁓ The Modern Revival ⁓

Darksome night and shining Moon,
Hell's dark mistress, Heaven's queen,
Harken to the witch's rune,
Diana, Lilith, Melusine!
Queen of witchdom and of night,
Work my will by magic rite.

DOREEN VALIENTE, *THE WITCH'S CHANT*

As we have seen, the first of the three kinds of people we might think of as witches did not in fact see themselves as witches but as witch doctors or anti-witches.

The second kind – those who were accused by the witch hunters of 'skin-turning' into the form of animals, of riding on broomsticks and of copulating with the devil – may have included some of these witch doctors, or cunning-folk, but it also included people who never practised any kind of magic.

It is only with the third category that we find people proudly calling themselves witches, redeeming the term and reversing its previously accepted meaning, so that today witchcraft is considered by many a religion. It is taught in books and on the internet, discussed in conferences and celebrated throughout England and, indeed, the world.

This kind of witchcraft emerged in the middle of the twentieth century thanks to the writings of Gerald Gardner, a civil servant who had spent most of his life in the East. When in retirement he returned to Britain and immediately set about meeting the occult intelligentsia of London. During the war he moved to Christchurch in Dorset to avoid the air raids, and there he claimed that he was initiated into a coven of traditional witchcraft. In 1954, a few years after the Witchcraft Act was repealed, he published a book recounting his experience, *Witchcraft Today*, which he followed several years later with another, *The Meaning of Witchcraft*. These two books succeeded in founding a new religion, which he termed 'Wica', and which later came to be spelt 'Wicca', from the Saxon, meaning wizard, sorcerer or magician.

Professor Ronald Hutton, who has written the definitive history of modern pagan witchcraft, *The Triumph of the Moon*, writes: 'No academic historian has ever taken seriously Gardner's claim to have discovered a genuine survival of ancient religion.' The magical religion that Gardner outlined in his books, and which others developed and elaborated, has mysterious origins but it is most likely that Gardner himself created it from a number of sources, including medieval magical texts and the work of Aleister Crowley.

Gardner's genius, however, lay in offering to the world a way of spiritual celebration that was admirably suited to an era dedicated to throwing off the shackles of sexual repression. The first known coven of this new religion was formed in a nudist resort part-owned by Gardner, near St Albans in Hertfordshire, just north of London, that still exists. It was in this region that Queen Boudicca attacked the Roman town of Verulamium and laid it to waste. It was here too that Britain's first martyr St Alban died in the fourth century where the great abbey now stands. It was also here that Sir Francis Bacon, revered by generations of British occultists, lived out his final years, and where a mural painted in his day, filled with esoteric symbolism, can still be seen, protected by a glass panel in a shop on the High Street beside the White Hart Inn.

Just outside the town, in a reconstructed Elizabethan cottage in the grounds of the Five Acres Country Club, Gardner held his first coven meetings. From the 1940s right through into the 1960s, the club attracted not only witches, but Druids in the shape of Ross Nichols, founder of the Order of Bards, Ovates and Druids, and a leading Sufi, Idries Shah, who wrote Gardner's biography. The rock band Pink Floyd famously spent a wild psychedelic evening at Five Acres after a concert in 1966, and the witches' cottage still stands in the resort's grounds, a forgotten shrine of the one religion England has given to the world.

GERALD GARDNER, 1884–1964

Gerald Gardner, the founding father of modern Wicca, was born in Blundell Sands, near Liverpool. Because he suffered from the 'magician's disease' of asthma (so-called because notable figures in the occult world, such as Aleister Crowley, Allan Bennett and Ross Nichols suffered from it), the family nanny took Gerald on numerous holidays to warmer climes – West Africa, the Canaries and the Mediterranean. When he was seventeen, she took him to Ceylon, where she became engaged to the heir of a tea plantation. Gerald worked on the plantation, receiving no formal education, and for the next thirty-five years he lived in the East, in Ceylon, Malaya and Borneo, working as a tea grower, rubber planter, government inspector and Customs officer.

He became fascinated by weaponry and wrote a book that became the standard work on the Malay *kris* dagger. He also became interested in anthropology, native magic and archaeology, carrying out excavations in Johore, and travelling to China and French Indo-China (now Vietnam) in search of archaeological material. On retiring in 1936, he returned to England with his wife Donna. His doctor recommended nude sunbathing to treat his asthma, and Gardner became an enthusiastic naturist.

When war was about to break out, he moved from London to the New Forest, where he came across the Rosicrucian Theatre in Christchurch, Hampshire (now Dorset). The theatre put on plays about Druids, Pythagoras and other themes of a mystical nature, and was run by a magical group, the Rosicrucian Order Crotona Fellowship. Gardner claims that it was here that he met members of a New Forest coven who initiated him into traditional English witchcraft.

In the years that followed, Gardner came into contact with many key figures in the world of English magic. Not only did he become an ordained Christian priest in the obscure 'Ancient British Church', but he also became a Druid and participated in summer solstice ceremonies at Stonehenge. He came into contact too with Aleister Crowley and joined his magical group known as the OTO, the Ordo Templi Orientis.

During this period Gardner began to mix with members of the occult 'salon' that met at the Atlantis Bookshop in Museum Street, London. The owner ran 'The Order of Hidden Masters' from the shop, which had a meeting room in the basement. The bookshop published his second novel on magic. It was here, and at the Spielplatz naturist resort, that he met Ross Nichols, who later became a key figure in the Druid world, and who edited Gardner's book *Witchcraft Today*, published in 1954. It succeeded in launching his particular brand of witchcraft, which became known as Wicca, to a public who were by turns scandalised and fascinated by a religion so openly erotic and magical.

Thanks to the work of Doreen Valiente, one of his High Priestesses, amongst others, Wicca began to flourish throughout Britain and abroad. Raymond Buckland, a Londoner who was initiated into Wicca and met Gardner in 1963, introduced the path to the United States. In 1964, when reading a book on magic on board a ship returning from Lebanon to Britain, Gardner died of a heart attack and was buried in Tunis. Donna, his wife of thirty-three years, had died a few years earlier, having never participated in her husband's magical pursuits.

Some view Gardner as a rogue – and he certainly was cavalier with the truth. Others believe that he was an inspired genius. A year after his death, the writer Justine Glass captured the diverging views of this founding father of the modern witchcraft movement: 'Opinions about Dr Gardner are so divergent that it seems the truth must lie somewhere between the extremes. He has been described to me as a brilliant scholar, and a man with a veneer of learning; as a loveable, delightful character, and a "messy old man". Some say he was a master of witchcraft, others that he had no real knowledge at all.'[8]

✍ The Swinging Sixties and ✍ Witch Royalty

Gardner gave Doreen Valiente the task of rewriting the rituals he had constructed, making them shine with a poetry that is inspiring and erotic. In the process, Wicca became perfectly aligned with the spirit of the times – the Swinging Sixties in London. It also began attracting flamboyant personalities who had at last found a religion that was sexy, for not only did meetings take place in the nude, but new initiates were given the 'Fivefold Kiss' – by the High Priest if they were a woman, and by the High Priestess if they were a man – and the leaders of the coven could celebrate the Great Rite that depicted the union of the God and Goddess, either symbolically by dipping the ritual dagger into a chalice of wine, or by making love ritually within the circle.

Gardner courted the press, which lavished their attentions on him and his coven, catering to the English need to take their sensationalism with a patina of disapproval. Gardner himself loved the attentions of the media, however unflattering, and after his death he was followed in this enthusiasm by the self-proclaimed 'King of the Witches', Alex Sanders, and his wife Maxine, who survives today as one of the wise elders of the craft.

As the Swinging Sixties and seventies moved into the more psychologically mature eighties, Wicca, or witchcraft as it was also now known, became interesting to many in the feminist and burgeoning 'goddess consciousness' movements, who adapted Gardner's model to focus their worship mostly or exclusively on the Goddess. After centuries of male-dominated religions the opportunity to participate in a female-centric religion was exhilarating. Women-only covens soon evolved and 'Feminist Witchcraft' was born, first in the USA and then in Britain.

As the environmental crisis loomed in the nineties, Wicca again proved to be a valuable framework that could be developed to encourage a greater reverence for nature.

The story of modern pagan witchcraft is a fascinating one because its genesis is recent enough, and is sufficiently well documented, for us to observe the way in which a religion can grow from a combination of different influences into a belief system that can sustain communities, nourish them intellectually and spiritually, and offer a satisfying alternative to what is already on offer.

The reason that it gained popularity so quickly was that – even if it was constructed with materials not always directly connected to old English witchcraft or cunning-craft – it felt as if it were.

A theatrical moment at the Hallowe'en Bash, London.

In addition, it fulfilled a genuine need for a spiritual practice that celebrated sensuality, sexuality and, above all, the feminine, which had been so repressed by Christianity. At last there was a religion that empowered women to be priestesses. Wicca not only brought magic back into religion but placed it centre-stage, not just by celebrating one of the most magical aspects of life – sexual energy – but by including in its rites the practice of magic: invocations to the gods, the raising of power and the casting of spells.

There is a simple and powerful reason why modern pagan witchcraft is the most widely practised form of magic in England today: thanks to Gardner's eclecticism, modern initiates of the craft engage in magical practices that take their inspiration from virtually every kind of magic practised in these lands and from every epoch. In it you will find elements that draw their inspiration from the Druidic and Celtic era, from the folk magic of the Anglo-Saxon shaman, from the alchemist and the medieval magician. Witches today use the magic of the cabbala and the Tarot; they draw on elements inspired by Freemasonry, spiritualism, the sex magic of Aleister Crowley and the ritual magic of the Hermetic Order of the Golden Dawn, as well as, more recently, Jungian psychology. And they succeed in doing all this in a way that is structured as a workable system – most often in groups that meet for 'esbats' (at the time of the full moon) and 'sabbats' (at the time of the old Celtic festivals and at the solstices and equinoxes). A host of influences that at first glance would seem unmanageable somehow fall into place in modern witchcraft and suit many – although by no means all – aspiring magicians.

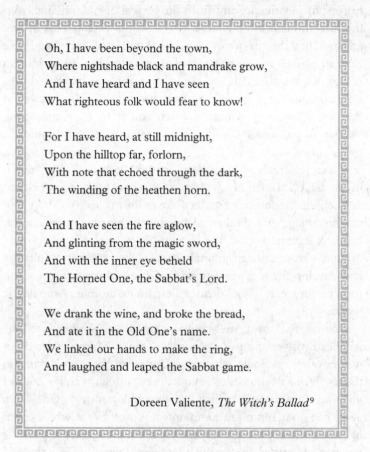

> Oh, I have been beyond the town,
> Where nightshade black and mandrake grow,
> And I have heard and I have seen
> What righteous folk would fear to know!
>
> For I have heard, at still midnight,
> Upon the hilltop far, forlorn,
> With note that echoed through the dark,
> The winding of the heathen horn.
>
> And I have seen the fire aglow,
> And glinting from the magic sword,
> And with the inner eye beheld
> The Horned One, the Sabbat's Lord.
>
> We drank the wine, and broke the bread,
> And ate it in the Old One's name.
> We linked our hands to make the ring,
> And laughed and leaped the Sabbat game.
>
> Doreen Valiente, *The Witch's Ballad*[9]

VIVIANNE CROWLEY

Vivianne Crowley (no relation to the infamous Aleister) is a Wiccan Priestess, an author and a respected teacher of paganism. She has a doctorate in psychology and has trained in transpersonal psychotherapy.

Wicca as we know it today draws on pagan religious and magical practice from our pre-Christian past, from European folk magic, and from the revival of ritual magic from the fifteenth century onwards. It is a vast encyclopaedia of lore and practice that draws on the herbal magic of the village wise woman as well as esoteric mystical practices that unite human beings within the Divine. Much of what was practised was unacceptable until the mid-twentieth century. It threatened the power interests of both Church and state; by empowering people, in particular women, it was seen by its very nature as being subversive.

Wicca was revived in England in the 1950s and soon caught my interest. I started my first coven at school at the age of eleven and joined the famous Sanders' coven in my teens. The art of making magic still fascinates me. It can be taught, of course, but it is strongest when the initiate has natural psychic powers or comes from a magical family that teaches children to nurture and develop the magical powers that many children possess but soon forget when school thrusts them into a more unsympathetic world.

One of the most well-known magical techniques used by witches involves the use of 'poppets', doll-like images made of wax or other materials, which got themselves such a bad name in the witch trials. Another technique, very popular with the coven I joined, is 'cord magic', which has a very long history. One witch alone can do it, but more commonly it is used by the whole coven in a 'cord wheel', where everyone binds cords together to raise the power and concentrate on the intent, and then releases a slipknot to seal the cord.

The strongest magic involves invocation, evocation or the creation of thought-forms or familiars. Invocation means bringing the Divine into our psyche to expand our consciousness and is an act of spiritual growth. Evocation means to 'call forth' or 'call up', and it involves manifesting spiritual entities. The creation of familiars is often harder for modern people to accept, as to do this we need to break off part of our psyche, separate it off from ourselves and let it fly free of the circle to work on its own, while still remaining somewhat under our control. To use this separated consciousness, it must have a form or body. This is created by the circle through what is known as 'etheric energy', which is formed by the disciplined use of the chakras, which are the energy centres of the body. The energy can be manipulated by the mind and formed into shapes by visualisation. Serious magic of this kind is hard work, which is how we often refer to it, and must be treated with the greatest respect. Without proper discipline it can get out of control and can damage the practitioner.

People always ask me about the intent of witchcraft and what it is used for. The answer in 'white' covens is simple: it is to use these powers for good amongst the circle and its friends. For example, if someone is ill, the coven can imagine them bathed in a golden, healing light and concentrate the intent on improving their health. There are obviously other, more selfish aims, such as the acquisition of money, power, etc., but in my experience if such gifts are not earned they will often turn against the person who requests them. 'Black' magic, when used purely for selfish ends, corrupts the user and can lead to psychological disintegration.

'White' magic can be learnt safely within the circle and will eventually lead to a heightened state of consciousness, which will fill your everyday life. This is the true joy and excitement of Wicca.

Initiation is of immense importance in Wicca. The training period lasts for many years, with three levels of initiation. At the first level, initiates are brought blindfold and bound to the circle. The passwords for the first initiation are 'perfect love and perfect trust'. The coven becomes for us a home, a place of wholeness, truth and love, where one may grow to spiritual maturity. Nakedness, which is often dismissed as a licence for sexual abandon, is in fact nothing of the kind. Instead it is a symbolic removal of barriers to friendship and intimacy.

The second two levels of initiation increase the initiate's commitment to Wicca, providing them with a number of tools to increase the power created with their magic and ensure they can control any unfortunate repercussions from the spirit world. The second stage also recognises that the initiate is now fully equipped to teach others and start their own coven if need be. The third stage recognises that the initiate has progressed into a deeper relation with the spiritual and Divine worlds around us. Above all, initiation recognises that the ability to deal with unseen worlds can be terrifying at first and give rise to panic when individuals realise that unseen factors can influence their lives. This is something that primitive people accept readily, but it is not part of our culture.

In setting out on this initiatory path, it is important to remember the maxim, 'know thyself'. You should always be the guardian of your destiny. Some initiates decide that they will go no further than the first level, and this may well be wise. Another danger is when initiates put their initiators on pedestals and let them have too much control over their destiny. Again, let your own common sense prevail. Your instinct is always the best judge of what is right for you.

As for myself, I have found that Wicca is a starting point in a journey that can enormously enrich life. Most of the magic talked about in introductory books on Wicca is about what I call 'small magics', useful improvements to everyday life. For greater power, you need to make a deep contact with the Divine, and be willing to dedicate yourself to the gods and the Great Work, which is the transformation of human consciousness. What starts as a quest for power becomes instead the way of the seeker; not a seeker of power but a seeker of truth. The quest is not to do magic, but to become magic. All ritual and teaching then becomes, like the musician's technique, the bedrock and foundation of inspiration, but not the music that is created. That is a sublime mystery about which we can speak only in riddles. The way to it is through the maxims that guard the first step on the path – to keep silence, to dare, to know and to will – and the maxim that lies beyond those – to become. For those who seek a teacher and an entry point, I would say: 'When the student is ready, the master will appear.' For me, she was sitting next to me on the top deck of a London bus. When we are ready to see, our path is revealed to us.

———————————

What is a Spell?

In its widest sense a spell is simply a wish expressed in a magical way. It asks for healing or blessing, or for something concrete and specific such as a new house or job. Unfortunately, it can also be used to ask for something unpleasant, as in a curse, which is also a wish but a destructive one.

Wiccan authors Janet and Stewart Farrar write in *The Witches' Way* that 'a spell is a ritual for raising psychic power and directing it to a specific and practical purpose'. The psychologist Vivianne Crowley mentions in her *Principles of Wicca* a number of techniques of traditional spellcraft, including candle and cord magic, chanting, wild ecstatic dance and the use of talismans.

The Yorkshire poet Robin Skelton, writing in *Spellcraft*, has objected to the breadth of such definitions, believing that we should see a spell specifically as an act of verbal magic involving the pronunciation of words, in one's mind or out loud, as distinct from any other magical act, such as the making or wearing of a charm or talisman, or the practice of ritual.

⁓ Spellcraft ⁓

Spellcraft can be found amongst the magical traditions and indigenous cultures of virtually every country on earth, for the desire to cast spells simply represents the innate human desire to influence circumstances. Since the earliest of times, when people were ill or poverty-stricken, robbed or deceived, yearning for a lover, or longing for a better home or a bounteous crop, they turned to spell-makers in an effort to either make their dreams come true or to punish their enemies.

A study of early English spells shows that they were often concerned with ensuring the protection of livestock and crops from theft or illness. An eleventh-century spell to ensure that swarming bees stay on the owner's land involved throwing a handful of soil over the swarm while saying: 'Settle ye, war-women, sink to the ground! Never should you, wild, to the wood fly. Be ye as respectful of my welfare as is every man of food and shelter.'[10]

Albrecht Dürer, The Four Witches, *1497.*

Being a Christian represented no barrier to the use of spells: a twelfth-century method for recovering stolen livestock involved dripping the wax from three candles on the footprint of the missing beast while singing: 'Let the Cross of Christ bring it back. The Cross of Christ which was lost by theft was found again. Let Abraham close to you paths, roads, hills and rivers. Let Job bring him [the thief] bound to judgement.'[11]

Imagining the impact that the theft of livestock could have

upon a family helps us to understand how something as disturbing as 'black magic' or evil sorcery could arise. A husband or wife betrayed by their spouse, a couple who lose their child after giving it the remedy of a local wise-woman, a family ruined by theft: all might be tempted to utter a spell that curses the person they believe has harmed them.

Once you believe in the efficacy of spells and curses, then it follows that you need charms or counter-spells to protect yourself from their power. Here is such a charm found in Powys: 'Lord Jesus Christ be the preserver of William Pentrynant his cows, calves, milk, butter, cattle of all ages, mares, suckers, horses, of all ages, ewes, lambs, sheep of all ages, pigs, sows and prosper him on this farm to live luckily saved from all witchcraft and evil men or women spirits or wizards or hardness of heart amen.'[12]

Today most witches insist that their spellcraft is used only to good ends: to heal and bless, or to achieve positive results such as success in finding a new home, job or lover. Many spells found in modern books are reminiscent of the 'positive affirmations' found in pop psychology and New Age teachings, which are designed to influence the subconscious mind. While some believe that these affirmations have a 'placebo effect' – working solely by programming the mind – magicians and witches who use spells believe that other forces are also at work. A primary tenet of the magical world-view is that everything is connected in a web of subtle energies. By casting a spell, the witch or wizard not only affects his own subconscious but also sends an impulse across this web to influence other people or situations.

Science is slowly catching up with this magical view. We now know that the placebo effect is real and can be used to our benefit; merely suggesting something to our minds can have a powerful impact on our health and on our bodies. And now that studies in parapsychology and telepathy suggest that the human mind could influence other humans and animals at a distance, the idea that spell-casting might work no longer seems implausible.

Witches today use a variety of methods for casting a spell. In a coven they might use the combined energy of the whole group to 'project' the spell into the web, by dancing ecstatically round and round until at a signal they all drop to the ground, imagining the spell winging its way through the skies. Or they may use cord or knot magic, which involves holding cords across the circle and tying knots while uttering the spell.

A witch alone might use a spell-box or candle magic to help cast her spell. With a spell-box, once the spell is written, ideally on parchment at a special time and accompanied by a special ritual, it is placed in a small wooden box, which is then hidden or buried outside, to be opened only once the spell has been fulfilled. With candle magic, a spell is cast while lighting a candle, with the intention that, by the time the candle has been consumed, the spell will have succeeded. If the witch is in a hurry, a needle can be pressed into the wax some way down the candle, in the hope that the spell will succeed when the flame reaches the needle.

A spell might also be cast by offering the parchment that it is written upon to the elements – to the earth, to a candle-flame, to the wind atop a hill, or to running water or a deep well. Someone wishing to make their partner 'sweeter' might write their name on a piece of paper and add it to a jar of honey, which they then keep in a special place.

This kind of sympathetic magic, which symbolically depicts the desired outcome, is as old as humanity. Anthropologists believe that cave paintings of successful hunts were probably made prior to the hunt to magically create the desired result, and much modern spell-casting uses such sympathetic magic. Janet and Stewart Farrar in *The Witches' Way* write of casting a spell on two people who were having difficulty communicating. They consecrated and named two chess pieces after the protagonists, then placed them at either ends of a mantelpiece. Each day they recited their spell and moved the pieces a little closer together.

✒ Traps for the Sorcerer's Apprentice ✑

Spell-making will either fascinate or repel you. You might be itching to cast one now or you might have an instinctive fear of such an activity, which feels like meddling in matters best left alone.

Enthusiasts of spell-casting claim that it empowers people. Robin Skelton, in *Spellcraft*, says:

> Anyone who turns to spell-making . . . with compassion for others
> and the desire to use his or her psychic energies to enhance the
> quality of life, will find that, while spell-making is not a mystic
> way or path to spiritual illumination, it can result in a certain inner
> peace, for the maker of spells is rewarded by a feeling that he or
> she is making full and proper use of his or her emotional life and
> is no longer irritated by the continual repetition of that frustrating
> feeling that 'There is nothing I can do about it.' There is, for the
> spell-maker, always something that can be done about it.[13]

Critics of spell-making point to the ethical dilemmas it can create, which are not easily resolved, even with the best of intentions. Often the spell-caster assumes they know what is best, which can be a dangerous supposition. What if the two people whose representatives were being drawn together on the mantelpiece were better off not speaking to each other? What if the new job or house you want is not really meant for you, but for someone else? A spell designed to give you more time in your life might achieve its result by getting you fired from work, or a spell to attract a lover might deliver someone who becomes your lover for a while before becoming the bane of your life.

It is easy for spell-making to become a sort of spiritual consumerism where people try to use spells to get all the things they think they need – boyfriends or girlfriends, cars, jobs and money. In this way the intention comes from a sense of lack – or a perceived lack – rather than from an inherent trust in life.

Books on witchcraft will often warn their readers of the risks involved in spell-making, emphasising the idea that spells should not be made to harm other people. However, they will also go on to suggest spells for attracting a lover, for example, which are coercive or appear to interfere with their free will, as in this spell: 'Every Friday night [Friday being the day of Venus, goddess of love], culminating in a Friday on which the moon is full . . . throw salt onto the fire from your right hand, saying "It is not salt I turn to fire but the heart of the man I seek; let him have no peace of mind until he comes to me."' Another spell concludes with this demand: 'This I lay upon you: when we meet open your thighs and call me into you.'[14]

Spell-casting can also involve the making of 'poppets' – small dolls that are used as representatives of the recipient of the spell. In black magic they are stuck with pins to cause harm, but in 'good magic' they are used for healing or blessing. In a coven, the High Priest and High Priestess might symbolically or actually make love and then 'give birth' to the poppet, which will then be blessed and named, before having the spell cast upon it.

Again, while some books insist that such techniques should be used only for sending healing or positive energies, others suggest that it is acceptable to use such a poppet in other ways, such as for 'binding spells'. If someone is engaging in malicious gossip, for example, the poppet's mouth can be sewn up. During the massacre of the Kurds by Saddam Hussein's troops, some magicians named poppets after the dictator, bound them tightly with string and placed them in their fridges, in an effort to prevent him causing more harm.

While it might seem quite reasonable to attempt to stop malicious gossip or mass killings, wise advice to a sorcerer's apprentice would be to avoid all attempts at binding spells. If the web of subtle connections between all things does exist, working in such a way will forge a link between yourself and the recipient of the spell. Even if you do not believe in the web, a link will be forged in your subconscious. Love spells are best avoided, too, unless they ask not for a specific person but simply for more love to come into your life. Even healing spells can be problematic if their effect is to alleviate symptoms without affecting the underlying cause. Before a spell is cast, you should think carefully about any unintended consequences that its fulfilment may cause. It is often advisable to finish a spell with the words: 'If it be for the Greater Good'. By inserting this rider at the end of the spell, you are acknowledging that there may be reasons why your spell should not succeed that are beyond your ken.

☉ *How to Perform a Love Spell*

In spellcraft, as in life, one's chickens return to roost.

ROBIN SKELTON, *THE PRACTICE OF
WITCHCRAFT TODAY*

Most people who work with spells will have a tale or two to tell you about love spells that have gone wrong. However much you think a particular person will be perfect for you, however much you *know* that So-and-So needs to be paired up with So-and-So, your knowledge is partial and life has a nasty way of teaching you how wrong you can be.

A cardinal rule is never to meddle in other people's love lives, so perform a love spell only for yourself and never 'target' a particular individual in an effort to make him or her your lover. Instead, get to the root of the matter, which is your need for love, and cast a spell to simply bring more love into your life. To do this you might like to try candle magic.

Modern witches often cast spells by using candles as their 'means of delivery'. Much of the lore of 'candle magic', as it is known, came to England from the southern United States. In nineteenth-century New Orleans, the indigenous religious and magical practices of the African Americans, with their extensive herbal lore, merged with the Roman Catholic practice of lighting votive candles, to become a major spell-casting medium of a tradition that has come to be known as 'Hoodoo'. In the mid-twentieth century,

through books published in America, this practice was picked up in England by Gerald Gardner and others.[15]

To cast this spell all you need is a single green candle and some pure olive oil or aromatherapy oil. Some practitioners like to write their spell on the candle, or to carve symbols such as runes or pentagrams in the wax with a knife, but this is not essential. On a Friday, which is magically associated with the planet Venus, the goddess of love (as is the colour green), make sure you will be undisturbed for a while, and focus on your intention. Imagine yourself bathed in feelings of love and contentment. Visualise yourself happy, full of love for the world, and deeply fulfilled.

Now dip a finger in the oil and 'anoint' the candle by starting in the middle and smoothing the oil towards each end. As you do this, create a strong visual image of yourself in this happy state. Then light the candle and as you do this say: 'May my life be filled with love. May love flow through me from dawn to dusk, from dusk to dawn, all the days of my life.'

The beauty of candle magic is that you can now leave the candle to burn, with the idea that it is radiating out its message through its flame. Allow it to burn about one seventh of its length, then snuff out the flame saying: 'So may it be!'

Relight the candle the next day and repeat the spell, and do this each day until, after a week, it has been consumed.

MAXINE SANDERS

Maxine Sanders grew up the solitary child of an eccentric mother and an abusive father. She would take wild rides on her pony, sleeping in haystacks overnight to get away from adults who, she believed, were living a lie. When they spoke, Maxine could often see how their voice 'colours' became different to those of their bodies and betrayed the fact that they were not telling the truth. This was not the only natural psychic power that Maxine developed. Very quickly she found she could create 'astral journeys', which she used to visit her much loved grandmother, while her mother made Maxine use her astral skills to spy on her elusive husband.

When she was older, and after she had attended a meditation group for some time, a friend of the family introduced her to a circle that worked with the Egyptian Mysteries. She proved an apt pupil and was eventually initiated into the group in the depths of secret Cheshire caves, in a terrifying twenty-four-hour ceremony that included walking through fire.

In her teens a more normal life ensued, until her mother met Alex Sanders, a man known to be a witch. She describes him as 'a small-framed man in a blue raincoat and Trilby hat. How could he be so ordinary?' He had a reputation as a powerful healer in those days and impressed Maxine when he appeared to restore a full crop of hair to a woman who had gone bald. He lived in a small terraced house in Manchester, where the activities that took place soon drew Maxine like a magnet. Sanders taught Maxine that witchcraft was a magical religion that provides new insights and feelings into every waking moment. He also taught her what he believed was the difference between the 'craft' of witchcraft, or Wicca, which raises power by people working together in a coven, and the work of a magician, who works alone to get even greater results by conjuring spirits from a dimension other than this world. Alex practised both.

Maxine's mother was not pleased by her daughter's growing interest in witchcraft and sent her to work as a nanny in London, but Maxine soon became bored and returned to Manchester, where Alex now initiated her into his coven, not just as a witch, but as a witch queen to symbolise the goddess at rituals. The beautiful teenager became a powerful presence in Alex's circle, where they would celebrate their meetings naked, often in evocative places in the local countryside, such as Alderley Edge in Cheshire.

At one of these meetings, Alex, who enjoyed being in the media limelight, organised a local press photo shoot. Next morning the paper screamed: 'Ex-convent girl in witchcraft rites.' The nationals soon took it up. The editor of the News of the World once remarked: 'The Sanders witches were a godsend when news was thin on the ground.' The impact on Maxine was considerable. A Catholic priest, accompanied by two censer-swinging 'altar boys', came to exorcise her. Her relationship with her parents hit an all-time low.

Shortly afterwards, Maxine took up witchcraft full time, often with strange results. The oddest was when she attempted to create 'elementals', which are small helpers created with magical visualisation, having only a short lifespan. Maxine imagined these as little 'Homepride' flour men from the TV ads. However, she was so successful that the flour men multiplied all over the house like mice, and it took a long coven meeting to get rid of them. Alex was not amused.

The coven moved to London and, in no time at all, would-be initiates from every walk of life were beating a path to their door. This was the Swinging Sixties, and becoming a witch was the coolest of the cool. Although the hippie movement embraced Wicca wholeheartedly, the attitude of the establishment was not so forgiving. The police in particular would take to arresting Alex and Maxine with all sorts of accusations, although Maxine claims many members of the force were now joining up and could easily be identified by their shoes. They were even accused of being involved in the Ian Brady moors murders and had to sit though agonising sessions, listening to tapes of the crimes.

Alex and Maxine's version of witchcraft soon spread to the USA and Europe, alongside the more well-known Gardnerian variety. But with growth came a loosening of standards, as Maxine explains:

'The harmony and dedication of a coven is all. It is like training a team of shire horses to pull a coach containing that most precious item of all: the human soul. Very rarely has the pursuit of magic alone led to true spirituality. More commonly it has become a pursuit for power, resulting in a dangerous inflation of the ego, trapping the initiate in a circle of illusion from which they may never escape.'

After the break-up of their marriage and Alex's death, Maxine began to take less of a part in organised witchcraft and moved to Snowdonia, where she still lives. She speaks of her concerns about where the craft is now heading.

The craft seems so very complicated today. When I was initiated in the sixties, everything was much simpler. We went in, did a simple spell and that was that. But this simplicity no longer works for modern man. I was a ceremonialist and found that people wanted something complex, so I am partly to blame for satisfying their wishes, but now the surroundings of ceremony and practice are knocking out the magic. I believe that, eventually, we will go full circle and the simplicity will come back, but until this happens more and more of the best covens are becoming secret, as they distance themselves from those who, they believe, practise the form but not the true substance of magic.

The numbers involved are now huge. More than six thousand people attend the 'Witchfests' in England every year, and the growth in America has been fantastic, yet this growth has weakened the dedication and quality of new initiates. When we started, we selected only those with real psychic potential and got rid of those who could not complete the training. Now covens search everywhere for new recruits and training has turned into one long counselling session to keep people involved. New joiners seem to be older too, sometimes more weird and 'Gothic' looking – not at all like the Beautiful People of the sixties.

As to the future, I believe that the craft is firmly here to stay, driven by man's worries about the future of our planet. In the sixties it was the atom bomb; now it is global warming, something for which there appears to be no solution, so people are drawn to the mystical side of life.

Witchcraft has been with us a long time. The post-war revival simply packaged together a lot of the old rituals into new ceremonies, but the underlying magic goes back a very long way. Above everything, witchcraft is real. We are all constantly being bombarded through the media with Hollywood's version of a magic and mystical world, but have no idea about whether or not this exists in reality. So we are left with a yearning for adventure but no means of satisfying it. Witchcraft provides a tangible way of introducing us to a world that cannot be explained in scientific terms, but can dramatically influence our everyday life.

The danger is that those who teach new initiates can gain power over them, just as a hypnotist can gain influence over their subjects. In the worst cases this power can be used to take money from the initiate, control his or her life unduly, or even to force them into sexual relations against their will. I know so many people in the occult world who have become corrupt. The black side is stronger than ever and you cannot police it, but the magic itself sorts out the wheat from the chaff. There is a great appetite nowadays for more public ritual, but to me this is like group sex, and I am very choosy about whom I get into bed with.

I still firmly believe that the majority of people practising Wicca are sincere and worthy of respect. Teachers may not be as strong as they were, but the previous generation left some extraordinary written material. I have just been studying the beliefs of [the esoteric group] Builders of the Adytum, which is superb occult stuff.[16] If people want to acquire the discipline and put in place the safety keys, my advice is to follow the best teaching available and be very selective about which group they join and who are the teachers.

Despite the ups and downs of my life as a priestess of witchcraft, I would have no hesitation in recommending it to those who have the ability and the appetite to take it seriously. I would, however, counsel all those who stand on the threshold of a serious involvement with the craft to use their own common sense in deciding what is best for them. Your subconscious is always your best friend in keeping you out of trouble. Above everything, don't be fooled by those who dress up the magic in complexity and ceremonial. There are many paths to magic. If it works, just use it. As for myself, I have gone back to being a witch, listening to my inner voice and trusting in the magic that came so naturally to me as a child.

✍ Things to Do ✍

✾ The single most effective way to learn about the influence of witchcraft in England is to visit the Museum of Witchcraft at Boscastle in Cornwall. The museum is over fifty years old and has been completely renovated since the village was flooded in 2004. It began life in 1951 as

the Museum of Magic and Witchcraft on the Isle of Man,
and was started by former MI6 agent, Cecil Williamson,
who employed Gerald Gardner as the 'resident witch'.

Walking through the museum today, you cannot fail
to be impressed by the richness of magic and folklore
that is on display, including items from the Richel
Collection – the world's finest collection of ritual sex
magic artefacts. Tintagel Castle, where it is said that
King Arthur was conceived, lies a short distance away.
Above the museum a library holds one of the world's
best collections of literature on magic and witchcraft. See
www.museumofwitchcraft.com

❋ Take a free course in Wicca online. One-time deputy
headteacher and specialist in medieval history, Keith
Broad, who writes under the name Pino Longchild, and
his jazz-singer wife, Chantal Santos, formed the Magicka
School in 2004 to offer online training in witchcraft
and the Tarot. Now thousands take Pino's free courses

and discuss their experiences in numerous specialist forums on the school's lively message board. See www. magickaschool.com

❧ Subscribe to Britain's oldest magazine on witchcraft and related subjects, *The Cauldron*, published quarterly. See www.the-cauldron.fsnet.co.uk

❧ Visit a 'Witchfest'! A London-based group, 'The Children of Artemis', publish a glossy magazine, *Witchcraft and Wicca*, and hold an annual Witchfest at Fairfield Halls in Croydon. This is one of the largest gatherings of witches in the world. Mingle unobtrusively with pagans, wizards and witches, and attend talks, workshops, a witches' market, live music and a rock club. A visit to the Witchfest offers an ideal opportunity to check out the ideas and practices of modern witches in England today. See www. witchcraft.org

❧ Celebrate the traditional festival time of Beltane or Samhain in London at a pagan and witchcraft event known as the 'Beltane Bash' or 'Hallowe'en Bash', organised by the Caduceus shop. These colourful events, which have been taking place for the last fourteen years, include stalls selling books and paraphernalia, rituals, morris dancing, live music and performances, and the 'oldest Pagan Pride Parade' outside Conway Hall in Red Lion Square, Camden. See www.paganfestivals.com

❧ Visit the Anne of Cleves House in Lewes, East Sussex, where you can see a wax poppet, complete with nail-hole, found in a nearby garden, or the Steyning Museum, West Sussex, where you can see shoes that were found plastered into walls to ward off evil and bring good fortune. Find out whether your local museum has any artefacts related to witchcraft or folk magic.

⚜ If you're a naturist, or at least don't mind taking your clothes off in the interests of research, consider paying a visit to the Five Acres Country Club in Bricket Wood, Hertfordshire, near St Albans. This was once the naturist resort partly owned by Gerald Gardner, and it was here that he held coven meetings in the Witch's Cottage, which is still in the grounds.

The Elizabethan cottage originally came from Herefordshire and had no known connection with witchcraft. A friend of Gardner's had it dismantled and re-erected in a folklore museum in Barnet, and when the museum closed relocated it to Five Acres. Photos of the interior of the cottage, complete with 'skyclad' witches in ceremonial poses, began to feature in newspapers and books from the 1950s.

A day visit to the club will cost you £16 and you may have to do some magic to persuade the management to show you the interior of the cottage, where you can still see the coven's ritual circle and pentagram inscribed on the floor. See www.fiveacrescountryclub.com

⚜ Visit Manningtree in Essex, where the Witchfinder General, Matthew Hopkins, began his vicious witch hunt. Manningtree lies on the southern bank of the River Stour and claims to be England's smallest town. Depending on your beliefs, you might want to make an offering in memory of the people who were hanged here for witchcraft, perhaps by strewing coins or flowers into the river where the bodies were later thrown, or by lighting a candle in the town's fourteenth-century church, St Mary's, Lawford, or even at the St Mary and St Michael Church at Mistley, where Hopkins is buried.

'Latimers', in Highcliffe, Dorset.

- Make a 'Wiccan pilgrimage' to Dorset to visit two key sites in the story of modern Wicca: Christchurch, where Gardner claimed he met the witches of the Rosicrucian Theatre (demolished in the 1960s), who initiated him into English witchcraft; and 'Latimers' in the village of Highcliffe, where Gardner claimed he received his initiation.

- Near the village of Minstead, in Hampshire, visit the possible site of the witches' magical 'Battle for Britain' in the New Forest, near to the Rufus Stone – the site of the legendary death of King William II. The anthropologist Margaret Murray suggested in the 1920s that William had been a member of the witch-cult and had voluntarily and ritually sacrificed himself at this spot. Historians no longer accept Murray's suggestion, or her thesis that an organised 'secret religion' of witchcraft, rooted in the Neolithic era, which practised human sacrifice, was once in existence throughout Western Europe.

❧ Resources ❧

BOOKS

Buckland's Book of Saxon Witchcraft, Raymond Buckland (Red Wheel, 2005)

Complete Book of Witchcraft, Raymond Buckland (Llewellyn, 1986)

The Druidcraft Tarot, Philip and Stephanie Carr-Gomm (Connections, 2004)

Druidcraft: The Magic of Wicca and Druidry, Philip Carr-Gomm (Thorsons, 2002)

Fire Child: The Life and Magick of Maxine Sanders, 'Witch Queen', Maxine Sanders (Mandrake, 2007)

The Green Hedge Witch: A Guide to Wild Magic, Rae Beth (Robert Hale, 2008)

Hedge Witch: Guide to Solitary Witchcraft, Rae Beth (Robert Hale, 2008)

Real Witches' Handbook, Kate West (Llewellyn, 2008)

The Triumph of the Moon, Ronald Hutton (Oxford Paperbacks, 1995)

Wicca: The Old Religion in the New Age, Vivianne Crowley (Thorsons, 2000)

Witchcraft for Tomorrow, Doreen Valiente (Robert Hale, 1993)

A Witch Alone: Thirteen Moons to Master Natural Magic, Marian Green (Thorsons, 2002)

A Witches' Bible, Janet and Stewart Farrar (Robert Hale, 2002)

CHAPTER SIX

TRANSMUTATION AND TRANSFORMATION

The World of the Alchemists and Puffers

I had discovered, early in my researches, that their doctrine was no mere chemical fantasy, but a philosophy they applied to the world, to the elements, and to man himself.

W.B. YEATS, *ROSA ALCHEMICA*

Some people believe that we leave traces behind us – vibrations or mysterious magnetic changes in the walls and atmosphere of the houses in which we have lived. Psychics say they can read these traces like the recordings left on a magnetic tape.

To anyone walking through the rooms of Wilton House near Salisbury, for example, such an idea seems utterly possible, as if the life once lived between these walls is only a breath away. Here in the sixteenth century one of the most unusual and talented women in England's history – Mary Sidney, Countess of Pembroke – maintained an alchemical laboratory, assisted by Sir Walter Raleigh's half-brother Adrian Gilbert, who also created an elaborate magical garden in the grounds, based on sacred geometry. And although the garden and house have undergone many

Wilton House, near Salisbury

changes since their time, through fire and restoration, it still seems as if its former inhabitants were here only yesterday.

Mary Sidney is remarkable for being one of the few women whose names appear in the history of alchemy in England and, indeed, the world. She was also the first English woman to achieve a significant literary reputation. Some even believe that it was her genius that lay behind the plays of William Shakespeare, which they claim she either wrote herself or collaborated upon with the group of literary luminaries that she patronised.

Raised at Ludlow Castle in Shropshire, Mary Sidney was one of the most highly educated women of her time: she was trained in rhetoric, music, scripture and the classics. Not only was she fluent in French, Italian and Latin, but she may also have known some Greek and Hebrew. She created a recipe for invisible ink and sent coded messages to friends, embedded in musical compositions that used measures to represent the letters of the alphabet.

While the world of folk magic – of cunning-craft and witch-craft – flourished in the villages, many of the educated and the wealthy found themselves attracted to the equally magical but more abstruse and demanding world of alchemy. As with folk magic, this involved potions and prayers – a fascinating mixture of physical and spiritual activities that were designed with one aim in mind: to effect change. In folk magic, the change desired was in the well-being of the recipient – in their wealth or health. Alchemy was more ambitious in that the change it sought was transmutation: of lead into gold, or of the soul of the alchemist into an illumined state.

Both kinds of magic called on the power of prayer; both turned to astrology to calculate the most propitious times for their operations; both used materials from the natural world for their magical recipes. But while folk magic used simple ingredients, close to hand, and minimal equipment, the alchemist needed pure ingredients and expensive materials that included furnaces and all the apparatus of a laboratory. It is no wonder, then, that it became the pursuit of those with access to funds and to education, such as Mary Sidney, who must have been influenced by the visits she almost certainly made to the alchemical laboratory and library of Dr John Dee, astrologer to Queen Elizabeth I.

By engaging in her chemical and alchemical experiments, Mary Sidney was pursuing an activity that fascinated many intellectuals of the day, a study whose roots lay in the Graeco-Egyptian world of Alexandria, or probably deeper still – in the mysteries of ancient Egypt.

Mary Sidney: 1561–1621

'In her time, Wilton House was like a College, there were so many learned and ingeniose persons. She was the greatest Patronesse of witt and learning of any Lady in her time. She was a great Chymist, and spent yearly a great deale in that study. She kept for her Laborator in the house Adrian Gilbert (vulgarly called Dr Gilbert) half-brother to Sir Walter Raleigh, who was a great Chymist in those dayes and a Man of excellent naturall Parts; but very Sarcastick, and the greatest Buffoon in the Nation; cared not what he said to man or woman of what quality soever.'

JOHN AUBREY, DIARIES

✎ The Origins of Alchemy ✎

Alchemists were – and are (because a few still exist today) – concerned with the process of transmutation. Some have focused all their efforts on trying to transmute base metals into gold, while others have used alchemy as a way of transforming themselves as human beings. These two goals may seem completely different, but many alchemists have attempted to pursue both at the same time.

This arcane science emerged into recorded history in Alexandria, in the West, and in China and India, in the East, at about the same time: the fourth to the third century BC. No one is sure whether this happened independently, or whether it first arose in one part of the world and was then carried by travellers to the other, which would certainly have been possible: Greek philosophers travelled with Alexander the Great when he invaded India in 325 BC, by which time the Silk Route, which connected East and West for trade, was already in operation.

Although Western and Eastern alchemy share common features – an interest in gold and mercury, for example – in the East alchemy was almost exclusively concerned with discovering spiritual liberation and an 'elixir of life', which would increase longevity or even confer immortality. In the West the Graeco-Egyptian culture of Alexandria was mainly concerned with using the principles of alchemy to work with metals and minerals, but often in a way that combined a spiritual understanding with a manipulation of the world of matter.

This branch of alchemy almost certainly emerged out of one of the earliest and most powerful magical traditions in the world: that of ancient Egypt. There are no written traces of this early Egyptian alchemy, due to the destruction of the great library of Alexandria, but the legend that the Egyptian god Thoth was the founder of alchemy echoed on until the medieval era. It was then that Latin and Arabic translations of lost Greek and Syriac

Hermes Trismegistus.

texts appeared, claiming that Alexander the Great had found an emerald tablet in the tomb of this god, whom the Greeks called Hermes-Thoth, Hermes Trismegistus, or Thrice-Great Hermes, who reveals the key principles of alchemy in the text of the fabled Emerald Tablet, which begins: 'True it is, without falsehood, certain and most true. That which is above is like that which is below, and that which is below is like that which is above . . .'[1] Another eleven statements follow, summarising the philosophy of alchemy and cryptically explaining the creation of the world.

Alchemical ideas, also known as 'Hermetic doctrines' after Thrice-Great Hermes, spread from the Graeco-Egyptian world throughout Europe. The combination of alchemy as a mystical discipline and as an experimental procedure involving metallurgy at first seems bizarre. However, a consideration of the magic of the Celts and Druids provides us with a clue as to why alchemy has exerted such a universal appeal, and why it became so popular in England, as well as all over Europe, from the very earliest times.

The underlying phenomenon that alchemy addressed was the mystery of transformation – of the way one thing changes and gives birth to another. All around us we see this mystery being acted out: in the plant world as seed turns to bud and fruit; in the human and animal world as coupling creates a child; and in the mineral world as crystals grow and metals are forged.

In the days of the Celts and Druids, the blacksmith was accorded magical status. It was through his art that the tribe was kept safe from attack. It was he who forged the cauldrons that cooked the food and held the brews of the healers. The daily art of the blacksmith seemed to symbolise the way in which life worked: the heat of the fire, the blows of the hammer, were like the trials and tribulations of life, and it was reassuring to sense that, by analogy, out of these hardships could come beauty, utility and strength.

The Celtic goddess Brighid, known as Bride in Scotland, and Brigantia in the North of England, was the goddess of the forge, and of the two elements used by both smith and alchemist: fire and water. She was also the goddess of healing, midwifery and poetry, all of which emerge from the 'forge' of the body or soul. Such ideas can be found in many mythologies and cultures, and the language and ideas of Hermeticism built naturally upon them.

✍ Robert of Chester and ✎ the Islamic Influence

By the seventh century, however, we hear little of alchemy in Europe. Instead, it was being developed in the Islamic culture of the Arab world, which eventually reached  into Spain. And it was there, in 1144, that an Englishman, Robert of Chester, the Abbot of Pamplona, produced the first known translation of an alchemical text into English: *The Book of the Composition of Alchemy*. It appeared at a significant moment when intellectual life in Europe was undergoing a revival. Robert's translation helped to initiate one of Islam's greatest contributions to European thought, and prompted the beginning of the renewal of European interest in the art.

Robert of Chester was primarily interested in alchemy as an experimental science that explored the nature of matter and the natural world. Stimulated by his book, scholars throughout Europe – particularly in Germany, France and the Low Countries – began to concern themselves with alchemical experimentation.

✸ Roger Bacon and the Spires of Oxford ✸

A hundred years later, Roger Bacon, a thirteenth-century Franciscan friar who taught at Oxford University, became fascinated with alchemy and the experimental method. Having already formed a deep interest in mathematics, astronomy and chemistry, he decided that he would explore alchemy in two directions. He wanted to perfect the knowledge of how to purify metals so that they became gold, but he also wanted to know how to make effective medicines and elixirs to prolong life, just like the alchemists of the East.

At some point in his career he was imprisoned for a period – reports range from its being a term of one year to fourteen years – but it seems likely that whatever he endured was as a result of his unorthodox researches and interests, which included astrology. A local legend – that Bacon and a fellow friar, Thomas Bungay, blew themselves up in a bungled alchemical experiment in Oxford – was later turned into a comedy, *The Honourable History of Friar Bacon and Friar Bungay*, by the Elizabethan playwright Robert Greene. Magic features strongly in the story, with Bacon magically transporting the hostess of a tavern from one place to another, and engaging in a magical contest with a German magician. The play ends with him renouncing magic altogether and turning to a life of repentance.

In reality, Roger Bacon was an outspoken man, a visionary and one of the earliest pioneers of the empirical method, comparable in stature to his namesake Francis Bacon, who would play a key role in the development of the scientific method three hundred years later. In his writings, Roger Bacon anticipated many later inventions including microscopes, telescopes, spectacles, aeroplanes and steamships. Such was his contribution to science that a statue of him can be found outside the Museum of Natural History in Oxford, a city that would become important again in the story of English alchemy in the seventeenth century.

∾ Geoffrey Chaucer, Royal Licences ∾ and the Reign of the Puffers

In the centuries after the time of Roger Bacon, the most interesting developments in alchemy occurred abroad – particularly in France and Germany – while in England it became dominated by an increasingly frantic search for material gold, rather than the search for the spiritual 'gold' of illumination.

'Puffers', as alchemists came to be derisively termed because of their need to tend their furnaces with bellows in hand, reigned supreme. Charlatans, who used conjuring or simple tricks such as covering small amounts of gold with a substance that could then be dissolved in such a way as to give the appearance of transmutation, began to proliferate.

Geoffrey Chaucer satirised this state of affairs in one of his *Canterbury Tales*. In 'The Canon's Yeoman's Tale', the yeoman recounts the tricks used by his canon to obtain gold. Chaucer clearly knew his alchemy and recounts in detail the materials used by the alchemists of his day, including urinals, sublimatories, alembics, bull's gall, brimstone, valerian and moonwort.

In the end there was so much trickery that the Crown limited the conducting of alchemical experiments by a system of royal licences, which were granted in the hopes of obtaining treasure to prosecute the French wars.

⁊ George Ripley and his Scrolls ⁊

Chaucer's canon may have been a rogue, but it was a gifted Augustinian canon, George Ripley, whose contributions in the fifteenth century signified a return to the magical roots of the Great Work, as the alchemical process was called.

Ripley studied in Louvain, in Rome and on the island of Rhodes, where the Knights of St John of Jerusalem encouraged him in his alchemical researches. In 1477 he returned to England and settled in a monastery in Bridlington, Yorkshire, where he continued his experiments, despite complaints about the noxious fumes that sometimes emanated from his study.

His great contribution was to bring his powers of pictorial and poetic imagination to bear on the Great Work. His *Compound of Alchemy*[2] describes the alchemical process in verse as twelve stages or 'Gates', and was highly influential; manuscript copies circulated widely. His *Ripley Scrowles* depicted the various stages in pictorial form, like images from a dream or play. He was particularly concerned with the observation of the changing colours of the alchemical matter.

With his work it becomes easier to understand the way in which an alchemist could develop spiritually by contemplating the various stages of the process. Despite Ripley's romantic and elegant imagery, which hinted at the transformation of the soul rather than matter, rumours abounded that he was indeed able to make gold. It was even said that he donated £100,000 a year to the Knights of Malta and St John to support their war against the Turks.

Over twenty-five works are attributed to Ripley, although whether he wrote them all is doubtful. Certainly his *Scrowles* and *Compound of Alchemy* are two of the most important alchemical texts of all time. Fittingly for someone who devoted himself to the Hermetic art, Ripley ended his days in an anchorite hermitage near Boston in Yorkshire.

✒ The Alchemists of Bristol, ✒ Bath and Salisbury

Although the idea of transmuting ordinary metals such as lead into gold seems fantastical to us, sincere believers in its possibility continued to exist into the sixteenth century and reports of their success continued to circulate. Thomas Norton, reputedly the Mayor of Bristol and a contemporary of Ripley, is said to have produced enough gold by this means to have financed the rebuilding of the church of St Mary Redcliffe in the city.

In his *Ordinall of Alchemy*, Norton suggested that a team of four helpers was needed by the alchemist to obtain the Philosopher's Stone, which in its turn would produce gold. His conviction that the stone could be obtained through chemical means, as well as hearsay of his success, encouraged future generations of experimenters, the most famous of whom were the magician and astrologer Dr John Dee and his disreputable colleague, Sir Edward Kelley, of whom we shall hear more in the next chapter.

A less well-known figure is Thomas Charnock, who learnt his art from a master in Salisbury. Unfortunately his master died in 1554 and a fire destroyed his laboratory and records, leaving Charnock bereft, since he could not remember all the details of the procedures he had learnt.

William Holway, the blind and dispossessed Abbot of Bath, came to his rescue and offered him guidance. When Holway's abbey was dissolved in 1539, local legend recounts that he hid a vial of alchemical elixir in a wall, but was unable to retrieve it. After he had surrendered his house and revenues (totalling £617) to the king, the monastic life of the abbey came to an end, and it must have been pleasing to Holway to find in Charnock a younger man he could teach.

⮐ The Elizabethan Age ⮐

'Tis generally reported that Doctor Dee, and Sir Edward Kelley were so strangely fortunate, as to finde a very large quantity of the Elixir in some part of the Ruines of Glastenbury-Abbey, which was so incredibly Rich in vertue that they lost much in making Projection, by way of Tryall; before they found out the true weight of the Medicine. And no sooner were they Masters of this Treasure, then they resolved to Travell into Forraigne Parts . . .

ELIAS ASHMOLE, *THEATRUM CHEMICUM BRITANNICUM,* 1652

With the Spaniards plundering the gold of South America and threatening Britain with their armadas, it was not surprising that Queen Elizabeth was interested in a potential source of wealth closer to home, and it was said that her astrologer, John Dee, and his colleague, Edward Kelley, had found in Glastonbury a red powder that could turn lead into gold.

It was in this atmosphere of fascination with tales of transmutation that the talented Mary Sidney grew up. When Mary was fourteen, following the death of her sister Ambrosia, the Queen invited her to join the royal household. Mary accompanied the Queen on her 'progresses' through the realm and came to know Dr Dee. By the time she was installed in Wilton House, building a laboratory would have seemed the most obvious thing to do – and if Marie de'Medici, Queen Consort of the French king Henry IV, could have her own alchemical laboratory, so could Mary, Countess of Pembroke.

But as the Elizabethan era drew to a close, the world of English alchemy was set to change for ever, chiefly thanks to scientist and legendary Rosicrucian, Robert Fludd.

✎ Alchemy as Medicine – The ✍ Extraordinary Art of Spagyrics

Born in Bearsted in Kent in 1574, Robert Fludd took his MA at St John's College in Oxford before travelling to Europe in 1598

to study medicine, chemistry and occult philosophy. It was here that he encountered physicians who were working with a system of alchemical medicine taught by Paracelsus. This remarkable Swiss doctor had died – there were rumours that he had even been murdered – in Salzburg fifty years earlier.

Paracelsus pioneered the use of chemicals and minerals

in medicine, and his great contribution to alchemy was to insist that the true goal of the alchemist was not to find material wealth, but to heal the sick. He wrote: 'Many have said of Alchemy, that it is for the making of gold and silver. For me such is not the aim, but to consider only what virtue and power may lie in medicines.'[3]

For Paracelsus, creating medicines and elixirs that could bring health and longevity, which had always been the preoccupation of Eastern alchemy, became his life's purpose, and he travelled as far as Asia Minor in search of knowledge. Instead of applying the various processes of alchemy – heating, distillation and so on – to metals in an attempt to transmute them into gold, he used these same processes on plants and minerals to create medicines. He coined the term 'Spagyric' to describe his art, from two Greek words, meaning 'to separate' and 'to recombine', since he believed he was separating the various components of his ingredients, purifying them and then putting them back together again.

Fludd studied Spagyrics in Europe, returning to Oxford in 1604 to obtain his medical degree. By 1609 he was a member of the London College of Physicians and had established a practice in London using Spagyric medicine, which included the use of a patient's horoscope to determine when to take the remedies. His practice was so successful that he was able to establish an apothecary with a dedicated laboratory to prepare his alchemical remedies.

◉ *How to Make a Philosopher's Stone*

Let the keynote of your work be the desire to know the wonders of nature and the desire to help others. The highest form of medicine is love, says Paracelsus.

MANFRED M. JUNIUS, *THE PRACTICAL HANDBOOK OF PLANT ALCHEMY*

The magical arts of the astrologer, herbalist, and natural healer come together in a branch of alchemy favoured by many modern

The Alchemist, *by William Fettes Douglas, 1853*

alchemists and known as herbal alchemy, which is often seen as a branch of Spagyrics. Today you can buy medicines commercially produced by this alchemy.

Spagyrics can be applied to metals and minerals, as well as animal and vegetable matter. Each of these can yield a 'Philosopher's Stone', which the alchemist believes paves the way to the creation of 'gold'.

The easiest stone to create is a vegetable stone, which can then act – if you believe the alchemists – as a catalyst that will improve your health and help open you to states of spiritual consciousness.

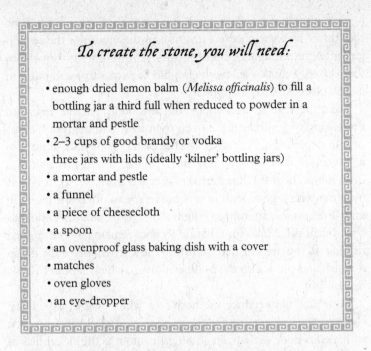

To create the stone, you will need:

- enough dried lemon balm (*Melissa officinalis*) to fill a bottling jar a third full when reduced to powder in a mortar and pestle
- 2–3 cups of good brandy or vodka
- three jars with lids (ideally 'kilner' bottling jars)
- a mortar and pestle
- a funnel
- a piece of cheesecloth
- a spoon
- an ovenproof glass baking dish with a cover
- matches
- oven gloves
- an eye-dropper

Alchemists used astrology and an awareness of the planets in their work; every metal and plant was associated with a planet. Lemon balm is ruled by Jupiter, which rules Thursdays, so you should begin this process just after sunrise on a Thursday. Mark Stavish, the author of *A Short Course in Plant Alchemy*, recommends that you 'Start with prayers to God that the mysteries may be revealed to you and your place in the Universe restored'.

Grind the dried herb to a fine powder in the mortar and pestle, concentrating on the idea that you are helping to release the magical potency of the herb in this way.

Fill one of the bottling jars a third full with the powder, then add the alcohol until the jar is about half full. If you are using a glass kilner jar with a rubber seal, simply seal the jar now. If you are using a jar with a metal lid, use clingfilm to create a seal so that the alcohol fumes don't make contact with the lid.

Put the jar in an airing cupboard or wherever there is a fairly constant warmth. Leave for several hours, or a day or so.

Once the alcohol is dark green, it is ready for the next step. Line the funnel with the cheesecloth, sit it in the mouth of the second jar and pour the alcohol out of the first jar through the funnel into the second. Seal this jar (with clingfilm if necessary) and put it in a dark place, such as a cupboard.

Take the first jar and spoon out the debris of the herb into the baking dish. Preheat the oven to at least 230 degrees Celsius or 446 degrees Fahrenheit. Take the dish outside and stand it in a safe place clear of anything inflammable. Light a match and drop it into the dish. The herbal matter will burn like a Christmas pudding with a good deal of smoke. Every so often stir the herb and, if necessary, attempt to relight it, to ensure all the alcohol has been burnt off. Make sure that no alcohol remains by sniffing the residue. If you are satisfied, return to the kitchen, place the lid on the dish and put it into the preheated oven, which should by now be very hot.

Your goal is to reduce the herb to a white or grey ash. Keep checking the process. In an ideal situation, you would have an oven with a glass door so that you could gaze into it as the alchemists of old would gaze into their furnaces and glass alembics.

When you can see only ash, turn off the oven and wait for everything to completely cool. Then tip the ash into the mortar and grind it with the pestle until it is a fine powder. Pour this powder into the third jar and then, with the eye-dropper, slowly add the alcohol extract that you obtained earlier. Keep adding drops until the ash has absorbed as much as it can. You will then find that you have created a waxy substance, which is the vegetable stone. It will look whitish or grey. Seal the jar and place it in a cool, dark place. Over time, it will change its colour and consistency.

Alchemists believe that if you mix a small amount of this vegetable stone with water and drink it, you will improve your physical and spiritual health and will also have made one small step towards discovering the elixir of life.

'An Alchemist's Story'

Our Alchemist – who wishes to remain anonymous – has always had an interest in the occult and joined a coven at the age of 15. He became a practising herbalist, but was drawn to the practical (as opposed to the philosophical) side of Alchemy through the writings of Israel Regardie, who was largely responsible for recording and publishing the magical practices developed by the Golden Dawn. He has made a speciality of 'Spagyrics' – plant alchemy – which he now practises full time from his well equipped laboratory on the Welsh borders.

My lifelong interest in Alchemy was kindled by Israel Regardie's book *The Philosopher's Stone*. It was hard to see my way into the subject and how to get started as alchemical texts are full of mysterious symbolism and very hard to decode. This either puts people off completely or sets them on a road of creating sexual or philosophical interpretations, much as Jung did. Once I began to understand the subject better, I realised that it is, above all, a practical discipline to be pursued with great application and self-questioning: '*Ora et Labora*' – 'pray and work' – as the alchemists used to say. I started collecting alchemical glassware and trained as an herbalist, but my breakthrough in fact came through my other occult work.

I was living in mid-Wales at the time and experimenting with spirit invocation, using the *Key of Solomon*. I was particularly interested in a lunar spirit, known as 'Sophiel', who is described as one who 'teacheth the knowledge of herb and stone'. This seemed particularly relevant to alchemy, where the beginner starts by working with herbs and gemstones, before attempting the more difficult transmutation of metals. I did an evocation ritual on a Monday at the full moon, which is the best time for lunar spirits, but as there was no resulting physical manifestation I felt it had failed. I asked for help in understanding the alchemical texts, but didn't hold out any great expectations of success. I was proved wrong as it turned out. Exactly nine weeks later (nine is the Lunar number in the cabbala), I was attending a conference and an elderly American walked straight up to me and asked, 'Are you interested in Alchemy?' We arranged to meet afterwards and he later spent a full 24 hours helping me to make sense of the whole subject. He also put me in touch with a group of practical alchemists in the West Country, with whom I could build my skills. The evocation had worked after all!

From this moment on, I felt a sympathetic flow between the work and my own emerging understanding and I always knew what to do next. Alchemy is associated with the early attempts to transmute metal into gold, but, as far as I know, there is still no direct evidence that this has ever been achieved. Instead, I decided to start with 'Spagyrics', Plant Alchemy, which complemented all my experience as an herbalist and added the new dimension of creating substances with magical properties to help me with my occult work. In particular, I discovered how alchemical substances could be used to enhance the preparation of rituals. I also helped to set up a group of three alchemists, three skryers and three ritual magicians – note the number nine coming up again. We work very well together and the different disciplines complement each other, as magicians have discovered since the very early days of the Neo-Platonists.

I have built myself an extensive laboratory over time. You need specially made glass retorts and surprisingly, there are still craftsmen today who have an interest in the old art. I also discovered you have to be quite careful . . . I had a massive explosion whilst distilling pepper and still have the scorch marks on the ceiling to remind me! Israel Regardie ruined his lungs distilling Antimony and many old prints show the dangers of the art.

Spagyrics is the art of producing plant elixirs, which are very potent herbal preparations that combine medicinal and magical properties. Alchemy works on the separation of the three principal elements of Mercury, Sulphur and Salt. In the plant world these elements are represented by their spirit: Mercury by the natural alcohols that can be extracted from plant materials and contain the life force of the spirit, Sulphur by the plant oils, which represent the personality of the plants, and Salt by that which remains after the plant material

An Alchemical Laboratory

has been burnt to ash or evaporated. These salts have particular properties that alchemists value. They are used to catch what they refer to in their writings as 'quick fire', which is then combined with the Sulphur and the Mercury to produce an alchemical concoction with medicinal or magical properties. The symbolism of this process lies at the very heart of Alchemy. The Mercury is usually referred to as the 'White Queen', the 'Red King' is Sulphur, and the Salts are the body. Their combination is the Alchemical Wedding.

The whole alchemical process is long and the practitioner must understand all the different nuances of elemental combinations, laboratory work, timing of the process against the right astrological positioning, exposure to fresh air and nature. The books and 'recipes', unlike modern cookbooks, give you only an overall framework and a set of hints; it is the success of the learning process itself that will determine if you are to become a real alchemist or not.

The first process, releasing the Mercury, involves distilling the purest alcohol possible. Chemically, this is Ethyl Alcohol (C_2H_5OH), which is never found free within nature and must be distilled several times from the 'Menstruum', the water and

Marriage of the White Queen and the Red King.

alcohol solution that the plant is soaked in before you begin, in order to get rid of excess water. This is often referred to in old alchemical texts as 'letting seven eagles fly'.

The 'volatile' Sulphur, or plant oil, is extracted by steam and will float on the surface of the condensate. This is similar to the individual plant oils you find in Aromatherapy. The Menstruum, after extraction of the alcohol, can then be boiled dry to provide the 'fixed' salt of Sulphur. This substance, which is usually black, must be subjected to prolonged heating, and then covered with hot distilled water, which is gently evaporated to produce a pure white salt. The plant salts can also be extracted by burning the remaining plant material, then carefully washing the ashes to remove impurities in a process known as Calcination.

The art of alchemy lies in the separation and rejoining of the three elements within a magical domain, where astrology, ritual and prayer are all important. Each plant will have a governing planet – Jupiter, for example, is the governing plant of Sage – but you must also consider its aspect to the other heavenly bodies and their influence for good or evil. The moon, especially, rules the ebb and flow of nature and plant energies and should be waxing during your alchemical process.

'Our work starts in darkness and in death,' the old practitioners of alchemy would say. The herb that one is working with must be reduced to its 'chaos', that is its component parts, which we must separate, purify, then conjoin, so that the whole will be greater than the sum of its parts. This is the essence of plant alchemy. The finished concoction should be left in the night air, so that the salts will suck into their body the natural force of creation. Successful alchemy in this way will create a new element, which contains all the medical and magical properties of the herb, but at a higher level. This element is represented in alchemical texts by the lion. Sometimes it takes the shape of a stone, which can be consecrated on a magical altar with extraordinary results. I recently photographed this process and when the film was developed it showed a glowing orb, which had no visible presence in my ceremonies. On closer investigation I could make out the shape of twins, curled around each other within the orb. The herb I was working on was Fennel, which is ruled by Gemini. Was I actually seeing a manifestation of the living spirit of the plant?

What is the benefit of such creation, one might ask? Eternal Life, the Philosopher's Stone – the red powder of transformation – and the transmutation of lead into gold, are, to my mind, more symbolic than practical. On a more realistic level, one of Alchemy's favourite practices is the production of the 'Primum Ers Melissae', which was held in high esteem by Paracelsus. This is a compound that promotes the vitality and life force that diminish as one gets older. It is distilled from the herb 'Melissa', or lemon balm, which is common enough in many English gardens. Recreating such practices today are a challenge and an adventure for the small but dedicated band of alchemists.

Has not Alchemy been overtaken by science? This is a question that everyone asks. From my perspective, I believe that Alchemy is addressing many phenomena that science still cannot explain. Detailed research, for instance, has shown that human attitudes can affect the shape of crystal formation (*Hidden Messages in Water* by the Japanese scientist Masuru Emoto explores this) but how can such a thing be possible? There is a deep relationship between the energies here on earth, those above and the formation of all beings: 'As above, so below', as the magicians say. For me, practical alchemy provides an extraordinarily rich experience in working with the very substance of creation. You are exploring God's world – the miracles of the divine.

———————

Applying the Hermetic doctrine of 'As above, so below', found on the Emerald Tablet of Hermes Trismegistus, Fludd proposed that the heart was responsible for circulating blood, reasoning that the heart resembled the sun and the blood was like the planets that orbited around it. His friend William Harvey later explained the process in more scientific terms, whilst still referring to Fludd's analogy.

Fludd wrote prolifically, not only on alchemy and philosophy, but on his musical theories and on his many designs for a perpetual motion machine. His defence of the mysterious group known as the Rosicrucians, whom we will encounter in Chapter 10, led many to claim that he was a member of this secret brotherhood, although historians believe this is unlikely, particularly since the Rosicrucians themselves may not even have existed.

Even in the first half of the seventeenth century there were signs that the age of the 'puffers' was coming to an end. At the height of Fludd's success, Ben Jonson's comedy *The Alchemist* was performed for the first time in Oxford and then in London in 1610. The play satirised the credulity and greed that Jonson saw all around him, epitomised in the search for gold and the elixir of life. By the middle of the century, chemistry had separated itself from its parent, alchemy, while a mechanistic, as opposed to a magical, world-view was gaining ascendancy. Nonetheless, at the same time, the last of the famous English alchemists were hard at work.

✐ The Ashmolean Museum and ✐ the Confiding of the Secret

This is the famous stone
That turneth all to gold;
For that which God doth touch and own
Cannot for less be told.

GEORGE HERBERT

The last English proponent of alchemy of any note was Elias Ashmole, the founder of the famous Ashmolean Museum in Oxford, whose world we shall explore in Chapter 9. Fascinated by astrology, magic and Rosicrucianism, in 1652 Ashmole published his *Theatrum Chemicum Britannicum,* a collection of dozens of alchemical documents. In it, he surveys the extant literature and draws conclusions.

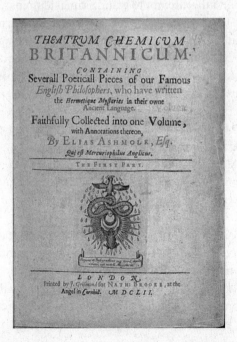

Regarding the Philosopher's Stone, for example, he mentions that alchemists have described a vegetable stone – and even an angelic stone too. He believed that the vegetable stone was probably responsible for 'the Wallnut-Tree which anciently grew in Glastenbury Church-yard, and never put forth Leaves before S. Barnabies Day, yet then was fully loaded with them'. He also believed that the stone could 'discover any Person in what part of the World soever, although never so secretly concealed.'[4]

One year after the book's publication, an alchemical philosopher, William Backhouse, revealed to Ashmole the inner secret of the *materia prima* – the basic material from which the Philosopher's Stone was prepared. From his notes we even know the day on which this revelation occurred: it was 13 May 1653.[5] From that moment until he died in 1692, for reasons unknown, Ashmole wrote nothing more on alchemy.

As the seventeenth gave way to the eighteenth century, the two strands that had been running together in alchemy – the attempt to alter matter and the attempt to gain spiritual illumination – finally came apart. The science of chemistry waved goodbye to its quirky parent. Thanks to the alchemists, a whole range of compounds had been discovered, including sulphur, nitric acid, mercuric oxide, potassium sulphate and hydrochloric acid. Innovative processes had been developed too: in the preparation of alcohol, in the introduction of chemicals into medicine, thanks to Paracelsus, and in the process of tanning leather. But the Enlightenment encouraged new thinking and a rejection of doctrines that could not be proved by reason. Alchemy's reliance on visions and dreams, on obscure texts and concepts that defied logic, ensured its demise as a discipline concerned with attempting to produce gold or a material elixir of life.

However, it proved to be a long and protracted goodbye. The Royal Society was founded in 1660 to encourage scientific research, but even its most famous member, Sir Isaac Newton, the pioneer of the mechanical model of the universe, was taken with Hermetic ideas and conducted alchemical investigations in secret.

The end of a period of over five hundred years of attempts

at making gold in England is perhaps best marked by the tragic death of Dr James Price of Stoke village near Guildford in Surrey in 1783. Price claimed he could effect the transmutation and in front of an invited audience of the social elite of the day, including Lord Palmerston, he appeared to be successful.

Price was then challenged by the Royal Society to perform the miracle again – but this time under the scrutiny of a committee led by Sir Joseph Banks. Price prevaricated and delayed before finally agreeing. Once the committee had assembled at his house, he drank an acid poison and died before their eyes.

‍⟋ J.K. Rowling and ⟍‍
the Magic of Harry Potter

I've never wanted to be a witch, but an alchemist, now that's a different matter. To invent this wizard world, I've learnt a ridiculous amount about alchemy. Perhaps much of it I'll never use in the books, but I have to know in detail what magic can and cannot do in order to set the parameters and establish the stories' internal logic.

J.K. ROWLING, INTERVIEW WITH
THE *HERALD*, 1998

One of the reasons why the Harry Potter stories appeal to adults as well as children lies in the fact that J.K. Rowling has based her books on a knowledge of real magic. Her work is not simply 'fantasy', but draws upon the rich seam of images and ideas found in traditional magical lore. This underpinning of the Harry Potter books means that the stories carry the same power as myth, using symbols familiar to the collective psyche for centuries.

Rowling draws on the lore of folk magic and witchcraft for her descriptions of spell-making and seership, and on Tarot symbolism when she uses such imagery as the lightning-struck tower and the hanged man. But she is clearly most attracted to the world of alchemy, and in this she is following an established tradition in

English Literature of writers who have used alchemical imagery – from Shakespeare to C.S. Lewis.

The alchemical dimensions of Rowling's work are explored in detail in John Granger's *Unlocking Harry Potter: Five Keys for the Serious Reader* (Zossima Press, 2007). Hans Andréa, who devotes a website to exploring the spiritual significance of Rowling's work (at www.harrypotterforseekers.com), points out in the following passage the many similarities between the stories and a famous Rosicrucian work, *The Alchemical Wedding of Christian Rosenkreutz*, published in 1616:

> Harry Potter goes to an ancient castle for seven years; in *The Alchemical Wedding*, Christian Rosycross (CRC) goes to a castle for seven days. Both heroes are given a letter of invitation during a violent storm. To reach the castle, Harry travels across a lake with mermaids in it; to reach the Tower of Olympus, where the actual alchemy is performed, CRC travels across a sea with mermaids in it. Harry is faced with being sorted into one of four houses; CRC faces four paths to choose from at the beginning of his journey to the castle. Both books mention Paracelsus. A number of mystery animals are mentioned in both books, for example the phoenix, the unicorn and the griffin. In both the Tower of Olympus and Harry's castle lives a very ancient man who is in control of the whole proceedings. In both stories the meals are served up by invisible servants in a hall lighted by floating candles. In both stories there is a funeral where a phoenix appears. There are many more similarities – too many to be coincidence.

Perhaps J.K.Rowling agreed with Goethe when he wrote to his friend Frau von Stein in 1786: 'I have read through the Wedding of Christian Rosenkreutz. There is a good fairy tale to tell there in good time, when it will be reborn. It cannot be appreciated in its old skin.'[6]

Teacher of Celtic shamanism, Dr Geo Trevarthen, believes that

Rowling's work answers a pressing need of our times – for a sense of magic and meaning – and says that we can use Harry Potter's example as 'an alchemical antidote to the culture of complacency'. In her book *The Seeker's Guide to Harry Potter* (O Books, 2008), which explores the mythic and sacred dimension of the stories, she writes: 'We fully attain the [Philosopher's] stone by giving it to others, as Harry does . . . [His] greatest message is love's generosity in the face of loss.'

Geo Trevarthen, Hans Andréa and Professor Ronald Hutton, a specialist in the history of witchcraft, Druidism and paganism, shared a podium at the 2008 Accio Conference, 'From Quidditch Flyers to Dreaming Spires: Exploring the Worldwide Influence of the Harry Potter Novels', held at Magdalen College, Oxford. The title of their joint discussion was 'Paganism and Christianity in Harry Potter'.

Books of the papers presented at the 2005 and 2008 conferences are available from Accio at www.accio.org.uk.

⋘ Perfection of the Soul ⋙

We hear little of alchemy in the nineteenth century, apart from one tantalising glimpse afforded by the story of Mary Anne Atwood who in 1850 published *A Suggestive Enquiry into the Hermetic Mystery*. Her father, Thomas South, had a large library of rare books on religion and philosophy, and his daughter, knowing Greek and Latin, had helped him index the collection.

Mary learnt from her father that there was a secret thread that connected the teachings of the European alchemists with those of the ancient mystery schools of Egypt and the classical world. She became interested in spiritualism and hypnosis, becoming convinced that the alchemists knew the secret of the perfection of the soul. But no sooner had the first hundred copies of her book been sold than Mary Atwood panicked because her father feared that she had revealed too much, and she tried to buy back as many copies as she could.

Thomas South and his daughter made a pyre of every copy they could find, together with a long manuscript poem about alchemy that he had written, and on the lawn of their house in Gosport they set fire to it. The book was republished a century later from a copy that escaped the fire, and the story that surrounded its strange fate inspired Lindsay Clarke's alchemical novel, *The Chymical Wedding*, first published in 1989.

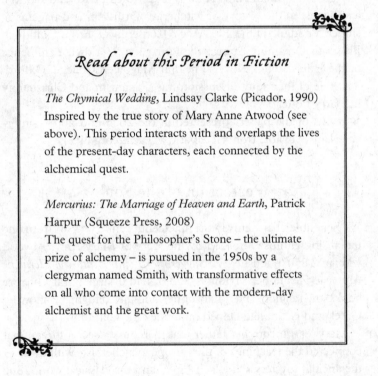

Read about this Period in Fiction

The Chymical Wedding, Lindsay Clarke (Picador, 1990)
Inspired by the true story of Mary Anne Atwood (see above). This period interacts with and overlaps the lives of the present-day characters, each connected by the alchemical quest.

Mercurius: The Marriage of Heaven and Earth, Patrick Harpur (Squeeze Press, 2008)
The quest for the Philosopher's Stone – the ultimate prize of alchemy – is pursued in the 1950s by a clergyman named Smith, with transformative effects on all who come into contact with the modern-day alchemist and the great work.

By the end of the century, the secrets that South and his daughter had been scared to reveal were acting like leaven amongst the Victorian magicians of the Golden Dawn, illuminating their work and providing them with powerful symbols and vocabulary.

By the middle of the following century, thanks to the pioneering work of the psychologist Carl Jung, alchemy began to be seen as a metaphor for the psychological work of maturation and development, which he and his followers termed 'individuation'. This was the 'gold' of spiritual maturity sought by the depth psychology of Jung, who believed that alchemists had discovered a way of working towards integration and illumination, using external means to reveal and explore inner processes.

✶ The Adept of Eastbourne ✶

While most interest in alchemy now comes from psychologists and psychotherapists keen to mine its symbolism, a few people still practise laboratory alchemy in England, and all the equipment, ingredients and instructions can now be purchased on the internet.

The last recorded example we have of a successful alchemist was Archibald Cockren, who died in the 1960s. A pioneer of electro-massage who worked as a masseur in a medical unit during the First World War, he published a book in 1940 titled *Alchemy Rediscovered and Restored*. In it he described his experiments, and his success at obtaining 'the Mercury of the Philosophers, the Aqua Benedicta, the Aqua Celestres, and water of Paradise':

> The first intimation I had of this triumph was a violent hissing, jets of vapour pouring from the retort and into the receiver like sharp bursts from a machine-gun, and then a violent explosion, whilst a very potent and subtle odour filled the laboratory and its surroundings. A friend has described this odour as resembling the dewy earth on a June morning, with the hint of growing flowers in the air; the breath of the wind over heather and hill, and the sweet smell of the rain on parched earth.

A persistent rumour recounts that he did indeed find the elixir of life, and that he never died but continues to live in Eastbourne – an alchemical adept over 130 years old.

The Most Well-Known English Alchemists

Robert of Chester, fl. 1140–1150

Roger Bacon, 1214–1294

Thomas Bungay, c.1214–c.1294

Sir George Ripley, c.1415–1490

Thomas Norton, c.1433–c.1513

Thomas Charnock, 1524x6–1581

William Holway/Hollewell (Gibbs), fl. 1520

John Dee, 1527–1608

Sir Edward Kelley, 1555–1597

Mary Sidney/Herbert, 1561–1621

Robert Fludd, 1574–1637

William Backhouse, 1593–1662

Sir Kenelm Digby, 1603–1665

Sir Thomas Browne, 1605–1682

Elias Ashmole, 1617–1692

Thomas Vaughan, 1622–1666

Sir Isaac Newton, 1642–1727

J.P. Kellerman 1779–18??

Archibald Cockren, c.1880–c.1960

PATRICK HARPUR

Patrick Harpur is a practical, everyday philosopher, who has spent many years examining the four great pillars of Renaissance magic – Hermetic philosophy, the cabbala, Neoplatonism and alchemy – in order to rebuild the pre-scientific world-view that he finds most congenial to true knowledge. He has taken a number of temporary jobs to fund his research, as well as working in publishing and writing two novels. He has also written widely on the reality of daemons and how they can appear through that great collective imagination of which the Romantics, such as Blake and Coleridge, spoke so eloquently. He lives alone in a cottage in Dorset.

My grandmother was a very good medium and she passed on her interest in spiritualism to my mother. My father was Irish and psychic, too, but came from a long line of Church of Ireland vicars; so for much of my life I have been trying to find a view that reconciled the heretical and the pagan with the Christian picture.

Thanks to my parents, I was given the best education money could buy – public school and Cambridge – but after graduating I felt that I had not been taught what I wanted to know. I eventually became attracted to alchemy and, having thought I could crack it in a month or so, in fact spent four years reading weird texts – some of them in the original Latin – for my alchemical book, *Mercurius; or, the Marriage of Heaven and Earth.*

As I immersed myself in this new knowledge, I realised that alchemy describes the workings of the imagination itself. It describes how our psyches work: there is endless circulation, making the volatile fixed and the fixed volatile, separating and conjoining. Alchemy is the chemical counterpart of artistic creativity, because it is, at root, a real soul activity, i.e. both material and non-material. Separate all your elements and bring them all together. Any playwright knows that you do this, which is why I suspect that when alchemy began to decline in Europe at the turn of the seventeenth century, it released its myth-laden gases into the English air, which were inhaled by

Shakespeare and the great Jacobean dramatists whose plays are full of alchemical imagery. How else can we account for such a sudden burst of brilliant plays out of nowhere?

When you come to the twentieth century, you see the same flash of understanding in C.G. Jung, the great Swiss psychologist. When he stumbled across his first alchemical text, he recognised that it was the historical counterpart to his psychology of the unconscious. Alchemy is going on in all of us, all the time, whether we like it or not. It is a description of how the deep imagination and the collective psyche work. That's why Jung's last great books are about alchemy.

I bummed around in my twenties, until I discovered Jung. He was a great key for me and I got a first glimpse of what I was after. I took part-time jobs to feed my habit, which was reading books and writing. I just earned as much money as I needed to take a few months off and study. I had an idea that I wanted to be a poet and a mystic. I failed on both counts . . . I took every kind of job, from gardening to market research. Then I'd knock off and live incredibly cheaply somewhere.

My most successful book was a thriller, *The Serpent's Circle*, then a novel titled *The Rapture*, about an autistic child and his search for a self.

It was then that I became enthralled to Lady Alchemy. And she led me to Hermetic philosophy, and especially to those followers of Plato, the so-called Neoplatonists, who first flourished in Alexandria between about AD 100 and AD 300. During these two centuries, the place became a huge melting pot of mystics, early Christians, Gnostics, Hermeticists and so on, leading to a great flowering of thinking. All philosophical and religious ideas were embraced and considered equally, a bit like Hinduism. It ended when the Emperor Constantine adopted Christianity and declared everything else heresy. The different threads then separated and went their own way.

As I read about the period, I found a great insight, which has stayed with me ever since. As part of the scientific revolution, we are trapped in a vision that there has to be either a material or a spiritual world. You must have one or the other. The Platonists believed rather that there is a *metaxy*, an in-between world, which combines both forms. They were experts in this in-between world and the daemons who inhabited it, mediating between us and the gods. They believed that we are all given a personal daemon at birth to guide us through life (a concept that inspired Philip Pullman).

You will find this view in the 'myth of Er' told by Socrates towards the end of Plato's *Republic*. The daemon is selected at random and assigned to each of us at birth to act as a kind of blueprint for our lives, guiding and protecting us, which is where we get the idea of a guardian angel.

One of the most alluring ideas of the Neoplatonists was their notion, derived from Plato's dialogue *The Timaeus*, that there is a soul of the world. This is the 'in-between' world I mentioned earlier – what Jung called 'psychic reality'. It underlies what we call reality and it contains all the images of everything that is, including ourselves. For we are not, it turns out, the solid, literal beings we project ourselves as. Our souls are but individual images in the collective soul of the world. It is a humbling idea to consider that, as the poet W.B. Yeats said, we think we are the deep when in reality we are a little foam upon the deep! We think we have created new ideas and new inventions, yet we see that they all pre-existed in the mythic patterns within the world-soul.

That all our modern science is in fact a replication – but in literal form – of older myths is something I spend a long time describing in my book *The Philosophers' Secret Fire*. We begin to see, too, that the 'magic' of modern technology is only a literalisation of traditional magic. The shaman's ability to fly, to do harm at a distance, to exercise telepathy, for example, are all made literal by aircraft, missiles and telephones. Television is nothing other than a literal attempt to re-create the Other-world of imagination itself, where daemonic 'little people' grip us with their 'glamour'.

For each individual, the task is simple. We have to clear away our negative preoccupations and link ourselves to this world-soul. It is where we come from and where we go to when we die. If we achieve this connection – it involves, of course, a 'dying to oneself' – we begin to participate in a world that hitherto we only observed from the outside. We become a wise man or woman, a philosopher, a shaman. We must make the Other-world journey, meet the daemons, making allies of some, defeating others. From this comes power through wisdom, healing and magic, because you now have access not just to your own psyche but also to the great collective psyche. But you cannot, by definition, abuse this power, as it would mean abusing yourself.

The world of imagination as reality is very hard for us to grasp. It was not until the Renaissance, thirteen centuries after the Alexandrian revolution, that the idea was rekindled and it led to a huge outpouring of art and science. Marsilio Ficino was the great intellect of this age. He was the first man to reread and translate into Latin the Neoplatonists, and the original Hermetic texts, which poured into Florence in the fifteenth century. He set up his own villa, just like Plato's 'Academy', specifically to practise natural magic – *magia naturalis* as he called it.

He was most interested in how invoking the gods themselves would allow their powers to be drawn down for beneficial use. For instance, if you wanted to invoke the sun, you put yourself in a room with gold objects, perfumes and music that all corresponded to the sun. In this state, your invocations would create a sort of vessel that would automatically attract the solar powers, which could then be used either to transform yourself or be infused into sigils to benefit others. Ficino held rituals with groups of people to experience the effect of these invocations directly on their imaginations, rather like an early form of group psychotherapy.

Ficino envisioned natural magic as a whole philosophy of life, rather different from the later 'demonic magic' of Cornelius Agrippa, whose three books on the subject have had more influence on magicians right up to the present day than any other. Ficino focused on understanding which techniques of magic worked best and were most powerful. You will find this debate between magic as a source of power and as a source of philosophy central to any discussion of the subject.

The next great development of this intertwined view of magic came through the English magician John Dee, who can be thought of as the shaman for the tribe of the English. He could see that the English psyche was deeply torn between the Catholic impulse to worship the old Goddess in the form of the new Queen Elizabeth, and the emerging Puritanism. He saw too that there was a need for a new blend of spiritual beliefs.

Dee became the mentor of a movement that Shakespeare called 'The School of Night', which included such luminaries as Sir Walter Raleigh and Sir Philip Sidney. It was to be almost a new religion, made up of a synthesis of Neoplatonism, Hermeticism, alchemy and cabbala – the same four strands that had fired Ficino and his followers. They all believed that they had hit upon a *prisca theologia*, a 'pristine theology', made all the more attractive for being, as they thought, older than Moses and certainly older than Christianity and the divisions it had produced.

Unfortunately, the movement dispersed and broke up into its component parts. Alchemy, for instance, passed into Jacobean drama, into modern chemistry and, finally, via Jung into depth psychology. The alchemists saw themselves as forming a 'golden chain' down which the secret of alchemy was passed from master to pupil. But the secret of alchemy is also the hidden, 'occult', imaginative view of the world found in the poetry of William Blake and W.B. Yeats, as well as in the psychology of Jung.

In my more optimistic moments I see myself as a small link in the chain, trying to reintroduce traditional Neoplatonic, even 'magical', thought to my generation. But 'thought' is the wrong word. Imagination is better. And through imagination you see the world anew as the alchemists and Romantic poets saw it – enchanted, animate, ensouled.

This is why the alchemists always insisted that the secret of their art is right there for everyone to see. It's right under our noses. But we don't see it. We don't see it because we cannot learn how to see it. The secret is not on any curriculum. We have to be initiated into it – and that of course always involves the inconvenience of dying to one's self and being reborn . . .

My own initiation came, I suppose, through my labouring at

alchemy when, suddenly, I felt the centre of my personality shift. Something else was writing through me, my daemon perhaps, who was none other than Mercurius, the alchemical personification of the world-soul. And I saw how humans are constituted in the same way as the cosmos, each of us an aspect of the great source of all imaginative life, the soul of the world. It's one of the joys of the golden chain that, when you discover one link in it, as I discovered Jung, then you soon discover all the other links, back through the Romantics to the Renaissance magi, back to the Neoplatonists, the cabbalists and the Hermetic philosophers.

Unfortunately, not many people these days have the time or the interest to pursue these ancient truths. We are obsessed with more immediate matters like acquiring money or being loved, and want self-help techniques for getting enough of these, but we also want to be mysterious. This is not new. Even the ancient magicians had to fight the temptation to make a quick buck now and then through their power.

But if you get it right, then magic becomes a 'philosophy of the soul'. However, this can never be a doctrine or a system because it depends on a particular vision of the world and on subtle imaginative insight. Like the soul itself, magical thinking shape-shifts and, as we've seen, appears down the ages in different guises – now as thinking, now as chemistry, now as poetry, now as psychology, and so on. This is why I have written three books and am writing a fourth. Even with this I will not have expressed 'the truth' and all that I want to say because, as Heraclitus remarked, 'no one can fathom the soul, so deep is its extent'. As some wit has said, the truth is that which cannot be Googled.

I'm driven by my personal daemon, but I hate the act of writing. It's an absolute pain and I have to live in penury and get by, while not eating or sleeping. But I shouldn't complain. I have a lovely life in Dorset, where it feels as if I'm on a permanent holiday; and although writing is difficult and does your head in, it brings the reward of a life that has meaning.

Besides, my 'daemonic reality' is not all stick and no carrot. My own daemonic allies have come to me one by one over the years.

The key to becoming better acquainted is to understand, as Robert Graves describes in *The White Goddess*, that you must first learn your daemon's name and then keep it totally secret. I invoke my daemonic allies to do simple things, like finding a parking space or getting someone to give me their old computer. Daemons are good at specifics, like coming up with a new washing machine, but don't ask them to help you win the lottery or take their advice on when the world is going to end.

It is possible to get help from your personal daemon to increase your powers, but meddling in this way can be fatal. Think of all the dangerous people, like Stalin, Hitler and so on, who must have had immensely powerful personal daemons, but twisted this power for their own ends.

My basic belief is that magic is not possible without the sort of philosophy that existed before the Industrial Revolution: that there is a correspondence between the universe and us – the macrocosm and the microcosm: 'As above, so below', as the alchemists believed. It made perfect sense to them that what you did affected the cosmos, and vice versa. The link was through the world-soul from which everything flowed, and of which we are all just individual manifestations.

✍ Philip Pullman, the Rosicrucians and Dust

In the closing years of the twentieth century, three children's fantasy novels, known collectively as *His Dark Materials*, which had taken Philip Pullman seven years to write, achieved a success rivalled only by J.K. Rowling's Harry Potter series. A play, based on the trilogy and lasting over six hours, was produced by the National Theatre, and *The Golden Compass*, a Hollywood film version of one of the books, was released in 2007.

Pullman's books, set in a 'multiverse' of parallel worlds that include magical creatures, witches and angels, have been criticised as being atheistic, with the *Catholic Herald* even suggesting they should be burnt. Pullman, however, does not deny the value of the religious impulse, which he believes 'includes the sense of awe and mystery we feel when we look at the universe, the urge to find a meaning and a purpose in our lives, our sense of moral kinship with other human beings – [it] is part of being human, and I value it. I'd be a damn fool not to. But organised religion is quite another thing.'[7]

While disdaining established religions, Pullman says he has experienced mystical states three or four times in his life, when 'with enormous excitement, I could see that the universe was alive and I was part of it. I saw this so clearly and intensely that I don't think I could sustain that state for very long.'[8]

Just as J.K. Rowling seems to have been influenced by the Rosicrucians, so too has Philip Pullman. When asked about the inspiration for the magical device that appears in his books, the alethiometer, a mechanism capable of divining the truth, Pullman replied: 'The alethiometer came out of my interest in the Renaissance, the world described so vividly by Frances Yates in *The Art of Memory* and *The Rosicrucian Enlightenment*. During the Renaissance there was a rediscovery of Greek philosophy, and a fascination with what we now call the occult, astrology and alchemy.'[9]

The alethiometer is reminiscent, too of the Archeometer of the French nineteenth-century magician Saint-Yves d'Alveydre, which he claimed was an instrument for predicting events and co-ordinating all human knowledge. That in turn was probably inspired by the Polish mystic Hoene-Wroński's 'Prognometer', a similar device made of three globes and two pyramids mounted on a carriage of gilded copper.

Another striking feature of Pullman's stories are the animals known as 'daemons', which accompany each character and are a manifestation of their inner nature and conscience. Pullman says he does not know where the idea for them came from, but since he acknowledges his interest in the Renaissance it seems highly likely that he had absorbed the Neoplatonic idea of daemons, well known in that era, which is used in Hermetic magic and certain psychologies to represent aspects of the soul or divine nature.[10]

In crafting his trilogy, Pullman mounts a polemic against the forces of repression and orthodoxy, which he calls The Authority, and here we can clearly see the influence of John Milton, William Blake and Gnostic ideas, all of which Pullman acknowledges, and which were all – like Rosicrucianism – opposed to the established hierarchy of the Church. Some commentators, however, believe that behind the devastating critique of established religion that is conveyed in *His Dark Materials*, Pullman is offering us his own version of 'Quantum Mysticism', drawing on his fascination for 'Dark Matter' and depicted in his concept of 'dust' – a substance that allows magic to occur and that enables witches to fly and cast spells.

～ Things to Do ～

❃ Explore Mary Sidney's world by visiting Ludlow Castle (www.ludlowcastle.com), where she spent her childhood, and Houghton House in Ampthill, Bedfordshire – now a ruin administered as an ancient monument by English Heritage – where she lived at the end of her life (see www.english-heritage.org.uk). Houghton may have been the model for the 'House Beautiful' in John Bunyan's masterpiece, *Pilgrim's Progress*. Most important of all, visit Wilton House, near Salisbury. Although her laboratory is long gone, there is much to see including the story of 'Arcadia', depicted in the panels of the Single Cube Room. Her brother, Sir Philip Sidney, dedicated his 'Arcadia' to his sister. See www.wiltonhouse.co.uk

❃ Experiment with using alchemy in an oracular way with *The Alchemy Stones* by M.E. Warlick (Connections, 2002).

❃ Take a course of in-depth study of the world of the English alchemists on a CD ROM with expert Adam McLean, or

take his advanced study course on the Ripley Scroll. See his
'The Alchemy Website', which is the most comprehensive
on the subject, at: www.alchemywebsite.com

❋ Take a home-study course in alchemy. Laboratory
equipment and lesson materials are mailed to you. See
www.flamelcollege.org

❋ Take a residential course in alchemy on the Isle of
Wight with Bob Plimer, philosophy lecturer and
member of the International Alchemy Guild. See
www.alchemycoursesatthecourtyard.com

❋ Study alchemy with the Rising Phoenix Foundation,
through distance learning and in gatherings in London,
Gloucestershire and elsewhere. See www.rpxf.org

❋ Combine an understanding of the eightfold seasonal
cycle, celebrated by Druids, Wiccans and pagans,
with alchemy by reading and working through
Glennie Kindred's *The Alchemist's Journey* (Hay House,
2005).

❋ Visit the alchemical section of the virtual 'Museum of
Lost Wonder' at www.lostwonder.org

❋ Consider joining the International Alchemy Guild, a
group of alchemists from around the world who come
together to exchange views, news and research in the
Hermetic arts and all forms of practical and spiritual
alchemy. They publish a journal, organise conferences,
and maintain an online shop and archives. See www.
alchemyguild.org

❋ Attend the International Alchemy Conference, usually
held over three days in Las Vegas, which includes

demonstrations, lectures and workshops in spiritual and practical alchemy and Spagyrics. See www. alchemyconference.com

✳ Follow courses in Spagyrics and alchemy, and order videos of workshops on these subjects from www. triadpublishing.com

✳ Browse the Spagyric medicines available online at www. australerba.com.au and www.spagyricmedicine.com

✳ Follow Jay Ramsay's lucid guide to using alchemy as a path of self-development in his *Alchemy: The Art of Transformation* (Thorsons, 1997), or use alchemy to help you in your closest relationships with his *Crucible of Love: The Alchemy of Passionate Relationships* (O Books, 2004).

✳ Make a pilgrimage to Oxford, where alchemists Roger Bacon, Robert Fludd and Elias Ashmole studied or taught. Visit the Ashmolean Museum and see the statue of Bacon outside the Oxford Museum of Natural History in Parks Road.

✐ Resources ✐

BOOKS
The Alchemist's Handbook: Manual for Practical Laboratory Alchemy, Frater Albertus (Red Wheel/Weiser, 1987)
Alchemy: Science of the Cosmos, Science of the Soul, Titus Burckhardt (Fons Vitae, 2000)
Alchemy: The Secret Art, Stanislas Klossowski De Rola (Thames & Hudson, 1973)
Ars Spagyrica – being a rendition of the Alchemical Arte of Spagyrics, G St M Nottingham, (Verdelet Publishing, 2005)

Isaac Newton: The Last Sorcerer, Michael White (Fourth Estate, 1998)

Medicine and Magic in Elizabethan London: Simon Forman: Astrologer, Alchemist, and Physician, Lauren Kassell (Oxford University Press, 2007)

On Becoming an Alchemist: A Guide for the Modern Magician, Catherine MacCoun (Trumpeter Books, 2009)

Path of Alchemy: Energetic Healing and the World of Natural Alchemy, Mark Stavish (Llewellyn Publications, 2006)

CHAPTER SEVEN

THE QUEEN'S ASTROLOGER

The Man Who Conversed with Angels

❧❀❧

Would to God in heaven I had awhile . . . the
mysticall and supermetaphysicall philosophy of
Doctor Dee.

GABRIEL HARVEY IN A LETTER TO
EDMUND SPENSER, 1573–1580

Magicians rarely work alone. Although periods of seclusion and hermitage may sometimes keep them from human company, their sole desire is for relationship, connection, union. They want to explore the strangeness of the world, to delve into the deepest mysteries of existence and to converse with the brightest minds and greatest souls that they can find – whether they are alive or have died and now live in the celestial realms.

Like the magic circle they draw around themselves in ritual, each magician has a 'circle' of influence, and if we are to judge the power of a mage by the nature and quality of that circle, then it is to the Elizabethan wizard Dr John Dee that we must award the title of England's greatest magician. Like the mythical Merlin who acted in the time-honoured role of the Druid as adviser to his sovereign, Dee became Queen Elizabeth's astrologer. Like the philosopher Roger Bacon in the thirteenth century, Dee was an alchemist as well as a scientist and a mathematician. Like the Freemason Elias Ashmole in the seventeenth century, he amassed the greatest collection of magical texts in the country, only calamitously to lose much of his collection. Like Aleister Crowley in the twentieth century, he attempted to commune with spirits, and was even prepared to resort to unconventional sexual relations if it seemed necessary to attain his magical ends.

And although each of these contenders for the title of the country's greatest wizard knew some of the most interesting intellectuals of their time, Dee's circle of influence extended far wider, to encompass many of the most talented hearts and minds of his age. Like an *éminence grise* directing operations from behind the scenes, the gaunt figure of Dr John Dee stands at the very heart of the English Renaissance of the arts and sciences that occurred during the Elizabethan era.

Dr John Dee, 1527–1608/9

✎ A Magician Born ✎

He that is a true magician, is brought forth a magician
from his Mother's Womb; and whoso is otherwise, ought
to recompense that defect of nature by education.

THOMAS RUDD, *THE NINE CELESTIAL KEYS*

Dee was born on 13 July 1527 in London, the son of a Welshman
who was a gentleman server to Henry VIII. He first attracted
attention as a precocious fifteen-year-old undergraduate of St
John's College, Cambridge, when he was already showing one of
the basic qualities needed by a magician – that of self-discipline.
For three years, so Dee says, he 'did inviolably keepe this order;
only to sleep four houres every night; to allow meate and drinke
(and some refreshing after) two houres every day; and to the
other eighteen houres all was spent in my studies and learning'.[1]
On graduating he was appointed under-reader of Greek at the
newly established Trinity College, and he was later made a
Fellow.

During his time at Cambridge he achieved notoriety – and narrowly escaped conviction for sorcery – by constructing a mechanical flying beetle for a stage production of Aristophanes' *Pax*. It was so realistic that it terrified members of the audience, who thought it the work of the devil. Dee was fascinated by mechanics and the mathematical principles behind this science. His interest in mathematics soon turned to a fascination with astronomy and astrology. Finding that England offered too narrow a perspective on the sciences, he took himself off to the University of Louvain, near Brussels – one of the finest in Europe. It was a smart move. The scientific world was buzzing with Copernicus's heretical notion that the sun, not the earth, was the centre of the heavens and Dee found a ready ally in the famous mapmaker, Gerald Mercator.

All his life Dee combined a passion for the sciences with an interest in magic. Even as he studied navigation with the Dutch geographer Gemma Frisius or discussed cartography with Mercator, he was preoccupied with his studies of alchemy and Hermeticism – subjects he had begun to research while at Cambridge.

During the two years he spent at Louvain he included law in his studies, 'for recreation', as he put it, and also wrote a work in twenty-four books entitled *Mercurius Coelestis* – never published and now lost. He visited Antwerp and the court of Charles V in Brussels, but it was in Paris that he achieved fame, with his lectures proving so popular that many students were forced to stand outside a packed hall and listen through the windows. By this time Dee was only twenty-three, but even then he was being sought out by some of Europe's leading intellectuals. Returning to England, filled with inspiration from his discussions with mathematicians, philosophers, cabbalists and classicists, he was introduced to King Edward VI, received the patronage of the Earl of Pembroke and began – deliberately or not – his work of influencing the English Renaissance.

He joined the household of the Lord Protector, the Duke of Northumberland, and tutored the duke's children. These included Robert Dudley, the Earl of Leicester, who was to become one of the country's greatest patrons of learning, and a favourite and

Robert Dudley, Earl of Leicester, 1532–1588.

rumoured lover of Queen Elizabeth. But until Elizabeth gained the throne, Dee suffered at her half-sister's hands when she succeeded Edward. 'Bloody Mary', as she became known after having nearly 300 Protestants burnt at the stake, had Dee arrested in 1555. He had drawn up astrological charts of the Queen and Princess Elizabeth, and was charged with 'lewde vayne practices of caculing and conjuring' to enchant Queen Mary.[2] After months in prison he was released without conviction.

Three years later Mary died and Dee was welcomed at Elizabeth's court. He became a favourite of the new queen, who called him 'her philosopher' and asked him to calculate the most astrologically propitious day for her coronation. A frequent visitor to the palace, he was given a wide range of tasks to perform,

Elizabeth I, 1533–1603.

including that of reforming the Julian calendar for England and, when an image of the Queen was found in Lincoln's Inn Fields with a pin thrust into its heart, of counteracting any evil that might have been directed towards her.

Now Dee was able to pursue his fascination for magic without fear of prosecution. Over the next few years we find him travelling often through Europe, building up his library from the flood of ancient texts or 'grimoires' (see the box overleaf) that emerged with the Reformation, and studying languages and cryptography. It was probably around this time that he started working for the spy network of his friend, Sir Francis Walsingham, in which it is suggested he had the code number 007.[3]

Sir Francis Walsingham by Willem and Magdalena de Passe, 1620.

During this time Dee's relationship with Elizabeth continued to flourish and he dedicated his new book, written over thirteen days in Antwerp in 1564, to his sovereign. It was entitled *The Monad, Hieroglyphically, Mathematically, Magically, Cabbalistically and Anagogically Explained*. In its frontispiece Dee wrote: 'Who does not understand should either learn, or be silent.' And although the book became famous, the response of the academic world was, indeed, silence – the book was ignored.

What is a Grimoire?

A Grimoire (derived from the Old French 'grammaire' – grammar, in other words a system of language) is a sorcerer's ritual handbook used for invoking angels or evoking spirits. Grimoires usually contain incantations, sigils, magical descriptions and lists of the spirits to be invoked for specific purposes. They may also feature 'Tables of Correspondences', showing how to enhance the ritual with colours, music, astrological conjunctions, herbs and alchemical potions.

Grimoires such as the famous *Key of Solomon*, the *Goetia* or the *Grimorium Verum*, represent a continuity of magical practice over a thousand years old, although there are many different versions of the texts, each with missing elements. Ancient grimoires survive in libraries, and much work has been done recently to restore them to their original forms.

One of the most influential grimoires has been *The Sacred Magic of Abramelin the Mage*, which seems to date from the fifteenth century. In this magician's manual, an elaborate ritual procedure is described which takes eighteen months to complete. Designed to give the practitioner the 'knowledge and conversation' of their 'Holy Guardian Angel', the 'Abramelin Operation' has been attempted by a number of modern magicians, most notably Aleister Crowley. This, and many other grimoires, can now be read on the internet at www.esotericarchives.com

✎ The Circle of Influence Widens ✎

Behind the scenes, however, Dee's influence was growing. As well as tutoring the Earl of Leicester, Dee taught the earl's favourite nephew, Philip Sidney, becoming an intimate associate of the Sidney family and their friends. It seems likely that Sidney's sister Mary received instruction from Dee. Her laboratory assistant at Wilton House, Adrian Gilbert, was a close friend of the wizard.

It was through the 'Sidney circle' that Dee exerted much of his influence. It numbered many intimates of the Queen, such as the Earl of Leicester, Sir Walter Raleigh and Sir Francis Walsingham, whose daughter Frances married Philip Sidney. In a manner entirely fitting with magic's long preoccupation with language and poetry, something we first detect in the Celtic bards, a number of Sidney's friends – including Edmund Spenser, author of the epic poem *The Faerie Queene* – were united in an informal association they called the 'Areopagus', which was concerned with reviving the use of measured verse. They, along with Dee, were inspired by the theory of musico-magic, developed by the Renaissance magician Marsilio Ficino, which held that chanting verses of perfectly written poetry could attract beneficent planetary influences.

Sir Philip Sidney, 1576, artist unknown.

Despite Dee's wide circle of friends and admirers, however, and the obvious affection of the Queen for her 'pet magician', circumstances conspired to ensure that Dee remained permanently short of funds. Lacking independent means, he moved into his mother's house at Mortlake in the 1560s, remaining there not only after her death in 1579 but for much of the rest of his life. There he built up a massive library and laboratory, which became a place of pilgrimage for scholars from across the Continent,

Sir Walter Raleigh. Portrait by Nicholas Hilliard, c.1585.

as well as his base for pursuing his magical studies. It was here that Dee, settled at last, wrote a number of important papers including a detailed analysis of Elizabethan England.

He became interested in, amongst other things, dowsing for treasure, and proposed to the government that, in return for half the spoils, he should be permitted to seek treasure on the Queen's behalf, giving him a monopoly over the activity. Unsurprisingly, he was turned down.

Dee's knowledge of mapping, learnt in the Lowlands, also became useful, and he helped plan the route of various expeditions to find a northern route to China. His position as a major influence on world events from behind the scenes is perhaps most clearly seen in the way he provided the ideological underpinning for the concept of the British Empire. He was the first person to use that term when he proposed to the Queen that England should challenge Spain's right to the new territories and build her own empire based on sea power.

He even offered counsel when the Spanish Armada threatened the country, predicting its destruction by storms. When his prediction came true, there were some who said the wizard had conjured up the storms himself.

Who knows what important political future Dee might have had if he had kept to this direction, as his relationship with the Queen was now at its strongest, and she often came to visit him at Mortlake, on one occasion accompanied by her court on her royal barge. A new enthusiasm, however, began to monopolise Dee's energies. Forever a seeker after Truth, he became convinced that the only way he could obtain the knowledge he sought would be not through science or reason, but through making contact with superhuman intelligences. The Dee expert, Rufus Harrington, explains the reasoning behind this ambition:

> The great sixteenth-century thinkers were intrigued by what we call today the 'Three World Philosophy'. This combined a physical model of the cosmos and a metaphysical map representing the relationship between humanity and the Divine. This vision of God's creation placed the earth at the centre of the cosmos as the terrestrial sphere, the realm of the elements of Fire, Air, Water and Earth. Turning around the terrestrial sphere was the celestial realm of the planets and the wheel of the fixed stars, and beyond that the super-celestial realm, a darkness that stretched into infinity.
>
> These three worlds were manifestations of the Divine, and they believed that communication with the Divine could be achieved by undertaking a journey from the terrestrial world, through the celestial world to the mysteries of the super-celestial realm beyond the circle of the fixed stars. The ambition they cradled was to use such a journey to expand their consciousness and understand all the mysteries of Creation, and for Dee it is clear that this was his mission – to seek communion with the Divine, 'to speak with God and his Angels'.

☙ Conversing with Angels ❧

If he was to achieve this communion, Dee decided that he would have to discover the language used by the Old Testament prophet Enoch, since, according to the Bible, Enoch was able to talk to God directly. Cabbalistic sources stated that Enoch lived for 365 years and then became the Angel Metatron. Here was proof for Dee that it was possible to speak to God, even to achieve angelic status. Believing that the language Enoch used had been destroyed with the Tower of Babel, he set about trying to rediscover it.

He decided that the magical technique of 'scrying' would be

the most effective way of attempting to obtain this information. Scrying was a favourite technique of the popular magicians known as cunning-folk who plied their trade throughout Britain during the Elizabethan era, and is familiar to us all in the image of the fortune-teller with her crystal ball. Gazing on to a reflective surface such as a mirror or bowl of water, the scryer would report visions that revealed the whereabouts of stolen goods, the identity of thieves, or glimpses of the spirit world and its inhabitants.

As Dee could see no visions when scrying himself, he began experimenting with people who claimed they possessed the skill. After limited success with several scryers, he met a man in 1582 whose destiny became intimately entwined with his own.

Edward Kelley was peculiar-looking. Often wearing a cowl to disguise the fact that his ears had been lopped, supposedly for forging coins, he was also crippled. Furthermore, he was rumoured to have dug up corpses for use in magical practices. He was, however, gifted in the art of scrying, and while some believe he was a charlatan who tricked Dee, others feel he was an extraordinarily talented psychic, with the twentieth-century magician Aleister Crowley even claiming to be his reincarnation.

Edward Kelley, 1555–1597.

On being invited to scry by Dee, at his very first attempt Kelley succeeded in summoning the Archangel Uriel, dressed in purple and gold. Soon an even more powerful being, the Archangel Michael, appeared, and Dee's magical researches were catapulted into top gear.

The agenda for future contact with the angels was set by Michael. Dee was to be taught the original language of fire spoken by these celestial beings. But first a complex set of 'Magical Tables' was revealed, which linked the forty-nine different angel functionaries to different aspects of life, such as wisdom or commerce (in much the same way as the notion of 'houses' works in astrology). The minutiae given in each of the forty-nine cells of the tables was extraordinary – and Dee copied down everything meticulously in his diaries.

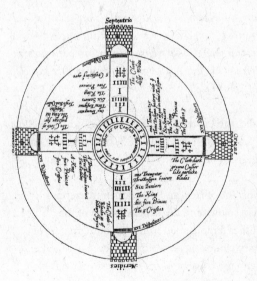

A gold disc, now in the British Museum, engraved with the 'Vision of Four Castles' experienced by Dee and Kelley in Krakow in 1584.

In further scrying sessions the angelic language was dictated by Kelley to Dee, soon to be accompanied by other revelations. The pair, inspired by the angelic advice, began looking around England for sites of buried Danish treasure.

After scrying revealed one such site, Kelley was sent off in March 1583 on an expedition to recover the treasure. Dee was overjoyed when he returned from Blockley, in the Cotswolds, with a 'certayne moniment of a boke' on magic and alchemy. It was allegedly written by St Dunstan, the tenth-century Abbot of Glastonbury, who some believed was an alchemist. Kelley claimed to have found the book on Northwick Hill, to the north-west of Blockley, together with a quantity of red earth and a scroll containing a diagram or map of ten locations of buried treasure, of which details were given in a strange cipher. A local man, Master John Husey, had assisted Kelley and they had discovered the site 'by the direction and leading of some such spirituall creature'.[4]

ROBIN COUSINS – *Dee's Lost Treasure*

Robin Cousins was born in Norfolk into a family that always had psychic abilities. Now retired from a career in information science and librarianship, he has researched Dee's treasure-hunting activities in detail and is well known for his lectures about the magician's travels, titled 'In the footsteps of John Dee'.

Dee quickly guessed the cipher on the scroll found by Kelley to be encrypted Latin. On 11 April 1583, he broke the code, which revealed the diagram to be:

A table of the locations, the objects and the hidden treasure of Menaban of Gordanili, soldier and the expelled King of the Danes and of many other famous men from the southern part of Britain near the military camps there, which I ordered here to be hidden and buried, with the consent of those closest to me, for the benefit and advantage of those of us returning at some future time. Which [table] having been interpreted, they may easily bring what was hidden to light.
     The ten places decipher as:

1. Gilds cros hic o . . . meridioonali. ot on. 2. BlankisSuterscroces. 3. Marsars got cros. 4. Huteoscros. 5.

Fledsgrenul. 6. Mons Mene. 7. Mounteglesarnid. 8. Lansapant.
9. Cortsnelds. 10. Mnrrmerse.

The names appear corrupted, which unfortunately makes their identification difficult today. Illustrations on the map depict a number of traditional hiding places for treasure, including five village crosses, three mounds or hills, two fields and at least six trees. The mass destruction of ancient crosses in the pursuit of treasure and, later, by Parliamentary decree in the 1640s, makes the treasure hunter's task difficult, but two possible locations can be identified.

Huteos or Huet's Cross was probably located on Northwick Hill. Dee notes in his diary on 23 March 1583 that the hill was where the map and the other items were found, but on 11 April he refers to them being discovered at the cross. The sketch of the Huteos Cross reveals that it was already severely damaged with only part of the shaft remaining. Unsurprisingly, not even the slightest fragment is traceable in the area today, but the find was undoubtedly the 'treasure' of Huteos Cross.

The other site on the map located with certainty is Mons Mene, now known as Meon Hill in south Warwickshire on the north-eastern edge of the Cotswolds near Mickleton. Unlike the other places, the hill is easily traceable in the *Concise Oxford Dictionary of English Place-Names*. Folklore relates that Meon Hill itself was supposedly created by the devil. The escarpment has long been a meeting place for witches' covens, and a silent black dog (the Keeper of the Treasure?) is traditionally said to haunt the hill. Treasure of sorts was actually found there in 1824, when a hoard of 394 iron currency bars was unearthed near the centre.

Meon Hill is notorious for the murder of Charles Walton, a hedge-trimmer from nearby Lower Quinton, who as a boy claimed to have seen the ghostly hound at least nine times. At the age of seventy-four, Walton was found slaughtered on the lower slopes of the hill on 14 February 1945, apparently as a ritual sacrifice for St Valentine's Day. It was said that he had paranormal powers and had carried a small black scrying stone concealed in his pocket watch. Other tales had him casting spells and vindictively blighting the crops. Walton was supposedly killed in order to release people from his enchantments. Not only was his throat cut by a billhook, but a crude cross had also been slashed on his chest and he had been pinned to the ground with a pitchfork through his neck, thereby allowing his blood to flow freely and revitalise the earth.

Police investigations drew a blank. The villagers were silent on the matter and the murder remains unsolved to this day.

Obtaining the treasure on the map was not as simple as Dee had first thought. With Kelley as his scryer, Dee consulted the angels for advice with increasing regularity. They counselled him to avoid trouble with the law by digging up just the red earth from each site, which could later, by alchemical means, be used to make gold. Little more is heard of the treasure, although some of the red earth from Northwick Hill was used by Kelley in Prague to convince the Emperor of his alchemical powers.

The failure of Kelley's treasure-hunt to find a source of funds undoubtedly depressed Dee, but help was at hand in the shape of an eccentric Polish adventurer, Prince Albert Laski.

In June 1583, the Polish prince was accompanied by Sir Philip Sidney to Oxford, where – on the orders of the Queen – he was lavishly entertained with plays, banquets and public disputations with, amongst others, the Italian philosopher and mage Giordano Bruno who was then visiting the city, effectively in an attempt to revive the magical religion of ancient Egypt.[5]

On their way back from Oxford, Sidney called on his friend Dee in Mortlake, bringing with him the Polish prince, and bearing tales of Bruno and his theories. By this time Dee was already uncertain about his future within the spy-ridden Elizabethan court and he was also worried about his chronic lack of funds. His angelic helpers encouraged him in his concerns, and the appearance of Laski proved the catalyst for Dee's greatest adventure – covertly conveying himself, Kelley, both their families and the choicest books in his library, first to Poland and then to Prague, to meet the Holy Roman Emperor. Once all was ready, the expedition set sail in conditions of great secrecy, passing in two 'wherries' or barges down the Thames in the middle of the night, and then embarking at Greenwich on to a large ship for the crossing to Holland on the night of 28 September 1584.

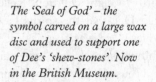

The 'Seal of God' – the symbol carved on a large wax disc and used to support one of Dee's 'shew-stones'. Now in the British Museum.

Poland was to prove only a temporary stop and soon the expedition continued to Prague, then the capital of Bohemia and ruled by the Holy Roman Emperor, Rudolph II. Dee and Kelley were received warmly and enjoyed a personal audience with the Emperor, but soon court politics and Dee's unwillingness to hand over his secret angelic writings began to sour the relationship. Not in the least discouraged, Dee and Kelley continued their work and were astonished to be told by a spirit that they would now receive the ultimate revelation in a completely new angelic language, but the price of this knowledge was to be the burning of all their records to date. With considerable trepidation Dee committed twenty-eight volumes of his precious notes to the flames. Shortly afterwards, Kelley declared a miracle, restoring the papers undamaged to Dee. He had found them, he said, 'in the very mouth of the furnace'.

The Pope, scandalised by all he heard about this pair of

Englishmen, demanded their extradition to Rome. Rudolph banished Dee and Kelley from the Holy Roman Empire, but they found a protector in Count William Rosenberg, a patron of alchemy, who put them to work in his laboratories in the quiet village of Trebon in southern Bohemia. Kelley, who had always been more interested in alchemy than Dee, now began experiments into the nature of the Philosophers' Stone, using the 'red earth' he had found in England.

For a time Dee and Kelley worked together amicably and continued their scrying conversations with the angels, until there came an episode that destroyed their partnership. Kelley had never been able to father children with his wife Joanna, nor was their marriage a good one. Dee's wife Jane, however, had given birth to eight children. Kelley clearly took a fancy to Jane and told Dee that the spirits had requested they share each other's wives. Dee was sceptical at first, and Jane herself was far from enthusiastic. 'I trust,' she said, 'that though I give myselfe thus to be used, that God will turn me into a stone before he would suffer me in my obedience to receive any shame or inconvenience.'[6] Eventually, however, she agreed to the arrangement, but this quickly led to a breakdown in their friendship and a parting of the ways when Kelley took himself off to Prague to seek his fortune on his own.

For a while, Kelley's reputation as an alchemist brought him wealth, royal patronage and the ownership of large estates until, like so many of his kind, he failed to deliver on his promises. He was imprisoned in a local castle and in 1597 died whilst trying to escape. Today a statue of Kelley stands in the grounds of the castle, with another in the wax museum in Prague, where there is a pub called Magister Kelly, that serves drinks in alchemical retorts.

Separated from Kelley and summoned home by the Queen, Dee returned to England with his wife and children. On 15 December 1589, after six years in Bohemia, they arrived back at his house in Mortlake, only to receive an unpleasant shock. The house, and in particular Dee's library and laboratories, had been ransacked. At least five hundred books had been stolen, his reading room had been stripped of its furniture, and most of his scientific instruments had been taken including two globes given to him by Mercator. Some histories recount that the house was ransacked by an angry mob, but it seems that in reality it was stripped of its assets by people known to Dee.[7]

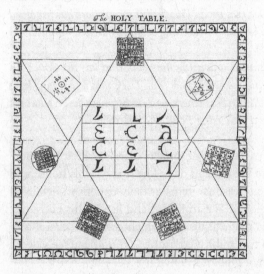

The design for Dee's 'Table of Practice'. The crystal ball or mirror was placed at the centre. The letters displayed are Enochian.

Although England's greatest wizard lived for another two decades, the story of these final years is not a happy one. Even though the Queen granted him a living by appointing him warden of Christ's College in Manchester, he found the college inhospitable and he was separated from his old home in Mortlake. Most of his friends were now very old or dead, and amongst his countrymen he had acquired a dubious reputation for being a conjuror of spirits. His long-suffering wife Jane died from the plague, as did five of his children. The death of Elizabeth in 1603 and the crowning of James I led Dee to return to London in the hope of a new beginning, but it was not to be. He died at Mortlake in 1608 or early 1609.

STEPHEN SKINNER

Stephen Skinner is one of the foremost experts in the traditional magical techniques used by John Dee. He was the first to republish Dee's original diaries and, together with co-author David Rankine, he restored to their original complete form many of the magical manuals, or 'grimoires', that Dee had used. This painstaking effort has involved more than thirty-five years of researching original magical manuscripts all over Europe.

Stephen is also a skilled practising magician and has developed his own approach to getting the best results from Dee's magic. He now lives most of the year in Malaysia, where he has become the best-known non-Asian to become a practising Feng Shui master.

D r John Dee kept two sets of parallel diaries, which have survived largely to the present day. The first was his household diary, recording such personal items as daily expenses, details of his visits to the Queen at Westminster, and lists of his accounts. The second was his magical diaries, which come in several sections, one of which was published in the 1660s after Dee's death by Meric Casaubon, a Doctor in Divinity.

The only copies available in the 1970s were in major libraries or enormously expensive, so I decided to produce a facsimile edition, which was published in 1974. It was entitled: *A True and Faithful Relation of what passed between Dr. John Dee (A Mathematician of great fame in Queen Elizabeth and King James their Reignes) and some spirits: tending (had it succeeded) to a general alteration of most states and kingdoms and with a preface confirming the reality (as to the point of spirits) of this relation: and shewing severall good uses that a sober Christian may make of all – by Meric Casaubon DD.* This must be one of the longest book titles in history, but it does describe accurately the challenge of interpreting Dee's work.

Dee was an extraordinary intellectual talent – for example, he was the first man to collaborate on the translation of the works of

Euclid from the original Greek to English, bringing the basis of geometry to England in a way that is still valid today – but, in the magical sphere, he quickly tired of academic learning and wanted concrete results. He was hampered in this by his own personal weakness in psychic skills, as well as by the inconsistencies and gaps in the published materials that had emerged after 1,300 years of Church repression since the great days of the Hermetic and Neoplatonist philosophers who had developed many of the practical techniques. Much of this magical lore is contained in grimoires – ancient magical manuals, such as *The Key of Solomon*.

In addition, there is a need for an invocational language to communicate with the angels and spirits that you wish to summon. Many of the ancient magicians used Latin, Greek and Hebrew for this purpose, but Dee decided to develop his own 'Enochian' language, named after the prophet Enoch of the Old Testament, who was reputed to be able to speak with the angels. When I started my work, considerable doubts were aired as to whether Dee's Enochian was in fact a language at all, rather than a made-up jumble of words.

Luckily, at about this time, Donald Laycock, a Professor of Linguistics at Canberra University, came to England and did an analysis, which proved to his satisfaction that the Enochian was a proper language with real syntax. To help others in their studies of the Enochian, I then published a complete Enochian dictionary, which lists the original words that Dee used in his manuscripts, as well as later misspellings by Aleister Crowley and the Golden Dawn. This dictionary is still used in the Reading Rooms of the British Library.

Dee's practical magic was firmly rooted in the grimoires known to have been in his library. The 'Magical Table', which he and Kelley used, was traditional grimoire apparatus, a kind of portable altar first mentioned in the thirteenth century. He used the *Liber Juratus*, also called the *Sacred Book*, written by the Greek Honorius in the early thirteenth century, to create his most vital sigil – or magical symbol, the *Sigullum Dei Aemeth*, a seven-sided figure full of spirit names, which then was cast in wax and used on his Magical Table. The same design was also used to insulate the table legs from the earth and support the scrying crystal. He used silk, which may have produced some sort of electrostatic effect. Dee would start each magical session with long prayers, which were very similar to the invocations in the grimoires.

After Dee's death, one of the first people to attempt to use his system was the little-known but important magician Thomas Rudd (1583–1656) who knew Dee, and who attempted a synthesis of his Enochian, together with the *Goetia*, one of the most important grimoires of the seventeenth century. It is assumed by many people that Dee simply created all his practical magic through Kelley's scrying, but this is untrue. There is no doubt that Dee already had a substantial amount of grimoire material in his extensive library before he met Kelley, and was already using it himself in a practical way, although he would have been very careful to avoid being caught using such 'demonic' material.

Producing a complete set of the original grimoires used by Dee has been a longer task, and my objective is to revise and republish most of the important ones. We completed Rudd's *Goetia* recently. It has taken a huge amount of time and research to synthesise this work since there are over 140 different manuscript versions of *The Key of Solomon*, in which the Goetia is found, but it is now complete and has just been published (*The Goetia of Dr Rudd: The Angels and Demons of Liber Malorum Spirituum Seu Goetia Lemegeton Clavicula Salomonis with a study of the techniques of evocation*, Golden Hoard Press *2007*).

The Key of Solomon, which probably originated from Byzantine Greek sources in the late fourteenth century, was translated into Latin, then into Italian, French and English. Some of the most extraordinary versions were owned by French royalty just before the French Revolution. Marie Antoinette's private scribe copied several of them, but when the owners lost their heads on the guillotine the manuscripts were sold at auction and made their way to England. Here they have survived up to the present day where one can still find them, slumbering in obscure libraries, sometimes badly miscatalogued.

Of course, as Dee realised, the whole point of assembling all this magical material is the practical invocation of spirit beings, so the study of grimoires is not an abstract activity; they should be used for real. One of the reasons I live in Asia is because I have the time, space and privacy to experiment with magic. The local magicians, the 'Bomohs', are accepted as a profession, available for hire like any other, and have a long and practical continuity in their art. Gerald Gardner, who was a colonial administrator in Malaysia, brought back a lot of these practices to England and incorporated them into Wicca, as these were amongst the most functional forms of magic he learnt.

Dee is not a blip in magical history, but part of a continuity. His combination of the academic and the practical approach is exactly what we need today. In the West, the true magicians are still groping a lot in the dark because, despite Dee's legacy, we have a lack of continuity in practice. The real breakthroughs are made by a handful of solo magicians working by themselves or with a few friends. There are temples, but they are mainly on Golden Dawn lines, obsessed with Masonic-type rituals of initiation and staged development, which were originated by Freemasons and the founders of the Golden Dawn. This approach often results in nothing more than formulaic ritual; with no spiritual creature manifesting itself in the glasses or triangles, it isn't really magic.

Kelley might have been a rogue and a villain, but he had genuine magical talent and seemed to have been a reasonably good alchemist. There is no doubt that Dee was gullible: for example, in the way he believed in Kelley's story about the burning of the books and the mysterious finding of them again, yet together they were a strong combination of the intellectual and the empirical. Both men played a hugely important part in England's magical history, although their magical achievements may well have more in common with the more practical approach taken in the East than with the formal Masonic-style rituals of the Golden Dawn and other, similar, latter-day magical orders.

Read about this Period in Fiction

The House of Dr Dee, Peter Ackroyd (Hamish Hamilton, 1993)
Set in modern and Elizabethan times, Dr Dee narrates much of the book, imbuing it with a hazy focus on a glittering other world of magic and alchemy, strange impressions from the alchemist's laboratory and an unfolding magical process.

The Angel of the Western Window, Gustav Meyrink (Dedalus European Classics, 1991)
This describes John Dee's and Edward Kelley's astrological and mystical experience, through the story of a descendant whose discovery of Dee's diaries leads to a search for immortality.

Aegypt, John Crowley (Overlook, 2007)
A series of four novels, sequenced around the scheme of the twelve astrological houses. In the first of the series, 'The Solitudes', an unorthodox historian and expert in ancient myths and superstition living in modern day America encounters the world of Dee. 'The Solitudes' helped earn Crowley the American Academy of Arts and Letters Award for Literature.

The Casebook of Dr Simon Forman, Judith Cook (Headline, 1993–2003)
A series of Elizabethan historical thrillers based on the original casebook manuscripts of Forman, and containing a combination of historical and fictional characters.

❧ The School of Night, Rosicrucians ❧ and the Golden Dawn

Dare one say that the German Rosicrucian
movement reaches a peak of poetic expression in The
Tempest, *a Rosicrucian manifesto infused with the*
spirit of Dee, using theatrical parables for esoteric
communication?

FRANCES YATES, *MAJESTY AND MAGIC*
IN SHAKESPEARE'S LAST PLAYS

Even though Dee's influence declined dramatically in the closing years of his life, he succeeded in handing on his magical legacy virtually intact to a series of discerning occultists from the time of his death up until the present day.

Authors Stephen Skinner and David Rankine suggest that soon after Dee died, the magician Dr Thomas Rudd began working

Prospero and Ariel, *by William Hamilton, 1797.*

with Enochian magic, as did members of the British aristocracy, including Baron Summers, and Sir Joseph Jekyll, a Master of the Rolls, and Goodwin Wharton, a Lord of the Admiralty.[8] Historian Dame Frances Yates has advanced the theory that Dee inspired Shakespeare's figure of Prospero in *The Tempest*, and influenced Rosicrucianism, which we shall explore in Chapter 10.[10] In the seventeenth century, the Freemason, alchemist and founding member of the Royal Society, Elias Ashmole, became in many ways Dee's spiritual heir, managing to preserve for posterity many of his copious notes and diaries. And in the nineteenth century, thanks to Ashmole, the founders of the Hermetic Order of the Golden Dawn were able to include Enochian magic within their curriculum, ensuring in this way that Dee's system would survive into the twentieth century and beyond.

RUFUS HARRINGTON

Rufus Harrington is a practising psychologist and one of the foremost experts on John Dee and his Enochian magic, in which he is a High Priest with his own temple. After an early experience with Wicca, Rufus became fascinated by Dee's work and determined to restore it to its original purity. He spent three years in the British Library, painstakingly copying from Dee's original manuscript diaries, and he has built a modern Enochian practice around the results.

My first lesson in Enochian magic proved an amazing experience. The High Priest of the magical group I had joined produced a beautiful scrying mirror and set me in front of it, then invoked, using the Enochian language. As the invocation progressed, I felt as if my psyche was being warped out of its familiar shape, and the physical and magical worlds were combining. The flame of the candle in the centre of the magic circle opened like a door, becoming larger than the candle itself. The flame had become radiant, filling the temple with an ethereal light, and I was part of that light. It was like looking into the fire of God. That moment more than anything transformed my life. It was a moment of true initiation. I knew I had to learn everything about Enochian magic.

I began with the Golden Dawn's approach to the Enochian system, which uses very powerful invocations and took me into an extraordinary alternative reality. I even woke after a night of ritual to find a strange liquid oozing out of the spine of the book of invocations I had been reading. These kinds of experience convinced me that Dr Dee had discovered a powerful, tangible magic that not even the psychologists could explain, and I decided, like Dee, to find both a scientific and a magical explanation for what I was experiencing.

I determined to read Dee's own diaries, which I knew were kept in the British Library manuscripts collection, and I went on to spend the best part of three years working on his original manuscripts. The experience was wonderful: having delivered to your desk thick, leather-bound books of magic that come straight out of every magical film you have ever seen – but these are real and contain John Dee's original, handwritten diaries, over four hundred years old.

As my research progressed I discovered that enough of Dee's diaries had survived to reconstruct the Enochia in its original form as given to Dee and Kelley. I found myself involved in an act of re-creation. It was easy to imagine myself with Dee and Kelley in their rooms at Mortlake, at work with them at the scrying altar. Dee would create the invocational atmosphere through intense prayer; then Kelley would use the scrying crystal to see the visions described in the very diaries I was now reading. It was like being in a time machine.

The Enochian system is deeply alchemical. It starts with the base metal of your consciousness and begins to transform it. My work with the Enochia was deeply woven with the quest to seek the knowledge and conversation of the Holy Guardian Angel. With fellow magicians I had hired a small castle in Wales. During a ceremony on the top of a tower, under the night sky as a storm gathered about us, I invoked my Holy Guardian Angel, which descended upon me, even spelling out its name, as the lightning shattered the darkness.

This experience activated a fundamental alchemical process in my psyche. I began a journey into the interior of my being, to the underworld, which was mirrored in my external life by my moving to Australia – literally to the land Down Under. As in a shamanic journey, I was travelling into the underworld, but, as with shamanism, there are physical side effects and I became increasingly ill. My body and my psyche were collapsing and even the doctors could not find what was wrong with me. In sheer desperation at the darkest point I prayed for help and had a vision of the Goddess, who shed a single tear, which washed over me and brought an indescribable sense of peace. It proved the turning point. I understand now that I was in the classic transformational phase of alchemy, passing through the 'Nigredo' – the darkness – into the 'Albedo' – the light.

My experiences armed me spiritually and made me realise that I could now help people on their own spiritual quests, so I returned to England and got involved with the pagan movement, then in its infancy. I also trained as a psychotherapist, and working first in the NHS, and then in private practice in Harley Street. Psychology has provided me with wonderful insights, but it in no way explains away the profound reality of magic. The inner world of the psyche and the outer world, seen as well as unseen, are connected, and the archetypes and spirits you encounter there can be confusing and threatening, but in facing these we grow both psychologically and spiritually.

The Enochia opens you up to the experience of other worlds, other levels of intelligence, but, as Dee and Kelley knew only too well, it is not a plaything. It is one of the deepest systems of magic. I teach that the dangers of magic are real and should not be minimised, but neither should the adventure and the potential of the magical arts. We are on an extraordinary journey. And we should thank Dee and Kelley for showing us the way.

If you stand in the British Museum today and half close your eyes as you gaze at the impressive wax seals and the shiny surface of Dee's obsidian mirror, perhaps for a moment you will be carried back in time until you see the old wizard in his study in Mortlake, kneeling in prayer before his scrying table, while Kelley gazes into the mirror. Candles sputter and burn, and slowly out of the surrounding darkness figures emerge into the candlelight – this time not of angels or archangels, but of those who have been influenced by Dee.

There is Sir Francis Bacon, Lord Chancellor, who visited the older Dee in Mortlake when he was a young man. Behind him stands Elizabeth in regal splendour. The poets Spenser and Sidney step forth from the shadows now, as do Walsingham and Raleigh, and other friends of Dee, who some say formed 'The School of Night' – a secret society of those who dared to think for themselves. His son Arthur is here, too, who like his father travelled east, to act as physician to the tsar of Russia for eighteen years. Still more come – magicians Thomas Rudd and Baron Summers; Kelley, his old companion, reconciled to him at last; Elias Ashmole, who a century later interviewed Dee's grandson while preparing to write his biography. And here too are all those occultists who in the nineteenth and twentieth centuries worked with Dee's Enochian system of magic: the founders of the Hermetic Order of the Golden Dawn – Wynne Westcott and MacGregor Mathers – and the 'Great Beast' Aleister Crowley, who so admired Kelley. Then, as swiftly as they came, the figures disappear, and you find yourself once more standing beside the glass case in the museum.

The language of the angels, brought to the world by Dee and Kelley, remains as mysterious today as ever, and whether it is really derived from the celestial realm we may never know, but what is certain is that for those practitioners determined enough to master its intricacies, it offers a powerful system of magical practice that has become one of the cornerstones of English magic. Perhaps the angels really did talk to Dee and Kelley all those years ago in Mortlake and Bohemia.[10]

SIMON FORMAN, 1552–1611

One of the most notorious magicians of the Elizabethan era was Simon Forman, who practised medical astrology in London during a time when it was racked by plague.

Born in Quidhampton, Wiltshire, in 1552, Forman spent an unhappy year at Magdalen College, Oxford, before working as a teacher in Salisbury. In 1592 he moved to London and set up a medical practice in Billingsgate, using astrology both for diagnosis and for determining when to administer remedies. When the plague struck, he stayed put, unlike many of the city's doctors, and it is said that he cured both himself and many patients of the dreaded illness. As a result his fame grew until he came to the notice of the Royal College of Physicians, which decided to fine him for practising without a licence. Nine months later a patient of his died after taking his medicine and Forman was jailed briefly. After seven years of wrangling he finally managed to obtain a licence from Cambridge University.

Forman had the same desire as Dee – to communicate with the spirit world – but he never succeeded. On several occasions he believed he had summoned the spirit of a black dog, but nothing else, and he was similarly unsuccessful in his alchemical work. He was never able to produce the Philosopher's Stone.

Despite these failures, his great contribution to the story of English magic can be found safely housed in the Bodleian Library in Oxford, where 15,000 pages of manuscript written by Forman detail his work with thousands of clients, the rules of his 'astrological physic', his alchemical experiments and even the intricacies of his love life. Most of these papers were donated to Oxford by that great Renaissance mage and antiquarian, Elias Ashmole. This treasure trove was appreciated only in the nineteenth century, when it was realised that Forman's notes contained perhaps the sole, authentic, contemporary account of performances of Shakespeare's plays at the Globe Theatre, although their authenticity has been questioned by some scholars.

A week before his death in 1611, Forman prophesied to his wife that he would die. The astrologer William Lilly recorded how he fell off a boat as he crossed the Thames. Enigmatically, his last words before he drowned were: 'An impost, an impost!' Four years later, when Lady Essex was accused of murdering Sir Thomas Overbury, Forman's wife was called to testify and his records were examined by the court. Lady Essex had consulted the wizard to obtain magical help in rendering her husband impotent, so that she could obtain an annulment and marry the man she really loved – Robert Carr, Earl of Somerset. Overbury had advised Carr against the liaison, thus becoming the target of Lady Essex's hatred. She was accused of arranging for him to be poisoned and, although convicted, was spared execution. She was banned from court, then later pardoned. The judge in the trial denounced Forman as 'a devil' – tarnishing for posterity the reputation of a man who until that time had been seen as a gifted healer and astrologer.

◉ *How to Perform Renaissance Astrological Magic*

Natural magic depended on a belief that the effluvia of the celestial bodies affected the lower world. Hermetic philosophers viewed the stars as superior organisms through which God channelled his powers.

PETER J. FRENCH, *JOHN DEE: THE WORLD OF AN ELIZABETHAN MAGUS*

 The very earliest magicians of prehistory were sensitive to the power of the night sky and the light of the moon and stars that slowly move across it. As astronomical and astrological lore began to evolve through the second and first millennia BC, the megalith builders of Britain and Europe ensured that much of this lore was preserved in the great stone circles and barrows they erected. Marking the rising and setting of stars as well as of the sun and moon, their monuments stand as a testament to our ancestors' belief in the significance of heavenly influences.

Celtic and Saxon sorcerers picked the plants they needed for their spells and cures in accordance with their knowledge of star lore, as did the later healers and magicians of the Middle Ages. By the Elizabethan period, the influence of the Renaissance was in full swing as hermetic and astrological texts from the Continent, and Italy in particular, circulated in Britain.

Elizabethan magicians such as John Dee and Simon Forman were steeped in an understanding and practice of the art. Although much study is needed to become an astrologer today, it is still possible to experiment easily with one of the most central ideas of magical astrology: that planetary influences can be encouraged within our lives.

☉ *An Experiment in Astrological Magic*

As above, so below.

HERMES TRISMEGISTUS, *THE EMERALD TABLET*

Astrology is based upon the idea that planets, and their relationship to each other in the sky, influence our personality and actions – even our destiny. Renaissance astrologers believed that by using the magical 'law of correspondences' they could attract favourable influences into their lives. This law of correspondences, or sympathy, is based on the idea that like attracts like, and so by surrounding themselves with sympathetic sights, sounds and smells, and by performing ceremonies with these ingredients, magicians believed it was possible to change their fate and character.

It may seem far-fetched to suggest that one's fate can be altered by such behaviour, but in reality the way our lives unfold is often determined by our character and how we react to circumstances. If we are able to make even small changes to the way we respond to events, our experience of life will change. Certain things will turn out differently, and in this way we will have 'altered destiny'.

If you are willing to try a small experiment using these ideas of astrological magic to see whether they have a positive effect on your life, take the following five steps:

1. Determine your sun sign. Most people know their sign of the zodiac, but if you don't, consult this chart. If your birthday falls within the dates specified, that's your sign.

♈	**Aries**	21 March–20 April. Planetary ruler: Mars
♉	**Taurus**	21 April–21 May. Planetary ruler: Venus
♊	**Gemini**	22 May–21 June. Planetary ruler: Mercury
♋	**Cancer**	22 June–22 July. Planetary ruler: Moon
♌	**Leo**	23 July–21 August. Planetary ruler: Sun
♍	**Virgo**	22 August–23 September. Planetary ruler: Mercury
♎	**Libra**	24 September–23 October. Planetary ruler: Venus
♏	**Scorpio**	24 October–22 November. Planetary ruler: Mars
♐	**Sagittarius**	23 November–22 December. Planetary ruler: Jupiter
♑	**Capricorn**	23 December–20 January. Planetary ruler: Saturn
♒	**Aquarius**	21 January–19 February. Planetary ruler: Saturn
♓	**Pisces**	20 February–20 March. Planetary ruler: Jupiter

2. Each of these signs is 'ruled' by a planet, whose influence is said to affect your personality and is listed in the chart above.

In the Renaissance, the outer planets of Neptune, Uranus and Pluto had not yet been discovered. Today most astrologers assign Pluto's influence to Scorpio,

Uranus's to Aquarius and Neptune's to Pisces. But some astrologers stick to the traditional way of using just seven planets, and we shall too.

See whether you can identify the effects of your planetary ruler on your character:

Mars On the positive side, Mars is believed to influence you to be brave, gallant, enterprising, energetic and independent. On the negative side, Mars is believed to influence you to be destructive, egotistic, coarse, cruel and quarrelsome.

Venus On the positive side, Venus is believed to influence you to be loving, cheerful, friendly, kindly, poetic, artistic and harmonious. On the negative side, Venus is believed to influence you to be sentimental, vain, lazy, lustful and vulgar.

Mercury On the positive side, Mercury is believed to influence you to be witty, literary, subtle, brilliant and sensitive. On the negative side, Mercury is believed to influence you to be unprincipled, worrying, conceited and gossip-prone.

Moon On the positive side, the Moon is believed to influence you to be magnetic, peace-loving, maternal and psychic. On the negative side, the Moon is believed to influence you to be frivolous, capricious, procrastinating and lazy.

Sun On the positive side, the Sun is believed to influence you to be dignified, vital, ambitious, optimistic, constructive and a lover of education. On the negative side, the Sun is believed to influence you to be ostentatious, pompous, despotic and lacking in ambition.

Saturn On the positive side, Saturn is believed to influence you to be faithful, analytical, systematic, tactful, responsible and studious. On the negative side, Saturn is believed to influence you to be pessimistic, secretive, avaricious, fatalistic and jealous.

Jupiter On the positive side, Jupiter is believed to influence you to be benevolent, wise, just, popular, magnanimous and sympathetic. On the negative side, Jupiter is believed to influence you to be extravagant, dissipated, fanatical, self-indulgent and hypocritical.

---

3. Decide which positive influence you would like to encourage in your personality. This could come from the planetary ruler of your star sign, or from another planet.

4. Now look at the list of traditional correspondences in the chart opposite and gather as many items as you can that are associated with the planet whose influence you wish to attract.

5. The magic itself is then simple: with the clear intention to attract the positive energy of the planet you have chosen, use as many of the items associated with the planet as possible. In other words, wear its colour, use its scent, drink tea made with the herbs it rules, listen to its music and so on. Do this for as long as you can – starting on the day of the week ruled by the planet, and continuing for perhaps three days or even a week – and then see whether you notice any effects in your life.

A Capricorn, for example, who feels the influence of her sign's planetary ruler Saturn strongly in her life, might be aware of her tendency to be responsible and studious, but also to suffer from a sense of pessimism

Table of Astrological Correspondences

Planet	Day of Week	Colour	Metal	Stone/s	Scent	Food	Herb/s	Flower/s	Essential Oils
Sun	Sunday	yellow	gold	amber ruby topaz	frankincense	honey grapes oranges cinnamon saffron	St John's wort	sunflowers daffodils	cedarwood neroli rosemary
Moon	Monday	white	silver	moonstone	camphor	nutmeg lettuce	lemon balm	lilies	jasmine lemon sandalwood
Mars	Tuesday	red	iron	malachite red hematite	hyacinth basil garlic	ginger onions mustard	bryony nettle	juniper	basil coriander ginger
Mercury	Wednesday	silver/ multicoloured	mercury	chalcedony sardonyx	vetiver marjoram	celery dill fennel	valerian cinquefoil	jasmine lavender	eucalyptus lavender
Jupiter	Thursday	blue	tin	topaz amethyst turquoise	myrrh	artichokes asparagus beets chicory	betony borage	daisies carnations	clove melissa anise
Venus	Friday	green	copper	jade emeralds	rose sandalwood	apples beans	burdock vervain	roses	cardamon rose
Saturn	Saturday	black	lead	onyx hematite garnet	patchouli	barley	mullein	solomon's seal	cypress patchouli

and fatalism. She might decide that the influence of the Sun could introduce in her a new sense of vitality and optimism. Using this magical method she would decorate her home with sunflowers and daffodils, and starting on a Sunday would wear bright yellow clothes, use the essential oil of neroli in a perfume, drink St John's wort tea and listen to songs like 'Here Comes the Sun' and 'Let the Sunshine in'.

Another person, who feels they need to be more assertive and wants to bring more 'Martian' energy into their life, might try to attract the positive qualities of Mars by starting their regime on a Tuesday: dressing in red, eating curries with plenty of ginger and garlic in them, and drinking nettle tea, while listening often to the 'Mars' section of Holst's *The Planets*.

Renaissance magicians were well aware of the influence that smell, music and colour could each exert on the human being – influences that have only recently become the subject of scientific enquiry. A rationalist might think that such a magical operation could have an effect as a result of subtle changes in the nervous system caused by these influences, together with a placebo effect that encourages the outcome we desire. The astrological magician will agree with the rationalist, but will also hold to the belief that planetary influences are mysteriously conveyed by the items used in the magic, through the law of correspondences.

❧ Traps for the Sorcerer's Apprentice ❧

Don't try the above experiment if you are a perfectionist or have a tendency to obsessive-compulsive behaviour. The anxiety generated by not being able to find all the right ingredients for your astrological magic, and the potential imperfections you might find in them (if only the candles were a deeper green!), are likely to outweigh any benefit you might gain.

❧ Things to Do ❧

❧ Visit the British Museum to see Dee's scrying mirror and other magical implements.

   In the Enlightenment galleries, you can come within a few inches of probably the most extraordinary and powerful magical equipment ever used by an English magician. There in the glass case in front of you lies John Dee's original 'magic mirror' or 'shew-stone', which was one of the many translucent or reflective objects he used for scrying. This obsidian mirror was reputedly originally Aztec. Aztec priests used such mirrors for divination and seeing visions, and were associated with Tezcatlipoca, the Aztec god of rulers, warriors and sorcerers, whose name can be translated as 'Smoking Mirror'.

   The antiquary Sir Horace Walpole acquired the mirror in 1771. A paper label in his handwriting explains that this is 'The Black Stone into which Dr Dee used to call his spirits' and that 'Kelley was Dr

Dee's Associate and is mentioned with this very stone in Hudibras [a satirical poem by Samuel Butler]. Kelley did all his feats upon The Devil's Looking-glass, a Stone.'

The mirror, or other objects that he and Kelley used as tools for scrying, was placed on a 'table of practice', and each leg of this table stood upon a wax disc that was elaborately carved with magical symbols. Two of these discs are displayed beside the obsidian mirror. A gold amulet engraved with a representation of one of Kelley's visions and a larger carved wax disc can also be seen: known as the 'Seal of God' (Sigillum Dei) this was used to support the 'shew-stone'. Finally, there is a crystal globe, six centimetres in diameter. This item remained unnoticed for many years in the museum's mineral collection and is possibly the one owned by Dee. You can see photos of all these items at www.britishmuseum.org

❋ Visit the vast British Library in St Pancras to study Dee's manuscripts and diaries under supervision in their Manuscripts department. This should be undertaken only by the serious scholar, since these texts are fragile and have survived solely through an extraordinary sequence of events.

On Dee's death, some of his papers and possessions passed into the hands of a famous collector, Sir Thomas Cotton, with the exception of four short manuscript books. These, distilling the knowledge derived from his scrying sessions with Edward Kelley, along with the manuscripts that constituted the Five Books of Mystery, were hidden by Dee in a compartment of a wooden chest. In 1642, the chest was purchased by Robert Jones, a confectioner living in Lombard Street. In the base of the chest, Jones found a small slit, which, on being probed with a knife, opened a secret drawer. The papers proved unintelligible to the Joneses, so they left them out in a pile of scrap paper for their maid, who being a thrifty individual used them for lining pie tins and lighting fires.

On remarrying, Susannah Jones showed the remaining papers to her new husband, Thomas Wale, a warder at the Tower of London, who in turn showed them to the scholar and magician, Elias Ashmole, featured in Chapter 9. Ashmole immediately recognised them for the extraordinary find they were – the surviving remnants of the Books of Mystery and the scrying diaries – and he preserved them for the world.

Much of the material in the British Library can now be found online, saving the manuscripts (and your feet) wear and tear: see www.esotericarchives.com/dee

The Old Ashmolean, Oxford.

Visit the Old and New Ashmolean museums in Oxford. In the Old Ashmolean on Broad Street (now the Museum of the History of Science), you can see one of Dee's Enochian tables, and in the New Ashmolean in Beaumont Street, you can see a rare portrait of the wizard.

If Dee's role as the first 007 and as a code-maker interests you, you might like to track down the rare *Doctor John Dee, or the Original 007* by Robin Brumby (Dacorum, 1977). To sense Dee's spirit, forever keen to defend England, hovering over future generations, visit 'Station X' at Bletchley Park in Buckinghamshire, where during the Second World War code-breakers cracked the German Enigma and Lorenz codes. See www.bletchleypark.org

❊ For those who like a challenge, a walk on Meon Hill
or Northwick Hill in the Cotswolds might provide the
inspiration needed to find the treasure never unearthed
by Kelley or Dee. Watch out too for the illustrated talks
held on Dee around the country by Robin Cousins.

❊ Visit the site of Dee's house in Mortlake, where he had
an observatory, laboratories and an extensive library.
The house was on the north side of Mortlake High
Street, across from and a bit to the west of the Church of
St Mary the Virgin. The space between the High Street
and the river is narrow and houses there generally had
gardens on either side of the road.

In about 1619, Dee's entire estate was purchased
for the Mortlake Tapestry Works, which stood to the
east of Tapestry Alley as far as Chitton Alley, opposite
Avondale Road. Tapestry Alley was broadened into an
open space in 1951 and again in 1980. The building
presently standing on the west of this space is a modern
block of flats known as Tapestry House. The area across
the road, the site of Dee's old orchard, is John Dee
House, an ugly council block.

Between the wars, a large stone globe was discovered
in the back garden of 94 Mortlake High Street, where
John Dee House now stands. When broken open, it was
said to reveal a glittering crystal. Whatever connection
this may have had with Dee has now been lost. Those
who have mastered dowsing might like to look for Dee's
lost books under the tarmac behind the flats where the
washing now hangs.

On the east side of the flats, there is a small section of
old bricks in the church wall. These are believed to be
the only physical remains of Dee's estate. Lean against
them for a moment, and see whether you can you sense
the spirit of the old magician.

Dee was reputedly buried in the chancel of the

Mortlake Parish Church of St Mary the Virgin, but no trace of his burial can be found there. In the late seventeenth century John Aubrey was shown a stone here with no inscription, but known as Dr Dee's stone and believed to be part of his tomb. The churchyard was restored in the 1980s and there is now an information plaque showing notable tombs, but Dee is not mentioned. The local rumour is that his stone was removed, but his body still lies under the chancel.

❧ In magic, images are believed to act as channels for specific energies, making the pictures you have on your walls affect your consciousness and environment. Even if you don't believe this, the fact that pictures trigger conscious (and unconscious) thoughts and feelings through the memories and associations that they evoke suggests you should choose your pictures with care. If you find Dee inspiring, you could decorate your study with a reproduction of an engraving of him. Three old prints are available, reproduced on card or mounted canvas in various sizes, through www.amazon.co.uk

❧ If you enjoy playing chess, or would like an unusual set of initials after your name, consider becoming a 'Master of Enochian Chess'. The Victorian magicians William Wynne Wescott and S.L. MacGregor Mathers, who founded the Hermetic Order of the Golden Dawn, devised this special chess game based on Dee's Enochian system. Although it is sometimes called Rosicrucian or Elemental Chess, it is most often termed Enochian Chess. You can take a course in it, leading to the qualification of MeC, or you can simply download PC software to play it on your screen, or buy a set of the four boards needed from www.enochianchess.com

These are all offered by the magician Steve Nichols, who has also revived an Enochian and Golden Dawn

Order, originally founded in the 1960s by the Cornish surrealist Ithell Colquhoun and the exotic Russian countess Tamara Bourkhoun. Now known as the Order of the Phoenix, it is described as following 'the tradition of the Phoenix Order of ancient Egyptian High Priesthood . . . with an affinity to the Harry Potter Order of the Phoenix . . . It is a twenty-first-century school of magic utilising Psychomorphological techniques.' See www.ithellcolquhoun.co.uk and www.orderphoenix.org

❧ Get friendly with your Guardian Angel. Dee's interests were wide-ranging, but the magical arts of astrology and angelic conversation were central preoccupations of his. To attempt a conversation with an angel you can try Enochian magic, but it is complex and difficult to master.

Thankfully, with today's explosion of interest in the mystical and magical, there are many books and courses available that offer to put you in touch with angels in general, and your Guardian Angel in particular, without the more demanding use of ritual magic.

The world's most famous New-Age spiritual community – Findhorn in Scotland – was started with guidance from angels. In England both Diana Cooper in Dorset and Theolynn Cortens in north London run distance-learning courses, train teachers and publish books on how to work with angels. See www.dianacooperschool.com, www.dianacooper.com and Theolynn's www.soulschool.co.uk

If the New Age style of these two schools feels too simple for you and the Enochian system of magic too complex, try David Goddard's approach. Goddard co-founded the Rising Phoenix Foundation, which teaches angel magic, alchemy and the cabbala through distance learning and in gatherings in London, Gloucestershire and elsewhere. See www.rpxf.org

❧ If you'd like to study astrology, there are hundreds of books, courses and websites that offer training. One of the most well-established organisations is the Faculty of Astrological Studies, founded in London in 1948, which offers distance-learning education, classes in London and a summer school in Oxford. Graduates receive a diploma entitling them to use the letters DFAstrolS after their name. See www.astrology.org.uk

❧ Resources ❧

BOOKS

The Queen's Conjuror: The Life and Magic of Dr Dee, Benjamin Woolley (Flamingo, 2002). The most authoritative and complete biography of Dee.

John Dee: The World of an Elizabethan Magus, Peter J. French (Routledge & Kegan Paul, 1972)

John Dee's Conversations with Angels: Cabala, Alchemy, and the End of Nature, Deborah E. Harkness (Cambridge University Press, 2008). An academic study of Dee's work in the context of Elizabethan thought.

John Dee's Five Books of Mystery: Original Sourcebook of Enochian Magic, ed. Joseph Peterson (Weiser Books, 2003)

The Diaries of John Dee, John Dee (Day Books, 1998). Dee's private journals and spirit diaries are brought together for the first time, compiled from the original documents in the Bodleian Library and the British Museum.

Practical Angel Magic of Dr John Dee's Enochian Tables, Stephen Skinner and David Rankine (Golden Hoard Press Ltd, 2004). An important primer for those who want to study the Enochia.

Dr Simon Forman: A Most Notorious Physician, Judith Cook (Chatto & Windus, 2001)

Working with Angels, Fairies and Nature Spirits, William Bloom (Piatkus Books, 2002)

Angel Inspiration: How to Change Your World with the Angels, Diana Cooper (Mobius, 2004)

Working with your Guardian Angel, Theolyn Cortens (Piatkus, 2005)
The Sacred Magic of the Angels, David Goddard (Red Wheel, 1996)

WEBSITES

Information on Rufus Harrington's Enochian work can be found at:
    www.enochianmagic.co.uk and www.templeofflame.com
Information on Stephen Skinner's books on magic and Feng Shui can be
    found at: www.sskinner.com

CHAPTER EIGHT

THE SHAG-HAIR'D WIZARD OF PEPPER ALLEY

Cunning-Folk, Girdle-Measurers and the Faery Faith

There be within England above five hundred conjurers as he thinketh . . . and specially in Norfolk, Hertfordshire, and Worcestershire and Gloucestershire.

FROM AN ECCLESIASTICAL EXAMINATION OF
A LONDON CUNNING-MAN IN 1549[1]

It's the seventeenth century. You're in London and you've got a problem. You might be in ill-health, you might have had something stolen from you, you might be short of money and keen to see whether 'treasure conjuration' could work for you, or you might just want a 'figure erected' – a horoscope cast – to see how you can get out of your current predicament.

One of the most popular topics of conversation in these times, whether amongst intellectuals in their coffee houses, or amongst simpler folk in their parlours, concerns the reputations and stories of the numerous wizards and 'cunning-folk' who ply their trade in town and country. Each have their speciality, and your friends will have plenty of advice to dispense as to whom it would be best to consult, as does the seventeenth-century playwright Thomas Heywood when his character in *The Wise Woman of Hogsdon* says:

> You have heard of Mother Nottingham, who for her time was
> prettily well skilled in casting of waters; and after her, Mother
> Bomby; and then there is one Hatfield in Pepper Alley, he doth
> pretty well for a thing that's lost. There's another in Coleharbour,
> that's skilled in the planets. Mother Sturton in Golden Lane,
> is for fore-speaking; Mother Phillips, of the Bankside, for the
> weakness of the back; and then there's a very reverend matron on
> Clerkenwell Green, good at many things. Mistress Mary on the
> Bankside is for 'recting a figure; and one (what do you call her?)
> in Westminster, that practiseth the book and key, and the sieve
> and the shears: and all do well, according to their talent.[2]

Perhaps you don't fancy having your waters cast by urinating into a bottle to have it heated over a fire for a diagnosis, or peered at for visions of the future. Instead, let's say that you have had a purse stolen and you want to find the culprit and retrieve your money. You know that the sieve and shears method can work wonders, but you decide to put your faith in Master Hatfield as you've heard good reports of this 'shag-hair'd wizard' of Pepper Alley.[3]

As you walk to his lodgings, you are engaging in an activity that has been undertaken since time immemorial in every country on earth. You are on your way to a magician in the hope of finding something. In your case it's a lost purse; in someone else's it might be lost health, protection from evil or famine, or consolation at the loss of a loved one, or indeed spiritual illumination.

Cunning-folk such as the shag-hair'd wizard can be found in English literature from the middle of the fourteenth century right through until the early years of the twentieth. These records show that for over half a millennium the wizard or cunning-person was a well-established feature of everyday life, both urban and rural. Dr Owen Davies, who has written their definitive history, describes them as a 'professional type that for centuries was as integral to English life as the clergyman, constable and doctor'.[4]

The average person today knows little or nothing about cunning-folk, but in some ways their like have never really left us: in almost every town you can find fortune-tellers, mediums and alternative practitioners – people who will offer to make contact with a dead relative, find a lost love, or heal an ache of the heart or body. Although you could say they are cunning-folk in all but name, there is one big difference between those wizards of old and the spiritual practitioners who offer services to the public today, and that is in their relationship to witchcraft. In the old days much of the work of cunning-folk revolved around combating bewitchment, which is hardly the case today.

We don't know when the name was first used, but it is derived from the Anglo-Saxon *cunnan*, meaning 'to know'. Just like the word 'wizard', which comes from the Old English *wis*, meaning 'wise', these terms denote a role that is rooted in the pre-Christian world – the animistic and pagan world of the Anglo-Saxon sorcerer-shaman, although it goes further back still to the world of the Druids and their predecessors, who conducted their magic in caves in the very earliest days of our history. They were also often termed witches by those who didn't like them, and their story is inextricably bound up with the story of witchcraft and magic.

Reaching Mr Hatfield's lodgings in Pepper Alley, you may have to join a throng of people waiting to see him. When it's your turn, you are shown into a room filled with strange objects – bottles containing dried animals, large books lying open to reveal complex diagrams – and you find yourself facing an elderly man with a great shock of wild hair and a penetrating gaze. Some cunning-men were known to dress the part as wizards, while others wore ordinary clothes, but Hatfield relies on his eyes and hair for effect.[5]

After you have explained your problem, the shag-hair'd wizard asks you for a list of suspects. As you give each name he writes it on a scrap of paper. Then he rolls each scrap into its own ball of clay and invites you to look into a bucket of water. One by one he drops the balls into the bucket, until they float on the surface and begin to disintegrate. All at once a ball dissolves completely and its scrap of paper lies floating on the surface. Triumphantly the wizard reads out the name. You knew it! It was your nephew who stole the purse! You will confront him with the truth as soon as you return. Handing Hatfield his fee, you leave his lodgings and make for home as swiftly as you can.

❧ JOHN LAMBE, 1545/6–1628

A BRIEFE DESCRIPTION OF THE NOTORIOVS LIFE OF IOHN LAMBE otherwise called Doctor LAMBE. Together with his Ignominiovs DEATH.

Printed in Amsterdam 1628.

This Jacobean wizard, who tutored the children of Worcestershire gentry, practised the arts of physician and fortune-teller. Reputed to be an 'entertaining juggler', he was also able to detect lost property and to advise clients on marital affairs. Like many wizards before and since, he adopted the

title of 'Dr' without bothering to acquire the usual qualifications. Many believed in his powers: it is said that he
predicted great sorrow as a result of an accident in water
to Lady Fairfax, and three days later her brothers were
drowned.

Between 1608 and 1610 he was arrested several times,
once for offering to conjure an angel in a crystal glass.
Imprisoned in Worcester Castle, he was later moved to
the King's Bench prison where he 'lived in style', consulted by the powerful and wealthy – his greatest patron
being the Duke of Buckingham. Accused of rape, he
was sentenced to death, but although he was saved from
execution through the influence of Buckingham, he was
later cudgelled to death by a London mob one night,
after returning from the theatre.

Toad Doctors, Charmers and Girdle-Measurers

For the five hundred years or so in which the cunning-folk are
mentioned in literature, other names were also used to describe
these magical practitioners. Terms such as wizard, conjurer, wise-
man or woman and necromancer were used interchangeably, but
there were names too for specialists. Charmers, fortune-tellers,
astrologer-physicians, toad doctors and girdle-measurers: all plied
their trade using specific techniques to achieve their goals, while
cunning-folk were usually in command of a range of methods and
offered their services for a variety of ends that included finding
lost property, identifying thieves, healing the sick and even locat-
ing treasure.

Charming was a particular and distinct magical tradition all of
its own. The charmer was usually known for their innate healing
touch or for a particular healing object that they owned, but most
often for their knowledge of one or more simple verse charms.

A charmer's gift was often inherited, passed with great secrecy from one generation to the next – sometimes at the deathbed. Unlike cunning-folk who charged for their services, charmers would accept only gratuities, or gifts in kind.

Fortune-tellers were on the lowest rung of the ladder of magical practitioners, usually charging just a few pence for their services, which included palmistry and scrying with a crystal ball or mirror.

Astrologer-physicians were more highly paid and better educated, since it required some skill to 'erect' a horoscope and interpret it.

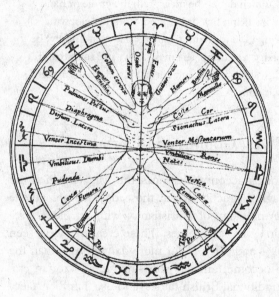

Diagram of the relationships between parts of the body and the signs of the zodiac. Taken from Robert Fludd's De Supernaturali, *1619.*

Toad doctors were found in the West of England and records show that they were still practising at the end of the nineteenth century. They offered to cure scrofula, and sometimes other ills, such as bewitchment, by putting a leg taken from a live toad in a muslin bag for the sick person to wear around their neck.

Girdle-measurers had mostly died out by the eighteenth century. Their skill lay in determining whether someone was bewitched or troubled by fairy folk by measuring their belts.

In this 1566 account of a Cambridgeshire girdle-measurer, Elizabeth Mortlock, we can see how Christian beliefs blended seamlessly with a magical world-view that included a belief in fairies. She started by reciting

> five Paternosters in the worship of the five Wounds of our Lord,
> five Aves in the worship of the five Joys of our Lady, and one
> Creed in the worship of the blessed Father, the Son and the
> Holy Ghost . . . Which done, she measureth the girdle or band
> of any such persons being sick or haunted, from her elbow to
> her thumb, craving God for Saint Charity's sake that if [they] be
> haunted with a fairy, yea or no, she may know, and saith that if
> it be so the band will be shorter and her cubit will reach further
> than commonly it doth.[7]

∽ Elves, Goblins and Fairies ∾

Elizabeth Mortlock's account illustrates the way in which the world of the magical practitioner in those days combined the doctrines and terminology of Christianity with an older, pre-Christian belief in spirits and fairies. These creatures were seen as more complex – and often as far more dangerous – than the images we have become familiar with since the Victorian era. Writers talk of 'traditional British fairies' and use 'fairy' or 'faery faith' as an umbrella term that denotes a belief in a whole range of spirits, which includes elves, goblins and even the souls of the dead.

We might yearn to spot a fairy usefully tending our garden for us, but most people in the old days were scared of fairies and sought to appease them. The Anglo-Saxons believed that many diseases were spread by elves and would often diagnose a patient as 'elf-shot'. Centuries later, people in England still described someone who was ill as 'fairy-taken' and believed that fairies stole new-born babies – replacing them with 'changelings', who were easily spotted by their unusual or fey appearance.

They believed, too, that fairies live in a parallel world to ours: they look like humans, wear human clothing, marry and mate, and display all the flaws and foibles of humankind. Some live within the earth or in wild and uninhabited places – deep in the forest, in caves or on mountains. But others live in people's houses, in 'antient buildings, and places of the slain', as one early modern writer claimed.[8] They are ruled by a King and Queen of Fairy – or Elfhame ('Elf Home') as their world was often called.

Puck *by Richard Dadd, 1841.*

Fairies can become invisible at will, can skin-turn (or metamorphose) into animal form and can fly great distances. Their bodies are made of a semi-material substance. Seventeenth-century Yorkshireman Durant Hotham wrote that fairies were 'lodg'd in Vehicles of a thinner-spun thred than is visible to our dim sight'.[9] The folklorist Katharine Briggs believes we can divide traditional British fairies into two groups: 'trooping' and 'solitary'.[10] Trooping fairies congregate far apart from human society, while solitary fairies are either of the domestic or non-domestic variety. Solitary

domestic fairies live alongside humans in their houses, outbuild-
ings or gardens. The non-domestic fairies, rather like hermits, live
far from human and other contact.

⤳ The Magician's Pact with Faery ⤳

Ordinary folk wanted to protect themselves from encounters with
fairies. They therefore never spoke ill of them, and sought to curry
their favour by leaving offerings of milk and food, even though by
the Middle Ages the Church condemned such activity. But people
also believed that fairies were gifted with supernatural powers that
enabled them to locate lost and stolen property, effect cures and
see into the future. It was the magician's job to work with the fairy
folk and to intercede on their behalf.

But how does a magician develop a relationship with a spirit or
a fairy? An analysis of the records of cunning-folk and of those
accused of witchcraft, or of practising cunning-craft, reveals a
common pattern. During a time of crisis, such as severe poverty
or bereavement, the person who is to become a magician experiences an encounter with an other-worldly being who offers them
a deal: if they will enter into a relationship (which is sometimes
sexual), the spirit will work on their behalf. This spirit is sometimes experienced as a deceased person's ghost, sometimes as
a fairy, sometimes as an animal. The individual then begins to

*Oberon, Titania and
Puck wih Fairies
Dancing, by William
Blake, c.1786.*

practise as a healer or cunning-person – often with reluctance, since they know that if their attempts fail they may well be accused of witchcraft.

The historian Emma Wilby believes that this same pattern can be traced in the experiences of shamans from diverse cultures, with parallels in the accounts of Christian mystics, and in *Cunning Folk and Familiar Spirits: Shamanistic Visionary Traditions in Early Modern British Witchcraft and Magic* (2005) she suggests six factors that would have encouraged these kinds of visionary experiences:

1. For many poor people chronic undernourishment from childhood was exacerbated by periods of famine. Add to this the fact that many women were almost continually pregnant or nursing, and were overworked, and you have the ideal conditions for destabilising normal consciousness. Mystics traditionally fast and engage in physical mortifications and asceticism to achieve similar physiological conditions.

2. Life in England in the early modern period (from roughly 1500 to 1800) was characterised by far more exposure to suffering than it is for most of us today. The scholar Barbara Rosen conveys this idea powerfully when she invites us to imagine a world in which 'treasured livestock suffer from inexplicable sicknesses; crippling diseases strike; and over and over again, children scream and suffer helplessly and die. There are very few literate people today who can enter into an existence in which one bears ten children and watches five of them die in infancy.'[11] It is no wonder that the world's major religions evolved distinct approaches to understanding suffering, and that magicians and healers have been in constant demand. Exposure to intense emotions, particularly of bereavement, are now known to be significant factors in the production of altered states of consciousness.

3. With the invention of electric light, none of us in the twenty-first century is aware of how it must feel to experience darkness consistently and have no control over it. Wilby suggests that 'the early modern poor would have lived much of their lives under the powerful thrall of darkness, and their perception of the world and its inhabitants would have been sculpted by its mystery.'[12]

4. In the days before television, and even books, people's imaginations were more powerfully developed than they are today. For centuries the storyteller and bard had conjured images from their audiences' minds out of nothing more tangible than darkness and firelight. Stories of fairies, elves and goblins, of witches and wizards, of King Arthur and Merlin, of Tom Thumb and Robin Goodfellow and scores of other heroes, developed the creative powers of the mind in ways lost to most of us.

5. 'Mind-altering' substances may have been ingested, either voluntarily or involuntarily. When available water was often suspect, beer was drunk by ordinary people in large amounts, and was stronger than modern commercial brews. For the malnourished this could produce hallucinations, as could psychoactive agents that may have entered the food chain in moulds, such as ergot, which grows on rye. There is much controversy in the scholarly world about whether or not 'flying ointments', composed of hallucinogenic plant compounds, were used by witches, and whether the indigenous psychoactive mushrooms *Amanita muscaria* and *Psilocybe semilanceata* were ever ingested deliberately by British shamans, such as the Druids. The balance of research suggests that psychoactive agents were not deliberately used by magicians in Britain, but it is still quite possible that visionary experiences may have been triggered involuntarily by them.[13]

6. Finally, Wilby suggests, to these five factors must be added a sixth: a powerful and ancient belief stretching back into pagan times in the reality of spirits and the spirit world.

✄ Charlatans or Shamans? ✄

Contemporary accounts of cunning-folk indicate that many engaged in trickery. Others, however, were clearly sincere in their belief that they were working with supernatural powers and, in an age when doctors were scarce and as likely to kill as to cure you, the local wise-person often provided much needed relief. As George Gifford said in 1587: 'Many in great distress have been relieved and recovered by sending unto such wise men or wise women, when they could not tell what should else become of them.'[14]

Much of their healing abilities may have been the result of the placebo effect, which science now reveals to be as potent as many a drug. Although most people were within easy reach of a wizard, they would often travel great distances to visit a particular wise-person, whose reputation they valued or who was rumoured to be successful with a certain type of complaint. As they were already primed to benefit from their visit by their faith in the practitioner, the appearance and surroundings of the wizard undoubtedly played their part in inducing a receptive state of mind. In an age when most people were illiterate, books were seen as symbols of power and of esoteric knowledge, and cunning-folk often displayed their books of astrology or magic to impress their clients.

Owen Davies, in *Cunning-Folk: Popular Magic in English History* (2003), points to one of the great ironies in the story of English magic. The Kentish gentleman Reginald Scot was one of the earliest sceptics to commit his ideas to print in his 1584 book *The Discoverie of Witchcraft*. In it he attempted to reveal the folly of the witch-hunts, and to debunk his contemporaries' obsession with magic, which he saw as superstition. But by filling his book with details of the magical methods that he sought to deride, he succeeded only in perpetuating and popularising these methods for generations to come. His book was a favourite of cunning-folk, as was the grimoire *The Key of Solomon*, which appeared in the fifteenth century and gave detailed instructions on how to detect thieves, find treasure, procure love and curse enemies, through magical methods that involved conjuring and commanding spirits to do one's bidding.

It was the same *Key of Solomon* that provided much of the ritual content for the revived form of witchcraft known as Wicca.

✎ The Grimoire of ✑ The Key of Solomon

The Key of Solomon, ever since its appearance in manuscript form, has exerted a major influence on English magic. Those

who studied and were inspired by this medieval grimoire include Dr John Dee, many of the cunning-folk, the Victorian magicians of the Golden Dawn and Gerald Gardner, the twentieth-century promoter of modern witchcraft. Here is an abridged extract from the 1904 edition by S. Liddell MacGregor Mathers:

If thou wishest to succeed, it is necessary to make the following experiments and arts in the appropriate days and hours, with the requisite solemnities and ceremonies contained and laid down in the following chapters . . . Before commencing operations both the master and his disciple: must abstain with great and thorough continence during the space of nine days from sensual pleasures and from vain and foolish conversation . . . on the seventh day, the master being alone, let him enter

into a secret place, let him take off his clothes, and bathe
himself from head to foot in consecrated and exorcised water,
saying devoutly and humbly the prayer, 'O Lord Adonai,' . . .
The prayer being finished, let the master quit the water, and
put upon his flesh raiment of white linen clean and unsoiled;
and then let him go with his disciples unto a secret place and
command them to strip themselves naked; and they having
taken off their clothes, let him take exorcised water and pour it
upon their heads so that it flows down to their feet and bathes
them completely; and while pouring this water upon them let
the master say: 'Be ye regenerate, renewed, washed, and pure,'
etc., . . . the master in sign of penitence will kiss the disciples on
the forehead, and each of them will kiss the other. Afterwards
let the master extend his hands over the disciples, and in sign
of absolution absolve and bless them; which being done he will
distribute to each of his disciples the instruments necessary for
magical art, which he is to carry into the circle . . . The first
disciple will bear the censer, the perfumes and the spices; the
second disciple will bear the book, papers, pens, ink, and any
stinking or impure materials; the third will carry the knife and
the penknife of magical art, the lantern, and the candles; the
fourth, the Psalms, and the rest of the instruments; the fifth,
the crucible or chafing-dish, and the charcoal or fuel; but it
is necessary for the master himself to carry in his hand the
staff, and the wand or rod. The things necessary being thus
disposed, the master will go with his disciples unto the assigned
place, where they have proposed to construct the circle for
the magical arts and experiments; repeating on the way the
prayers and orations . . . When the master shall have arrived
at the place appointed, together with his disciples, he having
lighted the flame of the fire, and having exorcised it afresh . . .
shall light the candle and place it in the lantern, which one of
the disciples is to hold ever in his hand to light the master at
his work. Now the master of the art, every time that he shall
have occasion for some particular purpose to speak with the
spirits, must endeavour to form certain circles . . . Now, in

order to succeed in forming such a circle concerning magical art, for the greater assurance and efficacy thou shalt construct it in the following manner . . . Take thou the knife or penknife, consecrated after the manner and order which we shall deliver unto thee in the Second Book. With this knife or penknife thou shalt describe, beyond the inner circle which thou shalt have already formed, a second circle, encompassing the other at the distance of one foot therefrom . . . And between the first and the second circle . . . thou shalt make four hexagonal pentacles, and between these thou shalt write four terrible and tremendous names of God . . .'

✎ Princes vs. Peasants – High vs. ✎ Low Magic

Students of magic have found it useful to divide magic into one of two categories: high and low.

Low magic was the folk magic of the peasant or rustic whose aim is practical – to secure health, love and wealth. It was often based on inherited lore and an oral tradition in a largely illiterate culture, and its purpose was not to understand the workings of the universe, but to alleviate suffering and achieve tangible, material ends.

High magic was the pursuit of the wealthy and the aristocratic, those in power. They had access to wealth – and, supposedly, health with their expensive physicians – so their magic developed in a literate culture. It was concerned not so much with material gain as with developing the practitioner's wisdom and understanding. As Owen Davies puts it, books of high magic 'contained holy orations on how to obtain good memory rather than good money'.

This division of magical aims can be seen clearly in the goals of the alchemists: some sought material gold, others the spiritual gold of illumination. Surveying the magical and related 'New Age' scene today, we see the same division: advertisements for books or courses stress either the practical benefits of more wealth and health, or the more 'spiritual' benefits of increased wisdom – even enlightenment. But human beings are complex creatures and sensibly want to have their cake and eat it. The more canny ads ask: 'Why not seek wealth, health *and* spiritual illumination?' Even in the fifteenth century a cross-over was occurring between the work of high and low magicians.

The Key of Solomon is a case in point. It drew upon much of what was considered 'high magic' and yet it also catered to the desire for love, wealth and power. As a result it circulated widely throughout Europe, exerting an influence on magical practice that continues to this day.

✎ Star Lore and Herbcraft ✎

When giving healing, the cunning-person would often combine herbal remedies with prayers or charms. Most of the latter were of Christian origin, but some older formulae were used. The word 'abracadabra', which we now associate with stage magic, was used by the Romans as a charm against disease, and as late as the seventeenth century we find the antiquary John Aubrey assuring his readers that it is effective against the ague.

Alongside charms sung or muttered to the patient, or written on parchment and concealed in bags hung from the neck, healers  would draw on their knowledge of herbal medicine, which in itself has a long and venerable history. The most sophisticated cunning-folk were able to combine their use of charms and herbology with astrology, aided to great effect by the work of Nicholas Culpeper, and the publication in 1652 of his *The English Physitian, or an Astrologo-Physical Discourse of the Vulgar Herbs of this Nation*, which has been described as the most successful non-religious English text ever published, since it has been in print continuously since the seventeenth century.

Culpeper's life displays much of the intellectual and magical influences that played themselves out during the three centuries or so of the early modern period. Whilst he aimed for reason as his guiding light, he was motivated both by the practical goals of 'low magic' to improve the lot of Everyman, and by the loftier aims of 'high magic' as expressed in the works of Hermeticists and alchemists.

⚘ NICHOLAS CULPEPER, 1616–1654

Although not a cunning-man, Culpeper significantly influenced the practice of cunning-folk with the publication of his *English Physician* in 1652 and his *Complete Herbal* in 1653.

Although he also held to the same beliefs – in the power of the stars and of plants, and of the magical relationship between them, and in Christianity – he was also keen to base his research on reason and experience.

He spent his childhood in Isfield in Sussex, was educated at Cambridge and was then apprenticed to an apothecary. Having married a wealthy woman, he set up a pharmacy in Spitalfields in London, obtaining his herbs from the nearby countryside, and treating as many as forty patients a day, using a combination of astrology and herbalism. Jealous of his success, the Society of Apothecaries accused him of witchcraft.

He joined the Republicans and fought in the English Civil War at the Battle of Newbury in 1643. He carried out battlefield surgery, but was wounded and returned to London, where he died of tuberculosis at the age of thirty-eight. Of his eight children, only one survived into adulthood.

Culpeper, the first of a chain of herbal shops inspired by him, was founded in London's Baker Street in 1927 by the herbalist Hilda Leyel, who also founded the Herb Society. Her goal was to re-create the 'still room' of Tudor England where seasonal herbs, fruits and plants were turned into distillations and elixirs, preserves and potions. There are now two Culpeper shops in London, and eight in other English towns.

By the early twentieth century a shift in understanding, which had begun much earlier, finally reached fruition. Reginald Scot's viewpoint, first voiced four hundred years previously in his *The Discoverie of Witchcraft*, was finally accepted wholesale: elves and fairies were no longer seen as harbingers of disease and, most importantly of all, witches were no longer believed to be the cause of misfortune.

Much of the cunning-folk's work revolved around curing bewitchment, and as Owen Davies puts it: 'When the unbewitching business dried up during the early twentieth century, cunning-folk soon ceased to exist both in practice and in popular discourse.'[15] That's why so few of us even know of the term that described one of the most ubiquitous figures in English public life for more than five centuries.

Despite this, the legacy of the cunning-folk lives on in the work of alternative healers who draw upon a similar understanding of magic, and there are even modern-day practitioners who have begun to call themselves by the same name.

⚚ BILLY BREWER, 1818–1890

The most famous cunning-man in nineteenth-century Somerset was Billy Brewer, known as the 'Wizard of the West'. This Victorian magician paraded the streets of Taunton in a long Inverness cape with a broad sombrero hat over his long curly hair. He travelled around Somerset, Devon and Dorset, selling the clay pipes that he made and offering the usual services of a cunning-man: charms, protection from bewitchment and fortune-telling.

CASSANDRA LATHAM

In a tiny cottage, known as 'The Doll's House', tucked away in a narrow alley in the village of St Buryan, near Penzance in Cornwall, Cassandra Latham earns her living as a 'village wise-woman' – declaring her occupation on her tax return as 'witch'.

After a difficult early life, she trained as a registered nurse, before being initiated into witchcraft by two friends. Rather than working in a group as a 'coven' witch, she has adapted the original notion of village wise-woman to the modern age, dealing with a variety of clients who come to her through her website or through personal recommendation.

It has always been difficult to figure out what I should call myself. 'Witch' is still a prejudicial and secretive term and the more correct historical description of myself as one of the 'cunning-folk' is also confusing. Cornwall has produced more than its fair share of such people, especially in the times before the NHS brought medicine more widely to poorer people, but the individuals themselves are remembered as having been pretty eccentric. Cunning-women were called 'Granny', 'Mother', 'Auntie' or 'An'

[Cornish] and there's a well-known turn-of-last-century story of Granny Boswell's first encounter with a car. She swayed in front of it, quite drunk, until she was blasted with the horn by an angry driver. Shouting curses, she predicted the car would never get further than the end of the street. Halfway there, it broke down with a loud bang and had to be towed away by a horse!

I have great respect for the 'craft' and its centuries-old knowledge, and still use it as the basis of much of what I do. I still use 'poppets', small figures of people or animals, to work spells, for instance, although I much prefer to call them by the Celtic term 'fith fath'. 'Fith' means shape-shifting and 'fath' means the magical words used for invocation. An old one goes:

> I sall goe until a Hare
> Wi' sorrow and sick mickle care
> I sall goe in the Devil's name
> An while I come home again.

If you want to be a practising witch who can be of help to the community, you need to be very much in touch with the seasons and the changing power of nature. Above everything, you have to feel when is the best time for magic and for dealing with the spirit world.

The most powerful magical energy comes at the time of the eight seasonal festivals. It is wild and anarchic, and symptomatic of the chaotic element of life that exists between death and rebirth – the primeval soup from where all things come. The traditional local festivals that took place at this time are still enormously important at a cathartic level. They formed a very specific function for hard-working people to kick over the traces and feel life from a different perspective.

For example, in some processions, ordinary people would dress up as mock mayors and bishops. Nowadays, you have the dreaded political correctness and 'nanny state' interfering. For example, at the May Day 'obby 'oss [hobby horse] festival in Padstow, the 'oss I dance with and tease is a skull-and-pole hobby horse and the 'clacker' of its tongue is made of wood and horse-hair, which is so important to raise the energy. Someone told me that such an object might be dangerous or unhygienic! Other festivals, such as the Tar Festival at Ottery St Mary, where barrels of blazing tar are pushed around, are equally wonderful, but no doubt also in danger from the 'nannies'.

How do I help people? I make amulets and charms, using magic and invocation, often made with elements from nature. For example, I used magpie claws for one of my clients, a local shopkeeper, who asked me to help combat a spate of shoplifting. I attached the magpie's feet, representing thievery, to a cross of rowan, which is an ancient symbol of protection. I surrounded them with a circle of ivy wrapped with lead, both of which have restrictive qualities. At the right time on the right day, I charged it with the appropriate energies. I saw the man a few weeks later and he said it was working . . . well, like a charm!

Much of my work nowadays is not so much in healing, in terms of helping people search for the cause of their problems, but more in helping them find their own solutions. We live in a world where there seems to be little connection made between spiritual and medical problems, yet your body does not lie. I see the connection between people's lifestyles and social history and the physical manifestations of their sickness. Doctors look only for physical symptoms.

I also help with wart curing, which has always been associated with witches. I used to think they occurred solely in old people, but I now believe they are more likely to occur in adolescent or pre-pubescent children as they try to grapple with a life slipping beyond their control. I tell them that I can make the wart go away – usually within a moon (a lunar cycle) – and then I help them express themselves better with aerobics, music, etc.

How do I find out about the problems themselves? I find Tarot the most useful tool. It helps summarise everything that I have picked up about a person. Sometimes the problem can be caused by a house with dubious energies, and I am often asked to help in such cases. Here, I use dowsing to find which parts of the house need attention. I don't try to exorcise the whole place as a priest might; instead I connect to the house spirits to find out what's going on.

Curing the problem can involve some of the oldest tricks of all, like 'spirit houses'. Spirits love activity centres and I use natural materials to build something intricate that will occupy their minds. You can see examples in the Boscastle Museum of Witchcraft. One I particularly like is a big glass globe full of 'hundreds and thousands'. In the middle of the globe is a charm, which attracts the spirits in, and then they just have to count the hundreds and thousands. In my own cottage I have 'witch balls', which are full of coloured threads to keep the spirits busy so they don't get up to no good.

People often criticise witches for the power they can gain over those who come to them. Just like 'transference' in psychiatry, this can be a real problem. My attitude is to encourage clients to move on, which usually works well. I feel a strong responsibility for the craft and work closely with the Pagan Federation, helping to organise conferences, answering questions, giving talks and so on. Most people don't know where to get answers if they are interested in one or other of the magical crafts and can get taken for a ride.

I still have huge respect for the past, but see myself as an adventurer and a pioneer. As you grow older, you want things to come to you, rather than running around. There are magical ways to achieve this, but I still love taking people around the countryside, showing them things that they have never spared the time to look at or feel before. As for my consultations, I have long ago stopped giving out my phone number to time wasters, but I find email a great help. If people spend the time to get their thoughts down in writing, they are halfway to understanding the problem. The main thing, though, is to have a continued sense of wonder. People who are always saying, 'I know, I know,' have stopped learning.

Read about this period in Fiction

The White Witch, Elizabeth Goudge (Hodder, 2005)
Herbcraft, gypsy lore, and white and black witchcraft at
the time of the Civil War. See www.elizabethgoudge.org

The Edge of Tomorrow, D.G. Finlay (Star Books, 1979)
The story of a witch joining puritans making their
way to the New World with an interesting subplot: the
telepathic communications and psychic battle between
the witch and a native American sorcerer.

Rudyard Kipling and Thomas Hardy include cunning-
folk in their stories. In Kipling's *Marklake Witches* a
'white wizard' cures people with herbs and charms, and
'conjurors' appear in Hardy's *The Withered Arm*, *The
Mayor of Casterbridge* and *Tess of the d'Urbervilles*.

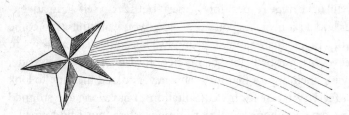

*Up until the mid-nineteenth century there may have been as
many as several thousand working in England at any given
time . . . The majority, roughly some two-thirds, were male.*

OWEN DAVIES, *CUNNING-FOLK: POPULAR
MAGIC IN ENGLISH HISTORY*

✧ The Magician's Grimoire ✧

A Compendium of Magical Techniques Used by Wizards and Cunning-Folk between the Fourteenth and Nineteenth Centuries

Most of the magical techniques of the village wizard had been inherited from the Middle Ages, and had direct links with Anglo-Saxon and classical practices.

KEITH THOMAS, *RELIGION AND THE DECLINE OF MAGIC*

◉ *The Benefits of Wizardry*

1. Earning a living or supplementing your income. In Tudor times the majority of cunning-men may have been professionals, such as clerics, schoolmasters, churchwardens and medics. But by the mid-eighteenth century the well-educated gentleman wizard was almost extinct, with one survey showing that from then on over 80 per cent were craftsmen, tradesmen or farmers.

   While most used their earnings from wizardry to supplement their income, some earned a good living from their cunning-work alone. In the eighteenth century, Hannah Green was said to have amassed savings of £1,000. Susanna Gore in Driffield, Yorkshire, accumulated 'a considerable amount of property' in the early nineteenth century. Thomas Atkinson in Kirby Lonsdale left 'quite a fortune' in the same era.

2. The satisfaction of seeing your fellows healed, given hope, and with whatever they have had stolen or lost restored to them, as James Mason in *The Anatomie of*

Sorcerie (1612) reported: 'there are diverse and sundry kinds of Maladies, which though a man do goe to all the physitions that can be heard of, yet he shall find no remedy: whereas sometimes they are cured by those which are called cunning folkes.'

3. Respect, even awe, from the community and the advantages of prestige. In the nineteenth century a Surrey labourer told a local magistrate that the wizard he consulted was a 'blessed man'. In 1593, George Gifford quotes someone asserting that the local cunning-woman did 'more good in one year than all these scripture men will do so long as they live'.[16]

4. The company of familiars and spirits to aid you in your work, including fairies. One commentator in the sixteenth century wrote that, in England, 'The opinion of faeries and elfes is very old, and yet sticketh very religiously in the myndes of some.'[17] Animal familiars reported as being used by cunning-folk were usually small mammals, but might sometimes be birds or insects.

⊙ *The Risks of Wizardry*

1. Arrest and trial by secular or ecclesiastical authorities, and being pilloried in the stocks, or executed by burning or hanging. However, most cunning-folk avoided prosecution. Out of the four hundred accused of witchcraft in Essex, only four were clearly cunning-men or women. The punishment that ecclesiastical courts meted out usually involved simply standing in church clothed in a white sheet, wearing a sign that explained the offence.

2. Possession by evil spirits. Some cunning-folk clearly suffered from mental illness. But if one accepts the reality of spirits, it is also possible that some were tormented by maleficent entities.

⊙ *Services Offered*

- ❊ Thief detection
- ❊ Love magic
- ❊ Sundry cures
- ❊ Astrology
- ❊ Fortune-telling
- ❊ Herbalism
- ❊ Unbewitching

⊙ *Attire*

Any clothes might do, but some cunning-folk decided to impress their clients by dressing up. A nineteenth-century Yorkshire wise-woman sat robed in a sheet covered with magical symbols and wore a conical hat. Around her, bunches of herbs hung from the ceiling and a stuffed lizard basked on her table.

⊙ *Methods*

Natural magic, which utilises the occult properties of nature, the four elements of Earth, Air, Fire and Water, and the powers of the animal, vegetable and mineral realms.

Celestial magic, which works with the influences of the stars.

Ceremonial magic, which calls for the aid of spirits.

Sympathetic magic, based on the doctrines of sympathy and antipathy, using like to attract like, and antipathies to repel and protect.

⊙ *For the Detection of Theft and the Recovery of Stolen Goods*

THE SIEVE AND SHEARS METHOD

'Stick a pair of shears in the rind of a sieve and let two persons set the top of each of their forefingers upon the upper part of the shears holding it with the sieve up from the ground steadily; and ask Peter and Paul whether A, B, or C hath stolen the thing lost, and at the nomination of the guilty person the sieve will turn round.'

REGINALD SCOT, *THE DISCOVERIE OF WITCHCRAFT*, 1584

THE BOOK AND KEY METHOD

Records show that this method was used from the medieval era up until the nineteenth century for identifying criminals. Pieces of paper carrying the names of suspects were inserted, one by one, into the hollow end of a key that was lodged between the pages of a book, usually the Bible or a psalter. When the guilty person's name was inserted, the book would move or even fall out of the hands of the person holding it.

TURNING THE LOAF
Four knives were inserted into the sides of a loaf of bread. Then a wooden peg was sunk into the top of it, so that it became like a spinning top. As a list of names was recited, out loud or internally, it would turn at the name of the thief.

SCRYING
Scrying involves gazing on to a shiny surface until one seems to see an image. Crystal balls, bowls of water, polished mirrors and even fingernails were used in this way, with the guilty party or the location of the lost items being revealed to the scryer's gaze.

ASTROLOGY AND THE CONJURING OF SPIRITS
Horoscopes were sometimes cast for detecting the whereabouts of stolen goods, and spirits were also conjured for help in this respect. Two cunning-men – the Master of Holbeach grammar school, John Lamkyn, and a Cirencester wheelwright, Edmund Nasche – were prosecuted in 1545 in the Star Chamber for falsely accusing a man of the theft of money and jewels as a result of their 'conjuring'.

⊙ *For the Detection of Witchcraft*

Some physicians and surgeons, as well as gypsies and exorcists – both lay and clerical – offered to unbewitch clients. But cunning-folk provided the widest range of techniques to combat witchcraft, including preventative charms and the identification of the offending witch, as well as cures for their 'maleficium' (evildoing). Until the mid-nineteenth century, many ills of the body remained undiagnosed, and 'bewitchment' offered an explanation, which in itself may have given the sufferer a measure of relief.

For diagnosis, some wizards used the herb vervain, known since classical times as the 'Enchanter's Herb' and reputedly used by the Druids. A decoction of vervain was used to wash the patient. If

the run-off from this washing was filled with hairs or changed colour, witchcraft was clearly afoot.

Bubbles in urine were often taken as signs of bewitchment, and urine-scrying was used to determine the culprit. In the seventeenth century, for example, Joan Peterson, a cunning-woman from Wapping, used the following method to determine whether a client's cow had been bewitched: she boiled some of the animal's urine and scryed one of the bubbles produced in this way, seeing within it the face of the woman the cow-keeper already suspected.

Vervain, *by Will Worthington.*

As well as diagnosing bewitchment, many cunning-folk offered protection from witches' spells and the influence of evil spirits. To do this they often made 'witch bottles', which they buried outside a property, under the hearth, or plastered into the walls. The bottles were usually small – 3 inches high and made from blue or green glass – but larger bottles were also used, known as 'Greybeards' or 'Bellarmines', which were about 9 inches tall, and made from glazed stoneware decorated with fierce bearded faces designed to ward off evil. Inside the bottles, the hair and urine of the person who needed defending were mixed with nails, thorns and pieces of sharp glass. The idea was that the witch or spirit would be attracted to the hair and urine in their search for their victim, and would then be injured by the sharp objects. In addition, the bottle was symbolic of the witch's bladder, and through sympathetic magic it was designed to inflict excruciating pain on the offending witch. Witch bottles were particularly popular during the Elizabethan era, and were used throughout the sixteenth and seventeenth centuries, particularly in East Anglia.

*A 'Bellarmine' witch bottle
(seventeenth century).*

Sympathetic magic of the same ilk was used for bewitched livestock. The heart of a dead animal was pierced with pins and thorns and hung from the chimney. Soon the witch's heart would be seared with pain and she would stop her 'maleficium'.

To treat the results of witchcraft, the most common cures were a combination of written charms and herbal medicine. Fumigants of bay, rue, sage and rosemary were sometimes used, and for internal consumption concoctions of marigold, rosemary, angelica, true-love and St John's wort. Nicholas Culpeper's *The English Physician or Herball*, published in 1653, was widely consulted by cunning-folk. In 1854 it was recorded that a Somerset wizard prescribed an unbewitching ointment of sage, wormwood, jack-in-the-hedge and lard, to be applied to the back of the ear.

⊙ *For Success at Gambling . . . or Anything Else*

Wizards were not averse to using magic for their clients to succeed at virtually anything – from gambling to playing the lute. For these purposes they used charms or spirit conjuration, in which a spirit was invoked and commanded to set to work. Dr Elkes, an Elizabethan conjurer, supplied a ring that when worn guaranteed success at the gambling table. A spirit was enclosed within it and it was engraved with words of power in Hebrew.

Adam Squire, Master of Balliol College, Oxford, 1571–1580, was said to have sold gamblers a 'fly' (or familiar spirit) who ensured success at dice. And a conjurer told Lord Neville in 1544 that the spirit Orpheus would help him 'play as well on the lute and virginals as any man in England'.[18]

⊙ *For Protection*

Amulets, sigils and charms were sold by wizards to protect the purchaser or their house from lightning, vermin, fire, burglary and even wounding in battle. Shoes were sometimes plastered into walls to protect the house from evil spirits. In the early nineteenth century, John Parkins offered a charm to naval and military officers that would 'not only protect and defend the British Army and Navy in all those times of the greatest danger, but also give them the most complete victory over all their enemies, both foreign and domestic'.[19]

Charms were supposed to be written on 'virgin or unborn parchment'. Virgin parchment was made from the skin of an

animal that had not reached sexual maturity. Unborn parchment was made from the skin of an aborted animal. The charms were usually worn in bags around the neck, or sewn into clothing. But they could also be placed above doorways, in tin boxes that were plastered into the walls, or rolled up and inserted into holes in beams.

'Abracadabra' was one of the oldest charms used, which originated in the classical period. Other charms were of Christian origin and written in Latin. One of the most popular reads in translation: 'Let every spirit praise the Lord: they have Moses and the prophets. Let God arise and his enemies be scattered.'

Many protective charms combined biblical names with names of demons and sometimes gibberish, as in this example from an old hall in Bradford:

Aon + hora + Cammall + + +
Naadgrass + Dryadgrass + + +

Arassund + yo + Sigrged + + +
dayniss + Tetragrammaton E
Inurmed E Soleysickle + + +
domend + Ame + dias + hora + + M
Fiat

Holy water, consecrated candles, crosses and rosaries were all used in magical ways to offer protection to clients, particularly once the Church of England broke away from the Roman Catholic Church in the sixteenth century and Protestantism held sway. An enduring popular attachment to Catholicism, and to the magical protective and healing power of religious relics and holy objects, rendered them powerful tools in a wizard's arsenal. They were also used by ordinary folk even without a wizard's help: holy water was drunk as a cure for sickness, given to animals and scattered on fields. Communion bread was slipped under the tongue or smuggled out of church, uneaten, and used in a similar way.

Unlike today's witches, who draw their inspiration from paganism but aspire to some of the work of cunning-folk, the wizards of the early modern period were essentially Christian believers.

⊙ Love Magic

Cunning-folk often provided love charms and aphrodisiacs. Eleanor Cobham, Duchess of Gloucester, was tried in 1441 for using magic against Henry VI. She was accused of paying an astrologer, the canon of St Stephen's Chapel, Westminster, and a cunning-woman named Margerie Jourdayne. The cunning-woman was accused of supplying the duchess with love potions and was burnt at Smithfield for treason.

Most of the work done by cunning-folk in this field was fortune-telling – using astrology, palmistry or scrying to find out whom their client would marry, or how problems in relationships could be resolved.

A seventeenth-century wise-man from Newcastle, Peter Banks,

offered women a service to make their husbands treat them better. This involved wearing a written charm next to the heart, slipping herbs into their husband's tea, and burning his urine in the fire while saying the Lord's Prayer. In the same century the use of love philtres was publicly debated four times at Oxford University.

◉ *For the Discovery of Treasure*

Magicians often used dowsing to look for treasure. Sometimes their rods were called 'Mosaical rods'. In 1634, the Dean of Westminster gave his permission for the King's clock-master, David Ramsey, to use such rods to dowse for treasure in Westminster Abbey.

Spirits and fairies could be persuaded to reveal the whereabouts of treasure too. Thomas Heather, of Hoddesdon in Hertfordshire, was convicted in 1573 of conjuring up spirits in a local wood to help him find treasure. In 1607, fairies told Susan Swapper that a pot of gold was buried in a field outside Rye.

But these spirits were not always helpful, and sometimes it was considered necessary to exorcise a demon or evil spirit who guarded treasure, which was usually located in old burial mounds, under castle ruins or beneath wayside crosses.

Charms were also used for treasure-hunting: such a charm was offered by a wizard to Anne Bodenham in 1652 to find £1,000, which she believed the Earl of Pembroke had buried in the garden of Wilton House (For more on Wilton House see Chapter 6).

◉ *For Fortune-Telling*

Cunning-folk offered their services to predict and influence the outcome of courting, marriages, lawsuits, contests and bets. While many gypsies and women plied their trade as fortune-tellers using palmistry, some cunning-folk used astrology and scrying as means of divination. Since a person's fate can be influenced by their character, cunning-folk often employed methods such as physiognomy, whereby the face is 'read' for character traits. At a simpler level, lines on the forehead and moles on the face were 'read' in this way.

Cunning-folk also developed their own secret methods of fortune-telling, such as Joan Mores of East Langdon in Kent, who in the sixteenth century told the future from the croaking of frogs.

Other Influences on English Magic

Magic in England has never evolved in isolation. Instead it developed as a result of a continuous stream of influences from abroad, which included those of Nordic culture from the ninth century, alchemical ideas from Arabia in the thirteenth century, Neo-Platonic theories from Italy in the fifteenth century, Rosicrucian mysticism from Germany in the seventeenth century, and a cluster of influences from France during its nineteenth century occult revival.

The most powerful influence of all came from the Jewish mysticism of the kabbalah, which reached the world of 'high magic' in England in the sixteenth century. By the late nineteenth century it had become central to the majority of ceremonial magic being practised in the country.

Romany (Gypsy) traditions have also been a continuous feature in England since the sixteenth century, but have been less influential, due to a lack of written texts, and remained confined to the world of 'low magic': of fortune-telling, charming and herbal healing.

⚘ TAMSIN BLIGHT, MID-NINETEENTH CENTURY

Tamsin Blight achieved fame as one of the greatest Cornish cunning-women of her time.

Known as the 'White Witch of Helston', she was born at the end of the eighteenth century. She began practising as a conjuror in 1830 and married another of her profession in 1835 – the wizard James Thomas. They were such a successful double-act that people travelled from far and wide to consult them for cures and prognostications. Their downfall came when James propositioned a man in St Ives, who reported him to the police. He fled Cornwall, leaving his estranged wife behind to continue her practice.

Such was her fame that the following story grew up around a reputed incident in which she attempted to conjure the spirit of an old woman, in St Stythians graveyard, to find out where she had hidden the cash that her male relative believed was rightfully his:

> She then marked out a circle by drawing her Staff on the ground three times round the man, at the same time mumbling in her unknown tongue [Cornish]. This done, turning to the sailor, she said, 'Now, mind you don't move out of this charmed ring which I have made to protect ye, and if you are still determined I will now begin and summon the Spirit.'
>
> The Witch, holding out her Staff towards the spot where the old woman was buried, began her incantation, or citation, with long, strange words, slowly pronounced. Then she continued in a louder tone, 'Spirit of Jane Hendy, in the name of all the powers above and below, I summon thee to rise from the grave and appear before me and this man! By the spirits of Fire, Air, Earth, and Water, I summon thee to arise! Come hither, appear,

and speak to this man! Come!' This she said three times, raising her voice at each repetition until it ended in a shriek.

The Witch paused. All was silent for a moment, and then were heard, most fearful, because unusual, sounds, which more than any other earthly noise resembled the crashing or rending of wood and stones, mingled with painful moans, groans and shrieks, which seemed to come from the old woman's grave. The Witch, stretching out her arms, her red cloak and grey hair streaming back on the wind, pointed with her Staff toward the place whence these frightful sounds proceeded, and said, 'Behold, it cometh: be thou prepared!'

(From a Cornish folk tale, 'The Ghost of Stythians', William Bottrell's *Traditions and Hearthside Stories of West Cornwall*, 1870)

RECOMMENDED BOOKS FOR A WIZARD OF THE EARLY MODERN PERIOD (1500–1800)

The Key of Solomon, Anon. (late fifteenth-century)

There are numerous editions of this, one of the most influential books on the magical art and a common source book for cunning-folk. In the mid-twentieth century, Gerald Gardner drew upon it to fashion his witchcraft revival known as Wicca, thereby aligning it with the magic of many cunning-folk who practised in England from the sixteenth century onwards.

The Book of Secrets, Albertus Magnus (mid-sixteenth century)

This describes the magical properties of animals, stones and herbs.

The Discoverie of Witchcraft, Reginald Scot (1584)

This one volume, although written to debunk the work of wizards, reproduced so many of their formulae that ironically it served to perpetuate and propagate their methods more than any other book on the subject.

The English Physitian (1652) and *Complete Herbal* (1653), Nicholas Culpeper

The Fourth Book of Occult Philosophy (1655)

This, falsely attributed to Cornelius Agrippa and translated by Robert Turner, was one of the most notorious magical textbooks in Western Europe. Unlike the famous *Three Books of Occult Philosophy* that Agrippa really did pen, there was little theorising here, but plenty of practical instruction on magical techniques.

A True and Faithful Relation of what passed for many years between Dr John Dee . . . and some Spirits, M. Casaubon (1659)

This is a record of the seances held by Dee and Kelley (see Chapter 7), along with many others, and it recounts in detail the techniques they used to conjure spirits.

The Brittish Physician: or The Nature and Vertue of English Plants, Robert Turner (1664)

Turner was an astrologer, an occultist and a botanist.

A Compleat System of Magick; or, The History of the Black-Art, Anon. (1727)

This is almost certainly written by Daniel Defoe, the author of *Robinson Crusoe*. Although, like Reginald Scot, Defoe is a sceptic, this 400-page work provides much information on the work of wizards, conjurors and cunning-folk.

◉ *How to Make Herbal Remedies*

Many cunning-folk operated a successful 'front' as herbalists, offering their more magical solutions to clients behind closed doors. Herbal remedies often make use of powerful ingredients and it is not wise to experiment without sufficient knowledge. Thankfully the tradition of herbal medicine in Britain is well established, due to the pioneering work of figures such as Nicholas Culpeper, Mrs M. Grieve, and Mrs C.F. Leyel, and is also indebted to the work of the National Institute of Medical Herbalists. As a result, many excellent practitioners exist within reach of most people.

Some simple remedies that would have been used by cunning-folk can be safely made at home. To make an infused drink of hawthorn brandy that can be beneficial to the heart, try filling a jar a quarter to a third full of hawthorn berries and then top the jar up with brandy. Store in the dark and shake daily. After a month or so the brandy will be ready to drink and will have a delicious 'woodland' flavour.

To make a herbal tincture, use the highest-proof alcohol available, which is usually brandy or vodka. If you do not drink alcohol, use vinegar. Pick nettles (which act as a good tonic) and macerate the fresh or dried leaves with a mortar and pestle or a knife. Fill two-thirds of a scrupulously clean jar that has an airtight seal with the bruised leaves. Pour the alcohol or vinegar over the herbs so that they are just covered. Label the jar and place in a dark room or cupboard for a full lunar month. Every day shake the jar vigorously, concentrating on the idea that by doing this you are helping the plant release its powers.

When the moon is full, take your jar and leave it outside all night so that your tincture can be charged with the magical powers of moonlight. At the end of the lunar month, filter through muslin or a paper coffee filter, and store in a dark place. To use your tincture, with an eyedropper add about twenty drops to a glass of water and drink it immediately.

✎ Things to Do ✎

❋ Visit a website devoted to folk magic in Britain that explores specifically the range of unusual objects that have been discovered hidden within the walls and under the floors of old buildings in Britain, such as dried cats, horse skulls, old shoes, written curses and charms, witch bottles and ritual marks. These objects were usually concealed in buildings, or sometimes buried outdoors, for use as spells or counter-spells. See www.apotropaios. co.uk

❋ Many of the exhibits on display at the Witchcraft Museum in Boscastle, Cornwall, relate to the practices of cunning-folk. See Chapter 5 for details. You may also find related exhibits in your local museum, such as shoes found hidden in old buildings as protective charms, or witch bottles.

❋ Explore the work of Marian Green, a prolific author on magic and witchcraft in the style of the village wise-woman. See her *The Gentle Arts of Natural Magic: Magical Techniques to Help You Master the Crafts of the Wise* (Thoth, 1997) and details of her distance-learning and residential courses at www.theinvisiblecollege.co.uk

❋ Often cunning-folk were herbalists, skilled in the medicinal use of herbs and plants. To find a qualified herbalist or to enquire about training as one, contact the National Institute of Medical Herbalists: www.nimh. org.uk

You might also want to join the Herb Society, established in 1927, whose headquarters are in the sixteenth-century Sulgrave Manor, Oxfordshire. They publish a magazine, offer online forums, and there is a bookshop and a herb garden. See www.herbsociety.co.uk

❧ Visit one of the many herb gardens open to the public. *English Herb Gardens* by Guy Cooper, Gordon Taylor and Clive Boursnell (Weidenfeld & Nicolson, 1986) lists over forty that you can visit, including spectacular examples such as the Chelsea Physic Garden in London, which was established in 1673 by the Worshipful Society of Apothecaries, and contains 4,500 different species of plant. See www.chelseaphysicgarden.co.uk

Visit the Museum of Garden History, described as 'one of London's best-kept secrets', in Lambeth Palace Road, which builds on the legacy of John Tradescant – friend of the magus Elias Ashmole – mentioned in Chapter 9. See www.gardenmuseum.org.uk

❧ If you visit the herb garden of Knebworth House, Hertfordshire, you can also bask in the atmosphere of one of England's most famous magicians, Sir Edward Bulwer-Lytton. The novelist and occultist frequented the occult bookstore of John Denley, just a street away from Treadwell's bookshop mentioned in the Introduction. As you walk through the library at Knebworth, you can see books on the shelves that he probably bought in Denley's shop.

❧ Wise-women were often referred to as 'Mother'. The most famous of these – Mother Shipton – may well be more mythical than real, but her cave and well in Knaresborough, Yorkshire, became England's first commercially developed tourist attraction when it opened its gates in 1630.

Mother Shipton

Mother Shipton was said to have been one Ursula Southeil, born around 1488 as an illegitimate child in the famous cave beside the River Nidd. In 1512 she married a carpenter, Toby Shipton, and soon – according to the story – performed her first act of magic, and a typical feat of a cunning-person: she detected a thief and ensured the return of the stolen property. It is said that it was then that she began telling fortunes and she continued making prophecies until her death in 1561. Her predictions were published with great success from 1684 onwards.

The publisher Richard Head later admitted that he had invented most of the biographical details and prophecies, which were added to and changed in later additions, and author Charles Hindley admitted that he had faked more prophecies in 1873. 'England's Nostradamus' – as she was termed – turns out to have been largely fabricated by the book industry.

Even so, a visit to Mother Shipton's Cave will reveal something just as magical as the birthplace of a mythical or part-mythical seer: a 'petrifying well' – the only one of its kind in the country. The water that tumbles over ferns and an overhanging rock turns whatever is put beneath it into stone. For example, if a visitor leaves a teddy bear they can return a year later to see a stone bear in its place – the result of calcite crystals forming. This strange sight, combined with boat rides on the river, a park, a wishing well, a museum and the inevitable tourist shop, make Mother Shipton's Cave a good place for a visit with children. See www.mothershiptonscave.com

'*Mother Shipton's House*' *from*
Charles Mackay's Extraordinary Popular
Delusions and the Madness of Crowds
(nineteenth century).

❊ If Surrey is nearer, you may prefer to visit cunning-
woman Mother Ludlam's cave, near Moor Park, a few
miles outside Farnham in Surrey. Although you can't
get inside you can peer through the grille into the dark
interior where one legend records that Mother Ludlam
brewed her potions in a cauldron.

Then climb the hill south of Frensham village called
Stony Jump, to see where one poor soul reputedly asked
the fairies, by whispering through a hole in the huge
outcrop of rock on the summit, whether he could borrow
the cauldron. Because he did not return it on time, the
cauldron chased him to the village church where he
collapsed and died.

✎ Resources ✎

BOOKS

Cunning-Folk: Popular Magic in English History, Owen Davies
(Hambledon and London, 2003)

*Cunning Folk and Familiar Spirits: Shamanistic Visionary Traditions in
Early Modern British Witchcraft and Magic*, Emma Wilby (Sussex
Academic Press, 2005)

Religion and the Decline of Magic, Keith Thomas (Peregrine, 1978)

The Archaeology of Ritual and Magic, Ralph Merrifield (Batsford, 1987)

*The Witch of the West: Or, the Strange and Wonderful History of Thomasine
Blight*, Jason Semmens (Semmens, 2004)

WEBSITES

You can learn more about Cassandra Latham from her website: www.
villagewisewoman.co.uk

See Owen Davies's website on cunning-folk at: www.cunningfolk com

CHAPTER NINE

'THE ENGLISH MERCURY LOVER'

Freemasonry and the Power of Numbers

Woe is me, a very great man comes to an untimely end: a rot of sheep and men. Is any Nobleman beheaded? What if may be? Justice took place.

WILLIAM LILLY, *ENGLAND'S PROPHETICALL MERLINE*, 1644, PREDICTION FOR 30 JANUARY 1649, THE DATE CHARLES I WAS BEHEADED

In the winter of 1679 a fire raged through one of the most important collections of magical texts ever assembled under one roof. Standing in the ashes and debris of his library in Middle Temple, London, Elias Ashmole, one of England's greatest magicians, must have been reeling from the implications of this devastation. Thirty-three years of meticulous collecting had been devoured by the flames of an accidental fire that began in a neighbour's chambers. Treasured volumes on his favourite subjects – alchemy, hermetic magic, astrology, history, the arts and sciences: all were destroyed, along with almost nine thousand coins and medals, which melted in the heat, not to mention the most comprehensive collection ever made of ancient manuscripts and seals relating to the English nobility.

For a man obsessed with the search for truth and meaning, Ashmole must have wondered at the grim irony of this moment. He was suffering the same fate as his great hero of the previous century, the magician he most admired – Dr John Dee – who had returned from his travels abroad to discover much of his treasured library destroyed.

Elias Ashmole was no stranger to suffering and devastation. He had lived through one of the most turbulent times in English history, the civil war, when the country was torn apart by factions and the King had been beheaded – on the exact day predicted by astrologer William Lilly in his book *England's Propheticall Merline*, published five years before the King's execution. His mother and his first wife had both died from the plague, which became known as the Great Plague as it reached its height in London in 1665. And he had lived through the Great Fire of London the follow-

'The greatest virtuoso and
curioso that ever was known
or read of in England before
his time. Uxor Solis [the
spouse of the sun, i.e. Luna,
or Minerva, patroness of the
arts and sciences] took up
its habitation in his breast,
and in his bosom the great
God did abundantly store
up the treasures of all sorts of
wisdom and knowledge.'

(ANTHONY WOOD,
1632–1695)

ing year. If he could force himself to think positively at such a
moment, he might have remembered the alchemical belief that
with fire comes destruction but also a cleansing and the possibility of rebirth.

This Renaissance man, standing amongst the ashes towards the
end of his life, had been born in a city that some believe is the
spiritual centre of England – Lichfield in Staffordshire, where a
startling number of ley lines cross.[1] In the early days it was probably a Celtic settlement where the goddess Danu was worshipped.
It was later a centre of Saxon belief, until the arrival in 669 of the
ascetic Christian hermit St Chad. Although St Chad would have
rejected the ways of the Saxon sorcerer and the Celtic Druid, such
was his reputation for saintliness (standing naked by his well to
sing to his creator at every dawn) that the dust from his coffin was
used by the citizens of Lichfield for healing.

The old ways of magic die hard. The Venerable Bede, writing
in the eighth century of the cures effected in this way, described
'a wooden coffin in the shape of a little house with an aperture
in the side through which the devout can take out some of the

Lichfield Cathedral.

dust, which they put into water and give to sick cattle or men to drink, upon which they are presently eased of their infirmity and restored to health'.[2]

A great cathedral rose up in the town and Lichfield became a major centre of Christian pilgrimage. It was here, amongst the narrow cobbled lanes of the fortified city, that Elias Ashmole was born in 1617. As a boy he was entranced by tales of the fairy folk told to him by a piper, and throughout his life he was captivated by every kind of magic practised in the country-side. He was the archetypal Renaissance magus – one of those rare figures who became adept at a vast range of interests and disciplines.

In addition to his first love of 'Natural Magick', he was an avid antiquarian and founder of the world's first public museum, the Ashmolean in Oxford. Fascinated by dreams, he kept a personal dream diary, which was studied by Jung. It offers the earliest sub-stantial record of dreams in the seventeenth century, just as his notes on his initiation into Masonry offers the earliest account of that experience.

Ashmole was a mathematician, a scientist, a founding member

of the Royal Society, a lawyer, an astrologer and an alchemist. And, just like the legendary figure of Merlin, who acted as wizard to King Arthur, and the historical figure of the Druid who was counsellor to kings, at the height of his career Ashmole became the adviser to the court of King Charles II.

This extraordinary man, who liked to call himself 'Mercuriophilus Anglicus' (the English Mercury-Lover), stands alongside Roger Bacon, Francis Bacon and John Dee as one of the most influential figures in British cultural history – both magical and mundane.

ᴄ Civil War ᴐ

By some strange coincidence, both the wizards Dee and Ashmole, although separated by a century, experienced intense periods of cultural destruction.

In Dee's lifetime, Henry VIII presided over the despoiling of the nation's ecclesiastical buildings and most of its libraries in the 1530s. Dee's spiritual heir, Ashmole, lived through England's second great period of destruction when, in the 1640s, Oliver Cromwell's troops replayed history, burning books and stripping churches of valuable artefacts.

As an antiquarian, Ashmole was a conservative by nature – he loved the past and tradition, and was the first person to be called a 'Tory'. Once civil war broke out, it was natural that he would support the King. He was appointed a captain in the King's cavalry and was sent to Oxford to defend the city. It was here that – again like Dee – he busied himself with codes and ciphers on behalf of the Crown. He found time, too, to study alchemy, and attend to the needs of his prodigious libido, falling in love at the same time with Lady Thornborough and her daughter, who both confided their dreams to him.

The Democratisation of the Magical Tradition and the Ragley Hall Circle

In the middle of the seventeenth century, with the upheaval of the civil war and the Interregnum, a watershed was reached in the development of magic in England. A spate of translations of works on magic and alchemy from the Continent were published, with more books on alchemy appearing between 1650 and 1680 than before or since. The democratisation of magic was beginning.

During this same period, as Elias Ashmole was preoccupied with alchemy – compiling his master-work the *Theatrum Chemicum* and visiting his mentor William Backhouse – a gifted woman at Ragley Hall in Warwickshire was also studying alchemy and the cabbala. Like Mary Sidney, in the previous century (see Chapter 6), who had been fascinated by alchemy and had patronised a circle of intellectuals around her at Wilton House, Lady Anne Conway's 'Ragley Hall circle' included the alchemist Francis Mercury van Helmont, who stayed as a guest for nine years and eventually persuaded her to become a Quaker. Towards the end of her life she wrote *The Principles of the Most Ancient and Modern Philosophy*. A life-long sufferer from severe headaches, she died early – at the age of 47 – but not before inviting a renowned Irish spiritual healer, Valentine Greatrakes, who in 1666 visited Ragley Hall in an unsuccessful attempt to cure her.

By the summer of 1646 it was all over. The Royalists surrendered and Ashmole returned to Lichfield to discover his mother dead from the plague and the cathedral ruined, its central spire smashed by

Cromwell's cannons. This triple blow was followed that autumn by his initiation into the mysteries of Freemasonry. Ashmole's record of this event, which took place at 4.30 p.m. on 16 October of that year, is the earliest written account of a Masonic initiation.

◈ Initiation into Freemasonry ◈

When the candidate returns to the lodge, all lights save that of the master have been extinguished. The candidate may dimly perceive the design of the third degree tracing board, placed in the centre of the lodge. On it is depicted a coffin. A vivid skull and crossbones rest upon it. A plumb-rule, level and maul [two-handed hammer] rest upon it. Across the coffin a sheet is spread. It depicts a third chamber. A veil is partially drawn over the Holy of Holies at the far end. A figure approaches that place's golden glow. Within the light, the Ark may just be made out. From the top of the coffin, a sprig of acacia grows.

The candidate is led by the junior and senior wardens to a kneeling stool. The candidate kneels as the wardens cross their wands over his head. A prayer, addressed to the 'Great Architect of the Universe' is said . . .

TOBIAS CHURTON, *FREEMASONRY: THE REALITY*

The origins of Freemasonry are controversial. Dr Robert Plot, first curator of the Ashmolean, recorded the belief that 'it was brought into England by St Amphibal, and first communicated to St Alban'.[3] Others, including William Stukeley (see Chapters 1 and 2), believed that it existed in Britain before the time of the Druids, and that during the Roman rule lodges and conventions were held regularly. It then almost died out until it was reintroduced into England by the saints Amphibal and Alban.

Both of these legendary origins for the 'craft', as Masonry is known, are pleasing for advocates of the theory that Sir Francis

Bacon, Viscount St Alban, was instrumental in the restoration of philosophical and esoteric Freemasonry. St Albans, originally the Roman town of Verulamium sacked by Boudicca, was where Alban, Britain's first martyr, was beheaded in the fourth century. Bacon lived here as a young man and in his last days. His mansion at Gorhambury, just outside the town, now lies in ruins, but in the High Street, on the wall of a shop beside the White Hart Inn, you can still see a mural painted in his time that seems to contain esoteric and Masonic symbols. Perhaps it was here that lodge meetings were held, before the 'brothers' repaired to possibly the oldest surviving pub in England: Ye Olde Fighting Cocks – visited by Sir Walter Raleigh and Oliver Cromwell, amongst others.

Whether Francis Bacon was really a Freemason is open to question; our knowledge of the movement's history before the eighteenth century is limited. It fully emerged into the written record only with the founding in London of the Grand Lodge of England in 1717 – appropriately in

Francis Bacon, 1561–1626

another tavern: The Goose and Gridiron Ale House in St Paul's Churchyard. But this date marks simply Freemasonry's conversion from being primarily an oral tradition into a practice that began to be recorded and codified. Prior to that date we have clues scattered here and there that hint at the existence of this brotherhood well before the founding of the Grand Lodge. The diarist John Evelyn noted that 'Sir Christopher Wren (architect of S. Paules) was at a convention (at S. Paules 18 May 1691), of Free-masone adopted a Brother of that Society'[5] and references can be found to Freemasons or 'freestone masons' in England as far back as the thirteenth century.

But what exactly is Freemasonry? In the opening pages of this book we talked about Freemasons' Hall, the headquarters of the Grand Lodge, near Treadwell's bookshop, and of the way in which Freemasons still conduct rites there that involve the use of darkness and wands – just like those of the very earliest magicians in the depths of caves. Many Freemasons today treat their lodge activities as purely social and charitable. Whilst some conspiracy theorists like to believe that Masonry is a dangerous cult, most people perceive it as a rather peculiar and outdated social club, burdened with quaint customs that involve members wearing aprons and rolling up their trouser legs for initiation. There are, however, many other Masons (both male and female) who experience Freemasonry as a path of initiation into the Mysteries. And, for centuries, Masonry has played a key role in the development of English magic.

๑ The Origins of Masonry ๑

Modern Freemasonry is termed 'speculative' to distinguish it from the 'operative' masonry from which it evolved. Operative masons were architects and builders who formed themselves in medieval times, or possibly earlier, into trade guilds and used secret signs and admission rituals designed to safeguard their profession. By the late sixteenth century, speculative Freemasonry had evolved from operative masonry, building upon their signs and rituals to create a path of moral and spiritual development.

Dividing Masonry in this way, however, belies the fact that, in

 practice, Masonry from its earliest days was steeped in esoteric lore, with an elaborate mythology and a belief in the Divine nature of geometry and mathematics.

In *Freemasonry: The Reality* (Lewis Masonic, 2007) and *The Magus of Freemasonry* (Inner Traditions Bear and Company, 2006), Tobias Churton argues persuasively that Masonry was influenced by encounters with stonemasons and Sufis from the Middle East. In 1686, Robert Plot wrote that although Masons could be found all over the country, the highest concentration of them was in the Staffordshire moorlands. Research reveals that a knight crusader returned from the Holy Land to the moorlands with Saracens, one of whom was a stonemason. These Saracens were the ancestors of the dark-skinned 'Biddulph Moor men' who live in the region to this day. Other Saracens also made their way to other parts of Britain; the city of Chester had a Saracen mayor in the early thirteenth century.

On the moors were three Cistercian abbeys. St Bernard, founder of the Cistercians, also wrote the rules for the Knights Templar, and many Templars found their way into Cistercian abbeys at the end of their active duties. There had been contact between Britain and the Holy Land since Saxon times. The great series of crusader castles were built with the help of masons from the East as well as from the West, and the influence of Syrian or Phoenician styles is particularly noticeable in the church of St Chad in Stafford.

During the thirteenth century, followers of the Sufi Sheykh Adi, in what is now northern Iraq, pursued a mystical Gnostic version of Islam, whose hymns resonate with Masonic symbolism.

A Sufi influence is even suggested in the earliest recorded 'secret word' whispered to the Masonic initiate as the secret handshake was demonstrated:

> Standing close With their breasts to each other, the inside of Each other's right Ankle Joints the master's grip by their right hands and the top of their Left hand fingers thrust close on ye small of each other's Backbone, and in that posture they Stand till they whisper in each other's ears ye one Maha – the other replies Byn.
>
> (Sloane MS 3329, British Library, c.1700)[5]

Details of the words spoken and the 'grip' can be published here because they were changed by the Grand Lodge some time ago. But what might that secret word mean? The Sufi fraternal greeting is almost identical: *muhabba*. The potential meaning of the first recorded 'secret word' of Freemasonry is revealed in all its simplicity and nobility: *muhabba* means 'love'.

One of the distinctive features of most traditions of magic is the way in which they rise above sectarian and religious allegiances. Most magicians share a common belief in the primacy of love as a universal force and in the existence of a 'Perennial Philosophy', which has existed throughout the ages and which attracts to it a 'brotherhood' and 'sisterhood' of men and women who are more interested in the discovery of truth, the development of the soul and its powers and the practice of virtues, than in the restrictions of an orthodox faith.

Freemasons, like alchemists, were and still are drawn from every religion, and Masonry has been highly influential in the development of the Western magical tradition. It inspired not only William Stukeley, Elias Ashmole and their contemporaries in the seventeenth and eighteenth centuries, but the ceremonial magicians of the nineteenth century, and the witches and Druids of the twentieth.

✒ The Influence of Freemasonry ✒ – Theosophy and the Fivefold Kiss

Masonry even came to influence many of the leaders of the Theosophical Society, one of the most significant occult groups ever created, and in particular the writer and activist Annie Besant.

What is Theosophy?

Theosophy (meaning literally 'God wisdom' from the Greek) was used as a term by Neo-Platonists, Renaissance philosophers, and the Swedish mystic Emmanuel Swedenborg, who lived in London for four years in the early eighteenth century. In 1875 Helena Petrovna Blavatsky and her colleagues founded the Theosophical Society to promote a study of world religions and metaphysics. Although not specifically a magical group, many magicians joined the society, and by the end of the nineteenth century Theosophy had become – alongside Freemasonry and the Hermetic Order of the Golden Dawn – one of the three most important influences on the development of magic in England.

Besant, a pioneer of women's rights and birth control in England, campaigned tirelessly for humanitarian and social-ist ideals. In 1902 she travelled with six friends to Paris, where they were all initiated into the first three degrees of a Masonic lodge that allowed women into its ranks. Thanks to the women's suffrage movement and a growing feminist awareness in France towards the end of the nineteenth century, this new form of Masonry was adopted enthusiastically by many who saw the need for change, although it was shunned by orthodox Masons. A new organisation was formed in Paris, which later became known as the International Order of Co-Freemasonry. On her return to England, Besant founded the first Lodge of Co-Freemasonry (or Co-Masonry in its abbreviated form) in London, with eight other lodges soon appearing in other parts of the country.

Annie Besant in Masonic regalia.

Co-Masons, many of whom were Theosophists, were determined to focus on the occult or spiritual nature of Freemasonry, restoring it – in their eyes – to its true purpose as an esoteric rather than a purely social and charitable movement. To this day a large building in the leafy suburb of Surbiton houses two temples dedicated to Co-Masonic rituals, and in Notting Hill Gate another two temples can be found in a quiet side street where a breakaway movement meets – the Order of Women Freemasons.

In these temples, and in all Masonic lodges, Masons work their way through a series of 'degrees' conferred upon the candidate in initiation ceremonies. There are more than thirty-three of these degrees and over the centuries dozens of rites have been added to the corpus of ritual material available to the keen Mason. As if climbing a ladder of spiritual mastery, the Mason is supposed to feel a sense of increasing illumination as each degree is attained.

The occult teachings of Freemasonry are transmitted during these rituals, which are magical because they follow the age-old tradition of the Mystery Schools of ancient Greece and Egypt in using symbolism and ritual movement in a way that stimulates the candidate's consciousness and development. Many of the rituals can now be found in books, but their effect can be known only through experience, which is why a leading Freemason explains that 'The magic of Freemasonry is a felt experience as a result of "doing" the rituals with other masons. It is a self-protective mechanism whereby you have to be initiated to appreciate its inner meaning which is almost impossible to explain in words.'[6]

Gerald Gardner, the proponent of the modern witchcraft movement of Wicca, must have realised this when he discovered Co-Masonry through meeting the members of a Rosicrucian group in Dorset in 1938, one of whom was Annie Besant's daughter. By the time Wicca's initiation ceremonies were being performed twenty years later in the secluded setting of the witches' cottage in the Five Acres Naturist resort, they had incorporated most of the features of a Masonic initiation, with the added excitement of being undertaken entirely in the nude and with some light ritual flagellation administered by the High Priest or Priestess as an ordeal.

Initiation into Freemasonry from Duncan's Masonic Ritual and Monitor, *Malcolm C. Duncan, 1866.*

In the Wiccan initiation, just as in the Masonic, the pentagram is used as a key symbol, and the novice is blindfolded and led by a 'cable-tow' tied around the neck. They are challenged before entering the magic circle at the point of a sword, and are then led sunwise around the circle, stopping at each of the cardinal directions.

Again, just as in a Masonic initiation, they are asked to swear an oath of allegiance and are shown the 'working tools'. In Masonry these are displayed on the altar as a square and a compass; in Wicca these are the four implements shown on the Magician card of the Tarot: the cup, wand, sword and pentacle.

In Masonry, candidates are instructed with 'Charges' exhorting them to lead upright lives; in Wicca the Charge of the Goddess, coming originally from Italy, is more thrilling, as this excerpt shows:

> Whenever ye have need of anything, once in the month, and better it be when the moon is full, then ye shall assemble in some secret place and adore the spirit of Me who am Queen of all witcheries. There ye shall assemble, ye who are fain to learn all sorcery, yet have not won its deepest secrets; to these will I teach things that are yet unknown. And ye shall be free from slavery, and as a sign that ye are really free, ye shall be naked in your rites, both men and women, and ye shall dance, sing, feast, make music, and love, all in my praise.[7]

In the earliest English catechisms of Masonry, the secret word was passed from brother to brother in an embrace known as the 'Five Points of Fellowship' – a kind of geometrical hug in which the heels, knees and hands of the initiator and the candidate were connected in imitation of the operation of a compass point and square. Gardner, or someone unknown, must have enjoyed converting this strained embrace into a more reverential and sensuous experience by introducing into Wiccan ceremonies the 'Fivefold Kiss', whereby the initiator kisses the candidate on the feet, knees, just above the genitals, and on the breasts and mouth. Freemasonic ideas had hit the ground of the mid-twentieth century running – just in time for the sexual revolution of the 1960s.

✎ A High Magician Uses Low Magic ✎

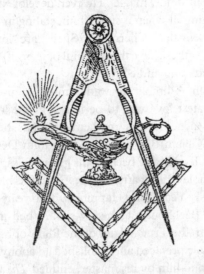

Elias Ashmole could never have dreamt that the simple initiation ceremony he underwent in 1646 would inspire such a radical reinterpretation, but such was his curiosity, his love of women, and his fascination for all things magical, that perhaps he would have appreciated the innovation.

Despite being a conservative, he was certainly willing to explore the unconventional. Suffering from the ague, he followed Robert Burton's advice in *The Anatomy of Melancholy* and hung three live spiders around his neck, curing himself in the process. From his youth he had begun using astrology to determine whether he would succeed in love, and in his old age he was still keen on the art: in 1682 he attended an Astrologers' Feast in London. Near Uttoxeter in Staffordshire, he participated in an invocation – asking the summoned spirit whether his friend would recover from his illness. The spirit replied in the affirmative, and he did indeed recover. Ashmole learnt Hebrew to study the cabbala from a rabbi in London, cast magic sigils in lead to help rid his house of fleas and attended a trial of witches at Maidstone Assizes in 1652.

Despite being a 'High Magician' who concerned himself with scholarly and antiquarian pursuits, Ashmole was not averse to using practical, so-called 'low magic'. He even developed a justification for lowering himself when it suited him, stating in *Prolegomena to Fasciculus Chemicus* that 'Charms, or Spells' are 'low and inferior assistants . . . yet these have their several powers, if judiciously and warily disposed and handled'.[8]

Even though Ashmole allowed himself to use charms and spells, his greatest love was to be found in the lofty heights of philosophical alchemy and mathematics. His heroes in these realms were William Backhouse and Dr John Dee respectively. The alchemist Backhouse became his guru – his spiritual father – in 1651, Ashmole writing afterwards, 'From this blest Minute I'le begin to date My Yeares and Happines'. Two years later Ashmole recorded that Backhouse, as he lay sick in bed in Fleet Street, revealed to him 'the True Matter of the Philosophers Stone', and in 1658 Ashmole prefaced and published an anonymous alchemical work given to him by his master, entitled *The Way to Bliss*.

Backhouse was an enthusiast of the Rosicrucian movement, which had originated in Germany earlier in the century. As we shall see in the next chapter, the Rosicrucians, real or imagined, played a significant part in English and European magical life from the moment they came into existence. A key element of British Rosicrucian interest centred upon the magical nature of numbers – a concept originating in the days of Pythagoras.

Ashmole's other hero – Dee – was also convinced of the power that numbers held, writing in his *Mathematical Preface* (1570): 'Many other artes there are which beautifie the minde of man: but of all other none do more garnishe and beautifie it, then [than] those artes which are called Mathematicall.'

And it was the power of numbers, of course, that lay behind the geometry so beloved of Freemasons and so necessary to the architects of cathedral, mosque and temple.

◉ *How to Use Numbers Magically*

Number is the ruler of form and ideas and is the cause of gods and demons.

PYTHAGORAS, ACCORDING TO IAMBLICHUS

PYTHAGORAS.

The Greek philosopher Pythagoras, the 'Father of Numerology'.

According to magicians, your name and birth-date have information encoded within them that can tell you a great deal about your character and soul – even your future. To crack this code you need to learn one of the basic magical arts: numerology.

The Greek philosopher Pythagoras is credited with introducing numerology to the classical world, but the origin of this art and the magical use of numbers can be traced further back to ancient India and China, Egypt, Assyria and prehistoric Europe.

From the moment people began counting, they discovered that alongside the practical use of numbers came power. The number of landmarks to pass before reaching a destination, the number of stars in a constellation, the number of days it took for a sown crop to begin sprouting, the number of animals owned, the number of warriors who will rally to your call – here we have the beginnings of early humanity's discovery of how to manipulate the universe around them. And with this we witness the birth of magic and astrology as well as of political and economic might.

Later, just as the science of chemistry gradually untangled itself from the 'superstition' of alchemy, so the science of mathematics managed to free itself from magical notions surrounding numbers. Most scientists today believe that numerology is simply nonsense. But magic treads in a realm beyond the reach of the scientist, and it is for you to decide whether the numbers hidden within your name or birthday really can help you in that first task of the magician: to 'know thyself'.

A FIRST EXERCISE

There are many different ways to use numbers magically to try to gain insight into your character and potential, or to get a glimpse of what the future might hold for you. Start with this simplest of methods – try it out on your name and the names of your friends and family – and either the results will surprise you with their accuracy or they won't. If they do seem uncannily insightful, you can explore the subject further in the 'Going Deeper' section below, in the recommended books and on specialist websites.

If the results of this first dip into the world of numerology are unconvincing, don't give up. Working with this exercise is like determining which astrological sign you belong to. Sometimes the thumbnail portrait of your sign of the zodiac will be spot-on but, as a professional astrologer will tell you, you will often need to look at far more information to get a really accurate picture. In the same way, the thumbnail portrait associated with your number might seem spookily accurate, but equally it may not. You may need to try some of the techniques listed at the end to see whether they are more helpful, or you may even want to consult a professional numerologist to explore your personal code more deeply.

ANALYSING YOUR NAME

When English magicians first started to work with numerology, they used the Pythagorean system, which equated the letters of the alphabet with numbers. Adapting it from the Greek, they created a grid that equated A with 1 and so on, like this:

1	2	3	4	5	6	7	8	9
A	B	C	D	E	F	G	H	I
J	K	L	M	N	O	P	Q	R
S	T	U	V	W	X	Y	Z	

The number derived from your full legal name is said to indicate the qualities you were born with, whilst the number derived from the version of your name that you use every day is said to describe how you will tend to experience yourself now. Choose which name you want to analyse (or choose both!) and, using this grid, translate your name into numbers, like this:

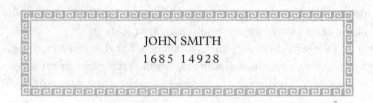

JOHN SMITH
1 6 8 5   1 4 9 2 8

Now add the numbers together = 1+6+8+5+1+4+9+2+8 = 44
Next reduce this number to a single digit between 1 and 9 by adding the two digits together: 4+4 to get your result = 8. Repeat if nesessary. Then read the relevant thumbnail sketch below and see whether it sounds like you.

1 **A leader: adventurous, courageous, determined, pioneering, inventive, original, individualistic, independent**

Someone whose name adds up to number One is likely to be a determined individual who likes to take the initiative and may well be in a position of leadership.

On the positive side they can be original, creative, and inventive – acting as a catalyst to action for others. Often courageous, they are always seeking a new challenge and can find it hard to finish what they have started. Strongly individualistic, they run the risk of becoming 'loners' who find it hard to get close to other people, and in extreme cases they can become opinionated, intolerant and egotistical, determined to have their own way whatever the cost.

2 **A peacemaker: gentle, sensitive, intuitive, diplomatic, cautious, indecisive, considerate, kind, co-operative, charming**

Someone whose name adds up to number Two is likely to be a gentle, charming individual who likes peace, harmony and beauty in their home and relationships.

Often highly sensitive and intuitive, they make good friends and partners, and are tactful and diplomatic – always seeking to mend broken relationships and hurt feelings. Their desire to make things better can sometimes lead to them being 'walked all over' and the danger for a Two is that their need for peace can mean they avoid challenging others or expressing their true feelings.

A Two will always try to seek balance, but this can sometimes mean that they are plagued with indecision – taking forever to choose their meal in a restaurant, or to make even the simplest decision.

3 **A creator and performer: inspired, imaginative, animated, enthusiastic, expressive, joyful, artistic, loquacious**

Someone whose name adds up to number Three is likely to be a person who is naturally optimistic, who knows how to enjoy themselves, and who is a born performer or actor, having a gift for self-expression.

Artistic and sociable, a number Three will tend to be happy only if they are creating or presenting something. They love bringing colour and joy into people's lives, and are good at being the life and soul of a party. They excel in their use of language, and tend to be talkative and often sexually charged. They are likely to expend their energies in too many directions at once, and although they are often highly creative and successful people, they can worry unduly about their abilities and may lack confidence.

4 A worker: practical, dedicated, industrious, conscientious, efficient, organised, stable, disciplined, hardworking, respectable

If you want a job done, look for someone whose name adds up to number Four.

Although they can sometimes be plodding and lacking in imagination, at their best Fours are the 'salt of the earth': stable, solid, reliable people who work hard and efficiently, and are used to organisation and discipline. They can be inflexible and dislike changes of plan, and can also suffer from fits of depression or rage, but they are often deeply concerned for the welfare and needs of others, and make excellent doctors and nurses.

A Four tends to be conservative and conventional, likes detail and routine, and enjoys building the foundations of an enterprise.

5 An adventurer: lively, resourceful, sensual, fickle, quick-witted, resilient, volatile, risk-taking, restless

Someone whose name adds up to number Five is likely to be a lively character who hates being tied down or stuck in a routine.

Fives get bored easily and love variety, adventure, risk and travel. On the positive side they thrive on change, are flexible and inventive and make sensual lovers. On the downside they resist commitment, can be volatile, and may have a tendency to enjoy gambling and unnecessary risk-taking.

Fives can be visionary and resourceful, excel at 'thinking outside the box' and can make good communicators. They enjoy working in the media, in films, theatre and television – but as directors or producers rather than actors.

6 **A family-loving home-maker: happy, balanced, responsible, protective, nurturing, harmonious, trusting**
Someone whose name adds up to number Six is likely to be well balanced, affectionate, and faithful.

Working well within organisations, teams and communities, they are loyal and dependable. Above all, a Six loves family life and is happiest beside their own hearth. They make good home-makers and love children and beauty, usually preferring a life of quiet domesticity rather than one of too much change and excitement. This can sometimes lead to them becoming smug and self-satisfied, but if their gift for friendship and their innate kindness and desire to be of service are cultivated, they are likely to lead successful and fulfilling lives, in which giving is more important to them than receiving.

7 **A scholar, philosopher and mystic: introspective, serious, reclusive, reserved, dignified, intuitive, studious**
Someone whose name adds up to number Seven is likely to be a natural recluse or hermit who prefers study to socialising, and who is more interested in spiritual or philosophical enquiry than in amassing fame or fortune.

A natural mystic and scholar, a Seven is happiest when exploring religious or esoteric subjects, or when engaged in analysis or research. Often highly sensitive and intuitive, a Seven needs regular periods of solitude. They tend to bottle up their emotions, keeping their feelings to themselves, and need to find ways in which they can relax and let go. They run the risk of seeking escapism rather than engaging fully in the world around them, and to find happiness they often need to give expression to their spiritual needs through following a religion or developing their own ideology.

8 A worldly person: powerful, practical, strong-minded, efficient, political, tenacious, ruthless, materialistic, hard-working

Someone whose name adds up to number Eight is likely to be deeply involved in worldly affairs – perhaps in business or politics.

They will tend to focus on material goals and be concerned with status and power, sometimes to the detriment of others. Although Eights are good at organising and delegating, and have a knack for bringing things together, they can be selfish, unscrupulous and ruthless in the pursuit of their goals. While Eights can often be successful, their success does not usually come easily and the prospect of catastrophic failure may always haunt them.

They have a great love of travel, and can achieve lasting and meaningful success if their ambitions are tempered with idealistic or spiritual values.

9 An idealist: determined, strong, compassionate, visionary, philanthropic, humanitarian, stubborn, romantic, passionate, impulsive

Someone whose name adds up to number Nine is likely to be a person of great charm and warmth, who is a visionary and an idealist.

Passionate and inspiring, some might find a Nine too impractical or unorthodox, but others will be impressed by them. With a strong desire to serve humanity, Nines make brilliant scientists, teachers and artists. They are determined and courageous, but can be stubborn and will dig their heels in if pushed too far. Once they have decided on a course of action, nothing will deter them or stand in their way.

Although usually generous and unselfish, they can be impulsive, rebellious, and highly egocentric – but all the time they will most likely be true to themselves and, ultimately, their ideals.

✐ Going Deeper ✐

For Number is the Mother and the Key
Of Arts; gives lyfe, and opens to a Sea
Of knowledge . . .

ELIAS ASHMOLE, 1653[9]

With this first exercise you have just dipped your toes in the water. If you want to go deeper, try some of the following methods:

Some numerologists say that the number derived from adding together the values of just the vowels will give you an idea of your inner soul qualities, while the number derived from the consonants will give an insight into your outer self – your personality. See whether this works for you.

Others say that the number derived from your day of birth symbolises how you see yourself. If you are born between the first and the ninth of the month, just read the thumbnail sketch that relates to your number and ask yourself whether that is how you see yourself. If you are born from the tenth onwards, use the method of adding the two numbers together (known as the 'Fadic method') to derive a number between 1 and 9 (for example, if you are born on the 28th of the month you see yourself as a 1: 2+8=10, 1+0=1).

Adding together the numbers of your full birth-date is said to give your destiny or fate number, which indicates what you deserve in this life. As an example, someone born on 28 November 1957 would be a 7: 2+8+1+1+1+9+5+7= 34 = 3+4 = 7.

Just as there are dozens of systems of astrology, so there are many different ways of working with numerology. Some numerologists use the Hebrew cabbalistic system, for example, which treats the numbers 11 and 22 as special, while others relate their system to astrology.

✷ Traps for the Sorcerer's Apprentice ✷

When former President Ronald Reagan and his wife
Nancy retired to California, they forced officials to change
their address from 666 to 668 St Cloud Road. No word
on whether the former president, whose full name is
Ronald Wilson Reagan, was bothered by the number of
letters in each of his first, middle and last names.

MARIO LIVIO, *THE EQUATION THAT COULDN'T BE SOLVED*

Once you know what numbers mean magically and symbolically, you can start to analyse and extract meaning from all sorts of things, such as place names, house numbers, telephone or car registration numbers, and historically significant dates.

While this sometimes might provide valuable insights, it's important to remember that numbers cluster in ways that can sometimes seem uncanny, as any follower of the lottery will know. There is no 'inner meaning' in this – it's not magic; it's just the way randomness works. Our brains are wired to see patterns, and to attribute meaning to patterns, so when we see a series of numbers that form a pattern or that 'miraculously' recur in different contexts we tend to think it must be meaningful.

When the novice magician first discovers the way numbers can encode information and reveal powerful truths, they can fall into the trap of seeing meaning in even coincidental or chance occurrences. Conspiracy theorists are particularly prone to this delusion. The 9/11 attack on the Twin Towers has spawned a host of speculation about the coincidences that $9+1+1=11$, that 911 is the number of the US Emergency Services, that the first plane to hit the World Trade Center was American Airlines Flight 11, that the State of New York was the eleventh state to be added to the union, and that the names George W. Bush, New York City, Air Force One, Afghanistan and the Pentagon all contain eleven letters.

The message? Don't look for magic and meaning everywhere. The way chance operates can sometimes make it look as if there is something mysterious afoot, when there isn't. The sorcerer's apprentice needs intelligence and the discernment to distinguish between the truly magical and mere coincidence.

NIGEL PENNICK

Nigel Pennick is an expert on a number of aspects of magic and a prolific author, with forty-nine books published to date, the last under his own 'Spiritual Arts and Crafts' imprint. After graduating at London University, he took a further degree in Botany and Biology at Cambridge and worked for a scientific research unit until the mid-1980s. He is particularly interested in the influences of the Germanic and Norse traditions of the Vikings and Scandinavians on the development of magic in England, and is also a skilled musician, painter and maker of stained glass. He lives near Cambridge.

A particular interest for me has always been the variety of spiritual influences on the development of craft skills, something now most associated with the Freemasons, but equally rooted in many rural guilds and associations.

When I was at Cambridge I met an old countryman, John Blackthorn, sitting in the corner of a pub, and I bought him a pint. He had been a horse expert since the First World War, but one evening he asked me out to help him plant his allotment potatoes. I wondered how on earth we would be able to set out straight rows at night, but he produced his rig, plus a couple of pointed sticks called 'Dods', wound with string, which he then aligned using the Pole Star. In a short time, we had a set of exactly parallel trenches lined up north and south, the best direction for potatoes to grow. It was an example of the practical use of astronomy without all the ritual stuff that gets in the way of magic. For me this was a spiritual initiation.

As I extended my studies, I soon realised that this spiritual association with arts and crafts had been common knowledge since the third century. Plotinus, one of the most famous Neoplatonist magicians, wrote in his *Enneads* that 'the arts are not an imitation of nature, but human-mediated expressions of the spiritual source of which nature is only the outward form.'

To me, art is the operative link between the imagination and the final result, which is what Tolkien called 'sub-creation' – using the given materials of creation in a new way that nevertheless operates according to the 'five principles':

1. suitability for purpose
2. convenience in use
3. proper use of materials
4. soundness of construction
5. subordination of decoration to the above

When art has the convincing inner conviction of reality, then a secondary world has come into being. For example, in the six-teenth century, the spiritual teacher Giulio Camillo Delmonico recalled: 'in Egypt, there were statue makers who were so skilled that when they had given a statue perfect proportions, it was found to be animated with an angelic spirit: for such perfection could not be without a soul'.[10]

Probably the best visible expression of this type of spirituality lies in the churches that Sir Christopher Wren built after the Great Fire of London. Wren was adopted into the Fraternity of Accepted Masons on 18 May 1691. Records of the Lodge Original, No. 1, mention him as being Master. He believed in the Freemasons' principle that sacred geometry is essential to spiritual architecture. 'Buildings cer-tainly should have the attribute of the eternal,' he wrote in 1721. His motto was 'numero, pondera et mensura' – by number, weight and measure: a saying ascribed to Solomon, the geometry of whose temple in Jerusalem is at the very core of Freemasonic belief.

Principles of sacred geometry involve combining basic forms, such as squares, cubes or circles, into an overall symmetrical struc-ture, which is then linked to various forms of numerology and astrology. Every church in the period immediately after the Great Fire of London was built according to such principles and is easily recognisable today. For example, Wren used the number seven in St Paul's Cathedral to determine the heights of the columns. This practice has produced beautiful and harmonious 'ensouled' structures, which continue to resonate three centuries later. Just visit them yourself and compare them to modern church architecture and you will see what I mean.

In 1711, Sir John Vanbrugh wrote that a church should create an image of solemn and awfulness in the beholder. Even now, when you go into one you are conscious of a feeling of reverence. In those days, people genuinely felt in church that they were experiencing God's will coming through the architecture.

The crafts and guilds, of which the Freemasons are an example, protected their knowledge tightly. Delegates at a craft conference in the fifteenth century were advised that the skill 'To take an elevation from a plan' should not be shown to anyone outside the craft. Complex initiation rites were designed to be both spiritually and physically frightening enough to persuade members of the order to keep its secrets. These rites still exert considerable power with societies, such as the Freemasons, but, alas, the craft basis of the movement has now, along with that of other guilds, been seriously eroded.

East Anglia, where I live, still has extensive records of these craft skills such as those practised by the Horsemen's Guild. Initiation involved various mental and physical ordeals, including putting a noose around a blindfolded apprentice's neck in a midnight barn ceremony, then make him jump to his apparent death. In fact, the noose would be detached from its beam at the last moment, so the apprentice would simply fall into a bale of hay.

Some of these secret guild skills were considered to be a species of witchcraft such as the making of 'drawing' oils, for example, to get a horse to move towards you. These were compounded from mixtures of cinnamon, fennel, oregano and rosemary, and were soaked into a cleft stick. Stopping and starting horses can be done using similar tricks. Clothes soaked in your own sweat strengthen your hold over the animal and the same principle can also be used with dogs. It was believed that the powdered liver of a weasel would stop a horse, as nothing will make one walk past it. Local witches soon learnt this trick and would hold a horse stopped until the owner paid them to release the spell. Magic has to have a practical use to survive. The witches were just employing an earlier version of a protection racket.

A closer relationship with witchcraft is associated with those who were ranked as 'Toads men and women', through carrying a powerful amulet known as the 'bone'. To gain the 'bone', one must bury a toad in an ants' nest and leave it until all the flesh has decayed. The bones are then taken to a stream, which runs north–south (like the rows of potatoes), and floated in the running water to separate them. The bone that appears to turn against the current is the 'bone' and it can be used to gain power over not just horses, but men and women too.

Our modern world tells us to ignore these ancient arts as superstition, but I would counsel caution. There is no doubt that some of the darker forms of magic are still practised. Visiting a local church recently, I discovered three human bones of varying sizes laid out symmetrically by the door. Using male, female and children's bones in this way is supposed to be a skill of a craft of sextons and gravediggers – the 'bone men'. In their initiation ceremonies, candidates would be led into a graveyard at dead of night where they would see two skulls. One would be that of a nobleman, the other that of a serf. The initiate would have to figure out which was which. The right answer was that you could not tell – all dead men are equal.

Other country rituals have got lost in translation into our modern world. The habit of washing doorsteps comes from a way of protecting houses through marking hearthstones and other entry points. In the old days, these would be neatly bordered with white around a row of nine crosses, sometimes rubbed with elder, dock or oak leaves to leave traces of green sap.

Sometimes, the last experts in a dying craft consciously destroyed their knowledge. For example, the labyrinths, still seen as mazes throughout England, once had a magical function of trapping spirits. Fishermen would construct them to trap these sprites, which stopped the wind blowing, and there are examples that are over a thousand years old. Yet the last great 'Labyrinth Master' refused to pass on his skills as he thought no one was worthy enough.

'Chronomancy', the art of doing everything at precisely the right time according to the cycles of the stars, is another lost skill. Runic magic stresses the importance of tapping into the right power on the right date, and consecration ceremonies used to abide strictly by such guidelines. Church-building ceremonies used to rely on 'electional astrology' to find precisely the right moment to lay the foundation stones.

I deeply regret the way we live in a world of strangers, where everything we use and see is brought to us through the anonymity of mass production, and is not 'ensouled', like Wren's churches, by sacred geometry and individual belief.

Attempting to redress the balance by searching out the ancient meanings is hampered by long periods in our history when magic and superstition were outlawed. For example, there was a miller in Huntingdonshire at Great Granston, who owned the last great book of witchcraft, titled *The Devil's Plantation*. His family were so frightened of its power that they burnt it. Often all that remains of the past is a few bits of paper hidden behind old stones, or a few little *Books of Shadows* that carry the past when there is no official record left. People no longer do things because their ancestors did them; it is no longer part of our culture to pass things on to the next generation.

⁀ Things to Do ⁀

❈ Visit Freemasons' Hall in London's Great Queen Street. There you can see for yourself the interior of the Grand Temple, and you can even buy books and unusual items such as a deck of Masonic playing cards from a small shop, which also sells regalia to the initiated. Tours take place five times a day and photographic ID is required.

Upstairs a reference library is available for research. It contains a comprehensive collection of printed books and manuscripts on every facet of Freemasonry in England, as well as material on Freemasonry elsewhere in the world, and on subjects associated with Freemasonry or with mystical and esoteric traditions.

There is also a museum containing an extensive collection of objects with Masonic decoration, including pottery and porcelain, glassware, silver, furniture and clocks, jewels and regalia. Items belonging to famous and royal Freemasons, including Winston Churchill and Edward VII, are on display, together with examples from the museum's extensive collection of prints and engravings, photographs and ephemera.

See www.ugle.org.uk for general information, and www.freemasonry.london.museum for information on the library and museum, which are open Monday to Friday, from 10 a.m. to 5 p.m.

Freemasons' Hall is a short walk away from the delights of Covent Garden and three of the capital's most interesting magical bookstores: the Atlantis Bookshop in Museum Street, Treadwell's in Tavistock Street and Watkins in Cecil Court.

* If you are more interested in the magical and esoteric significance of Masonry than in its social and charitable work, explore Co-Masonry, which is open to women as well as men. The UK headquarters are in Surbiton, Surrey, in a large building that houses a library and two temples. Lodges also exist in other parts of Britain. See www.droit-humain.org/uk

* If you'd prefer to become a Mason in the company of women only, consider joining the Order of Women Freemasons, established in 1908, with headquarters and two temples in Pembridge Gardens, West London. In June 2008 the Order held centenary celebrations at the Albert Hall with over five thousand members and friends

in attendance. Over three dozen 'craft lodges' can be found throughout Britain. See www.owf.org.uk

❃ You can also join and study with 'esoteric Masons' with distance-learning. See the 'Ancient, Accepted and Esoteric Freemasons' at www. esotericmasons.com

❃ The Canonbury Masonic Research Centre, located in Sir Francis Bacon's Islington home of Canonbury

Tower (*left*), holds an annual conference and lectures through the year on spiritual and magical subjects as well as 'esoteric Masonry'. See www.canonbury.ac.uk

❃ If studying or joining Masonry doesn't appeal to you, try sitting back and capturing its essence by listening to Mozart's opera *The Magic Flute*. Mozart was a keen Freemason and conveyed its central ideas in probably the most accessible opera ever written. For a real treat, rent or buy a copy of Ingmar Bergman's film version.

❃ Visit the Ashmolean Museum in Oxford. After a £61 million refurbishment completed in 2009, it is even more stunning than it was before. As you walk through its displays, remember the magician who founded this institution – the inspiration he found in his study of magic and alchemy, and the importance he attached to appreciating the gifts of the past. See www.ashmolean.org

If you can't manage a physical visit to the museum, you can take a virtual one to see it as it was in 2003, through a series of navigable, 360-degree panoramic views of each gallery, by visiting www.chem.ox.ac.uk/ oxfordtour/ashmolean

❧ Visit Lichfield, Staffordshire, considered the 'spiritual heart of England' by some esotericists, who point to the many ley lines converging on this old centre of pilgrimage. St Chad, patron saint of the insane, prayed naked beside the well now named in his honour, and Lichfield Cathedral is built over his bones.

 You can see a plaque honouring Elias Ashmole's birthplace in Breadmarket Street. Visits to Gaia Lane, Borrowcrop Hill, St Chad's Well and the cathedral (which displays a statue of Ashmole holding a model of his museum) are all worthwhile, particularly if combined with the Lichfield Heritage weekend or Lichfield Literature Weekend in September. See www. visitlichfield.co.uk

❧ Visit St Chad's Church in Stafford to see evidence of Saracen architecture, which may point to early Sufi influences on Freemasonry.

❧ Visit Ragley Hall in Warwickshire, site of the home of Lady Anne Conway and – for nine years – of the

Ragley Hall

alchemist van Helmont. The design of the current building was begun a year after her death, but work was not completed until the eighteenth century. See www.ragleyhall.com

❧ Explore the work of the Francis Bacon Research Trust, which offers itself as a 'Gateway to the Western Wisdom Tradition and Its Initiates'. Dedicated to exploring the esoteric, Masonic and Rosicrucian significance of Sir Francis Bacon's work, it organises conferences and pilgrimages, and offers a series of books by the Trust's founder, Peter Dawkins. The 'Treasure Trail' on its website presents an exciting way of exploring esoteric ideas through a website. See www.fbrt.org.uk

✏ Resources ✏

⊙ *Freemasonry*

BOOKS

An Encyclopedic Outline of Masonic, Hermetic, Qabbalistic and Rosicrucian Symbolical Philosophy, Manly Palmer Hall (Forgotten Books, 2008)

Freemasonry: The Reality, Tobias Churton (Lewis Masonic, 2007)

The Golden Builders: Alchemists, Rosicrucians and the First Free Masons, Tobias Churton (Red Wheel/Weiser, 2005)

The Magus of Freemasonry: The Mysterious Life of Elias Ashmole, Scientist, Alchemist and Founder of the Royal Society, Tobias Churton (Inner Traditions, 2005)

Isaac Newton's Freemasonry: The Alchemy of Science and Mysticism, Alain Bauer (Inner Traditions, 2007)

Freemasonry: Symbols, Secrets, Significance, W. Kirk MacNulty (Thames & Hudson Ltd, 2006)

The Secret Science of Masonic Initiation, Robert Lomas (Lewis Masonic, 2008)

The City of London: A Masonic Guide, Yasha Beresiner (Lewis Masonic, 2006)

Western Esotericism and Rituals of Initiation, Henrik Bogdan (State University of New York Press, 2007). This offers details of the Masonic influence on Wicca, the Golden Dawn and other movements.

WEBSITES

Purchase Masonic regalia or simply browse at www.thefreemason.com

The Philosophical Research Society was formed in 1934 by the Freemason Manly Palmer Hall, author of the monumental *An Encyclopedic Outline of Masonic, Hermetic, Qabbalistic and Rosicrucian Symbolical Philosophy*. The Society and its university offer DVDs, books, and distance-learning degrees. See www.prs.org and www.uprs.edu

Lectures by Manly Palmer Hall and a forty-minute video, 'Passing the Lamp – The Life of Manly P. Hall', can be viewed at www.video.google.com

Lewis Masonic, at www.lewismasonic.com, offer books, CDs and DVDs on Masonic and related subjects, including a twin DVD set of Tobias Churton's films: *A Mighty Good Man: Elias Ashmole and the Initiation* (a drama-documentary that includes a reconstruction of the first, personally recorded, Free Masonic Initiation into a Lodge anywhere in the world), and *Fama Fraternitatis: The True Story of the Rosicrucians*.

⊙ *Numerology*

To find out more about the power of numbers, use the modern magic carpet of your computer to fly into cyberspace where dozens of sites will teach you about numerology. Alternatively, investigate the books listed below, which will give you an even better grasp of this arcane art.

BOOKS

Action, Attraction Integration, Christopher Power (available from www.actionattractionintegration.com)

Numerology: The Spiral Path, Elen Sentier (Capall Bann, 2006)

Numerology: The Complete Idiot's Guide, Kay Lagerquist (Alpha, 2004)

To go deeper still, explore the most sophisticated development of
    Numerology, the Enneagram, in the following books:

H. Palmer, *The Enneagram* (Harper San Francisco, 1991)

S. Maitri, *The Spiritual Dimension of the Enneagram: Nine Facets of the
    Soul* (Tarcher Putman, 2000)

A.H. Almaas, *Facets of Unity: The Enneagram of Holy Ideas* (Diamond
    Books, 1999)

CHAPTER TEN

THE SPIRITS OF
DEAD MAGICIANS

Secret Chiefs, Hidden Masters and Adepts of
the Rosy Cross

*Consulting dead magicians may strike us as
highly sensational,
but it is a magical procedure with a perfectly
respectable history.*

SUSANNA CLARKE, *JONATHAN STRANGE &
MR NORRELL* (BLOOMSBURY, 2004)

The eighteenth century was the Age of Reason. Magic still flourished in the alleyways of the cities, and the countryside was dotted with its fortune-tellers and cunning-folk, but as the effects of the Enlightenment gained momentum it was science that increasingly held sway amongst the intelligentsia. There were some scientists, particularly in the earlier half of the century, who still clung to aspects of the magical world-view; one such was Isaac Newton, who experimented with alchemy until the end of his life in 1727; but in general, as the stranglehold of religion diminished through this era, so, too, did a preoccupation with magic.

Sir Isaac Newton, 1643–1727.

As conscious interest in the subject waned, however, a peculiar phenomenon occurred: more and more people began engaging in activities that were in essence magical, but without seeing them as such. This was due to the success of Freemasonry. To be led blindfold in bare feet or with one foot slip-shod, with clothes rearranged to expose parts of the body to the gaze of unseen initiates, to be challenged at the point of a sword, to have a noose around one's neck like a prisoner bound for the gallows or a foetus entangled with its umbilical cord, and to swear loyalty before being 'reborn' into the light and welcomed into a select group: this is an experience that is based upon the same principles that were used by the Ancient Mystery Schools. They can also be observed to this day in the rites of passage of indigenous peoples around the world. Clearly such a ceremony touches upon the most basic human experiences of birth itself, of fearing death and of surviving ordeals – and it was this activity, clothed in all the pomp and ceremony required to make it acceptable to eighteenth-century gentlemen, that made Freemasonry such an enduring and successful phenomenon.

But there was a price to pay for that success. As the institution of Masonry grew, its original founding impulses of mutual support, the protection of trade secrets and the use of secret rites were so appealing that these ideas were imitated and adopted almost wholesale by many trade institutions. Millers, coopers, printers and dozens of other similar groups developed rites that involved Masonic-style initiations. In 1830, the Shoemaker's Union in Cheshire, for example, bought 'a full set of secret order regalia, surplices, trimmed aprons, etc., and a crown and robes for King Crispin', the legendary patron of their craft.[1] Magic had crept into the professional life of England through the back door.

The attraction of mutual support in a time before the existence of the National Health Service or a well-developed insurance system also meant that 'Friendly Societies' proliferated; towards the end of the century their members numbered at least 4 million Britons. Like Freemasonry and the trade societies, these were organised into lodges, and the largest became national institutions, some of which still exist in greatly diminished form. They developed pseudo-histories and gave themselves grand titles, such as 'The Royal Antediluvian Order of Buffaloes', the 'Ancient Order' of Foresters, Shepherds or Druids, or simply 'The Society of Oddfellows'. At their meetings they wore robes, held initiation ceremonies that followed the Masonic pattern and promoted themselves through successive 'degrees'.

They sometimes invented new ordeals for their candidates. For example, Foresters had to fight a ritualised duel by sword, Buffaloes had their hair cut or singed, while Oddfellows were tossed blindfold into a pile of brushwood or had their heads thrust into a tub of water.[2] However strange this might have seemed, a visit to the opera to see Mozart's *The Magic Flute* would have reminded the initiate that Pamino, too, had to face his ritual ordeals.

By the end of the nineteenth century the extraordinary situation existed that millions of Englishmen were engaging in magical ceremonies without actually realising it. Rather than enrolling in a magical lodge, they believed that they were joining a social and charitable organisation, as do most Freemasons today. Even so, a Jungian psychologist would argue that you cannot enact rituals that use such primal symbolism without it affecting the psyche – even if only at an unconscious level.

Such was the power of the Masonic impulse that its impact was felt not only by trade bodies and Friendly Societies throughout the country, but on the world of organised magic and religion too.

Joseph Smith, the founder of Mormonism, a Christian sect now with over 12 million members, was influenced by Freemasonry and also, almost certainly, by that old wizard Dr John Dee. Smith, like Dee, tried to divine the whereabouts of buried treasure, used a black 'seer stone' for scrying, had 'conversations with angels',[3] was fascinated by the prophet Enoch, and established a religion that in its early years allowed polygamy. He and many of the early 'saints' of his church were Masons, and Masonic influences can be found in Mormon architecture and in the Mormon Temple ceremonies.[4]

‸ The Hermetic Order of the Golden ‸ Dawn and the Brotherhood of the Rosy Cross

While Masonic ideas made their way into only one branch of Christianity, they succeeded in influencing almost every aspect of ritual magic in England and Europe. Until the advent of Masonry, most ritual magicians had relied on the medieval magical workbooks known as grimoires which advocated lengthy and solitary procedures for evoking Holy Guardian Angels or for summoning demons who would do the magician's bidding. As Ronald Hutton in *The Triumph of the Moon* drily observes, this latter kind of magic, usually known as Goetia, was 'at basis an elaborate way of ringing for room service'.[5] With the arrival of Masonry, and its system of initiations and numerous grades, ritual magicians were given a structure that they could use as a basis for whatever kind of magic they liked – and it was a system that allowed for organisation, with a network of lodges that encouraged a pattern of cellular growth.

The 'Emerald Tablet of Hermes' from The Secret Symbols of the Rosicrucians, *Altona, 1785.*

Nowhere was the influence of Freemasonry on the development of magic more obvious than in the creation, towards the end of the nineteenth century, of an organisation that was to profoundly influence the development of magic throughout the world. Formed in London in 1888 by three high-ranking Freemasons, the Hermetic Order of the Golden Dawn took the structure of Freemasonry, with its rites and degrees, and used it to train magicians by informing it with lore derived from medieval grimoires, the cabbala and astrology. Furthermore, they added to this potent mixture a phenomenon that had intrigued and inspired generations of occultists and intellectuals: the Rosicrucians. These 'brothers of the Rosy Cross' were reputed to be advanced adepts who moved anonymously through the world, working for the good of humanity.

The Rosicrucians have had a major impact on the Western magical tradition and they continue to do so today, acting as one of many sources of inspiration for the magical worlds created by J.K. Rowling and Philip Pullman. Many thousands of people belong to the Rosicrucian groups listed at the end of this chapter.

But to understand why they have had such an impact, and why they are still influential today, we need to travel back to the early years of the seventeenth century.

Between 1614 and 1616, a trio of publications appeared that announced to the world the existence of a mysterious brotherhood. The first, published in Kassel in Germany, was titled *Fama Fraternitatis, dess Löblichen Ordens des Rosenkreutzes* (*The Declaration of the Worthy Order of the Rosy Cross*). The second, issued in 1615 and also published in Kassel, bore the title *Confessio Fraternitatis, The Confession of the Laudable Fraternity of the Most Honourable Order of the Rosy Cross, Written to All the Learned of Europe.* The third, *The Chemical Wedding of Christian Rosenkreutz,* was published in Strasbourg the following year and was perhaps the most interesting of all.

From The Secret Symbols of the Rosicrucians, *Altona, 1785.*

The *Fama* set the scene, revealing the existence of a fraternity founded by a nobleman and former monk, Christian Rosenkreutz, who lived from 1378 to 1484. He had travelled to the East in search of wisdom, visiting 'Damcar' (which might mean Damascus), Jerusalem and Fez, where he had been initiated into the secrets of Arabian magic. On his return he founded the brotherhood in 1408. Members of the order travelled incognito, healing the sick, and studying the laws of nature and her hidden forces, reuniting every year at the headquarters of the Order – the mysterious 'House of the Holy Spirit'. When Christian Rosenkreutz died, he was buried in a secret location that remained undisclosed for the next 120 years. Its discovery at the beginning of the seventeenth century, so the *Fama* reveals, heralds a new age.

Johann Valentin Andreae, probable author of The Chemical Wedding of Christian Rosenkreutz.

The *Confessio* echoed the message of the *Fama* and revealed a Protestant agenda: holding out the promise of a reformed world with an end to the tyranny of the Pope. *The Chemical Wedding* reads quite differently and recounts a story, filled with alchemical symbolism, of the wedding of a king and queen in a wondrous castle. Although all three works were published anonymously, *The Chemical Wedding* was almost certainly written by Protestant theologian Johann Valentin Andreae, who may well have written or co-written the *Fama* too. No one knows who wrote the *Confessio*.

From its inception the Rosicrucian phenomenon caused a furore. On the one hand there was a clear Protestant motivation behind the texts, and Andreae even confessed that *The Chemical Wedding* had been a 'ludibrium' – a sort of joke or game. Whether or not *The Chemical Wedding* was intended as a jest, the first two documents, known collectively as 'The Rosicrucian Manifestos', were clearly designed with serious ends in mind: philosophical, religious and even political.

The *Fama* ended by offering an invitation to 'all of the scholars and rulers of Europe' to promote the ideals of the brotherhood and to 'declare their minds in print', promising 'that whosoever shall earnestly, and from his heart, bear affection unto us, it shall be beneficial to him in goods, body and soul'.[6] No address was provided, but this omission was in reality a stroke of genius, worthy of the most sophisticated PR or advertising executive. The thought of a club that was so exclusive that it was impossible to contact – whose members were so dedicated and noble as to delve into the secrets of nature and heal the sick without a moment's thought for fame – was irresistible. All over Europe eager intellectuals sought to attract the attention of the Order by writing books praising their ideals and demonstrating why their authors should be admitted to its ranks, while others fulminated against it.

When no mysterious adepts emerged to welcome these authors, necessity being the mother of invention, a number of ingenious people felt moved to start their own Rosicrucian Orders. Fiction became fact and what had started as a 'Bardic' impulse succeeded in creating innumerable secret brotherhoods. The idea, to use internet marketing jargon, 'went viral'. From being little more than a story dreamt up by a few young Protestants in Middle Germany, it took on a life of its own and succeeded in replicating itself over and over again.[7]

The story of Rosicrucianism highlights an issue that in the end must be confronted by every student of magic and its history. The magical quest is – in one of its deepest senses – a philosophical quest for the truth, and yet the story of magic is one of endless fantasies, fibs and fictions. Much of the recounted history, certainly before the end of the twentieth century, of Druids, witches, Freemasons, alchemists and Rosicrucians is simply not true. Sometimes this is the result of deliberate deception, sometimes of poor scholarship combined with wishful thinking.

The question then becomes: 'Is it all worthless nonsense, or, like gold hidden in dross, is there something valuable at the heart of it all?' Sceptics quickly dismiss magic when they discover the duplicities of famous magicians, or the lack of substance behind most 'lineages' of so-called secret traditions. However, there is another way of understanding these things, which allows us to accept the fact that magical traditions can be founded upon fictions, as the writer Alan Moore explains:

> Might not the entirety of Magic be described as traffic between
> That Which Is and That Which Is Not; between fact and fiction?
> If we are to speak of Magic as 'The Art', should we not also
> speak of Art as Magic? . . . The magician conjures angels or else
> demons, out of nothingness into manifestation, while the novelist
> does likewise with her ideas and her characters. Again we have a
> commerce between the existent and the non-existent, something
> out of nothingness, the rabbit from an empty hat that is perhaps
> the very crux of magical endeavour . . . Sometimes things
> come through. Sometimes, things trade position with their own
> reflection. Real works of Magic are exposed as fictions. Works of
> fiction are revealed as Magic.[8]

From this point of view, the Rosicrucian phenomenon is an example of one of the most powerful acts of magic ever undertaken. The 'Manifestos' manifested the very thing that they described, with the result that there are today many 'secret fraternities' (most with an internet presence), training 'adepts' to be of service in the world.

A representation of the Rose Cross, created by the Hermetic Order of the Golden Dawn in the nineteenth century.

The most successful magical or occult groups of the last three hundred years have followed a similar pattern, including the Freemasons, the Theosophical Society, the Hermetic Order of the Golden Dawn, and the various groups of modern witches and Druids. All have seemingly been endowed with pseudo-histories that have since been exposed, and yet each has provided a vehicle for thousands of initiates to deepen their experience of life. Behind the fictitious or semi-fictitious histories of these groups, however, strands of influence can be found that often stretch far back in time. Currents of Gnostic, Hermetic, folkloric and other influences stand behind their genesis, and the casual researcher who dismisses the validity of magical groups on the grounds of their distorted pedigrees has merely failed to dig deep enough.

Read about the World of Rosicrucians and Hidden Masters in Fiction

Zanoni, Edward Bulwer-Lytton (Waking Lion Press, 2008). Morality is explored in the context of longevity. Zanoni, the archetypal white magician, is an initiate of a brotherhood who knows the secrets of alchemy and immortality.

The Secrets of Dr Taverner, Dion Fortune (Aquarian, 1989). Dr Taverner is the quintessential adept. A series of short stories involve him with most aspects of occult pathology, during which he is revealed as the senior adept of a magical lodge that brings down retribution on occult malefactors.

The Initiate, The Initiate in the New World and *The Initiate in the Dark Cycle*, Cyril Scott (Red Wheel/ Weiser, 1991). These three books recount anecdotes and studies of the initiate's encounters with an adept and 'a very well-known Englishman'.

Jonathan Strange & Mr Norrell, Susanna Clarke (Bloomsbury, 2004). In 1806 the return of magic to England is prophesied, and a story of rivalry between two magicians during the Napoleonic wars unfolds.

Even though the original Rosicrucians were a fiction, the ideas and images evoked in the 'Manifestos' and *The Chemical Wedding* were not merely imaginary. The idea of a secret society of initiates has existed ever since the days of the Ancient Mysteries, and entwined in the idea of the 'brothers of the Rosy Cross' one can sense the worlds of German knightly orders and medieval brotherhoods, combined with the sophistication of the academies of Renaissance Florence.

Some writers have even suggested that the Rosicrucian movement originated in England – either through the direction or inspiration of Francis Bacon, who wrote of ideals similar to those of the Rosicrucians in his *New Atlantis* of 1623, or, with more justification, that it arose as a result of John Dee's influence. The monad symbol he used in his work *Monas Hieroglyphica*, is reproduced in *The Chemical Wedding*, and the first edition of the *Confessio* included a text entitled 'A Brief Consideration of the More Secret Philosophy', which was based on Dee's *Monas* and which quoted it extensively. Dee was in Bohemia in the 1580s, thirty years or so before the 'Manifestos' appeared, and it is quite possible that at least some of the inspiration for Rosicrucianism can be ascribed to the English wizard.[9]

Whether or not the 'Manifestos' received influences from Mortlake or St Albans, once the texts began to circulate Rosicrucianism very rapidly took on its own character in England. Many of the individuals we have already encountered in earlier chapters were fascinated by the Rosicrucians and either sought admission or claimed that they were in fact already brothers. In the seventeenth century, the alchemical philosophers Robert Fludd and Thomas Vaughan were the two main apologists for the fraternity, and the Royal Society, founded in London in 1660, was probably influenced by the Rosicrucian ideals of a brotherhood of learning designed to herald a new age of enlightenment.

Thomas De Quincey, of opium-eating fame, believed that Rosicrucianism was responsible for the establishment of Freemasonry in England,[10] while most scholars believe the reverse process occurred, with Freemasonry taking the Rosicrucian idea to its bosom, and creating, in the eighteenth century, a set of Rosicrucian degrees, accessible only to high-ranking Masons who could call themselves 'Knights of the Rosy Cross' after enacting the requisite rites. A hundred years later, in 1866, the Societas Rosicruciana in Anglia (the Rosicrucian Society

The Symbol of the Rose-Cross from The History and Practice of Magic, *ed. revd. Ross Nichols, Forge Press, 1952.*

in England) was formed in London by the Freemason Robert Wentworth Little. It was three members of this Masonic organisation, which still exists, who founded the Hermetic Order of the Golden Dawn.

CHRISTINA OAKLEY-HARRINGTON

Christina Oakley-Harrington read history at the University of Pennsylvania, then took a Master's degree and doctorate at University College London. She knows a number of 'dead' languages, including Latin, Old Irish and Anglo Saxon, which she learnt at Oxford. For some years a lecturer in medieval religious history, she left academia in 2002 to found Treadwell's bookshop in Covent Garden.

I first became interested in the Golden Dawn about fifteen years ago, and it was because the people involved in it in its heyday were so culturally creative – outgoing and lively poets, actors, scholars, painters, playwrights. Moreover, they were genuine searchers after higher truths, who worked very hard at ritual and meditation to seek genuine spiritual experiences. The Golden Dawn was founded in the 1880s, but had earlier magical roots through the emerging nineteenth-century interest in magic fuelled by figures like Eliphas Lévi. Lévi's treatise, *Dogme et Rituel de la Haute Magie*, set out many of the basic principles of occult belief. The three founders of the Golden Dawn came from the specialist Rosicrucian side of Freemasonry, but were apparently frustrated as this practised little actual magic and barred women members. Like Freemasonry, the Golden Dawn had initiations, rituals and a grade structure to help members who sought spiritual knowledge that would transform their lives. Soon after its founding a number of brilliant women joined, including Moina Bergson Mathers, Maude Gonne, Florence Farr and Annie Horniman.

The grade structure was based on the Sephirotic 'Tree of Life' from the Kaballah (cabbala), but the diverse cultural backgrounds of some of the young and enthusiastic intellectuals they attracted, like William Butler Yeats, led to a much wider scope for their practices and a pantheon of deities, which included everything from Celtic to Egyptian. The Golden Dawn flourished until about 1902, then began to break up into factions and disputes, not least on account of dramas surrounding one of the order's young initiates – Aleister Crowley.

By 1920 there were a number of breakaways, revivals, splinter groups and lodges independent of the Golden Dawn, and the plethora of these explains why much of the magical world looks so fragmented today. For example, the famed English magician Dion Fortune was initiated into a Golden Dawn successor lodge, but decided she wanted to go her own way, and concentrate more on changing the collective consciousness of the human race. To this end she founded the Society of the Inner Light, which is still in existence today.

Aleister Crowley, that upstart young Golden Dawn member in 1900, also left it to create his own version: the Ordo Templi Orientis (OTO). A more primal, vibrant and transgressive version of the Golden Dawn, it was started before Crowley's time in Germany, but it has now incorporated much that was uniquely Crowley's, and his influence is unmistakeable. For all its message of sexual and personal liberation, the OTO's aims are resolutely spiritual, even when the methods are erotic: the union of the individual with their truest nature and with the Divine. The OTO is in existence today and is currently enjoying something of a renaissance. It too, has had splinter offshoots.

The matter of the multiplicity of magical orders is heightened by the fact that there is a tendency for those who are specifically interested in practising invocational and more 'hard' magic to split off into even smaller groups of two or three, which are often short-lived. But these, too, add to the panoply of groups with which the outsider must contend, even if he or she only sees the name of the group mentioned in a journal or website.

What actually do Western Mystery orders do? Firstly, they are organised to give a person an experience of self-transformation, union with the divine, rather than to turn one into a person who can achieve particular results like winning the lottery. At the start of the journey through the levels of an Order's curriculum, the initiate normally performs a set of elemental ceremonies – one for air, one for fire, one for water and one for earth – to empower these elements in the self. Then one goes on to the work of contacting one's personal 'Holy Guardian Angel': a Christian tradition but an occult practice. This is done by prayer and petitioning ceremonies; the latter are normally variants of the Abramelin operation, the hugely complex ritual which originally could take up to 18 months to perform. In the subsequent levels, one tends to do further workings that aim for the annihilation of the ego self. Highest levels of magical spiritual work (ritual, meditation, contemplation) focus on the union of the male/female principles in the Universe, the male and female aspects of divinity – depending on the order one belongs to, this is done solely through meditative contemplation, ceremonial symbolism, or occasionally in actual physical love-making rites. Those who do this work spend a lifetime at it, and progress through levels achieving titles like 'adept'. The woman or man who attains the goal of this work becomes, one could say, a highly spiritually advanced person – a transformed being who lives in union with Divinity and whose life embodies it.

I am often asked about the relationship of the Western Mystery traditions to Wicca. There are, of course, a number of magical crafts which are practised by both traditions, such as John Dee's Enochian techniques for invoking angels and other spirits, but there is a fundamental difference in organisational approach. Gerald Gardner, who founded Wicca, was also a Freemason, but he decided that a complex and bureaucratic grade structure was too restrictive for the emerging magical world, so created something much more cellular (Wiccan covens have only 13 people) which would discipline itself through a community of like-minded and responsible people. Perhaps his experience of never going to school, being raised by a wayward governess, steered him in this direction, but I would argue that he was also hugely influenced by the very tribal approach to magic he found as a colonial administrator in Africa and South East Asia.

There are really good, professional and dedicated people around now as magic comes of age. It is time it moved out of the 'Black Magic' image of Crowley, all full of personality and self-destruction. Crowley himself delighted in being the world's wickedest man, reviled by the press, and left almost nothing behind in terms of organisation to carry forward his knowledge – but make no mistake, he was a genuinely brilliant magician.

AN ADEPT OF THE GOLDEN DAWN

This interview is with a member of one of the branches of the Order of the Golden Dawn functioning today. He spoke anonymously.

In my late teens I became absorbed by the mystery of being. It was an overwhelming, awesome, mystical experience, which has infused my adult life. From this I felt that there were secrets behind creation that I needed to understand. This intense search led me a few years later to astrology, which explains how fortunes are distributed in different lives. Although this satisfied my thirst for hidden knowledge to a great extent I wanted to know the relationship between the creator and astrology. My search continued and, along the way, I felt that entering an initiatic order would provide the missing link, so I went into Freemasonry. Craft Masonry focuses on the lesser Mysteries and my mentor, knowing of my interest in astrology and the higher mysteries, pointed me towards the SRIA, the Societas Rosicruciania in Anglia, a Rosicrucian Order, whose members have to be Freemasons. It informs its rituals with astrological symbols and encourages the exploration of mystical studies including alchemy and theosophy. Upon entry I knew that this was the initiation I had been looking for, most especially because it introduced me to the cabbala, which has a deep comprehension of the relationship between God, astrology and manifestation. Through the SRIA I then became involved in smaller, side orders which work with archangelic forces to advance the divinisation of the candidate and subsequently to a newly reformed Golden Dawn temple, modelled on the original founded by the SRIA leadership during the 1880s.

Much of the teachings of the Golden Dawn Outer Order confirmed my existing understandings and I rose through the Grades rapidly through passing the required examinations. These grades confer the building blocks of practical magic, but you are not allowed to practise any magic until you enter the Inner Order and become an Adeptus Minor. These building blocks include the four elements, the Hebrew Alphabet, the Tree of Life and the planets and zodiacal forces as well as protection and divinisation rituals. In each of the elemental Grades your practical, emotional, intellectual and wilful characteristics are broken down, purified and re-assembled and finally placed under the control of your spiritualised self.

Spiritual magic requires integrity and maturity, and the Order is not keen on letting people practise it until they have indicated they possess those qualities and have undertaken the Outer Order Grades. We distinguish between natural and divine magic, a distinction first made by Pico della Mirandola in the early Renaissance who promoted man as magus, based on the observation made in Genesis that man is made in the image of God and the cabbalistic understanding that man partakes of the four worlds – the divine, the intellectual, the astral and the physical. He dismissed natural magic or using it for personal gain, whether financial, amatory or vengeful, as sorcery. Divine magic is about enhancing your spirituality and putting the divine in charge of your life so that you become an agent of divine providence. If we use natural magic it is always with the recipient's direct request or permission and is always carried out from a position of ethical consideration.

Nowadays, the huge popularity of the Harry Potter books amongst the younger generation and many adults indicates that there is an innate thirst in all of us for understanding the universe and our own being in magical terms. Its success is a spur to the creative imagination, which is an essential part of magic. The big question is whether magic is created by the imagination and then gets a life of its own or whether it is real and separate – in other words, is it subjective or objective? The path we follow combines the two. For example, we invoke elemental spirits into some of our initiation ceremonies through a combination of intonation, ritualised actions and the imagination, but once invoked they have a life and a character of their own both in the imagination of the invoker and through a real participation in the ceremony. Many have a strong sense of joy and fun. Some of our practices such as travelling in the spirit vision are clearly shamanistic. Others are related to the deification techniques of the priesthoods of the Ancient World. The establishment of the Golden Dawn was probably, in part, inspired by the newly excavated religious artefacts on display in the British Museum during the mid-nineteenth century, which revealed that ancient western cultures were permeated with magical understandings and practices.

What was the appeal of Rosicrucianism? Why did it inspire so many people including the founders of the Golden Dawn? One reason may simply lie in the power of the term and its symbol: a rose on a cross takes an image associated with Christian devotion and replaces the familiar sight of a suffering man hanging on it with an essentially feminine symbol of delicacy and beauty. Since the cross can be seen as a phallic symbol, adding a rose to it unites the masculine and feminine principles, creating as powerful an image of union as that of the grail and the lance.

Another reason for its attraction may lie in the fact that Rosicrucian ideals appeal to the very best in human nature. What could be nobler than seeking enlightenment, and teaching and healing without thought for fame or recompense?

But there is a third and perhaps more potent explanation for the success of Rosicrucianism. Nothing is more tantalising than something that is just out of reach, and the idea of 'Hidden Masters', of mysterious adepts with supernatural powers moving unknown amongst us, is romantic and alluring. It is essentially the idea of the spiritually advanced being, common in the East, translated into Western terms as the 'superhero' who, like Clark Kent, works incognito, stopping to change into his wizard outfit or tight Superman pants only when duty calls.

WHAT IS IT LIKE TO BE A ROSICRUCIAN?

Most modern Rosicrucian groups, formed in the nineteenth or twentieth centuries, combine elements derived from Freemasonry, Christian mysticism and the rituals of the Hermetic Order of the Golden Dawn.

Imagine you have joined the Fellowship of the Rosy Cross, formed in 1915 by A.E. Waite, once head of the Isis-Urania temple of the Golden Dawn, author of a history of Rosicrucianism and creator of the world's most popular Tarot deck, known as the Rider–Waite deck. You're in London's Earl's Court just before the outbreak of the Second World War. In a few years, in 1942, the Order will die with its founder, but tonight you have made your way through the dark, wet streets to attend the initiation of a member into the grade of 'Practicus'.

Once you have arrived at the house you change into magical robes and along with other members of the Fellowship you enter the temple. You assist in the 'Solemn Ceremony of Opening the Temple'. This is followed by the rite of admission of the candidate. Most participants have learnt their scripts by heart. As proceedings draw to a close with the 'Solemn Office of Closing the Sacred Temple', you glance at your ritual book to refresh your memory:

The Master and Warden turn again to the West, and with his Wand again uplifted the Warden says: Powers of the waters that are within us, sea unfathomable. In the deeps of the heart let us pray for the Sabbath that is to come, when there shall be harmony and equipoise in the outer worlds, and in that hidden world which is our own.

Then, with raised eyes and uplifted arms:–

Master of the Temple – The peace of ELOHIM be upon you, and the Blessing of the Lord of Hosts. Depart in reconciliation, depart in light, O Brethren of the Rosy

Cross. Go forth and carry the tidings, the glad tidings of peace in the inward stillness.

The Guide of the Paths turns Westwards, with arms outstretched.

Guide of the Paths – Go, but return at your call to the work of consecrated hearts . . .

Master of the Temple – . . .The Hour of the Rite is over, and having attained our term therein, I direct you to close the Temple in the Grade of Practicus.

The Warden lifts up his Wand.

Warden of the Temple – Let purified hearts go forth, as vestals clothed in white . . . In the Name of the Lord of Hosts, I close this Holy Temple in the Grade of Practicus.[11]

The idea of a hidden elite of magician-sages who could save the world worked its magic for over three hundred years, reaching the height of its popularity in the nineteenth century. Bulwer-Lytton's widely read novel *Zanoni*, published in 1842 and mentioned in

A bookmark found in the ritual papers of a member of the Fellowship of the Rosy Cross.

the introduction to this book, thrilled its readers with its opening scene set in an occult bookshop that was based on the real shop, frequented by Lord Lytton, owned by John Denley in Covent Garden's Catherine Street.

Here the book's hero recounts his meeting with a 'mysterious gentleman' who turns out to be an adept:

It so chanced that some years ago, in my younger days, whether of authorship or life, I felt a desire to make myself acquainted with the true origin and tenets of the singular sect known by the name of Rosicrucians . . . On entering the shop, I was struck by the venerable appearance of a customer whom I had never seen there before. I was struck yet more by the respect with which he was treated by the disdainful collector [and owner of the shop]. 'Sir,' cried the last, emphatically, as I was turning over the leaves of the catalogue, –'sir, you are the only man I have met, in five-and-forty years that I have spent in these researches, who is worthy to be my customer. How – where, in this frivolous age, could you have acquired a knowledge so profound? And this august fraternity, whose doctrines, hinted at by the earliest philosophers, are still a mystery to the latest; tell me if there really exists upon the earth any book, any manuscript, in which their discoveries, their tenets, are to be learned?'

At the words, 'august fraternity,' I need scarcely say that my attention had been at once aroused, and I listened eagerly for the stranger's reply.

'I do not think,' said the old gentleman, 'that the masters of the school have ever consigned, except by obscure hint and mystical parable, their real doctrines to the world. And I do not blame them for their discretion.'

Here he paused, and seemed about to retire, when I said, somewhat abruptly, to the collector, 'I see nothing, Mr. D—, in this catalogue which relates to the Rosicrucians!'

'The Rosicrucians!' repeated the old gentleman, and in his turn he surveyed me with deliberate surprise. 'Who but a Rosicrucian could explain the Rosicrucian mysteries! And can you imagine that any members of that sect, the most jealous of all secret societies, would themselves lift the veil that hides the Isis of their wisdom from the world?'

'Aha!' thought I, 'this, then, is "the august fraternity" of which you spoke. Heaven be praised! I certainly have stumbled on one of the brotherhood.'

'But,' I said aloud, 'if not in books, sir, where else am I to obtain information? Nowadays one can hazard nothing in print without authority, and one may scarcely quote Shakespeare without citing chapter and verse. This is the age of facts, – the age of facts, sir.'

'Well,' said the old gentleman, with a pleasant smile, 'if we meet again, perhaps, at least, I may direct your researches to the proper source of intelligence.' And with that he buttoned his greatcoat, whistled to his dog, and departed.

Bulwer-Lytton hinted that he was a Rosicrucian himself. In 1870, nearly thirty years after writing *Zanoni*, he wrote to a fellow author: 'Some time ago a sect pretending to style itself "Rosicrucian" and arrogating full knowledge of the mysteries of the craft, communicated with me, and in reply I sent them the cipher sign of the "Initiate" – not one of them could construe it.'[12]

Madame Helena Petrovna Blavatsky 1831–1891.

One of Bulwer-Lytton's readers, Helena Petrovna Blavatsky, who founded the Theosophical Society in 1875 in New York, was so taken with his books that she described him as 'the master of my dreams',[13] and made use of his work in her own book *Isis Unveiled*, (1877),

Koot Hoomi, a 'Hidden Master' of the Theosophical Society.

whose very title, as the above passage shows, suggests that she will provide the insights the young man in the bookshop is seeking.

The idea of a chance meeting with a great adept found expression in the story of Blavatsky's own life, when she stated that she met an occult Master as a young girl visiting the Great Exhibition in London.[14] And it was Hidden Masters, or the 'Mahatmas', who were cited as the source of the inner knowledge of Theosophy. Madame Blavatsky claimed that she was initiated by two of them, Masters Morya and Koot Hoomi, in Tibet. In this she prefigured a similar claim made by the founders of the Golden Dawn, who derived their authority for founding their Order from 'secret chiefs' known only to themselves.

The Golden Dawn was overtly magical and focused on the Western traditions of Hermeticism and the cabbala, while the Theosophical Society was more philosophical and was preoccupied in the main with wisdom from the East. The two bodies shared, however, similar concerns: the improvement of humanity, research into occult doctrines and the development of 'special powers' including extrasensory perception. The TS and the GD, as they came to be known, represent the summit of the nineteenth-century occult revival and their influence on the development of occultism and magic into the following century was immeasurable.

Francis Barrett's 'Magus' and the Nineteenth-Century Occult Revival

If the eighteenth century was characterised by an increasing interest in reason and science, the nineteenth was destined to become the golden age of a renewal of interest in magic and the supernatural – or to become the Age of Unreason, depending on your point of view.

Francis Barrett, compiler of The Magus, *1801.*

Historian of the occult, James Webb, writes that 'Reason died sometime before 1865 . . . after the Age of Reason came the Age of the Irrational.'[15] The nineteenth century was an age of turmoil; there were no fewer than fifty violent attempts to overthrow established governments in 1848 alone; 1859 saw the historic publication of Charles Darwin's *On the Origin of Species*. All of these events and many more precipitated a crisis of consciousness that resulted in, amongst a number of reactions, a renewed interest in the world of magic, as a symptom both of a desire to return to traditional ways of thinking and of a search for new ways of understanding the world and the nature of existence.

As if to announce this agenda of the new century, right on cue in 1801 a magician's primer, entitled *The Magus or Celestial Intelligencer being a Complete System of Occult Philosophy*, was published in London by failed balloonist Francis Barrett, who added the initials FRC after his name to suggest that he was a Rosicrucian adept – a *frater* or brother of the Rosy Cross. Barrett had copied text after text from books lent to him by the bookseller John Denley in Covent Garden, producing from these copies his own textbook of alchemy, divination and ceremonial magic. Omitting to mention that he had not written them himself, he 'recklessly produced a work which incorporated in almost their entirety some of the great classics of European occult literature', as Francis King explains in his biography of Barrett, *The Flying Sorcerer*.[16]

The Magus was divided into six books, and at the end of Book II readers discovered an advertisement for Barrett's school of magic in Marylebone, which advised them that 'Those who become Students will be initiated into the choicest operations of Natural Philosophy, Natural Magic, the Cabala, Chemistry, the Talismanic Art, Hermetic Philosophy, Astrology, Physiognomy, etc., likewise they will acquire the knowledge of the rites, mysteries, magi, cabalists, adepts etc.' Promising that the school would have no more than twelve students, 'lovers of philosophy and wisdom' were invited to visit the author 'at any time between the hours of Eleven and Two o'clock, at 99 Norton Street, Mary-le-Bonne'.[17] No record remains of Barrett's school and only one of his pupils can be traced with certainty – a John Parkins who, at some point before 1810, established the 'Temple of Wisdom' in Little Gonerly, near Grantham, Lincolnshire.[18]

Although no traces of Barrett's school remain, we do know that his work was admired by Frederick Hockley, a Freemason who once worked in Denley's bookshop, and who continued in the tradition of John Dee by working with crystals and mirrors

Pages from The Magus.

to obtain visions, which he recorded in more than thirty volumes of notes. It is likely that, with his associate Kenneth Mackenzie, Hockley helped to found the 'Rosicrucian Society in England'. Mackenzie's definition of magic, cited in the Society's magazine *The Rosicrucian*, is worth noting: 'a psychological branch of science, dealing with the sympathetic effects of stones, drugs, herbs and living substances upon the imaginative and reflective faculties'.[19]

Barrett's influence also travelled abroad, and reached the two countries that provided much of the stimulus for the nineteenth-century occult revival. In America, when the body of Joseph Smith, the founder of Mormonism, was examined after he was

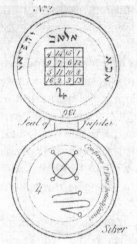

The Talisman of Jupiter from
The Magus

killed by a mob in 1844, he was found to be wearing Barrett's Talisman of Jupiter, depicted in *The Magus*. And in France, Eliphas Lévi, the writer largely responsible for the occult revival in that country, acknowledged the influence of Barrett's work, as did Bulwer-Lytton, who met Lévi when he visited England from May to August 1854.

The two men apparently attempted an evocation of elementary spirits in the London Pantheon,[20] and a friend of Bulwer-Lytton persuaded the French magus to turn his hand to summoning the dead. Bulwer-Lytton encouraged Lévi to write on magic, and the year after his return to Paris he released the first of a series of books that would popularise its study: *Transcendental Magic, its Doctrine and Ritual*. This was followed in 1860 by *The History of Magic*, and a year later by *The Key of the Mysteries*, which was translated into English by Aleister Crowley, who believed that he was Lévi's reincarnation.

✍ Spiritualism, Psychic Research and ✍ the Ghosts of Dead Magicians

While the occult revival was being stimulated by Levi's work in France, another phenomenon was tapping the same seam of interest in the supernatural: spiritualism.

The belief that spirits of the dead can be contacted, and that they can provide reassurance and useful information to those still living, can be found in every age, all over the world. But in the mid-nineteenth century, while much of Europe was in revolutionary turmoil, this belief provided the basis of a spiritualist movement in America that rapidly gained millions of converts and succeeded in stimulating the existing interest in Britain, so that by the 1850s séances had become fashionable throughout the country.

The concept of 'spirits' has always been the stock-in-trade of magicians. Spirits are beings without physical bodies who might be humans who have died, or angels, or demons, or 'nature spirits', or 'fairies'. Anglo-Saxon sorcerers, shamans and Druids were all believed to be in contact with the spirits of the ancestors; cunning-folk relied on their connections with spirits to provide them with the information their clients needed; and medieval wizards attempted to command demons from the safety of their magic circle. John Dee and Edward Kelley tried to communicate with angels, as did the early Theosophists, who were also interested in nature spirits. The arrival of spiritualism popularised this essentially magical activity.

Just as, with the invention of the telegraph in 1844 and the telephone in 1876, the world of science was proving that communication at a distance was possible, so the thought that our loved ones could speak to us from a faraway place was captivating for many people. A territory normally confined to a select group of seers was now a subject of widespread interest. Gladstone and Queen Victoria attended séances, Sir Arthur Conan Doyle and the distinguished physicist, Sir Oliver Lodge became enthusiasts, and various organisations were established in London to promote research into mediumship and the wider field of 'psychic studies'.

In addition to conversing with spirits, yet another domain that was traditionally the preserve of the magician became accessible to the world at large as these groups began to research and teach the development of extrasensory perception. 'Psychic studies' or ESP are catch-all terms that include abilities historically associated with the magician, such as the 'special powers' that enable a wizard to divine the future (precognition), to transmit and receive thoughts (telepathy) and to move objects at a distance (psychokinesis). By the end of the nineteenth century, the process had begun in earnest of making available to all the hidden secrets of magic.

DANIEL DUNGLAS HOME, 1833–1886

Daniel Dunglas Home:
The Flying Medium.

The Victorian passion for spiritualism threw up a number of fascinating characters, but none more so than Daniel Home, the 'Flying Medium'. Not only were his feats, which included levitation, witnessed by many of the important people of the age, but, unlike many of his contemporary spiritualists, he was never exposed as a fraud.

Home was born in 1833 to a Scottish family with a long tradition of 'second sight'. Adopted by his aunt and uncle, Home moved with them to America where they were eventually joined by his mother. After her death, which Home foresaw, he began to experience a number of disturbing psychic phenomena, including furniture moving around the house, and further startlingly accurate prophetic visions. The timing was right: the world was becoming obsessed with spiritual phenomena and Home's fame spread.

In 1855, at the age of twenty-two, Home moved to London where he conducted hundreds of séances, which were attended by many of the most important figures of the day, including Bulwer-Lytton and Robert Browning. He also toured Europe. Napoleon III invited him to the Tuileries, and even the Empress Eugénie was impressed when a spectral hand held hers and she recognised it as her father's. At another session, the spirit of Napoleon Bonaparte put in an appearance.

Back in London in 1871, Home was investigated by a well-known physicist, William Crookes. Despite a widely held belief that at last Home would be exposed as a charlatan, the report, which was published in the *Quarterly Journal of Science* in 1871, could find no evidence of fraud. Home retired the following year and died of consumption at the early age of fifty-three.

✒ Invoking the Spirit of a Magician ✑

If you're interested in magic and want to speak to someone who has died, it would make sense to talk to the ghost of a dead magician, which is exactly what the French occultist Eliphas Lévi did on his first visit to England.

The following extract is taken from his book, *Transcendental Magic, Its Doctrine and Ritual* published in 1855:

In the spring of the year 1854 I had undertaken a journey to London, that I might escape from internal disquietude and devote myself, without interruption, to science. I had letters of introduction to persons of eminence who were anxious for revelations from the supernatural world. I made the acquaintance of several and discovered in them, amidst much that was courteous, a depth of indifference or trifling. They asked me forthwith to work wonders, as if I were a charlatan, and I was somewhat discouraged, for, to speak frankly, far from being inclined to initiate others into the mysteries of Ceremonial Magic, I had shrunk all along from its illusions and weariness. Moreover, such ceremonies necessitated an equipment which would be expensive and hard to collect. I buried myself therefore in the study of the transcendent Kabalah, and troubled no further about English adepts, when, returning one day to my hotel, I found a note awaiting me. This note contained half of a card, divided transversely, on which I recognized at once the seal of Solomon. It was accompanied by a small sheet of paper, on which these words were pencilled: 'Tomorrow, at three o'clock, in front of Westminster Abbey, the second half of this card will be given you.' I kept this curious assignation. At the appointed spot I found a carriage drawn up, and as I held unaffectedly the fragment of card in my hand, a footman approached, making a sign as he did so, and then opened the door of the equipage. It contained a lady in black, wearing a thick veil; she motioned to me to take a seat beside her, showing me at the same time the other half of the card.

The door closed, the carriage drove off, and the lady raising her veil I saw that my appointment was with an elderly person, having grey eyebrows and black eyes of unusual brilliance, strangely fixed in expression. 'Sir,' she began, with a strongly marked English accent, 'I am aware that the law of secrecy is rigorous amongst adepts; a friend of Sir B— L— who has seen you, knows that you have been asked for phenomena, and that you have refused to gratify such curiosity. You are possibly without the materials; I should like to show you a complete magical cabinet, but I must exact beforehand the most inviolable silence. If you will not give me this pledge upon your honour, I shall give orders for you to be driven to your hotel.' I made the required promise and keep it faithfully by not divulging the name, position or abode of this lady, whom I soon recognised as an initiate, not exactly of the first order, but still of a most exalted grade. We had a number of long conversations, in the course of which she insisted always upon the necessity of practical experience to complete initiation. She showed me a collection of magical vestments and instruments, lent me some rare books which I needed; in short, she determined me to attempt at her house the experiment of a complete evocation, for which I prepared during a period of twenty-one days, scrupulously observing the rules laid down in the thirteenth chapter of the 'Ritual'.

The preliminaries terminated on 2nd July; it was proposed to evoke the phantom of the divine Apollonius and interrogate it upon two secrets, one which concerned myself and one which interested the lady. She had counted on taking part in the evocation with a trustworthy person, who, however, proved nervous at the last moment, and, as the triad or unity is indispensable for Magical Rites, I was left to my own resources. The cabinet prepared for the evocation was situated in a turret; it contained four concave mirrors and a species of altar having a white marble top, encircled by a chain of magnetised iron. The Sign of the Pentagram, as given in the fifth chapter of this work, was graven and gilded on the white marble surface; it was inscribed also in various colours upon a new white lambskin stretched beneath the altar. In the middle of the marble table there was a small copper chafing-dish, containing charcoal of alder and laurel wood; another chafing-dish was set before me on a tripod. I was clothed in a white garment, very similar to the alb of our catholic priests, but longer and wider, and I wore upon my head a crown of vervain leaves, intertwined with a golden chain. I held a new sword in one hand, and in the other the 'Ritual'. I kindled two fires with the requisite prepared substances, and began reading the evocations of the 'Ritual' in a voice at first low, but rising by degrees. The smoke spread, the flame caused the objects upon which it fell to waver, then it went out, the smoke still floating white and slow about the marble altar; I seemed to feel a quaking of the earth, my ears tingled, my heart beat quickly. I heaped more twigs and perfumes on the chafing-dishes, and as the flame again burst up, I beheld distinctly, before the altar, the figure of a man of more than normal size, which dissolved and vanished away.

I recommenced the evocations and placed myself within a circle which I had drawn previously between the tripod and the altar. Thereupon the mirror which was behind the altar seemed to brighten in its depth, a wan form was outlined therein, which increased and seemed to approach by degrees. Three times, and with closed eyes, I invoked Apollonius. When I again looked forth there was a man in front of me, wrapped from head to foot in a species of shroud, which seemed more grey than white. He was lean, melancholy and beardless, and did not altogether correspond to my preconceived notion of Apollonius. I experienced an abnormally cold sensation, and when I endeavoured to question the phantom I could not articulate a syllable. I therefore placed my hand upon the Sign of the Pentagram, and pointed the sword at the figure, commanding it mentally to obey and not alarm me, in virtue of the said sign. The form thereupon became vague, and suddenly disappeared. I directed it to return, and presently felt, as it were, a breath close by me; something touched my hand which was holding the sword, and the arm became immediately benumbed as far as the elbow. I divined that the sword displeased the spirit, and I therefore placed it point downwards, close by me, within the circle. The human figure reappeared immediately, but I experienced such an intense weakness in all my limbs, and a swooning sensation came so quickly over me, that I made two steps to sit down, whereupon I fell into a profound lethargy, accompanied by dreams, of which I had only a confused recollection when I came again to myself. For several subsequent days my arm remained benumbed and painful. The apparition did not speak to me, but it seemed that the questions I had designed to ask answered themselves in my mind. To that of the lady an interior voice replied – Death! – it was concerning a man about whom she desired information. As for myself, I sought to know whether reconciliation and forgiveness were possible between two persons who occupied my thoughts, and the same inexorable echo within me answered – Dead!

I am stating facts as they occurred, but I would impose faith on no one. The consequence of this experience on myself must be called inexplicable. I was no longer the same man; something of another world had passed into me.

LYN GUEST DE SWARTE

Spiritualist minister Lyn Guest de Swarte has an international repu-tation as a medium, spiritual healer and journalist. She edited the long-established spiritualist newspaper, Psychic News, *from 1996 to 2003, before creating her own successful newspaper,* Spiritual News. *She lives in Hove with her companion Cathy Gibb, who is a very powerful 'physical' medium and spiritual healer.*

From the age of eight, spirit people began to appear quite naturally to me and I felt that they were a normal part of my everyday life. My family was Jewish, a faith that has a deeply mystical element to it. I married and had my first child in my teens, and life was very difficult as I struggled for nine years with drug addiction.

In 1971 a desperate exhortation for help was answered. One night I was woken by a spirit woman who told me she would help me to change the conditions surrounding my life. I had seen many spirit people during my years of addiction, but this was the first time I'd had an actual conversation with such a wonderful person. As a result of that contact, I completely kicked the drug habit and my career as a speed skater, ice hockey player and sports journalist took off. By 1987, I was editor of *Sportsworld International* and was subsequently voted 'Magazine Sportswriter of the Year'. My spirit helper really seemed to be delivering the goods!

When my lovely father died in 1991, a skater friend persuaded me to go to the Croydon Spiritualist Church for comfort. I was full of trepidation, but found myself absolutely fascinated. On my next visit the medium startled me by claiming that my father was on the platform and he would be my 'shadow' for as long as I liked. She told me so many intimate details of his life, which she could not possibly have known, that I ended up convinced and wanted to learn more.

The Spiritualist Association of Great Britain advised me to join a 'circle' and I went to the Lewisham Spiritualist Church. There, I was advised of the three paths I could take: as a medium, a healer or a counsellor. Having had experience of training young skaters, I decided to try counselling and completed five years' training to become a certificated medium and healer. I am now ordained as a spiritualist minister.

I am often asked whether anyone can be a medium. We are all psychic beings. Some of us are able with training to become the exchange between the two worlds of spirit and physical matter. Just as we can all learn to play the piano but only a few of us can become a Rubinstein or a Liberace, so there are different levels of accomplishment as a medium. To develop your abilities you need to join a development circle, as I did, preferably within a spiritualist church, where a good teacher will teach you how to meditate and how to understand the mechanics of contact with those who live on in the higher world of spirit.

Once you have attained the ability to communicate with those who have passed over, you are responsible for proving their survival. I am not at all happy about the mass commercialisation of spiritualism by what I call 'bingo mediums' who ask questions such as: 'Is there anyone here who can "take" someone called Charlie, who passed over with a serious disease?' Throwing out generalisations like this is confusing and untrustworthy. I teach my students to be absolutely specific in their messages and to identify clearly the recipient as well as the communicator, leaving no room for doubt.

One of my own most convincing experiences was recorded on video. The medium used a physical technique to change her facial features to resemble the person coming through. Hardly believing my eyes, I asked: 'Is that really you, Mummy?' The reply came, 'You didn't always call me Mummy.' Then there was a pause, then, 'You once called me "Grumpy"!' Once – and only once – as a very young child, almost half a century earlier, I had called my mother 'Grumpy Hilda' – and had written it on the wall next to my bed.

Mediums are not always educated people and sometimes it helps if they are trained only to receive input and transmit, rather than to intellectually probe every message like a psychiatrist. Imagine yourself as an old-time manual telephone operator, just shifting the jack plugs and avoiding the temptation to listen in, or you would be driven mad.

Being a medium is like managing a long corridor full of impatient people – quite a daunting experience – and it is important to have 'doorkeepers' to manage the flow of spirit individuals who want to communicate. In my case I picked up two Chinese spirit guides at an early age who have been indispensable. Confusion often arises with those who claim to have Egyptian princesses or Native Americans as guides. This must not be taken too literally. Those in the spirit world will take a form that they think is most acceptable to the person they want to communicate with and through.

My strangest experience was when I was asked by the Magic Circle to be the last medium of the twentieth century to sit at the official 'Houdini seance'. The great magician always claimed that his last trick would be to beat dying. I sat in front of the audience with one of Houdini's old manacles on the table in front of me. I have arthritis and can scarcely bend my hands, whereas one of the secrets of Houdini's amazing escapes was that he was completely double-jointed. As I felt him come through me, I watched in amazement as my hand bent almost double, exactly as his had done. The whole evening was filmed by an Italian film company and one of the Italian magicians there told me he was overcome by the sense of Houdini's presence.

At the end of the seance Houdini told me that I must inform the audience that 'it had all been done by mirrors'. That seemed a daft thing to say to professional magicians, but he insisted and showed me a triple mirror, which I described to the audience. When I got home, I was astonished to find that the wrapped gift given to the key participants was a mirror box that makes objects disappear from view! It looked just like a triple mirror.

Spiritualism is in a way a philosophy of behaviour. It is firmly based in the certain knowledge that there is life after death. Everyone is psychic to some degree. The vital spark is linked to our sixth sense, what you might call extrasensory perception or ESP. Every person is surrounded by a form of energy, their aura, which contains all their knowledge and experience. It is this energy field that acts as an interface with the spirit world. A psychic is someone who can tune in to that energy field and read the information contained within it.

⊙ *How to Test Your Extrasensory Powers*

In the 1920s three books were published anonymously: *The Initiate, The Initiate in the New World* and *The Initiate in the Dark Cycle*, which recounted the life of a 'Hidden Master', an adept named Justin Moreward Haig, living in early twentieth-century London. The author of these novels turned out to be the prolific composer Cyril Scott (1879–1970), a member for a short time of the Theosophical Society. The books are still in print, now credited to the author, and they continue the grand tradition, found in Rosicrucianism, Theosophy and the Golden Dawn, of depicting an advanced soul who possesses occult powers. These souls, whether called 'hidden masters', 'secret chiefs', 'mahatmas', 'adepts' or 'initiates', are essentially magicians capable of using extrasensory perception – ESP – to survey both the past and the future, and to influence events at a distance.

Organised ESP research began in the nineteenth century in London, and now includes ongoing studies undertaken by a number of British universities. The internet offers an ideal medium for testing psychic abilities and at the forefront of this approach is the biologist Dr Rupert Sheldrake, who has initiated a number of ingenious online experiments. He also suggests research that you can perform at home with friends and family, using two experiences which could indicate that we all possess a degree of ESP since they are familiar to most of us: our ability to sometimes predict who is telephoning us, and our awareness of being stared at from behind our backs.

To try the staring experiment, sit in a chair blindfolded. A friend sits about a metre behind you and prepares by tossing a coin twenty times, recording the results on paper. 'Heads' will indicate that when the test begins they should stare at the back of your head for a few seconds, 'tails' that they should look away and think of something unconnected with the experiment. Rather than speaking, as the voice may convey subtle cues, they should then ring a bell or use a mechanical device to indicate the start of each of twenty attempts. Once you hear the sound, try to sense whether they are staring at you, and then call out, 'Looking' or 'Not looking', according to what you perceive. See whether your score is above the 50 per cent chance level. Thousands of tests of this kind have been conducted with the evidence overwhelmingly in favour of the theory that we have the ability to perceive when we are being observed, even if there is no explanation for this with currently accepted scientific models.

For detailed information and instructions on the experiment, see Rupert Sheldrake's website www.sheldrake.org and his book, *The Sense of Being Stared At: And Other Aspects of the Extended Mind* (Arrow Books, 2004).

Martial-arts experts, security guards and spies have long known that staring at people from behind can alert them to your presence, and it now seems that this is an example of genuine ESP, which defies materialistic explanation and reveals that adepts displaying psychic abilities, such as Justin Moreward Haig, really might exist. However much fantasy exists in the world of magic, we may soon discover that it is based on principles that can be scientifically proven.

LORRIE'S ANGELS

Lorrie Coffey O'Connor knew from her very early childhood that she had a strong calling to search for the truth, which was reinforced by some powerful spiritual experiences.

Until partial paralysis in her late teens ended her career, she was a talented sportswoman. After a disastrous marriage her life went sharply downhill. On the brink of suicide, she was drawn back to the spiritual visions she had had as a child, which led her first to becoming a healer, then a painter and finally, with her husband, Eugene, the creator of an extraordinary 'Angel Sanctuary'.

As a child I had a number of psychic experiences. When I was aged eleven, my mother and father were going through a difficult time together. One day my father took all of us children shopping, leaving my mother in the house. As soon as I got into the car I knew something was terribly wrong with my mother. I could see her in an armchair in our sitting room with her eyes closed and the smell of gas was overpowering.

When I told him, my father refused to take me seriously and just kept on driving. As I started to sob, I suddenly heard this beautiful voice saying: 'You know what you are seeing and feeling is true. You must tell your father that I am speaking to you and he must listen.' As soon as I did this, he turned the car around immediately and we went back home. As we opened the front door, the smell of gas poured out and there in the sitting room was my mother in the armchair, semi-conscious.

The experience of finding my mother like this was traumatic, but the communication from beyond was comforting and reassuring. I wasn't afraid; it had saved my mother's life.

Drawing on these memories helped me to survive later when my own life went badly wrong. At my lowest point I called to God for help. Three days later, I had one of the most profound and beautiful experiences I have ever known.

I had gone to bed as usual but woke because the TV was still on. I sat up to look for the remote, and there standing at the end of my bed was the most beautiful man. He appeared in a strange way timeless, both ancient and young. He wore brown robes, shining with golden thread, and an elaborate shoulder piece set with diamonds. His skin was like porcelain, almost transparent. He had warm brown eyes and dark hair brushed back to his shoulders. He spoke straight to my consciousness. In an instant I knew everything that I had to know to have the strength to carry on. It was an extremely holy experience.

The next morning every joy I had felt as a child burst back with redoubled strength and I had a heightened awareness of everything. As I walked down the street, I could see through people to the sources of their illnesses and deepest thoughts. I could hear and feel others' suicidal thoughts, loneliness and isolation, just as I had suffered. At the same time, I could hear this inner voice saying: 'You can help these people.'

This was where my journey really began. A couple of weeks later, I went into a little shop that I had passed hundreds of times before. Inside, there was a fascinating mixture of scents, and on display were strange things like crystals and singing bowls. I felt drawn into this exciting world and shared some of my experiences with the shopkeeper. He listened to me carefully, and then made a strange suggestion. 'There are many people who come here who could benefit from your gifts,' he said. 'If you'd like to practise your gift, use that chair there and see what you can do.' Five years later I was still there, and Eugene, the shopkeeper, had become my second husband as well as my partner in all that has happened since.

After some years of work at the shop, I began to feel a deep tiredness. Although I was offering guidance, people did not always listen to the direction given for their soul and treated me more as a fortune-teller. I questioned my own purpose and realised my life was once again at a turning point. I stopped work and immersed myself in stillness and nature for many weeks, until a door within me opened and I glimpsed my road ahead. The same voice came back to me and told me that I must start painting my spiritual visions. I had never painted before, but when I started to use my fingers and pastels, I was filled with a passion and excitement.

I gave myself wholly to the experience, as a result of which we sold the shop and found a lovely, remote country house. I was simply told to hang the paintings and my writings together, and to put a sign outside. Although it was challenging to begin with, over time word spread.

We founded our Angel Sanctuary just eight years ago. Each day we are surrounded by the magic we have been blessed to be part of and it has become our life's work. People come from all over the country; some are dying, others have suffered huge tragedy in their lives, whilst others are searching. Each is touched in their own unique way. I never set out to paint angels. It all came from within. We live from day to day, but both of us have this wonderful sense of magic, which for me is the Divine.

✒ Things to Do ✒

✳ Take courses in Golden Dawn magic, or research its teachings and history. A number of groups have an online presence. The most respected can be found at: www.osogd.org, www.hogd.co.uk,www. hermeticgoldendawn.org or www.goldendawntrust.com

✳ Explore the work of modern Rosicrucian groups, many of which offer distance-learning study courses, listed in the Resources section at the end of this chapter.

   Although historians point out that these groups have no historical connection with the seventeenth-century Rosicrucian phenomenon, and designate them Neo-Rosicrucian, each feels a spiritual connection with this secret society of Christian mystics, allegedly formed in late medieval Germany.

✳ Pay a visit to the Theosophical Society's headquarters in Gloucester Place, London. Entering the library, which offers for loan one of Europe's finest collections of esoteric books, is like stepping back in time a hundred years. The Society holds lectures, workshops and a summer school. See www.theosophical-society. org.uk

✳ If you're interested in ESP or psychic research, consider joining the Society for Psychical Research, founded in London in 1882. They publish a quarterly journal, hold annual conferences and bi-monthly lectures at Kensington Library, and maintain one of the world's most comprehensive libraries on this topic, which is open on Tuesdays and Wednesdays at the Society's headquarters in Marloes Road, Kensington. See www.spr. ac.uk

❧ Consider also the College of Psychic Studies in Queensberry Place, which began life in 1884 as the London Spiritualist Alliance. Arthur Conan Doyle was President in the 1920s. Today they offer a wide range of activities including courses on personal development, healing and psychic development. You can also have sessions of healing, guidance and counselling. Their journal is published twice yearly and you can borrow books from their library of over 6,000 volumes. See www.collegeofpsychicstudies.co.uk

❧ Travel to the Hogwarts-like Arthur Findlay College in Stansted, Essex, to take a residential course in 'psychic unfoldment', spiritualist healing and related subjects. Wander in the magnificent grounds, sit beside the lake, or visit the College museum and library. See www. arthurfindlaycollege.org

❧ If you're interested in mediumship, visit the Spiritualist Association of Great Britain in London's Belgrave Square, where you can book a private session with a medium, or attend lectures and classes. See www.sagb. org.uk

Arthur Findlay College

❧ Explore the work of the Anomalistic Psychology
Research Unit, based at Goldsmiths, University
of London, which researches unusual and
parapsychological phenomena. See www.goldsmiths.
ac.uk/apru

❧ Take a distance-learning course in parapsychology with
the Koestler Parapsychology Unit, a research group
based in the Psychology Department at the University
of Edinburgh. See www.koestler-parapsychology.psy.
ed.ac.uk

❧ Explore the work of Dr Michael Daniels, Senior
Lecturer in Psychology and Programme Leader for the
Master of Science in Consciousness and Transpersonal
Psychology at Liverpool John Moores University.
His website offers a wide range of video and audio
information as well as many ESP experiments that
you can perform online and at home. See www.
psychicscience.org

❧ Explore the work of Dr Rupert Sheldrake and
participate in online ESP experiments. Rupert
Sheldrake is the author of *Seven Experiments that Could
Change the World* and Director of the Perrott-Warrick
Project for research on unexplained human and animal
abilities at Trinity College, Cambridge. See www.
sheldrake.org

❧ Visit Cottingley in West Yorkshire to see the site
of the famous fairy photographs championed by
Sir Arthur Conan Doyle as proof of the existence
of spirits. The village is still much as it was when
the photographs were taken in 1917. Even though
in old age the two cousins who took the pictures as
young girls admitted that they were fakes, they still

maintained their belief in fairies. The atmosphere around Cottingley Beck, where the photos were taken, is enchanting, so take your camera. Before you go, get a full briefing at www.cottingley.net and at www. museumofhoaxes.com

◞ Resources ◟

BOOKS

The Rosicrucians: The History, Mythology, and Rituals of an Occult Order, Christopher McIntosh (Red Wheel/ Weiser, 1997)

The Rosicrucian Enlightenment, Frances Yates (Routledge, 2001)

The Rosicrucian Enlightenment Revisited, ed. Ralph White (Lindisfarne Press, 1999)

The Invisible History of the Rosicrucians – The World's Most Mysterious Secret Society, Tobias Churton (Inner Traditions, 2009)

Fama Fraternitatis: The True Story of the Rosicrucians (DVD), Tobias Churton, (Demand Media, 2008)

The Golden Dawn: An Account of the Teachings, Rites and Ceremonies of the Order of the Golden Dawn, Israel Regardie (Llewellyn, 1986)

The One True Adventure: Theosophy and the Quest for Meaning, Joy Mills (Quest Books, 2008)

Is There an Afterlife? A Comprehensive Overview of the Evidence, David Fontana (O Books, 2005). Written by the Professor of Transpersonal Psychology at Liverpool John Moores University and past President of the Society for Psychical Research, this book surveys the history of spiritualism and psychic research, including the most recent scientific research.

Cyril Scott and A Hidden School: Towards the Peeling of an Onion, Jean Overton Fuller, *Theosophical History: Occasional Papers,* volume VII.

The Traveller's Guide to Fairy Sites – The Landscape and Folklore of Fairyland in England, Wales and Scotland Janet Bord (Gothic Image, 2008)

The Door Marked Summer, Michael Bentine (Harper Collins, 1982).

A humorous and personally touching story of the well-known broadcaster's extensive experiences with Spiritualism.

Principles of Spiritualism, Lyn G de Swarte (Harper Collins, 1999).

WEBSITES

The Rosicrucian Fellowship, established in 1907 in California, offers books and distance-learning courses in esoteric astrology. See www.rosicrucianfellowship.org

AMORC, the Ancient and Mystical Order Rosae Crucis, founded in California in 1915, and now one of the largest esoteric organisations in the world, offers postal courses, books, podcasts, and open days in London and other cities. See www.amorc.org and its UK website: www.amorc.org.uk

The Lectorium Rosicrucianum, formed in Holland in 1935, also offers distance-learning courses. See www.lectoriumrosicrucianum.org

Visit Lorrie's Angels at www.angelart.bz

CHAPTER ELEVEN

OPENING PANDORA'S BOX

The Great Beast and the Priestess of the Sea

Still They teach eager pupils, showing the Path and guiding the disciple's steps; still They may be reached by all who seek Them, bearing in their hands the sacrificial fire of love, of devotion, of unselfish longing to know in order to serve; still They carry out the ancient discipline, still unveil the ancient Mysteries.

ANNIE BESANT, *THE ANCIENT WISDOM*, 1898

Victoria Street, London, July 1910. You have been invited to a performance of the 'Rite of Artemis' at the headquarters of the magical Order, the Argentinum Astrum, known simply by the initials AA, and run by the world's most infamous magician, Aleister Crowley.

At the door of the apartment that also serves as Crowley's London home, you are greeted by a robed figure holding a drawn sword. Having shown your invitation, you take your seat amongst the small and select audience. In the dim light you can see a statue and – wreathed in clouds of incense – several young men standing facing each other, clad in red, black and white robes. Crowley, robed entirely in black, enters the room and the ceremony begins.

Pentagrams are traced in the air, the room is ritually purified with a sprinkling of water and a wafting of incense, and the audience is invited to join the ritualists in drinking from the 'Cup of Libation'. The golden bowl is passed to you. You take a sip of the brew it contains, which smells of rotten apples, unaware of the fact that this mixture of fruit juice and alcohol contains alkaloids of the hallucinogenic drug mescaline, laced perhaps with an opium derivative such as morphine.[1]

During the course of the ritual you are invited to drink twice more, as the evening progresses with recitations of poetry, 'the dance of Syrinx and Pan in honour of our lady Artemis', and an exquisite performance on the violin by Leila Waddell, a beautiful young woman whose robe is embroidered with the design of the Rosy Cross.

Reactions to this fusion of ritual magic and artistic performance are enthusiastic. Crowley has laced the potion effectively – providing a stimulus to ecstasy but in such a diluted form that the participants attribute their feelings to the ritual alone.

Leila Waddell 1880–1932. One of Crowley's 'Scarlet Women' and the violinist in the Rites of Artemis and Eleusis.

Amongst your bohemian friends Crowley is considered an exciting, charismatic figure who dares to flout convention and explore the further reaches of his mind and his desires. He is wealthy – a man of independent means – and a courageous mountaineer. Members of the Alpine Club despise him because he obeys no rules. Shunning common sense, he climbs the vertical chalk cliff face at Beachy Head, finances expeditions to the Himalayas and ignores the advice of local guides. He is bisexual, sometimes wears make-up, and enjoys publishing his own erotic poetry and stories. And he is a magician dedicated to the mastery of every occult art. Your friends may consider him interesting and entertaining, since he is a witty raconteur, but soon the majority of the country will hold him in contempt, believing him to be the 'wickedest man alive'.

Today, just over sixty years after his death in 1947, opinions about this man – who loved to call himself 'The Great Beast' – are still divided. Many people dedicated to a spiritual and magical path steer well clear of him and of the magical organisations inspired by his work. They point to the fact that he died in penury as a heroin addict; that he apparently cursed people, invoked demons, took and gave to others all kinds of drugs; and that he could be cruel to animals as well as humans.[2] Others find him an attractive figure because he was immensely clever and amusing, and because he was a maverick who dared to strike out on his own, exploring every method available to him for altering consciousness and achieving his magical goals.

The young Aleister Crowley.

Crowley was born Edward Alexander Crowley in 1875 at the height of the nineteenth-century occult revival, and in the year that the Theosophical Society was founded. Brought up in a repressive household of parents who were members of the strict Christian sect known as the Plymouth Brethren, he was living in a period in which Europe and America had become fascinated by mediums, séances and hypnotism, and in which the Theosophical Society and the Hermetic Order of the Golden Dawn had stimulated an interest in magical and esoteric doctrines from both East and West.

Read about the magic of this era in Fiction

The Moonchild, Aleister Crowley (Weiser, 1994). This offers a uniquely personal description of the personalities of the Hermetic Order of the Golden Dawn (of which Crowley was a member) within the story of a magical experiment to produce a 'Moonchild' – a non-human entity who will incarnate into a priestess, and whose conception starts a magical war.

The Magician, W. Somerset Maugham (Penguin, 2007) and *The Winged Bull*, Dion Fortune (SIL, 1999). Crowley is portrayed as Oliver Haddo in Maugham's novel and as Hugo Astley in Fortune's. Dion Fortune also wrote a number of other novels, which she believed provided the key to fully understanding the system of magic described in her non-fiction. See also Jake Arnott's *The Devil's Paintbrush* (Hodder, 2009).

The Secrets of Dr Taverner, Dion Fortune (Alliance, 1996). This describes Fortune's real-life magical teacher, the Freemason Theodore Moriarty, and his occult school in Bishop's Stortford. In a series of short stories, Taverner – the quintessential adept – deals with most aspects of occult pathology, during which he is revealed as the senior adept of a magical lodge that invokes retribution on occult malefactors.

The Sea Priestess and *Moon Magic*, Dion Fortune (Red Wheel, 2003). The heroine of both books is a Priestess of the Moon, an old soul who has been incarnated to free the human soul from the stifling restrictions placed upon it by modern society. The finding of a suitable priest and the *modus operandi* of her magical workings are dealt with in fascinating detail.

But as a new century dawned, everything changed. Pandora's box was opened, and Crowley – of all magicians – was the one who would most eagerly plunge his hands into it to begin exploring its contents.

✎ The Great Beast Awakes ✎

Until the twentieth century, magic had been a practice that moved between the worlds of science, medicine, philosophy and religion. The great magicians of the past had been sages, had pioneered the experimental method, particularly with alchemy, and had been concerned with healing as well as with finding ways of communicating with other worlds and the Divine. But now a new discipline began to change fundamentally the world of the magician: psychology.

Although the modern study of psychology began in the last few decades of the nineteenth century, it wasn't until the beginning of the twentieth that it really started to exert an influence on the world. In 1900, Freud's *On the Interpretation of Dreams* was published, which articulated his theory of the unconscious and of the ways that its contents are denied access to our waking awareness through the mechanism of repression – particularly of sexual and aggressive urges.[3]

Although Freud detested the occult, his advocacy of the need for self-examination, through his newly developed method of psychoanalysis, followed exactly in the tradition of self-knowledge that lies at the heart of magic, epitomised in the injunction carved on the gateway to the Temple at Delphi: 'Man, Know Thyself'.[4] Freud's psychoanalysis used the analysis of dreams, and the free association of ideas and feelings, to slowly uncover repressed urges, with the aim of coming to terms with them in order to prevent them causing mischief, in the form of psychosomatic illness or neurosis. Freud believed that civilisation was based on the control of these urges, and that in their uncontrolled form they were highly dangerous. But he lived at a time when the rigid controls on society and the mind were already being loosened. As the twentieth century progressed, psychotropic drugs and the upheaval of two world wars would succeed in destroying many of these controls, but without the steadying influence that he believed could be obtained through psychoanalysis.

Mind-altering drugs had been used in magic in the past: there are accounts of Scythian magicians using cannabis in sweat-house ceremonies as far back as the second century BC. Various tribal cultures around the world used – and continue to use – them in their initiations and ceremonies, whilst some people have argued that the ancient Druids ritually used the two hallucinogenic mushrooms that grow in Britain, the fairy toadstool, *Amanita muscaria*, and the liberty cap, *Psilocybe semilanceata*, although most scholarly opinion believes this is unlikely.[5] In the nineteenth century Britain defeated China in two opium wars to ensure its right to continue exporting the narcotic, which was used by those exploring the occult – including Bulwer-Lytton and possibly the Theosophist Madame Blavatsky, who, it is said, also enjoyed smoking hashish.

Although hashish was a favourite opiate of Crowley's, he also indulged in every other kind of psychoactive substance that he could lay his hands on – including heroin, cocaine and morphine. He was particularly fond of ether, reportedly inhaling a supply purchased to relieve his wife's labour pains. To be fair to Crowley, he lived in a world in which the dangers of drug-taking were little understood, and he believed that taking the right kind of stimulant prior to a magical ceremony could be of practical benefit – opening the magician to mystical experiences and visions.

If it was Freud who pointed to the demons who lived in the basement, it was Crowley who grabbed whatever dynamite he could find to blow open the doors to that hidden world. And in addition to using drugs, he employed the very forces that Freud believed were at the root of the human psyche – sex and aggression – to try to access levels of reality that magicians had always believed in, but had often found hard to reach. He combined the taking of drugs with every conceivable kind of sexual activity within a ritualised setting to achieve his magical goals.

As a young man in London he joined the Hermetic Order of the Golden Dawn, quickly mastering its teachings, and just as quickly falling out with fellow members, particularly the poet W.B. Yeats, who detested him. He joined the OTO – the Ordo Templi Orientis – a quasi-Masonic group founded in Germany or Austria at the turn of the century, which claimed to teach techniques of sex magic. Crowley also started his own magical Order, the AA . . . which leads us back to that evening in London at its headquarters in July 1910.

In arranging the rite, Crowley was driven by two motives, common to many magicians: the desire to illumine himself and others, and to make money. While any reasonable person would find lacing drinks with drugs deplorable, Crowley's motivation was at least half sincere: he was attempting to provoke a blissful state and psychic illumination. But he also needed funds. Even though as a young man he had inherited the equivalent of millions of pounds (estimates vary between £2 million and £6 million), by his mid-thirties he had spent most of it. He had spiked the drinks not only to give his guests a good time, but also because he wanted them to publicise favourably a major fund-raising exercise: a series of seven similar events, entitled the 'Rites of Eleusis', to be performed in November 1910 at nearby Caxton Hall, whose tickets would cost five guineas – an enormous sum in those days, and the modern equivalent of several hundred pounds.

Due to lack of resources and insufficient preparation, the Rites were not a financial success, and the publicity, rather than being favourable, was instrumental in making Crowley the subject of one of the first smear campaigns of the British press. Despite this, the 'Rites of Eleusis' were landmark events that prefigured the experimental theatre of the 1960s, which involved the audience in an attempt to affect changes in consciousness – a central goal of magic. In the 1990s, the Rites were performed once again in London and included one of the most avant-garde performers in the world

*Aleister Crowley in the
'Rites of Eleusis', 1910.*

– Genesis P. Orridge, who, like the artist and film-maker Raymond
Salvatore Harmon and others, has been inspired by Crowley to
explore the very furthest reaches of the creative impulse.

THE REAL HOGWARTS

Early twentieth-century social reformers tried to create
the ideal environment for working and living – the
garden city, which would offer affordable housing in
pleasant semi-rustic surroundings. Idealists were soon
attracted to the idea: particularly Quakers, devotees of
the Arts and Crafts movement and Theosophists.

By 1907 the first garden city in Letchworth,
Hertfordshire, became the location for the Cloisters,
a Theosophical centre that also taught skills inspired
by the Arts and Crafts movement. An extraordinary

building, seen in a dream by the school's founder, was constructed at great expense using quantities of Swedish marble. It included a large room open to the air, an outdoor swimming pool, cloisters and towers. Residents, who slept in hammocks that descended from the roof, could enjoy nude bathing, a drink at the nearby Skittles – England's only alcohol-free pub – or a meal in the food-reform restaurant at the Simple Life Hotel. George Orwell described it in *The Road to Wigan Pier*, (1937) as a magnet for 'every fruit juice drinker, nudist, sandal wearer, sex-maniac, Quaker, nature cure quack, pacifist and feminist in England'. It was gifted to the Freemasons in 1948.

Beside the Cloisters stands a school established by Theosophists in 1915, that with a little poetic licence could be called 'the Real Hogwarts'. Although spell-

The Cloisters, Letchworth Garden City.

making and astral travel were not on the curriculum, the Garden City Theosophical School was founded on the high ideals and principles that are common to most magical philosophies. In 1920, the school changed its name to St Christopher's. Today it is a flourishing co-ed day and boarding school, whose only legacy from its foundation is its exclusively vegetarian catering.

⚬ Dion Fortune and the Rites of Isis ⚬

In involving an audience in a production that was part magical rite, part theatre, Crowley was turning to one of the earliest sources of our knowledge of magic: the classical world of the Ancient Mystery Schools where ritual dramas were enacted to provide participants with an experience of the transcendent.

Twenty or so years after Crowley's Caxton Hall performances, London was to witness another revival of this tradition of the Ancient Mysteries. This time it was the 'Rites of Isis' – directed by another magician, who stands in marked contrast to Crowley as a person of resolute moral stature. Violet Mary Firth, whose magical name was Dion Fortune, was born in 1890 and, like Crowley, she became fascinated at an early age with other worlds. She flirted with Christian Science, joined the Theosophical Society and enrolled as a student in a magical school, located in Bishop's Stortford, run by the charismatic Freemason, Theodore Moriarty.[6]

Dion Fortune,
1890–1946.

Before she studied with Moriarty, however, she had a frightening experience in London that was to profoundly influence her magical career. At the age of twenty, in the year that Crowley was organising his 'Rites of Eleusis', the young Violet Firth suffered a nervous breakdown. Caused by the psychological bullying of her employer, it was so severe that she believed it to be the work of black magic, or 'psychic attack', as she called it. She wrote about the experience in her book *Psychic Self-Defence*, a classic on the subject, first published in 1930, which is still in print.

As a result of her experience she turned to a study of psychology in an attempt to understand the power of the mind and, according to her, became at the age of twenty-three 'the highest-paid analyst in London', writing in *Psychic Self-Defence*: 'It was in order to understand the hidden aspects of the mind that I originally took up the study of occultism . . . And through all my experiences I was learning to interpret occultism in the light of psychology, and psychology in the light of occultism, the one counterchecking and explaining the other.'

The Belfry, West Halkin Street, Belgravia.

Between 1935 and 1939 she lived in a church known as the Belfry, a short walk from the Spiritualist Association of Great Britain in Belgravia. It was here that she wrote many of her occult novels, including her most successful, *The Sea Priestess*. She also held occasional lectures and, in the top room, performed the 'Rites of Isis' for invited guests. The climax of the performance involved her, robed as the goddess, rising from the depths into the room with the help of a lift installed by the owner, the eccentric Sir Vincent Henry Penalver Caillard. An intelligence officer and subsequently President of the Federation of British Industry, Caillard attempted to communicate with spirits with the help of two machines: a kind of typewriter used by a medium while in trance, which he called a 'reflectograph'; and a 'communigraph', which combined a pendulum with an ouija board.

Having joined the two great esoteric movements started in the previous century, the Theosophical Society and the Hermetic Order of the Golden Dawn, and finding both wanting, Dion Fortune started her own group, the Fraternity of the Inner Light, which still exists today under the name of the Society of the Inner Light. Her major work of non-fiction, *The Mystical Qabalah*, articulated the teachings of her mentor Moriarty and helped to continue the process of exploring the magical power of the cabbala that formed much of the work of the Golden Dawn and of Aleister Crowley.

While Crowley influenced artists and adventurers who enjoyed 'living on the edge', Dion Fortune succeeded in appealing to the mainstream of occult practitioners, which resulted in a proliferation of groups and teachers who continue to draw upon her work today.

Crowley, in his later years, became a spent force, but the 'magical current' that he initiated and called Thelema (after the abbey of the same name in Rabelais' novel, *The Life of Gargantua and of Pantagruel*) continued to exert its influence, most notably on Kenneth Grant, who combined the inspiration of Crowley with that of the science-fiction writer H.P. Lovecraft and the idiosyncratic magical system of the London artist, Austin Osman Spare, to produce a series of books that are denounced as the ravings of a madman by some and as works of great depth by others.

Grant, born in Essex in 1924 and now a recluse in his eighties, leads a magical order known as the Typhonian Ordo Templi Orientis. In the 1950s in collaboration with his wife Steffi, Grant began issuing a series of essays, known as the Carfax Monographs, which were designed to 'elucidate the hidden lore of the West according to canons preserved in various esoteric orders and movements of recent times'. These essays marked the beginning of half a century of contribution to Thelemic literature that includes poetry, biographical works, fact and fiction.

Grant's work, however, appeals to only a minority, and it is Crowley's influence on a different kind of magic, born in West Yorkshire in the 1970s and known as Chaos Magic, that may well prove his most lasting legacy. We will examine this in the next chapter.

◇ The Risks of the Magical Path ◇

Magic has always been considered dangerous, and even today many people are torn between a fascination with magic and an almost instinctive fear of it. Much of this fear comes from the fact that magic deals with 'hidden forces' and we are programmed to be fearful of the unknown. But are there any risks involved in the practice of magic?

Some people are so cautious by nature they adopt a policy of going nowhere near the subject. Others take a more reckless approach, in the style of the great conductor Sir Thomas Beecham, who said: 'In this life, try everything once, except incest and morris dancing.'[7] A middle way between these two extremes seems the most sensible.

Any exploration of the unknown carries risks, and when the unknown happens to involve the powers of your own mind, and of feelings and instincts that may be repressed, it is possible to experience discomfort or distress as these hidden parts of yourself begin to surface into awareness. In addition, the magical worldview involves a belief in spirits and the continuity of life after death, and anyone who takes on board such a view must be prepared for the possibility of encountering these beings. On the positive side, practitioners will say that they experience an increased sense of well-being as they come to know themselves and the universe around them in a deeper and more satisfying way. On the negative side, someone trying to follow the path of magic can easily find themselves in a world redolent with superstition and illusion.

For this reason, most magical schools and teachers recommend students adopt a gradual approach, so that any increased access to the untapped powers of their mind or sensitivity to the psychic realm is balanced by their developing self-knowledge and psychological maturity. This is fine in theory, but in practice the world of magic is still shot through with liberal quantities of delusion, grandiosity, naivety and superstition, which is why it can be so easily derided.

A major step forward in the evolution of magic occurred, however, in the late twentieth century, when a number of psychological approaches were developed, which have come to be known as the 'Transpersonal' or 'Spiritual' psychologies. With much of their roots in Jung's fascination with alchemy and mysticism, and his theories of the Collective Unconscious and Archetypes, these psychologies saw the human being as a spiritual entity possessing the untapped powers that magicians had always sought to develop.

Some magicians have embraced these new psychologies and incorporate much of their understanding into their work, but opinions in the magical community on this issue are divided, with traditionalists opposing any wedding of magic with psychology, which they see as rooted in a mechanistic view of the human being drawn from the worst arrogances of western culture.[8]

Proponents of the value of the new psychologies to a practice of magic believe that their great contribution lies in the fact that they work with the ideas of psychoanalysis and other psychotherapies, but with a spiritual perspective that accepts the reality of 'other worlds'. These approaches can then be used to promote ways of developing the self that can help avoid some of the pitfalls involved in the old-fashioned pursuit of magic. From their point of view, one of the best steps to take in a further exploration of magic is to experience transpersonal psychotherapy, or at least to learn more about it. (See the General Resources Guide in the Appendix).

The risks involved in the pursuit of magic are – put simply – either getting frightened by unpleasant perceptions or becoming deluded. Unfortunately it is possible to suffer from both symptoms at the same time. The delusion most commonly cited is known as ego-inflation in psychology, where access to archetypes or inner powers deludes a person into thinking they are vastly more important than they really are. In Golden Dawn work, for example, a magical technique is employed, known as the Assumption of the God-form, in which an Egyptian god is invited into the aura of the magician, to give its blessing. From a Jungian point of view, the power from the Collective Unconscious that might flood into the limited vessel of the magician's ego at this point could result in severe inflation or delusion. Such a risk is exacerbated by the use of the grand-sounding titles employed by many magical orders and inherited from Freemasonry or the Golden Dawn.

While severe ego-inflation may be rare, and good magical training warns its students against it, there are so many tantalising ideas, images and techniques in the world of magic, it is easy to fall prey to any one of numerous red herrings that can lure the unwary into a half-lit world reminiscent of that of obsessive conspiracy theorists. As Stephen Fry remarked, quoting Oscar Wilde: '"The true mystery of the world is the visible, not the invisible." How I wish mad new agers and the daftly superstitious realised that truth.'[9]

The other risk involves feeling 'spooked': feeling as if one is experiencing unwanted visitations from the spirit world or attack by invisible forces. Dion Fortune believed that she had suffered such an attack, and her *Psychic Self-Defence* (Weiser, 2001), which she wrote to offer advice on how to protect oneself magically, is still popular, as is Caitlin Matthew's more up to date treatment of the same theme: *The Psychic Protection Handbook* (Piatkus, 2005). Both books offer practical techniques for repelling the unwanted influences of malevolent spirits and human beings, and are valuable primers for anyone setting out on a magical path.

The mind is so suggestible, however, and the imagination often so vivid, it can be hard to determine the origin of any particular feeling or symptom, and even those who believe in the need for psychic protection recognise that the possibility of 'psychic attack' is extremely remote. However, in times of stress many people find relief and comfort from engaging in a specific act, such as wearing an amulet, repeating an affirmation or conducting a ritual of protection, whether this works by suggestion, through the placebo effect, or in a truly magical way.

Up until the nineteenth century, wizards or cunning-folk were often asked to offer magical protection. As we have already seen, before adequate policing and insurance, and when the causes of most ailments remained a mystery, the curses of malevolent witches or the baleful influence of spirits or elves, were often blamed. Rituals and spells were used to repel these unwanted forces, and today many magicians still hold that magical means are necessary to protect us from harm. Others, while sometimes using magical means in certain cases, believe that common-sense and discrimination offer us more protection than any number of magical formulae, which can be counter-productive when they encourage fear and superstition. The magician and essayist Lionel Snell writes: 'Don't waste time clutching crucifixes when terror- ised by psychic phenomena – it's far more effective to exorcise them with scientific scrutiny.'[10]

⊙ *The Magic of Tibet in Post-War England*

From the mid-1950s to the early 1980s, a popular series of books by an author known as Lobsang Rampa introduced many people to spirituality and the concepts of meditation, astral travel and magical powers through their romantic evocation of the world of a Tibetan lama.

After the success of the first book *The Third Eye*, in which the author describes his experiences growing up as a monk in Tibet and a trepanning operation that bores a hole in his forehead to render him clairvoyant, the Tibetologist Heinrich Harrer, dis- mayed by the book's fictions, hired a private detective to discover the true identity of the author.

'*Tuesday Lobsang Rampa*'.

It turned out to be Cyril Hoskins, born in Plymouth in 1910. He claimed that he had fallen out of a tree trying to photograph an owl, and while suffering concussion had given permission for a Tibetan lama, with the full name of Tuesday Lobsang Rampa, to inhabit his body. The British press accused him of being a charlatan and hounded him to such a degree that in the 1960s he went to live in Canada. He died in Calgary in 1981, having published nineteen books, one of which he claimed had been dictated to him by his cat.

His books have inspired many people but are scorned by scholars who see him as following Madame Blavatsky, the founder of the Theosophical Society, in a misleading tradition of 'pseudo Orientalia'.[11]

~ The English Tantrics ~

The story of magic in England in the twentieth century can be roughly divided into two phases.

In the first half of the century, the popularisation of psychology, combined with the work of Crowley and Fortune, resulted in much of magic freeing itself from the constraints of its past. As we have seen, other major factors were Freud's emphasis on the importance of sex, the upheaval caused by two world wars and the prevalent use of psychoactive drugs. In addition to this potent brew, the influence of the avant-garde and bohemianism, under-going a revival in London in the 1920s, contributed to an almost frenzied atmosphere of experimentation and the breaking down of inherited structures.

Although Crowley and Fortune were poles apart in their atti-tudes to drugs and sexual conduct, they both realised that sexual energy could be harnessed for magical ends. Whilst Crowley wrote openly about his experimentation in this area, Dion Fortune was more discreet, but her interest in the subject is quite clear, perme-ating almost every novel that she wrote. For her, the union of priest and priestess in a ritual act of love-making could release into the collective psyche potent forces for healing, and she believed that in this way she could help humanity free itself of sexual repression and guilt. There are some Fortune enthusiasts who believe that the era of sexual liberation that occurred in the 1960s was due, not so much to the invention of the birth-control pill, but to the rites that she carried out in Belgravia decades earlier.

Freud may have 'given permission' for sex to be explored by Westerners in the twentieth century, but in India the psychologi-cal and magical power of sexuality had been researched centuries earlier, and was included within the Tantric tradition of spiritual practice. Tantrics use sexuality to seek enlightenment and magical powers, and are divided by some into 'Left-Handed' practitioners, who deliberately break taboos and are capable of 'black magic', and 'Right-Handed' ones, who shun such practices. In the first half of the twentieth century, England attempted to catch up with India: Crowley epitomising the Left-Handed Tantric, Fortune the Right-Handed one.[12]

Dion Fortune died in 1946, Crowley a year later, but a third English Tantric soon appeared to build upon their work. In 1954, Gerald Gardner, whose life we examined in Chapter 5, pub-lished *Witchcraft Today*, a book that took elements from virtually every strand of magic practised in the country over the centuries. However, he also added a powerful dose of Tantrism by suggest-ing that magical work should be conducted in the nude, with the ritual use of a flail, and that rites should be led by a High Priest and High Priestess who would literally or symbolically couple at the climax of certain rituals. Aleister Crowley had spent decades exploring how sex could be used magically, while Dion Fortune had spent decades crafting novels and teaching in a discreet way the workings of 'polarity magic'. Now, without further ado, Gardner simply introduced the idea as standard magical practice in his new system of Wicca.

Magic had made a great leap forward. The increasingly permissive atmosphere of the twentieth century had allowed magicians to talk openly, for the first time, about a major source of power that fuelled their operations. Sexuality, however, was by no means their only concern. They were drawn to magic not so much by frustrated desire but by the age-old motives of the magician: the search for altered states of awareness, for communication with other worlds, for out-of-the-body travel in time and space, for the alteration of circumstances and the development of hidden powers.

As 'Tantrics', Gardner, Fortune and Crowley were pioneers, and each contributed to a resurgence of interest in paganism that would come to influence much of magic at the end of the twentieth and the beginning of the twenty-first century.

Students of MADELINE MONTALBAN
(1910–1982)

'Madeline Montalban' was the magical name of Dolores North, whose fascination with magic began as a child when she contracted polio. To while away the long hours, she started reading the Bible, as well as studies of folklore and magic. She was familiar with the magical scene in pre-war London, knew Aleister Crowley, frequented the Atlantis Bookshop (where members of Gerald Gardner's circle met) and typed the manuscript of his novel, High Magic's Aid. *During the war she served as a Wren in the Royal Navy, later claiming that she was really on Lord Louis Mountbatten's staff as his personal seer.*

Her legacy to the world of magic is a correspondence course (see

Resources, at the end of this chapter, for more details), which teaches practical ritual and self-development.

Interviewed below are Alfred Douglas and Rick Hayward, both of whom studied with Montalban, and Julia Phillips, a practising magician, who is currently writing Montalban's biography.

⊙ *Alfred Douglas*

Madeline believed that angels were real and existed to help man evolve. Her research centred round the book of Enoch, which is believed to be five hundred years older than the book of Genesis, and which seems to have inspired stories such as Adam and Eve and the serpent in the Garden of Eden. The book of Enoch was not thought to have survived, until a Scottish scholar, James Bruce, found no less than three copies in a cave in Ethiopia in 1773.

In the book of Enoch, the serpent of wisdom brings the light of consciousness to humankind, rather as Prometheus stole fire from the gods to give to mankind. According to this version of the story, the teaching angels descended to earth voluntarily to teach humans the arts of civilisation, rather than being rebels cast out from heaven by a vengeful God. The serpent's error was not in granting self-consciousness and intelligence to humanity, but in granting it before the human mind had evolved sufficiently to balance knowledge against wisdom.

Madeline believed that the ancient planetary deities of Babylonian times were one and the same entities as the fallen angels. As with other Hermetic traditions, one could invoke these forms of energy, using the most appropriate sounds, metals, perfumes, sigils, astrological conjunctions and so on, to bring about change in the material world. Madeline was very insistent on the practical use of magic, saying: 'If magic does not work, why bother about it?'

Madeline tended to work on two levels with her students. She made simple practices easily available to a fairly wide audience through her correspondence course, and through her articles on Tarot and astrology in *Prediction* magazine. But she also attracted a small number of gifted and powerful magicians who developed their own unique techniques unrestricted by the dogma of other Orders.

⊙ *Rick Hayward*

I met Madeline in 1967, when I was working as a session guitarist. She taught me that astrology should not be seen as some divination technique that works on its own, but that it is connected to everything else in the occult world and, in particular, to her form of magic.

The planets represent the different energies and qualities. Venus, for example, represents 'attractive' energy, the life force represented in sex, for instance, while Mars represents the driving power. Together, they represent every aspect of the divine power. In astrology, the planets symbolise the way that the primal energy of the universe is reflected in the different qualities of humans, animals and vegetables. Each is linked by a different 'ray', as Madeline would describe it.

The greatest magicians of the Renaissance would use these correspondences to redress defects in their personalities. Ficino, for example, one of the most powerful Renaissance magicians, was born under Saturn, which is a depressive, contracting energy, so he held rituals specifically related to the expansive energy in Jupiter, using appropriate music, colours, jewellery, etc. [See the 'How To' exercise in Chapter 7.]

As I began to practise Madeline's magic more intensely, I asked it to give me the freedom to devote my life to this new world. I was answered almost immediately, and soon found a job with *Prediction* magazine as an astrologer, which I still hold today. I also went back to guitar teaching, and here too I have found synchronicity with the occult. The octave is linked to the eight main planets in astrology. Rock music is based around three chords, the first, fourth and fifth – what I call the holy trinity of music. Anywhere in the universe, music must have this simple basis. It is a universal law.

⊙ *Julia Phillips*

Madeline was an extraordinary character. Today she would almost certainly have been a celebrity with a difference. She knew Crowley, but was not part of his Order, or, indeed, anyone else's magical group as she was far too much her own woman. She liked him as a person, but dismissed him as 'so much bluster, bravado and over-dramatised piffle to impress the weak willed'. When she died, a blanket box with a full set of Golden Dawn robes, sword and so on was found amongst her possessions, although there is no evidence – anecdotal or otherwise – to suggest that she practised magic in the style of the Hermetic Order of the Golden Dawn. Her life's work was in creating a truly unique magical system of her own.

During the latter part of her life, Madeline shared a big mansion flat off Shaftesbury Avenue with some of her favourite pupils. She actively practised magic herself, and believed that it was easier for women to create the force-field through magical power manifested on the material plane than it was for male magicians.

A number of modern occultists, including some Wiccans, have incorporated into their regular teachings extracts from Madeline's set of forty-two lessons. My own experience of working with her system is that she tapped directly into something both profound and original, and, like all genuine teachers, she was able to pass this on to others.

I have carried out one ritual that she taught me, the 'magical novena', twice in my life, and found it to be very accurate and powerful. Of course you have to be absolutely certain what to ask for before you start, but the ritual is not complicated and, for me, it really worked.

Unlike today, with all that the internet now offers, Madeline lived at a time when there was no easy access to occult secrets, and the main path in was through the secret groups. Her teaching, however, is so well rooted in the idea of a helpful spirit world, and offers such a practical and easy way to draw on these powers, that it has stood the test of time and is now attracting a much larger, world-wide audience.

✧ The Yorkshire Yogi and the ✧ Last Prosecutions under the Witchcraft Act

In 1935, at the height of the events that led to the abdication of Edward VIII, the Archbishop of Canterbury, Dr Cosmo Lang, revealed to the Prime Minister the results of his investigation into the influence on the king of a man who became known as the 'Yorkshire Yogi'.

Dr Alexander Cannon, who had a surgery in Harley Street, was becoming the confidant of the King while treating him with hypnosis for a drinking problem. MI5 investigated, a cover-up ensued and Cannon settled – in virtual exile – on the Isle of Man.

An article on Cannon, accused by some as a 'black magician', which appeared in 1936 in *Time Magazine* in the USA, reported:

He believes that man has not only an astral body which leaves the corporal shell in sleep or death but an etheric body even more refined than the astral. He has composed a kind of 'music' which consists of combinations of colors. He once offered to do the Hindu rope trick in London's Albert Hall for $275,000. He has invented a thought-reading machine called a psychostethokyrtographmanometer which he intends to demonstrate in the U.S. this year. He believes Armageddon may come in 1937. Like many another prominent mystic, he has no sense of humor.[13]

Armageddon did come, in its own way, a few years later than Cannon's prediction. Just before the decisive offensive of D-Day that would spell its end, MI5 acted once again to put a stop to an occult practice that it deemed harmful to the nation.

At a séance in Portsmouth, the medium Helen Duncan received messages from sailors drowned in the sinking of HMS *Barham*, months before the sinking was officially reported. Police arrested Duncan, who was put on trial at the Old Bailey and prosecuted for fraudulent mediumship under the 1735 Witchcraft Act. She was sentenced to nine months in prison, which conveniently kept her locked away during the D-Day operation and prevented her from revealing any more secrets during this critical time.

Helen Duncan, 1897–1956.

Duncan is often cited as the last person to be prosecuted under the Witchcraft Act, but six months after her trial, at the age of seventy-two, Jane Yorke became the last person to receive that honour, being fined £5. In 1951, the Act was repealed.

THE ATLANTIS BOOKSHOP

Described by one enthusiast as 'a hub for London's occult world, essential to the practising magus, pagan, shaman and witch', the Atlantis Bookshop was started in 1922 by John Houghton. Apart from providing you with a sympathetic atmosphere to browse their huge selection whilst classical music plays gently in the background, Atlantis hosts Moots, discussion groups, teaching workshops (for example on John Dee's Enochian Magic) and publishes under their own imprint, Neptune Press.

Whilst the original 'pegboard' where covens would recruit for members is no longer used, Geraldine Beskin, the shop's owner will often point people towards groups and contact points for those who want to explore further.

Geraldine is a magician herself and offers a good example of her conviction that occultists are sane and reasonable people, not oddballs. She talks sensibly and clearly about the subject, based on long experience with 'beginners' and believes that reading is a great way to get started, but for those who are serious, it is vitally important to 'do something practical' at least once a week.

'A lot of people are armchair magicians. My plea is to stay in one evening a week and get better at something. It may be embarrassing when you first try and call the quarters with only the cat for company, but you cannot drive a car just by reading the Highway Code. It is vital to understand that contact with spirits is the core to all of this and you cannot dodge this issue, or you are not talking about magic. If you feel nervous, find someone with integrity who you trust before you get in too deep.'

The shop is supposed to be haunted by a tall male, wearing old-fashioned grey clothing, striding towards the back door.

↶ The Tarot – Mirror of the Soul ↷

Tarot is a path of enlightenment, a way to realize the starlight within you. It teaches you to see things as they really are.

JAMES WANLESS, *VOYAGER TAROT*

'The Magician' from the Sharman-Casselli Tarot Deck.[14]*. The Tarot is made up of 78 cards. 22 are known as the 'Major Arcana', and 56 the 'Minor Arcana'. The first card of the Major Arcana is numbered 0 and is called 'The Fool', which is followed by Card number 1: 'The Magician'.*

The Tarot first appeared in Renaissance Italy in the fifteenth century, but it was not until it reached England, and became an object of fascination for Victorian magicians, that it began to reveal its full potential.[15]

During the occult revival of the nineteenth century in France, a number of writers began to look beyond the Tarot's use as a card game and fortune-telling device, to discern deeper meanings. They associated the letters of the Hebrew Alphabet and the paths of the cabbalistic Tree of Life with the twenty-two cards of the Tarot's Major Arcana. The founders of the Golden Dawn took this idea and taught its initiates a way of using the Tarot images as a system of 'keys' to unlock the secrets of the Tree of Life, through a technique known as 'path-working'. By strongly visualising a

Tarot image, and by working with its symbolism, the magician could gain access to each of the twenty-two paths of the Tree.

In addition to using the Tarot for path-working to explore the Otherworld and make contact with its inhabitants and powers, The Golden Dawn also used it as a tool for divination, and as a way of deepening their understanding of life. Each of the Major Arcana images were seen as symbolic of humanity's spiritual journey.

Two members of the Golden Dawn in particular were responsible for helping to create the most influential modern Tarot decks: Aleister Crowley who worked with the painter Lady Freida Harris to produce the Thoth Deck, with its powerful Art-Deco images, and A.E. Waite who inspired the artist Pamela Coleman Smith to create the Rider-Waite deck, which has become the most popular deck in the world, thanks to the way in which the 40 pip cards of the Minor Arcana are each painted with an imaginary scene. Traditionally these cards showed only the relevant number of symbols of the card's suit – Smith and Waite's stroke of genius was to portray each card with a story-like image that made reading the cards much easier. As a result of their work many decks today continue the practice of using scenes rather than symbols for the pip cards.

◈ A First Exercise ◈

A magician is someone who is wise. All the great spiritual traditions have developed methods of self-enquiry to pursue the goal of wisdom, and many of the modern methods of psychotherapy, such as psychoanalysis, can also help us deepen our self-knowledge. Magic offers tools for this as well, such as astrology, numerology, palmistry, and the Tarot.

In astrology twelve types of person are described, based on their zodiac sign. In numerology there are nine or eleven charac-ter types, and in the Tarot there are sixteen, depicted in the court cards of the four suits.

We're going to use the Tarot to deepen our self-knowledge, by determining which of the sixteen Tarot personality types we belong to. This will help us to acknowledge and build on our strengths, and to identify – and hopefully compensate for – our weaknesses.

As with many systems of 'typology', the idea of dividing up the whole range of human personality into just a few categories can sometimes seem crude, but the trick is to approach this field with an open mind. A magician is also a scientist – filled with curiosity, keen to learn more and prepared to venture into regions that some might reject out of hand. When it comes to Tarot's typology, there is support for its validity from the world of psychology: one of the most commonly used personality tests is called the Myers-Briggs Type Indicator. Using a questionnaire, it leads you to determine which of sixteen personality types you belong to, and these types can be correlated with the sixteen Tarot types that we are now exploring.

Each of these types is represented by one of the sixteen court cards of the Tarot deck, and to work out which of these you might be, you must first determine whether you are a King, a Queen, a Prince or a Princess. (Note that some Tarot decks use Knights and Pages instead of Princes and Princesses.) To do this, don't pay any attention to the gender or to the aristocratic associations of the terminology; instead ask yourself which of the following descriptions fits you the most closely. You may feel that several or all of the choices could describe you, but go for the one that your instinct tells you is most applicable.

(A) I feel young and innocent most of the time. Sometimes this makes me uncomfortable or embarrassed when I'm in the company of other adults who seem so 'grown-up'. I feel as if I have so much potential that I'm only beginning to explore.

(B) I like to get on with things. I want to be of use to the world, but I sometimes jump into things too impulsively. It makes me feel clumsy sometimes, but I prefer action to too much thinking.

(C) I feel quite mature and aware of myself and what I'm

doing in the world. I value creativity and compassion and like to nurture these qualities in myself and those around me.

(D) I feel in charge of myself and my life, and am considered an authority figure by some people. I have accomplished a good deal and try to be socially responsible.

If you're having difficulty choosing, ask yourself this question: 'If I had to choose just one of these four statements, which would it be?' (This is of course a 'trick' for the mind. But there's a place in magic for tricks!)

If you've chosen (A) your personality will be best described by one of the four Princess/Page cards; if you've chosen (B) one of the Prince/Knight cards; if you've chosen (C) one of the Queens, and if you've chosen (D) one of the Kings. But which one? Now you have to determine your suit. In playing cards there are four suits – clubs, diamonds, hearts and spades. In the Tarot these have become wands, cups, swords and pentacles.

To find out which suit you belong to, now ask yourself which of the following four descriptions best fits you:

(A) I'm an intuitive, enthusiastic person, who loves starting projects and tends to have ten new ideas before breakfast. I'm not so good at finishing things, though, and I can lack focus because I'm interested in so many things.

(B) I'm a sensitive, emotional person. I feel very deeply, and can cry easily. My heart goes out to people and animals who are suffering, and I feel drawn to the arts and the healing professions.

(C) I spend a lot of my time thinking and analysing. Some might call me an intellectual, and I can be accused of having my head in the clouds. I sometimes feel detached from everyday events and can find it hard to express my feelings.

(D)   I'm a practical person – I just like to get to work and
       do things, rather than endlessly theorising about
       them or talking about them. I'm good with my hands
       and like making people feel at home.

If you are an (A) your suit is wands; if you are a (B) it's cups; if
you are a (C) it's swords and for a (D) it's pentacles.

Now put the answers to these two sets of questions together and
you will know which of the sixteen Tarot personality types you
belong to. Read the thumbnail description for your type below.

❧ The Sixteen Personality Types ❧ of the Tarot

◉ *The Princess/Page of Wands*
enthusiastic, energetic, inventive

You are probably a lively, outgoing, playful
person, who is eager to experience life, to be
creative and to try out new things. You love
life, are a loyal friend and lover, and have a
burning desire to achieve. Your enthusiasm
is infectious, but you may sometimes act
theatrically or selfishly, using people and circumstances to achieve your own ends. On the
downside, you can sometimes be confused or
indecisive, and can feel so full of energy that
you find it hard to stay calm or focused.

◉ *The Princess/Page of Cups*
sensitive, tender, imaginative

You are probably a sensitive and highly imaginative person,
for whom the world of feelings and of dreams is particularly

important. You are likely to be attracted to artistic pursuits and to exploring the inner world, perhaps through meditation. You are a good listener and know when to offer sympathy and kindness. On the downside, you can sometimes feel that you are too easily upset and would like a thicker skin. It's also possible that to protect yourself from feelings of vulnerability you may actually have made yourself insensitive to others' needs.

⊙ *The Princess/Page of Swords*
inquisitive, objective, aloof

You are probably very bright – good at communicating clearly and diplomatically, and you enjoy intellectual challenges. You love a really good conversation and find it easy to be analytical, but because of the ease with which you can be objective and detach yourself from your feelings, some people experience you as distant or even aloof. It is easy for you to become overly critical of other people and even to be tempted into prying into their lives. You sometimes think that you need to get more in touch with your feelings but this makes you feel uncomfortably childlike, and your usual sense of certainty deserts you.

⊙ *The Princess/Page of Pentacles*
studious, self-reliant, good-natured

You are probably a very easy-going and good-natured person, and may well be a student or someone involved in study or in creative work. Realistic and practical, you may suffer a little from shyness and tend to spend long periods of time alone absorbed in your work. Although generally a diligent and hard worker, your weakness is that you can lapse into laziness.

◉ *The Prince/Knight of Wands*
passionate, eager, rebellious

You are probably full of enthusiasm and energy, especially for new ideas. You love to initiate projects and to come up with plans, but tend to have trouble completing them, since your eagerness is greater than your commitment to seeing things through to completion. You make an ardent and passionate lover, but you may well not be a loyal or a committed one. Your social conscience may sometimes make you act the revolutionary or the rebel, or you might channel your energies in the direction of commerce, sport or drama. For your personal development it would be wise to work on developing the qualities of reliability, attention to detail, commitment, and the ability to deliver on your promises to yourself and others.

◉ *The Prince/Knight of Cups*
idealistic, empathic, romantic

You are probably a caring, gentle, artistic and idealistic dreamer, who likes nothing better than the quest for love and beauty.

KNIGHT *of* CUPS

You will always follow your heart and your romantic dreams, and the challenge for you is to avoid the pitfalls of illusion and glamour. You are likely to be good at dealing with people and find it easy to empathise, which would make you a good counsellor or therapist. Sometimes you might find it hard to act because so much of your attention is in the world of dreams, and you may well be experiencing a conflict between what you feel in your heart and your need to take action in the world.

⊙ *The Prince/Knight of Swords*
intelligent, articulate, impetuous

You are probably intelligent, articulate and quick-witted. You enjoy an intellectual challenge and will often engage in argument or discussion for the sheer pleasure of using your analytical skills. Your youthfulness – either in age or attitude – means that you are not always capable of long and sustained effort, and can suffer from being too impetuous or too righteous. You may find it hard to spend time on your own, preferring to direct your attention outwards rather than inwards. Deep down you know that you need to develop more maturity and patience, but you cannot resist charging in where others would be more circumspect. You are, however, inventive, insightful, skilful – and brave and witty too, although your wit can sometimes be cynical or ironic.

⊙ *The Prince/Knight of Pentacles*
practical, realistic, sensuous

You are probably a steady, reliable and practical person, who is stable, uncomplaining and dependable in a relationship. You are ambitious, too, but know how to patiently and realistically work towards your goals. Beneath your respectable or conventional appearance you are sensuous and passionate, and feel strongly for the welfare of the land. You take pride in maintaining your home and investments, and may well be highly skilled with your hands. You value security, order and dependability, but the downside of this means that you may sometimes lack spontaneity, and you can become preoccupied with material ambitions, or obsessive about your health and sport.

⊙ *The Queen of Wands*
dynamic, confident, strong-willed

You are probably powerful and dynamic, with your passion expressing itself in generosity and creativity. Full of energy, and often wilful, you love challenge and excitement and make an excellent leader. You know how to get your own way, but usually you manage to do this with charm and flair. Your optimistic approach to life and your vibrant personality generate the charisma needed to pull together teams of people, making you good at communicating the big picture and inspiring others with your vision. Strong and warm as a lover and parent, you need to be careful not to become domineering, jealous or manipulative.

⊙ *The Queen of Cups*
loving, nurturing, intuitive

You are probably someone who is very much in touch with their emotions, and can often be highly intuitive or psychic. You are imaginative and compassionate, and make an excellent mother, therapist and friend. You may well be involved in artistic pursuits, the healing arts or relationship counselling, and since you have the creative ability to manifest your goals and dreams, you could feel drawn to working in the world of film or theatre.

⊙ *The Queen of Swords*
independent, graceful, analytical

You are probably a discriminating and perceptive person with high ideals, with a wisdom that comes from having known suffering and conflict, as well as joy and happiness. You are a lover of truth and freedom, are fiercely independent and, above all, you are in control of the powers of your mind. You are able to be discerning,

QUEEN of SWORDS

accurate and, if necessary, tough, and are naturally adept at analysing issues and situations. For this reason you would make a good lawyer or scientist. Some people might find you intimidating, but your honesty and your ability to be detached and to view situations objectively make you an excellent ally, friend or business partner. You can be an enigmatic lover, whose grace and intelligence are stimulating, but you may well not wish to devote yourself to a full-time relationship.

⊙ *The Queen of Pentacles*
generous, patient, pragmatic

You are the sort of person who trusts their instincts, and is eminently practical and generous. A warm host and excellent cook, you enjoy every aspect of home-making, including taking care of any children or animals that are in your life. You are probably a pragmatic, well-organised individual who handles their finances successfully, and makes a loyal and sensual lover. You make a good friend too, always offering a sympathetic ear, common-sense advice and practical help. Your desire to be of use can sometimes mean that you neglect your own health and needs.

⊙ *The King of Wands*
purposeful, enquiring, optimistic

You are likely to be a lively, amusing and ambitious person. Above all, you love freedom, but you are also able to commit to a vision once you have found it, and are a natural leader. For this reason you could be the ideal person to take charge of an organisation, since you can hold to a vision, and your enthusiasm and optimism can inspire others to co-operate with you. You make a passionate lover, but partners must be aware of your longing for freedom. You are decisive and strong-willed, but your failing is that you can be unsympathetic towards other people's negativity or weakness, since you experience these feelings so rarely. Your dynamic nature, dislike of routine and love of challenge will sometimes conflict with your strong will and ambition, which is keen to make significant achievements or forge a long-term career.

⊙ The King of Cups
tolerant, sincere, compassionate

You are likely to be an accomplished person who has attained some degree of success in an artistic or cultural field. As a jovial, caring, tolerant and sincere individual, you respond well to the needs of others, and are likely to have directed your creative imagination into socially responsible achievements. Others perceive you as wise and compassionate, with an artistic sensibility. Over the years you have learnt how to master your feelings, placing responsibility before your need for self-expression. This can sometimes create conflict, since your position, and the life you have built around you, often keep you away from the source of your inspiration. You might feel drawn to being a therapist, minister, or doctor, or towards working in the arts or the music business. As a lover, your intense feelings may be experienced as demanding, while in interactions with others your sensitivity and the deep currents of emotion that run through you may cause you to lose your objectivity and overreact.

⊙ The King of Swords
decisive, intellectual, discriminating

You are probably a person of ideas and action, discriminating and decisive. Your intellectual powers are finely honed, and you are at your best when making judgements and decisions. Friends turn to you for your ability to give an honest, objective opinion, since you are able to focus on an issue without being swayed by your feelings. You would make a good lawyer, accountant, surgeon, scientist, editor or computer specialist. As a lover you might enjoy fantasy and flirtation, but will tend to avoid the depths of passion. There is a risk that your ability to be decisive and analytical and to separate yourself from your feelings can make you act cruelly or heartlessly, and you may need to be careful to curb any tendency towards scheming or acting in a hurtful way.

◉ *The King of Pentacles*
responsible, steadfast, productive

KING *of* PENTACLES

You are probably a generous and patient person, exuding a sense of contentment and satisfaction with your life, home and family. A lover of fine food, earthy humour, sport and physical pleasures, you know how to combine knowledge with practicality to achieve your goals. You are reliable and responsible, and are capable of showing courage in adversity. You might well be successful and wealthy, having created a strong financial base through a consistent and often cautious investment in time, energy and money. You are sensual and passionate, and make a devoted partner, but your dependability can turn into inflexibility and stubbornness, and you may have a tendency to be coarse or vulgar.

✍ Going Deeper ✍

As you use the Tarot for personal development purposes you may begin to notice an increase in the number of synchronistic events in your life.

CATHERINE SUMMERS AND JULIAN VAYNE,
PERSONAL DEVELOPMENT WITH THE TAROT, 2002

Discovering which Tarot personality type you are is just a beginning. You can use this system to work out the strengths and weaknesses of your friends and family, and then you can use this knowledge practically. If you discover, for example, that your boss is a King of Wands, you will know that they are not a good person to turn to when you are feeling weak or vulnerable. Instead you need to turn to someone whom you've identified as being a Queen of Cups.

You can also explore the opposite side of your personality, which may be lurking in the shadows, longing for expression. To do this, 'translate' your court card in these two steps:

Step 1: Select the 'opposite' of your current court card by choosing the role shown below. (For example, if you are a King, select Princess.)

King	Queen	Prince	Princess
Princess	Prince	Queen	King

Step 2: Select the 'opposite' of your suit in the same way. (For example, if you are wands, select cups.)

Wands	Cups	Swords	Pentacles
Cups	Wands	Pentacles	Swords

So if you were a King of Wands, your opposite is the Princess of Cups. Now read the thumbnail sketch of your opposite to see whether that expresses some of the hidden or unexpressed side of your personality, and ask yourself whether there is anything you can do to help that side of you find fulfilment.

To explore the Tarot court cards more fully, read Mary K. Greer and Tom Little, *Understanding the Tarot Court* (Llewellyn, 2004), and Kate Warwick-Smith, *The Tarot Court Cards* (Destiny, 2003).

Once you have a grasp of the court cards and what they mean, you can move on to explore the other sixty-two cards of the deck. To do this, read Philip and Stephanie Carr-Gomm, *The DruidCraft Tarot* (Connections, 2004) or one of the books by Rachel Pollack or Mary Greer, such as Rachel Pollack's *Complete Illustrated Guide to Tarot* (Element, 2001) or Mary Greer's *Tarot for Your Self : A Workbook for Personal Transformation* (New Page, 2002).

Once you start to work with the Tarot, it is as if you start to get a glimpse of the 'secret levers' that operate the universe. The amount of serendipity and synchronicity in your life seem to increase. 'Serendipity' is a term devised by the writer Horace Walpole in 1754 to describe happy unexpected discoveries, whilst the word 'synchronicity' was coined by the psychologist Carl Jung to describe seemingly meaningful coincidences, which can often feel magical.

✧ Traps for the Sorcerer's Apprentice ✧

At the deepest levels, the Tarot's images defy analysis . . .
This is, in part, because the images themselves draw upon
the rich brew of Gnosticism, classical Greek philosophy,
alchemy, heretical belief and pagan myth. It is also because
the symbols are archetypal, reflecting characters in fairy
tales and dreams.

JANE LYLE, *THE RENAISSANCE TAROT*, 2005

Most people use the Tarot as a fortune-telling device, and the Tarot does have the uncanny ability to suggest what could occur in the future. However, it does this, not because that future is pre-ordained and destined to happen, come what may, but by helping you to see the direction you're headed: by throwing light on the underlying situation, and on your feelings, thoughts and motivations, which are perhaps only partly conscious.

Once you grasp this difference you can use the cards, not to predict what may happen as if it's something inevitable and fated, but as a way of gaining insight into your life so that you can actively help to influence and create your future through the choices you make.

Although using the Tarot for prediction might at first sight seem tempting, ultimately it will sap you of power – because it will lead you to act as if your life were determined solely by outside forces. Instead you need to use the Tarot as a means of gaining insight into the hidden dynamics of a situation or your soul. Then it will do the opposite – it will give you a sense of power and control over your life. It will increase your self-knowledge and as a result lead you closer to that goal of the magical art: wisdom.

ALAN RICHARDSON

Alan Richardson has written the definitive biography of Dion Fortune: Priestess: The Life and Magic of Dion Fortune *(Aquarian, 1987). His latest book is entitled:* The Google Tantra: How I became the first Geordie to Raise the Kundalini *(Ignotus Press, 2007).*

There's no denying that I was a weird child. By the time I was fourteen I knew that I was looking for some book, insight or experience that might crystallise or explain the inexplicable, which rattled inside me. Much of it hinged on the Theosophists' notion that 'when the pupil is ready, the Master will appear'.

I was ready enough for enlightenment, but I didn't suppose the Masters were too interested in visiting Ashington in Durham, even if the massive and encircling pit-heaps did look like the Himalayan mountain fastness of Tibet when they were covered with snow. What I needed was a good book.

For me, without doubt, it was *You – Forever* by Lobsang Rampa. I had never heard of the author before, or the controversy surrounding him, and there was nothing on the cover to indicate either any supernatural bias or spicy content to appeal to my exploding libido. Yet in the bookshop the book fell open of its own accord at a line drawing of a naked young woman and the astral body rising above her, connected to her by a silver cord. I felt as if I had been hit by a hammer. I just knew that this was real – that it was part of what I was looking for and part of me – and at that moment I knew I no longer wanted to be an ace fighter pilot: I wanted to become like unto a god.

Of course, as a rather pathetic and wimpish lad I wanted power so I could get a bit of revenge – especially on the dreaded Head of PE. I was no different from any other boy who tries to achieve power via football, sex, trade-union politics, marriage or a career, was I?

I had just enough money to buy the book. I couldn't wait until I got home to read it: I went to the bus-station toilets and sat in a cubicle devouring the contents while – there and then – trying to slip my astral body loose from the surly bonds of the flesh and send my spirit flying up – up! – into another realm beyond the pit-heaps. Nothing happened. Everything happened . . .

These days I'm obsessed with what might be termed the 'spirit of place', which is the notion that places have lives and consciousnesses of their own. Some places 'speak' to me, revealing and teaching me things. I've no interest in joining groups, though I don't knock them, nor in wearing robes, nor yet dancing naked in cornfields – and I don't knock that either. I'm quite happy to sit somewhere by myself and do my own thing, trying to link with the land, and the spirits of the land, and then get on with living in the real world. The real magicians I know don't festoon themselves with crystals and pentagrams, or wear the sort of clothes that make them look like extras in *Mad Max II*. They all have full-time jobs in the normal world, where their workmates know nothing about their 'other' lives.

I'm often asked how I know when magic is present. Sometimes I don't. I just know that when I'm 'plugged in' to something greater than myself, I feel intensely alive. As Crowley once wrote: 'Pure Will, without lust of result, is in every way perfect.' We're not in it for prizes. Dion Fortune and Co. once wrote that magic expresses itself in three different ways: through Power, Wisdom and Love. And to express these properly, you have to experience the opposite. You have to know what it feels like to be power-less and weak; what it's like to know nothing; and what it's like to suffer the agonies of being unloved. It's bloody hard. Psychic powers, spells, visions, astral projections, curses and healings and all the rest are very real, but they are only an extremely small part of the real magical path. Anyone who tells you magic is easy, or fun, needs a good slapping.

It sounds pretentious but your whole life has to be geared to magic. As someone from the Golden Dawn once wrote: 'You should regard every act, every incident, every idea, as a secret dealing between yourself and the innermost spirit of your gods.' Or something to that effect. Suffice to say that magic has given me a life of wonders: small miracles, great agonies, subtle delights, frequent bewilderment and no small degree of awe.

My most ambitious magical project has been 'raising the kun-dalini', something I wrote about in my book, *The Google Tantra*, although actually the book is more of a love poem for my partner, Margaret. The kundalini is a great reservoir of energy, based around the seven 'chakra' nerve centres of the body, focused espe-cially on the spine, with a strong sexual dimension. I have always been fascinated by energy and auras. I believe that we are envel-oped in an egg-shaped body of light, which I visualise as being as broad as your arms, extending above your head and below your feet.

To energise the chakras, you must visualise the seven locations and then direct consciousness towards them. It is a bit like rubbing a hurt part of the body to send blood flowing through it. I link them with the endocrine glands, of which I believe the chakras are the spiritual expression. When the kundalini is aroused, it roars up the spine, vitalising the chakras in turn with bursts of truly cosmic energy, and explodes out of the top of the head, giving the individual the whole-body orgasm known as 'horasis', as well as cosmic consciousness. It is such a powerful experience that it should not be attempted without due preparation and a wise teacher.

I persuaded Margaret to try one of the gentler techniques, a meditation described by the author Dale Goodyear as 'Raising the kundalini to the Lotus in the Heart'. This involves cajoling the kundalini gently up the chakras. Dale suggested visualising the 'Purple Lotus' in the heart centre, because wherever you place your attention a magnet is created, which draws energy to itself. Margaret and I weren't too sure what a purple lotus looks like, so we decided to visualise a rose instead.

We did the experiment standing, matching our breathing, and concentrating on sucking in the breath energy, the 'prana', visualising its brilliance. Touching her groin and visualising her base chakra, I talked her through it, getting her to visualise with me. On an impulse, I made the stem of the rose shoot down from her lowest chakra and take root in the earth. As I described this, she saw it and felt it. Then, using my hands as if drawing the energy up, we used the inhalation to rise up the stem as the exercise suggested. As it came to the heart chakra, we concentrated on seeing the rosebud open and the petals receive all the light of the stars, like a satellite dish. After we held it like this for a while, we reversed the visualisation, so that the rose closed up again, and the roots were withdrawn. And then it was my turn, Margaret matching what I had done to her.

This deceptively gentle 'flower' technique was openly powerful – at least in my experience. It didn't end in the physical region of my heart but carried on of its own volition to open up my whole head. It's hard to describe. It was as if the narrow cinema-screen of my consciousness was suddenly wraparound – four times wider and twice as high. I felt light, and swayed physically, as if I were no longer just flesh, but a sphere of light. It didn't last long. I closed the flower of my own volition, reversing the process again. Margaret, too, had felt the same sense of purity, of lightness, and the swaying. She was deeply moved. She looked all melting and lovely and I couldn't help but cuddle her. I felt like a teenager again.

Our experiments with raising the kundalini seemed to connect me to other experiences. One evening, just lying in bed, I felt as though I was suddenly in a different world. It was if my brow had opened up and I was looking into an empty classroom. It seemed to be in 1950s Scotland. There was no connection I could discern from my own childhood, but it seemed completely real.

Margaret and I decided to see whether working at a sacred site might further improve the experience, so we visited the Chalice Well in Glastonbury. As we sat there and tried to work with our inner fires, I can only say that things fell away. I felt as if I were perched on top of a steep cliff.

I believe we have probably all released kundalini energy. There may be no need for all the chakra exercises that Margaret and I have tried, but as Arthur Koestler said in his last days, there are only two important things in life: 'We must be connected to something, whether it's a person, place or object.' And 'It is more important to love than be loved.'

☙ Things to Do ☙

❧ If you've got plenty of money, consider applying for membership of Anton Mosimann's Private Dining Club in London's West Halkin Street. It may take up to three months to obtain approval, but once you're in, book a table in the Mappin and Webb room at the top of this

extraordinary building. The club now occupies the Belfry
– the church used by Dion Fortune and described in
her novel *Moon Magic*. As you dine you will be basking
in the atmosphere generated by Dion Fortune and her
fellow magicians as they performed the 'Rites of Isis'. If
you're short of cash, you might prefer just to explore the
building in 360-degree panoramas on a virtual tour at
www.mosimann.com

❄ Anyone exploring England's magical heritage needs to
visit Glastonbury (see 'Things to Do' in Chapter 4). As
you walk up the lane the Tor, the last house you can see
beside the footpath was once owned by Dion Fortune,
and it was here that she ran a retreat centre for her
magical group, the Fraternity of the Inner Light. You can
visit her grave too in the town cemetery.

At the top of the High Street, a left turn and a five-
minute walk along the main road towards Wells will
bring you past an imposing entrance to the cemetery
on the right. Ignore this and take the second entrance,
a wire-mesh gate. Fortune's grave is on the right of the
path leading up into the cemetery, slightly down and
in from a marker tree on a corner halfway up. Very
close is the grave of Charles Thomas Loveday, her
friend and supporter of many years, who died within a
year of her.

You might like to read her novel *Glastonbury: Avalon
of the Heart* (Red Wheel, 2003) while you sit on the Tor
or in Chalice Well Gardens.

❄ Pay a visit to the Atlantis Bookshop in London's
Museum Street, just across from the British Museum.
As you browse through their selection of books on
magic, remember the key figures in English magic who
have done exactly the same thing in this very place. The
bookshop organises talks in the basement of the shop

and 'The Moot with No Name' in a local pub, as well as occasional conferences on magical subjects. See www. theatlantisbookshop.com

❧ Explore the legacy of Aleister Crowley at the website of the Aleister Crowley Society: www.lashtal.com, and at the site of the 'Thelemapedia' – the Encyclopedia of Thelema and Magick: see www.thelemapedia.org. Explore the work of Austin Osman Spare and Kenneth Grant at www.fulgur.co.uk

❧ Explore the work of Dion Fortune's Society of the Inner Light (originally the Fraternity of the Inner Light). You can take a distance-learning study course, after which you can apply for entry through an interview at their headquarters in London, where members meet monthly. See www.innerlight.org.uk

❧ The books and website of Gareth Knight – the current head of the Society of Inner Light – are well worth researching. With over fifty years' experience of magical studies, Gareth Knight, in his own words, 'learnt a great deal through a long if bruising association with the redoubtable old occultist W.G. Gray and a creative interchange with a fellow one-time student of his, R.J. Stewart. See www.angelfire.com/az/garethknight

❧ R.J. Stewart was trained by the 'hidden Glastonbury adept' A.R. Heaver (1900–1980) and by W.G. Gray (1913–1992). With his many decades of experience, his books, workshops and trainings are well worth investigating. See www.dreampower.com and www. rjstewart.org

❧ Explore the work of the Servants of the Light, or SOL, which emerged from the Helios correspondence

course in the cabbala, started by W.E. Butler and
Gareth Knight. SOL offers correspondence courses
and workshops on ritual magic given by the school's
formidable director, Dolores Ashcroft-Nowicki. See
www.servantsofthelight.org and www.doloresashcroft-
nowicki.com

* Read the books listed in the Resources section of one
  of Dion Fortune's most accomplished pupils – the
  Yorkshire magician, W.E. Butler (1898–1978), who
  helped to found the Servants of the Light.

* Check out the Avalon Group. Founded by Dion
  Fortune's biographer and an expert on ritual
  magic, Gareth Knight, it is now led by author
  Wendy Berg, an authority on Egyptian, Celtic,
  Arthurian and grail magical traditions. The group
  offers distance-learning and group work. See www.
  avalon-group.org

* Madeline Montalban's correspondence course in
  practical magic is available from the Order of the
  Morning Star: see www.sheridandouglas.co.uk/OMS.
  html

* If a more philosophical and mystical approach appeals
  to you, explore the work of the Fintry Trust, which
  holds retreats and other events in Surrey, and which
  runs the Universal Order, founded in 1923, and the
  Shrine of Wisdom, which publishes source texts. See
  www.thefintrytrust.org.uk and www.shrineofwisdom.
  org.uk

✦ Resources ✦

BOOKS

The Ritual Magic Workbook: A Practical Course of Self-Initiation, Dolores Ashcroft-Nowicki (Red Wheel, 1998)

Polarity Magic: The Secret History of Western Religion, Wendy Berg and Mike Harris (Llewellyn, 2003)

Magic – Its Ritual, Power & Purpose, W.E. Butler (Aquarian, 1971)

The Magician – His Training & Work, W.E. Butler (Aquarian, 1972)

Apprenticed to Magic – The Path to Magical Attainment, W.E. Butler (Aquarian, 1972)

Magick in Theory and Practice, Aleister Crowley (Dover, 1986)

Christ, Psychotherapy and Magic – A Christian Appreciation of Occultism, Anthony Duncan (Allen & Unwin, 1969)

Applied Magic, Dion Fortune (Red Wheel, 2000)

Magical Images and the Magical Imagination, Gareth Knight (Sun Chalice, 1998)

Advanced Magical Arts, R.J.Stewart (Element, 1988)

CHAPTER TWELVE

THE WIZARDS' RETURN

The Renaissance of English Magic in the Twenty-First Century

❦

The world of magic is one of high imagination, and an art and science with applications as universal as those of mathematics. Yet its unique scope, encompassing both science and religion, has caused it to be denigrated in modern times. Physical science has discarded it as superstition or a pseudo-religion. Religion has regarded it, as it once regarded science, with deep suspicion, thinking it to be an impious attempt to trespass on sacred preserves. But I consider magic to be a middle ground between science and religion, reconciling them in a technology of the imagination, which can bring about personal regeneration and spiritual fulfilment . . . We have sadly neglected the contribution that the higher imagination can make in bringing about an ecological responsibility to science and a restoration of nerve to religion. Now that we and the environment are threatened with a Faustian disaster, could a re-appraisal of the function and importance of magic be the key to our survival?

GARETH KNIGHT, *A HISTORY OF WHITE MAGIC*, 1978

hrough the Second World War, during interludes when no German bombers threatened the skies above southern England, two men would sit in the nude on a Hertfordshire lawn, discussing their favourite subjects: folklore, magic and religion. Twenty years separated them in age, and they were almost polar opposites in character, but their common interests drew them together, and as a result they were to profoundly influence the development of magic in England, and the whole world, from the mid-twentieth century onwards.

The elder man, Gerald Gardner, had joined the Folklore Society in London immediately on his return to England after living in South-East Asia for thirty-six years. It was at one of their meetings that he may well have first met the younger man, Ross Nichols, or perhaps it was at the Atlantis Bookshop in Museum Street. Both were asthmatic and keen naturists who often visited Britain's oldest nudist resort, Spielplatz, just outside St Albans.[1]

As the old world order collapsed around them, both men were convinced of the need for a return to nature. Although a Christian, Nichols believed in the redeeming power of myth and in the need for a revival of folk customs. Just after the war he published a manifesto[2] calling for this, in association with fellow poet James Kirkup, who would achieve fame in the 1970s with his poem about Christ that became the subject of the last blasphemy trial in England.[3] Nichols also wrote a 'mythology for England', which he entitled *The Land of the White Bull*, and he edited Gardner's seminal *Witchcraft Today*, which launched his version of witch-craft, known as Wicca, in 1954.[4]

The revival of paganism in England had begun as early as the eighteenth century with the work of scholars such as Richard Payne Knight, author of *The Worship of Priapus* (1786).[5] But it was in the first half of the twentieth century that this primarily intellectual interest was translated into practical magic through the work of Crowley and Dion Fortune. It was then Gardner and Nichols in the second half of the century who took the revival to the next level by developing the 'calendar of worship' that has become the bedrock of modern pagan practice (see Chapter 2). To both of them, it seemed that humanity had got out of tune with the rhythms of the land and the seasons – and hence with the cycle of life itself. Their researches into folklore showed them that the old pastoral festivals had their roots in pre-Christian paganism. In addition to these four traditional festivals on the quarter-days of Lammas, All Souls, Candlemas and May Day, there were four others too – the solstices and equinoxes.[6]

Gardner's and Nichols's genius lay in putting together these two sets of festival times to create an eightfold calendar that offered the possibility of meeting once every six weeks or so to commune with the changing face of nature in a way that was both spiritual and magical. Into this eightfold scheme they introduced forms of celebration that drew widely from the magical heritage of Western Europe. Whilst Gardner's coven in Hertfordshire began celebrating the festivals in 1958, Nichols had to wait another six years before he could introduce them into his newly formed Order of Bards, Ovates and Druids.

Although there were some differences in their celebrations – Gardner's group celebrating 'skyclad', in private, Nichols's clothed in public – the similarities were striking. Both groups were organised like the Masons with three 'degrees' or 'grades'; both celebrated in a circle, invoking the four cardinal directions and the blessings of fire and water as primal elements.

In a strange echo of one of the world's oldest religions, the Jains, who in the first century had split in India into 'white-robed' and 'skyclad' sects, paganism in England 'came out' in the mid-twentieth century in the same two forms.[7] Since then, whilst these two 'traditional' approaches can still be found, so can many variations: some Wiccans now wear robes; some Druids like to be naked; some people don't want labels but hold similar ceremonies that they call neither Druid nor Wiccan but simply 'open' or 'pagan'. As a result, today anyone can witness a magical ceremony being held in public at one of many sites around the country. These public rites are peopled solely with clothed participants – skyclad rites are invariably private affairs.

In these celebrations one can detect traces, like strands of DNA, of many of the elements of Britain's magical history. On an equinox or solstice, go to Stanton Drew in Avon, or Avebury in Wiltshire, or the Long Man of Wilmington in Sussex, and you'll be able to spot the influence of the pre-Christian Druid, Celtic and Anglo-Saxon periods. Depending on the group performing the rite, there may also be inspiration drawn from the herb or star lore of the cunning-folk, from Elizabethan magicians and their love of angel and spirit invocations, and from Freemasonry and the Hermetic Order of the Golden Dawn. This is the outstanding legacy of Gardner's and Nichols's work, which has not only encouraged magic to stay alive but to be practised openly in the English countryside – and throughout the world.

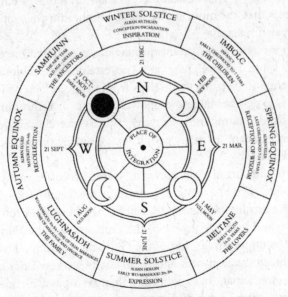

The Eightfold Calendar.

~ The 1980s ~
When We Finally Woke Up

Gardner and Nichols may have introduced this scheme in the late fifties and early sixties but it took until the eighties for it to really catch on. Until that time Wicca was mostly practised indoors, and was more concerned with spellcraft and connecting with the old gods rather than with the powers of nature. Druidic celebrations, on the other hand, were more focused on attuning to the seasons and local mythology, and were confined to a few groups holding more staid and formal open rituals on Glastonbury Tor, at Stonehenge or on London's Parliament Hill.[8]

But towards the end of the eighties a significant number of people finally woke up to the magnitude of the environmental crisis, and there was a wave of interest in indigenous traditions so huge that it reached even Prince Philip, who declared: 'It is now apparent that the ecological pragmatism of the so-called pagan religions . . . was a great deal more realistic in terms of conservation ethics than the more intellectual monotheistic philosophies of the revealed religions.'[9]

With the revival of paganism, magic was reunited once again with its close relative, religion. The established religions have always tried to distance themselves from magic, which by its very nature is experimental and empowering, and therefore threatening to fixed dogma and hierarchy. But by the closing years of the twentieth century many people were growing tired of conventional religion.

Wicca and Druidry, in contrast, seemed to offer many of its advantages, such as a sense of community and rites of passage for the major turning points in life, without the burden of too much doctrine, and with the power of the Goddess and the Earth recognised as important as that of the God and 'Heaven'. They also reintroduced magical rites and beliefs, which offered the opportunity to participate in ritual rather than be a passive consumer. In a sense, they gave people a chance to get in the kitchen and start cooking. In fact, many pagan books on magic today read like cookery books, and this is not surprising since Druidry and Wicca offer ingredients – ideas for rituals, stories, folklore, techniques – that can be combined in dozens of different ways to provide magical and spiritual experiences.

But not everyone is religiously inclined, and magic speaks not only to those seeking mystical experiences, but also to those who are more scientifically minded: who want to experiment, to explore, to pioneer and to learn about the workings of the universe as well as their own mind. The magician can be priest, but she or he can also quite easily be scientist too.

❧ Magic with Balls – the Whitby ❧ Conclave, Boggle Hole and the Ice Magick War

Over a thousand years ago, the windswept seaside town of Whitby in Yorkshire played host to one of the most significant Church synods in British history. The Synod of Whitby, held in 664, is seen by many as the turning point in the subjugation of the early British or Celtic Church to the power of Rome,[10] and it was here in the summer of 1970, in the house probably occupied by Bram Stoker, the author of *Dracula*, that a number of ritual magicians informally gathered to experiment with new ways of working magic.

Most of them, having imbibed not only Crowley's Thelemic magic but psychedelics too, disliked the obsession with hierarchy and protocol that afflicted groups such as the Golden Dawn and the OTO, influenced as they were by Freemasonry and Victoriana. As the author Sarah Whittaker writes:

Among the various magicians milling around at the time there was a degree of dissatisfaction with the state of magic as it stood. The general thought was that magic had gone stale. All that was about was either Gardnerian witchcraft or Victorian-derived ritual magic. Little had happened in the occult world since the twenties when Crowley had ceased to be as active as he had been in earlier years. And everybody knew that Crowley was a wanker, at least as far as the way he treated the rest of the world. The feeling was that it was time for something new. There was also a feeling that there was a need for magic with balls.[11]

These people wanted something wilder and freer that they could experiment with and push to the limits. Pagan celebrations of the seasonal cycle had not yet become widespread, and celebration and the religious impulse were of less interest to this group than research, experimentation and raw experience: they were scientists rather than priests or worshippers.

Throughout that summer they tried different techniques in their temple in the Whitby house and in the outdoor setting of nearby Boggle Hole. In particular they focused on techniques such as dancing and physical exhaustion that could induce altered states of consciousness, or the 'raising of power' as magicians call the sense that energy is being intensified.

By the end of the summer the experiment was over, but it had acted as a formative experience for the people involved, including the writer Ray Sherwin, Jo Sheridan and Alfred Douglas (whose interview appears in Chapter 11). This was especially true of the mercurial mathematician and ex-Eton schoolmaster, Lionel Snell, who, under the pen-name of Ramsey Dukes, has since become one of the most articulate and amusing advocates of new approaches to magic.

Meanwhile, similar ideas were whirling through the minds of magicians in other parts of the country, in particular in Bristol with aromatherapy oil importer, Peter Carroll. While the pagans, witches and Druids were influenced by the Romantics and the sixties era of flower power, this new generation of magicians was influenced by the edgier, tougher times of the seventies in which the Punks had reacted against the 'Peace and Love' message of the hippies, and when the influence of postmodernism allowed every assumption about life and magic itself to be questioned.

It was in this challenging atmosphere, in 1978, that Peter

Carroll and Ray Sherwin came up with the term 'Chaos Magic' to describe a new way of doing magic that cast tradition out of the window and – influenced by chaos theory in physics – would consider any technique that furthered the aims of the magician. They founded a group, the Illuminates of Thanateros, which after three decades is still the most successful and influential group working with this type of magic. In the same year, Peter Carroll produced a book that stripped the subject of its historical and cultural baggage, to create a work that some consider one of the most outstanding books on magic. Titled *Liber Null*, it was later published in conjunction with his *Psychonaut* (Red Wheel/ Weiser, 1987).

Perhaps out to shock, Carroll's book conveys a Nietzschean bravado, clearly influenced by Crowley, which describes the techniques of both 'white' and 'black' magic with startling clarity. Just as science avoids adopting an ethical stance, much to the dismay of the religious, so too the whole strand of Thelemic and Chaos Magic avoids stepping into the dualism usually needed to adopt an ethical approach to life.

To some, this is liberating; to others, it is disturbing and shocking. But the anarchist, the artist and the scientist are usually exhilarated when any attempt at moralising is abandoned. As an example of such an approach, here is a message posted on the internet forum of the Temple ov Psychic Youth – a magical group founded by the Crowley-influenced, avant-garde performer, Genesis P. Orridge, which makes use of weird spelling and very loud music to help its devotees achieve altered states of consciousness:

> Magick is the Ultimate weapon for the Artist, free thinker,
> freedom fighter, street sorceror, punk rock shaman, industrial
> Chaos magician, gothic witch, S and M alchemist, Pan
> worshipper, circus clown, Coyote, Kali, ghetto mojo daddy, body
> piercer, performance artist, junkie metal sculptor, antinomian
> magus, reiki mover, chi master, beat poet, acid head, rave god,
> and meditating MF. We are all of them and none of them and

some of them in turn and many more we have no idea about just yet. It is all Magick and there is no limit.[12]

Despite this comment, most magicians have been preoccupied with containment and limits – valuing secrecy and the protection of the magic circle. 'To Know, to Will, to Dare and to be Silent' is a traditional magical motto, and circles are often cast simply to protect the magician from the influence of evil spirits.[13]

But in banishing limitations, the new magicians, whether influenced by Crowley or Chaos, took hold of centuries of magical tradition in England and turned it upside down. Applying the philosophical approach of non-dualism obtained from the East by Crowley and others, they queried the very notion of good and evil, and suggested that, if you could work with spirits to obtain magical ends, it was irrelevant whether they were traditionally classed as 'good' or 'bad'. Ideas drawn from Buddhism and modern psychology – that, in the final analysis, spirits or demons come from the mind, and are all either delusions or temporary and relative forms – further freed the new magicians from any fear of engaging in this realm.

This understanding is well articulated in Ramsey Dukes's books, *What I Did in My Holidays: Essays on Black Magic, Satanism, Devil Worship and Other Niceties* (Mandrake, 1998) and *The Little Book of Demons: The Positive Advantages of the Personification of Life's Problems* (Aeon, 2005). Any concern that reading such books might encourage hurting other people quickly disappears as you discover Dukes's generous and brilliant mind, which explains why he has been described as 'a combination of Robert Anton Wilson and Tommy Cooper . . . the Peter Pan of the British occult scene.'[14]

⚶ Summoning the Spirits ⚶

Conjuring spirits stood at the cornerstone of magic for four hundred years in England. Between the twelfth and seventeenth centuries, the learned theory of magic insisted that every magical operation had to be accomplished with the aid of spirits. Even today the evocation of spirits forms an important strand of magical practice that can be seen in such varied forms as the general-ised request to the 'Great Spirit' to bless a pagan gathering, the channelling of spirits in New Age workshops, the communication with spirits in spiritualist circles and shamanic journeying, and the invocation of the spirits of each cardinal direction in Wicca and Druidry.

In all these cases, however, spirits are summoned in the hope that they are benevolent and in an appeal for blessings, healing or information. The new magicians adopted a more pragmatic and, many would say, more reckless approach. They took the 'black magic' of the old grimoires and, reasoning that since the demons described there exist only in a relative sense – perhaps as per-sonifications of unconscious complexes, perhaps objectively but at relative levels of reality – they could make use of the raw power that they offered.

From a traditional magical standpoint this was madness. The demons may be relative, perhaps even imaginary or useful metaphors, but to try to use their powers to gain advantage was courting disaster. Pointing to the evidence of psychiatry that psy-chotics often report being tormented by evil spirits, traditional magicians believed that only the most foolish or most degenerate would even consider such a path.

As evidence of the risks involved in such experimental approaches, which might attract the 'wrong sort', the Ice Magick war rocked the world of Chaos Magic in 1989. Peter Carroll explains:

> Sometime in '89, Frater U.D. formed an alliance with a secretive
> Germanic martial arts group and attempted to lead sections of the
> pact [the Illuminates of Thanateros] into it. The more I heard,
> the worse it sounded. Eventually I publicly accused Frater U.D.
> of abusing his position and of membership of an ultra right wing
> control cult with a seriously nasty agenda. All hell broke loose . . .
> The ice magick philosophy appeared to be a grim and paranoid

Thulean atavism [a return of an occult doctrine espoused by the Nazis] which might have had ghastly consequences if Frater U.D. had spread it through the fabric of western esoterics.[15]

Genuine demons, or fear of malevolent influences, could still affect even the most hardened Chaos magicians. The Ice Magick war soon passed, however, and today Chaos Magic still attracts some of the brightest minds on the magical scene.

Their brand of magic is hard to define because it encourages an experimental approach that rejects dogma and avoids definition. At its heart lies the concept of the magical paradigm shift in which practitioners are encouraged to work magic by adopting a belief system for some time before dropping it suddenly and switching to another, shifting – for example – from adherence to the beliefs of a medieval Christian magician, to those of a Sufi or a rational scientist or a Buddhist. Chaos magicians argue that this helps the practitioner transcend the limited viewpoint of any belief system, bringing with it a sense of power and flexibility that encourages access to each individual's creative genius.

For this reason, one of the most frequently cited tenets of Chaos Magic is that 'Nothing is True and Everything is Permitted'.[16] Although Chaos magicians mean by this that we are prevented from knowing objective truth by the limits of our perception, and therefore all things must be true and possible, the phrase has inherited the same flaw as the favourite saying of Chaos Magic's godfather, Aleister Crowley, whose motto was: 'Do what thou wilt shall be the whole of the law'. However much sophistry is employed to explain these phrases, the majority take them to mean 'Do whatever you like' and see at once the spectre of anarchy.

Indeed, how you judge the different kinds of magic available today depends to a great extent on your politics and your aesthetics. Chaos magicians are anarchists by nature, while Freemasons and Golden Dawners are conservative in their love of structure and tradition. Pagans find themselves trying to walk a middle way between these two extremes, seeming most like Socialists in their desire for egalitarianism and like Liberals in their attitudes to personal freedoms. To render these analogies concrete: a Freemason or 'traditional' ceremonial magician, such as one descended from the Dion Fortune line, will tell you that magic and drugs do not mix, whilst a Chaos or Thelemic magician might well encourage experimentation with drugs. On the other hand, most pagans would try to avoid making a statement altogether, believing it to be a matter of individual choice.

A similar spectrum of differences exists in musical tastes. As a generalisation, Freemasons prefer classical music and opera, pagans folk rock, Wiccans Gothic music, with Chaos magicians and Thelemites preferring heavy metal and Punk.[17]

In the colourful and varied world of magic in England today, Chaos magicians and Thelemites think of pagans and New Agers as 'fluffy bunnies', scared of the deeper powers available to those bold enough to experiment. New Agers are cautious of pagans and reject those influenced by Crowley as dabblers in darkness. Meanwhile pagans are dismissive of New Agers as rootless eclectics, yet share their concerns about the world of Crowley and Chaos. Although this might seem confusing to someone new to the world of magic, the variety of approaches available today are indicative of its vigour and potential. Monoculture is never healthy, and the magical scene in England instead displays the rich biodiversity of a jungle.

Here at least seven forms of magic flourish that originated in this country: Druidry and Wicca, the magic of the Anglo-Saxons and the Golden Dawn, the magic inspired by Crowley and Dion Fortune, and Chaos magic. There are many who regard Freemasonry as magical too, although whether its 'speculative' form originated in England or Scotland has not yet been conclusively determined.[18] But in addition to these seven or eight indigenous species, England is now home to a whole range of imported varieties of magic. With a few clicks of a mouse or the right introduction from someone in the know, you can find forms of magic imported from Africa, Latin America and the Caribbean, such as Voodoo, Santeria and Umbando. There are magicians and seekers studying the Nordic or Germanic systems, and types of magic can be found that were inspired by the practices of Native American tribes or Siberian shamans. Many people enjoy mixing and matching. Mirroring our increasingly cosmopolitan and globalised culture, in which we clothe and feed ourselves with material from all over the world, today's magicians enjoy an unrivalled ability to learn from every culture and tradition on earth. There are even some who look beyond the planet and human history, using science fiction as a way of turning for their inspiration to the future and the stars.

Limited minds might object to the sheer variety of cultures, languages and nationalities that have chosen to gather in this one small country, but England has gained far more than it has lost from this continuing multiculturalism, the roots of which lie in its first emergence in the tenth century, when the country was formed out of a mixture of Angles, Saxons, Jutes, Welsh, Irish, Norwegians and Danes. The magics that were born here may have originated in the English landscape but they were informed from the very beginning by different cultures. The Druids were influenced by the Classical world, as was that world by India. Alchemy was influenced by Arabia, Medieval magic by Jewish cabbalism. The Golden Dawn was inspired by German Rosicrucianism, the French Occult Revival, and the religion of Ancient Egypt. Thelema was a result of Crowley's explorations in Far and Near Eastern religion and magic, which informed Gardner's Wicca too. For Dion Fortune, Christ, the Egyptian gods and the gods of the British Isles were equally inspiring, and as for Chaos magicians: they would claim the Universe and the world of physics as their inspiration.

Freed of misinformed chauvinism, we can recognise this depth and breadth of inspiration from across the world, whilst still celebrating the unique role that England has played in the story of magic. We can marvel at the richness and variety of its magical history, and at the way so many kinds of magic originated in this country. We can remain surprised, too, at how little this rich vein of history has been studied and appreciated, particularly since many of the kinds of magic born in England are now the most significant and influential in the world.

Read about this period in Fiction

All the writers we recommend here are prolific and have produced series that explore the fictional worlds they have created.

• Although the thirty-six volumes of Terry Pratchett's *Discworld* series, published by Transworld Publishers, present an elaborate fantasy world that removes Pratchett from the genre of 'occult fiction', contemporary magicians enjoy reading his humorous portrayal of many of the ideas and figures that people the world of twenty-first-century magic. See www. terrypratchettbooks.com

• Phil Rickman has single-handedly invented a new genre of fiction in his *Merrily Watkins* series of ten thrillers, published by Pan Books, which follow the adventures of Hereford and Worcester's first woman diocesan exorcist. Rickman explores modern occult territory – under his own name and as Will Kingdom – with a stable of characters that includes a policeman, a New Age writer and a shaman who is also a transvestite entertainer. In addition to this series, readers will also enjoy his *The Chalice*, a thriller drawing on the Avalonian past of Glastonbury and a dark grail quest. See www. philrickman.co.uk

- The *Adept* series of five novels, published by Ace Books, written by Katherine Kurtz and Deborah Turner Harris, portrays a traditional hero, Sir Adam Sinclair, who is a psychiatrist and the leader of a secret brotherhood of magical police, in the best traditions of early twentieth-century writers of the genre. Sinclair's adventures deal with such diverse occult themes as the seal of Solomon, the magical battle of Britain, and the aftermath of Nazi occult involvement in back magic rituals and murder. See www.deryni.net

- The *Stonewylde* series of three books by Kit Berry, published by Moongazy Publishing, explores the world of magic in an alternative community in Dorset. Through the eyes of the adolescent heroine and her discovery of her own occult powers, we become aware of the darkness at the heart of a community founded on medieval precepts and pagan belief. See www.stonewylde.com

- The world of a modern Druid detective, *Gwion Dubh: Druid Investigator*, is explored by Penny Billington (Appleseed Press). Gwion, a mix of hard-boiled private eye and nature magician, enlists the help of the non-human peoples of the landscape, from dryads to dragons, as he battles dark forces, disseminating modern Druidic wisdom along the way. See www.druidauthors.com

- The ideas of Chaos Magic pervade the *Invisibles* series of comic books by Grant Morrison, published by Titan Books. See www.barbelith.com/bomb

PROFESSOR RONALD HUTTON

Ronald Hutton is Professor of History at the University of Bristol. Born in India, he was brought up with a love of the classics and went on to develop interests in both religious history and paganism. He has written a number of books on Wicca, modern Druidry and shamanism and, although not a practitioner of magic, is a well-known and respected figure within the occult world.

I cannot make spells or dowse and I am immune to curses, which is useful. I do not get bothered by spirits, which makes for a comfortable life, given the sort of people I study. I have, however, had sufficient personal experience of the occult world to understand what it must feel like to be a serious practitioner. For example, after I cleared out my mother's house after her death, things began to behave unusually. I noticed that electric lights began to turn themselves on and off and the central heating system developed a will of its own. I can only put this down to modest powers of telekinesis, combined with unusually strong emotions.

Twenty years ago I also had experience of clairvoyance and clairaudience – I could see and hear things at a distance. This ability came to me at a time of general illness when I felt I was drifting away from the real world, but it has weakened since. Thus, I feel that I have glimpsed a world that others inhabit. I think about a fifth to a quarter of people hear and see things that others don't. You can call it what you like, from body chemistry to shamanism, but it makes me sympathetic to real magicians.

I was brought up as a pagan on both ancient literature and modern works of fiction such as those of Kenneth Grahame and Rudyard Kipling, in which the natural world is full of spirits. I have never seen any reason to abandon this wonderful view. Although I have never had any direct evidence of anything in the spirit world, I am impressed by others' powers and sincerity, especially during the practice of ritual magic.

Ritual magic enriches personal life and provides huge pleasure. It is very creative and, as I see it, a way of consecrating action and giving meaning to it. This makes magical practitioners more self-aware as well as more effective as human beings. The beauty of modern ceremonial magic allows a big diversity of interpretation and everyone who participates can have an individually enriching experience. For example, a group may carry out a rite to Venus, but while one person believes they have seen a deity, another will have experienced love; yet another will have created a thought form they can work with, while another feels that they are in touch with an archetype. Gerald Gardner, the founder and publicist of Wicca, thought that each book of rituals should be different, and personal to the owner. I agree with this view.

Paganism is attractive to me because I like the deities of the ancient world and their contact with humanity. Established religions have created wonderful buildings, literature and spiritual achievements, but they are not ideally suited to a modern world of unprecedented mobility, individuality and choice. The fastest-growing forms of religion in the modern West are those that can be practised at home. Paganism answers to three modern needs. One is feminism. Another is a sense of reconnection to the natural world. The third is an ethic that encourages people to develop themselves, along with a responsibility towards others. The founder of the scholarly discipline of anthropology, Sir Edward Burnett Tylor, defined religion as 'respectable relationships formed by humans with spiritual beings'. To me that is the best definition, which has stood up well.

Paganism is growing fast in England. Every index, from the number of people signing up to internet sites to attendances at witchfests, suggests regular growth year on year. In 1996, I estimated that there were 10,000 pagan witches, but these were heavily outnumbered by non-denominational pagans, which take the number over 120,000. The established Church of England, still the most popular single denomination in the nation, now contains less than a million regular attendees, so the number of pagans is significant.

I like the basic principle of the relatively new tradition of 'Chaos Magic', providing that it does not fall into the trap that it was set up to avoid and become a dogma. It was founded in the 1970s by people interested in ritual magic who wanted to get outside the bounds of tradition and the feuding of different Orders, working practically with emerging ideas, whatever their source, that would get results.

Chaos Magic is built around two principles. The first is the need to create a state of focused consciousness to increase the effectiveness of ritual: what they call Gnosis. This can be achieved through excitation to the point of mental saturation via dancing, drumming, sex, etc., or through inhibition of the normal mental/emotional functions through prolonged meditation, stillness, breath control, etc. The second principle is the notion of 'belief shifting'. They consider a belief is only 'true' for the time of the magical action in which it is employed. Chaos magicians thus only get together to work on specific projects, like practising Crowley's Algerian workings, trying the keys of Dee's Enochia or, in one example I heard of recently, trying to arrange Rolls-Royces for every member of the group – the last, I suspect, was a very theoretical position.

What I really find interesting about magic is the magicians themselves.

Gazing into the Crystal Ball

If all the magicians of England, past and present – those who have been mentioned in this book and those who have escaped notice – were to gather one evening in the British Museum, what would they do?

With the great doors of the Museum closed to the public, they might well walk in a long and silent progress through the halls of looted, borrowed and acquired antiquities, pausing to pay their respects to all those who have influenced their work. Perhaps the spirits of Maori *tohungas*, of Aboriginal elders, of the guardians of Pharaoh Ramesses' burial chamber, of a thousand deities, would start to rise up from the statues and coffins and artefacts in these halls, to join the procession as it moves towards the Enlightenment Gallery. Coming to the one glass case that contains the obsidian mirror and crystal ball of Dr John Dee, the spirits and their earthly companions form a circle around it, and in a moment of tense expectancy, an atmosphere of utter stillness descends upon the room. Then, one by one, a select few amongst England's most important wizards step forward to gaze into the mirror and crystal ball.

After what seems like an age, each turns outward and makes their pronouncement. Francis Bacon smiles and explains that science will soon understand what magicians have been reaching towards for centuries; Roger Bacon notes that the advances of medicine, both conventional and otherwise, are – and will continue to become – more magical than he could ever have imagined. Mary Sidney and Lady Anne Conway speak of the radiance of the human heart, which will one day become as valued as the properties of the intellect. John Dee announces that our children will live to see the day when the existence of consciousness, independent of the body, will be proved beyond a doubt, and then Elias Ashmole, with tears in his eyes, speaks of the species that will soon be lost and of how he had never wanted his museum to house exhibits of creatures that would never walk the earth again.

A pause. An eternity. And then each spirit, each magician, returns to their homes, their statues, their memories.

✐ Next Steps in Magic ✐

Few magickians of any experience try to expand in one direction only. Magick implies the development of a wide range of skills or powers. To be a magickian is to be a Renaissance (wo)man, to be able to dance through a multitude of worlds and realities.

JULIAN VAYNE, *MAGICK WORKS: STORIES OF OCCULTISM IN THEORY AND PRACTICE*, 2008

Now that you have read this book, even though you may feel drawn to learning more, you might find it hard to decide what step to take next. The number of different approaches, eccentric characters and sometimes bizarre theories that fill the world of magic in England can seem overwhelming.

If your interests are scholarly, see the Appendix, which encourages the armchair magician to undertake further research. If, however, the practical sections in each chapter have whetted your appetite for actually becoming a magician, here are some ideas to help you.

In 1971, Luke Rhinehart wrote a novel, *The Dice Man*,[19] whose hero decided to make decisions with the throw of a dice. He began his adventure by telling himself, 'If I get a one I'll leave my wife, if a two I'll stay with her for ever, a three and I'll have an affair with the woman next door,' and so on. The book became a cult phenomenon that inspired plays, songs and a TV travel series, and in their search for liberation some people even tried to conduct their lives like the Dice Man.

If you want to begin exploring the world of magic in more depth, you could take the same approach: 'If I get a one I'll become a Freemason, a two and I'll become a witch, a three a Druid,' and so on. Chaos magicians would approve of this, as long as you threw the dice again after some months to get a fresh perspective.

Whilst this approach might suit some, a more considered way to proceed would be to begin your quest by asking yourself a few key questions. Central to all magical philosophies is the idea that deep down there is a part of you that knows what you are doing and why you are doing it, and which can answer the pertinent and sometimes difficult questions posed to it by the intellect. Different terms are used to describe this process of introspection, and the wise part of the self is called by some the 'god, goddess or spirit within', while others call it the higher self, the holy guardian angel or the soul. Many of the techniques of magic are designed to help our everyday awareness get in touch with this part of ourselves, so that our questing can achieve its goal and our questions can be answered.

See whether the questions, embedded in the account that follows, help you find the best steps to take next. Magic works with the imagination: using it, refining and strengthening it. Imagine you are in a wizard's study – perhaps you've made your way to Pepper Alley in early seventeenth-century London, perhaps to John Dee's library in Mortlake. As you sit comfortably amongst the old books and manuscripts, a shaft of sunlight slants through the mullioned window catching the dust, which seems to sparkle – just a little, just enough to draw your attention.

And then, there in the shaft of sunlight, stands the wizard who starts to address you:

Why do you wish to learn magic? Is it to satisfy your vanity, to distract you from the difficulties of your life, to puff yourself up in front of others and to lose yourself in fantasy, or do you aspire to the life of the magician because you want to know more, feel more, make more, help more?

There are many kinds of magic, and many kinds of magician. Some have been charlatans, some have been rogues, but most have been driven by the quest – the quest to explore the world of nature, of matter and of spirit, and by the quest to give and to love. Look at the work of the Rosicrucians, the alchemists, the adepts, who pored over their magical texts and tried experiment after experiment. True, they were sometimes – even often – driven by the lust for power, by the desire for wealth or fame, by selfishness or greed. But for many their deeper motives lay in the desire to ward off the evils of disease and ill-fortune, to increase the store of knowledge for humanity and to perfect their souls in the sight of God.

In the early days the practice of magic was firmly embedded within the practice of religion, which is why Sir Walter Raleigh wrote: 'The art of magic is the art of worshipping God.' But the magician is more than simply a worshipper: he is at heart a scientist and an artist. And so, even in the days of Raleigh – indeed, long before his time – the magician was tasting forbidden fruit: experimenting with the natural world and risking imprisonment, torture and even death if discovered.

Do you long to know more, to question everything – even
the most cherished beliefs of science and Church? And do you
long to create, to work with the magic of making something
from nothing but an idea, a spark of inspiration? Magicians are
creators: they long to produce, to fashion, to people the world
with the products of their minds and imaginations. Mystics seek
only union with deity, and in this respect they follow the path of
inaction. But magicians follow the path of action, and however
much they say they obey the magical injunction 'to Know, to
Will, to Dare and to be Silent', they cannot stop talking, writing,
painting, singing and dancing. They are the storytellers, the
word-weavers, who might also be the priests or priestesses who
help you with your marriage or funeral, who heal you with their
spells or hear you in your grief. Today they are as likely to study
psychology or complementary medicine as herbalism or arcane
lore, but essentially they are people who want to understand the
world with more than just their intellects. They want to use their
imaginations and their intuition too.

There are fools, of course, in every domain, and we are all
seekers on the path, but slowly progress has been made in the
world of magic. Yet even today it is sometimes cursed with
superstition, with unthinking adherence to outmoded beliefs and
preposterous delusions, but with every advance in science so, too,
is there an advance in the study of magic.

As the discoveries of medicine revealed the causes of many
diseases, magicians could abandon some of their more exotic
remedies and rites of protection, whilst still holding to their belief
in the magical power of the spirit and mind that science is now
beginning to reveal. As ways of communicating at a distance
were discovered, like the telephone and the internet, magicians
could see the manifestation in the physical world of those
powers of extrasensory perception that they had been exploring
for centuries, and they could harness these new tools to help
them in their work. As psychology released us from centuries of
repression, magicians were freed to explore the hidden powers of
the instincts as well as those of the mind.

Today a magician may want to rebel against the madness of the consumer society and the way in which we are destroying the earth, but he or she no longer needs to rebel against the prudery of the Victorian world. With the sophistication of leading religious thinkers, magicians don't even need to rebel against religion any more, and magic can once again represent – as alchemy once did – a secret tradition that transcends divides, uniting followers of every religion who aspire to the goals of magic.

There is still much room for improvement in magic, much that should change, but it is magic that inspires, magic that we need as our world struggles with the greatest challenges it has ever faced.

The wizard fades from view, leaving just the shaft of sunlight with its specks of dust floating in the air. You look around the room, with its old books and manuscripts piled on the table and lining the bookcases, and then you realise that a book lies in your hands, open at the page you are reading now. Your journey through the world of magic has ended. Or perhaps it has just begun.

DAVID CONWAY

David Conway was born the seventh child of a seventh child and he experienced psychic phenomena at an early age. After a distinguished academic career, which mixed study in London and the Sorbonne in Paris (where he ran off with a travelling circus), he joined the Treasury where, unsurprisingly as he was innumerate, he found the work baffling, as well as lacking in excitement.

This being the Age of Aquarius, he decided to turn his knowledge of magic into a no-nonsense guide that could be enjoyed by experts and the wider public alike. His first book, Magic: An Occult Primer *(Jonathan Cape, 1972), remains a considerable success with both adepts and novice magicians. He continued his career as a high-flying civil servant, while writing two more books:* The Magic of Herbs *(Jonathan Cape, 1973) and* Secret Wisdom: The Occult Universe Explored *(Jonathan Cape, 1985).*

In this latter book, he mentions the source of his esoteric knowledge, an extraordinary countryman and shepherd, 'Mr James', who combined inherited tradition, self-study and natural clairvoyance into a powerful magical practice, its roots seeming to stretch right back to the time of the Druids.

After the book appeared, David, who had never been part of the occult scene, retired from public view. He felt that there was something about his experience that was deeply personal and might risk being demeaned, were it to become a public spectacle. He is still a very private figure, living in a remote Georgian country house along with five ostriches, eleven cats, six dogs, five donkeys and an irascible cockatoo. This is the first interview he has given for over thirty years.

'Of course he's got second sight,' an aunt with occult leanings assured my mother on realising I was the seventh child of a seventh child. I never relished the notion of being different from everybody else, but a vivid experience, just after my fourth birthday, gave me little choice but to accept that I might indeed have access to a type of reality unavailable to 'normal' children.

Every night after my mother put me to bed, two elderly ladies would appear at my bedside. The taller one would stand back a little, while her companion made a big show of nodding and smiling and blowing kisses in my direction. At some point one of them, usually the taller woman, would lean over and tickle me. Every evening without fail, thin, bony fingers would reach down and begin the same relentless tickling while I, powerless to stop it, thrashed about in my bed. Throughout it all my tormentor's expression stayed blank, disconcertingly so, with no hint of a smirk or a scowl, just a mindless, unflinching resolve. Apparently my screams could be heard outside in the street.

Night after night my parents would try to persuade me it was all a bad dream, but some weeks later I was taken off to see our elderly family doctor.

'You say they talk to you?' he enquired.

I told him they did. I went on to describe them in detail and even provided him with their names, as well as the diminutives that they encouraged me to use. When I had finished, Dr Ellis asked the nurse to take me outside while he had a word with my mother. That night, on his recommendation, my bed was moved to another room and the mischief never recurred. Within days I lost all fear that my tormentors might return. But I never forgot them.

Several years were to pass before my mother disclosed what the doctor had told her. Years earlier, it seems, he had attended two patients in what was now our house, elderly sisters long since dead. Not only had I described them in remarkable detail – their hair, their clothes, even the consumptive cough of the older woman – but I had also given him their names as well as the pet names each used for the other. A mystery, he called it.

As I grew older, I realised that my experience was nothing unusual. 'Reality', as we know it, is more, far more, than what we ordinarily perceive. The smallest components of matter – molecular physics have partly confirmed it – straddle a frontier between the spatial–temporal world that we occupy and another, no less real, in which neither space nor time exists. In this multidimensional reality are found not only the memory of things that have happened (helping to nourish what Jung calls the Collective Unconscious) but also those non-physical entities indigenous to it.

Grasping this reality is a hard task for our imagination, accustomed as it is to functioning in only four dimensions. Worse still, our mind risks distorting whatever information it receives by adapting it to conform to our everyday experience, or by depicting it in terms that flatter our vanity and our sense of drama. That is why, for instance, we encounter in occult literature so many defunct Atlanteans, Red Indian chiefs, ancient Egyptians and the occasional extraterrestrial. The first magical lesson I learnt is that, before sticking one's head into the astral clouds, one should ensure that both feet stay firmly on the ground.

This, and most of what I know about magic, was taught me when I was a boy – a kind of 1950s Harry Potter – by an elderly sheep farmer, a friend of my father's named Mr James. It was in my Great-Uncle Davy's corner shop that I first set eyes on him, a giant of a man whose rough tweed suit, its colour an unsettling shade of ginger, helped somehow to exaggerate his size. He stood over six feet tall and was impressively broad shouldered, his head resting on a neck that put me in mind of a stocky young heifer. On top of it was a brown bowler hat, which might have looked comical on anyone else but on him looked strangely touching. His hands, coarsened and reddened by working outside in all seasons, were disproportionately huge, even for someone as solidly built as himself, as were his feet, squeezed into smartly polished boots. Whatever the weather, he carried on his arm a neatly rolled up umbrella, and rolled up it stayed, even on days when the rain was pelting down in buckets. Like the bowler hat, the brilliance of his polished toecaps and the silk handkerchief overflowing from his pocket, it was a disguise put together years earlier for his weekly trips into town. He had seen no reason ever to change it.

As I was a puny child, my father thought fresh air and exercise might do me good. Accordingly, both men agreed that every week I should leave early on Saturday mornings and cycle the twelve or so miles to the isolated farm where Mr James lived on his own. There I would help out by doing whatever tasks he set me.

I had another, quite different, reason for wanting to spend my Saturdays with Mr James: his reputation as a magician.

Over the following weeks, while the two of us set about our work – hauling bales of hay, repairing dry stone walls or treating sheep for foot rot – Mr James began to talk about the natural world around us, gradually introducing me to aspects of it that lay beyond what was evident to the senses. One day, for example, he pointed to a bramble bush and explained how its physical structure was merely the perceptible expression of unseen forces that determine its form. Working in and through a plant's inherent disposition, this formative force enables it to grow in a way characteristic of its species. Coaxed by Mr James, I was soon able to discern this subtle force at work (and brambles, being fast growing, are ideal to practise on), visible – just! – as a greenish light extending for about a centimetre, no more, beyond the tip of each leaf or runner.

These forces, peculiar to each type of plant, have their use in healing whenever they can be matched to the nature of a particular illness. For example, willow trees are adapted to thrive near water and so their characteristic force is deemed helpful in treating certain types of rheumatism, aggravated, as these often are, by damp conditions. And, true enough, when scientists got around to investigating the connection, they discovered that willow bark contains a glucoside, which, under the name of salicin (from the Latin *salix* or willow), would become an important resource in the treatment of rheumatism. As many will tell you, magic is often in advance of science.

The next stage of my apprenticeship involved 'close encounters' with what Mr James called the 'wider' reality, of which our everyday reality forms part. His belief was that, even though unremarked, this reality impinges on our sense of identity, giving human beings their individuality, just as it bestows a collective identity on other organisms or, indeed, on what appears to be non-organic matter as well. He assured me that even the planet we walk on is itself a will-impelled entity, not a lump of dead rock on whose surface living forms happen to thrive. 'Listen,' I have heard him whisper at midday, 'the earth's breathing in again.'

More difficult for a twelve-year-old to grasp was his teaching about the ascending stages of consciousness. Only when I grew older did I discover that these pathways to enlightenment feature in esoteric systems the world over – amongst them the cabbala – and were often based on the 'magic' number seven.

For Mr James there are seven so-called planes: four that manifest themselves (or, rather, are experienced) in physical terms and three others. All can be consciously enjoyed by human beings but the names commonly applied to them, even by someone as down-to-earth as Mr James, do little to render them intelligible. The first four are trance consciousness, deep sleep consciousness, dream consciousness and waking consciousness; the final three are psychic, super-psychic and spiritual-psychic awareness. For practical purposes, these planes – experienced through the appropriately corresponding colours, sounds and images – allow the trained magician access to that wider reality mentioned earlier. According to Mr James, the relevant correspondences are set out in a tree calendar compiled by the Druids and referred to by Robert Graves in *The White Goddess* (1948). (It appears also, in the earliest-known example of Celtic script, on a bronze fragment discovered just over a century ago at Coligny, near Bourg-en-Bresse in France.)

Once I had grasped (or managed to persuade him that I had grasped) the rudiments of magical theory, Mr James taught me how to put it into practice. The first technique I mastered was what is known as 'guided visualisation', an exercise nowadays used for training purposes by most magical groups. He would get me to look at a simple everyday object, a matchbox for example, then close my eyes and picture it in as much detail as possible, not just as I had seen it earlier but as if viewing it from a different angle or even, a hard one this, from all possible angles at one and the same moment. Harder still, but later demanded of me, was to imagine myself totally outside my body in order to observe the world from other points in space and even in time.

Another important lesson concerned the gateways, as Mr James called them, that exist in certain places, often at the junction of two 'energy' lines. These open up cracks, so to speak, between the worlds. When I was taken to one by Mr James, I was startled to hear a curious musical sound, curious because, while undoubtedly musical, it was not what music normally is. The source of it was the vibrational pattern found at any location where our space–time environment collides with a wider, multidimensional reality and adapts to it by opting to function, in the language of physics, as wave rather than particle. The experience only gave me gooseflesh but I have since learnt that it can seriously harm the unwary.

Never did Mr James tire of warning me that when dealing with supra-sensible realities, care should be taken to distinguish between what is objective (and outside us) and what is subjective or the product of our mind. Certainly, caution is needed, as well as a generous dollop of plain common sense. The latter, happily, was present in all Mr James taught me – he was never one for mumbo-jumbo or high-flown mystification. 'If you come across anything that seems supernatural,' he would say, 'the chances are that it isn't.' As a result I have made it my habit to look for a rational cause for what seems at first inexplicable before opting, when all else fails, for the magical.

Over the years spent in the company of Mr James I came across many events that were inexplicable and some that were incontestably magical. Take the evening we were both sitting quietly by his fireside, talking about the herb, vervain, which, he suggested, might help me remember my Latin declensions, at the time something of a challenge. I remember that the two dogs were first to notice that something was wrong. The one at my feet suddenly dived underneath the settle, while the other jumped down from my side and slunk into a far corner of the room. Mr James was unperturbed.

'Come in,' he shouted, and almost at the very instant there came a knock on the front door.

The farm we were in was miles away from anywhere, the night was rough and Mr James was never one to encourage visitors. Yet the man who entered the room was obviously familiar with it and, uninvited, drew up a chair by the fire.

'We were talking about vervain,' said Mr James without preamble, 'and I was about to tell this young man he'll find plenty of it a few miles away from here, up in the hills beside those old stones.'

'Have you ever seen them, those old stones?' asked the man. As he turned towards me I saw his face for the first time. And his eyes. These were not just blue, but seemed to convey the very idea of blueness, a blueness in which space and time had neither place nor meaning.

'First things first,' said Mr James, 'and for this little lad, it's time for bed.'

With considerable reluctance I took myself off to the small attic room. Not surprisingly after a hard day's work, I was out for the count before my head scarcely touched the pillow. The next thing I remember is finding myself at the dormer window, staring down at the bed in which someone who looked like my double lay sleeping. No sooner had I taken that in, and before I had time to be scared, there I was: outside, under a pallid moon. In front of me was a group of standing stones. I was not alone; our mysterious visitor was there as well.

With the calm, authoritative voice of the elderly preachers that I heard on Sunday nights in chapel, he spoke in the simplest yet profoundest terms of the magical path I was destined to follow. It was, he said, a journey that would take me into the innermost part of my being where in time I would discover the true self that dwelt within me. Reflected in that would be yet another self, different but essentially the same, at once part of me and, paradoxically, the whole of which I myself was a part. In other words within me, the microcosm, I would encounter the macrocosm, itself the creative and personal manifestation of the one, uncaused and self-existent Absolute.

Next morning, I awoke, refreshed and happy, not entirely sure that my experience had been anything other than a moonstruck dream. But, as the early sunshine ventured into the room, passing over the bedside table where my candle rested in a blue and white saucer, it appeared to linger awhile. And suddenly I saw a bunch of vervain, its grey-green leaves still wet with dew, its purple-lidded flowers only just half open.

Mr James is long dead, but the gift of magic that he bestowed on me remains. A few years ago I took the dogs for a walk down into the narrow valley where his farm now lies in ruins. Past the little stream we went, past the reed bed where, as a curious music in my head reminded me, there lurked one of those 'cracks' between the worlds. As I listened, a tall figure in fustian cloak and breeches emerged from behind some alder trees on the bank opposite. The sight of me appeared to startle him for he hurried off without a word or backward glance. For a second his blue eyes suggested he might be my mysterious companion on that moonlit mountaintop some forty years earlier. Or was he an ancient Druid, briefly restored to this world in order to complete some unfinished magical business? It might even have been old Merlin himself, back, as promised, to rescue our nation from a welter of crass materialism and spiritual apathy. On the other hand he might simply have been a poacher out that afternoon to catch a few brown trout. Mr James, ever the sceptic, would have plumped for the poacher. Myself, I prefer to think he was all of them combined. You see, magic and make-believe are not incompatible.

Fortunately, in my life there was always room for both.

ᵔᵒ Things to Do ᵒᵔ

❀ To explore the eightfold festival cycle, see Philip Carr-Gomm, *Druid Mysteries* (Rider, 2002). Ways of learning more about Druidry and Wicca can be found in Chapters 2 and 5 respectively.

❀ Discover the influence on the twentieth-century revival of paganism of two related groups: the Woodcraft Folk and the Order of Woodcraft Chivalry.

To see photographs and information on the Woodcraft Folk, visit the London Museum's virtual exhibition, entitled 'The 1920s – the Decade that Changed London'. Look out for exhibitions of this material following the museum's recent £20 million redevelopment. See www.museumoflondon.org.uk

The Order of Woodcraft Chivalry organised camps at Sandy Balls in Hampshire between 1921 and 1935, holding ceremonies in the woodland that combined elements drawn from paganism and Native American rites. This area of 120 acres in the New Forest has now become the Sandy Balls Holiday Centre, where you can take a holiday in one of their log cabins or caravans. See www.sandy-balls.co.uk

❀ Two magazines cater for those interested in pagan magic: *Pagan Dawn*, issued by the Pagan Federation, which also holds conferences, and *Pentacle Magazine*. See www.paganfed.org and www.pentaclemagazine.org

❧ Explore Chaos Magic through the archive at www.chaosmatrix.org and on the websites of its seminal thinkers. Peter Carroll's, at www.specularium.org, is subtitled 'A site exploring the hypothesis of Three-Dimensional Time' and includes essays such as 'Wizards Against Tyranny'. Phil Hine's, at www.philhine.org.uk, is particularly strong on 'Queer Magic' with essays like 'Bums in Brigantia', and includes an extensive archive, including contributions from Ray Sherwin. Dave Lee, another important figure in Chaos Magic, has a site with excerpts from his writing at www.chaotopia.co.uk

❧ If after researching these sites and reading some of the books listed below, Chaos Magic still appeals to you, you might like to approach the Illuminates of Thanateros, although this step is recommended only for serious and experienced students. Their site is at www.iot.org.uk

✒ Resources ✒

BOOKS

Liber Null and Psychonaut, Peter Carroll (Red Wheel/Weiser, 1987)

Understanding Chaos Magic, Jaq D. Hawkins (Capall Bann, 1996)

Condensed Chaos: An Introduction to Chaos Magic, Phil Hine (New Falcon, 1995)

SSOTBME Revised: An Essay on Magic, Lemuel Johnston and Ramsey Dukes (aka Lionel Snell) (The Mouse that Spins, 2002), which presents an intriguing fourfold typology of religion, science, art and magic.

Chaotopia! Sorcery and Ecstasy in the Fifth Aeon, Dave Lee (Mandrake, 2006)

Now That's What I Call Chaos Magick, Julian Vayne, Greg Humphries and Dave Lee (Mandrake, 2004)

᯽ Appendix ᯽

᯽ The Importance of The Armchair ᯽
in the Training of the Magician

The image of the Magus, a master of Magick, went
through many changes from pre-Christian times to the
stirring of Western civilization. A magus could be a
fraudulent purveyor of cheap tricks or the exalted bridge
between earth and stars. He could be a kind of arch-priest
evoking demons and invoking angels. He could be a
profound philosopher, an astrologer, an alchemist, a maker
of charms, and a foreteller of the future, or even, as in the
case of the legendary Merlin, a not-quite-human caretaker
of the vicissitudes of earthbound but heaven-destined
imperial British history – King Arthur's true friend (if
only he'd listened).

TOBIAS CHURTON, *THE MAGUS*
OF FREEMASONRY

People sometimes use the term 'armchair magician' to insult those who prefer curling up by a fire and reading a book about magic to actually casting a spell or performing a magical rite. Such a remark, born of an undignified utilitarianism, comes from a misunderstanding of the nature of magic and the value of reading. Most magicians spend decades in study and are often writers themselves. They understand the magical power of the written word, and its ability to transport us to other worlds.

By taking the path of the Armchair Magician the whole extraordinary world of magic is yours to explore. You could, for example, read your way through the history of English magic entirely through the works of fiction recommended in each chapter. You

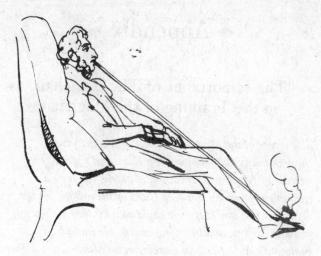

Edward Bulwer–Lytton understood that the armchair was an essential part of any serious magician's equipment even though this image shows him using an armless chair while smoking his pipe.

could take a biographical approach – reading the biographies and autobiographies listed in the next section – or you could go for 'micro-history' and focus on one specific topic by exploring the resources given in each chapter. Or if great sweeps of history appeal to you, take the 'macro-history' approach instead. To do this, a masterful and concise summary of the history of magic with particular reference to developments in England can be found in the opening chapters of Ronald Hutton's *Triumph of the Moon* (Oxford University Press, 1999), which can be supplemented by reading Richard Cavendish's *A History of Magic* (Penguin, 1991) or Gareth Knight's *A History of White Magic* (Mowbrays, 1978) followed by Nevill Drury's *The History of Magic in The Modern Age* (Carroll & Graf, 2000) which provides a detailed look at twentieth-century developments.

With three or four of these works under your armchair wizard's belt, you might like to plunge deeper, in which case try Keith

Thomas' *Religion and the Decline of Magic* (Penguin, 1971) which has been described by the *Times Literary Supplement* as 'perhaps the most important contribution to our understanding of English cultural history', and the books of Elizabeth Butler that explore the role of the magician in history and myth, including *The Myth of the Magus* (Cambridge University Press, 1948) *Ritual Magic* (Cambridge University Press, 1949) and *The Magical Art in England* (Kessinger, 2000). Complete your studies with historian James Webb's survey of the context in which recent traditions have arisen – *The Occult Underground* (Open Court, 1974) and *The Occult Establishment* (R. Drew, 1981) and an anthropologist's view of modern magical practice in Britain: Susan Greenwood's *The Nature of Magic: An Anthropology of Consciousness* (Berg, 2005).

Specialists in this arcane field may find themselves wondering why certain subjects have been left untouched or have only been mentioned in passing. As we began the task of describing the magic practised here for the last few thousand years we soon discovered that this was inevitable – particularly as we reached the early modern period. From 1500 onwards so much has happened, so many interesting movements have arisen, so much eccentricity and exciting developments have occurred, that it became impossible to mention them all, or even to give many of the movements and characters we were able to mention the attention they deserved. Our hope, however, is that these very omissions will provide a stimulus to those readers who cannot wait to begin their explorations.

The subject of magic provides a treasure-trove of fascinating material for the historian, the psychologist, the philosopher, the student of cultural history, anthropology and religion. For all of these, and for those who wish to become magicians themselves, the very best place to start is with a book in hand, which – like a magic wand – can conjure up a new world with every turn of the page.

~ Biographies & Autobiographies ~
of English Magicians

*Our English Philosophers generally, (like Prophets) have
received little honour . . . in their owne Countrey.*

ELIAS ASHMOLE, *THEATRUM CHEMICUM
BRITANNICUM*

The English Magicians: Roger Bacon, Dr. John Dee and William Lilly,
W. H. Davenport Adams (Kessinger Publishing, 2005)

The Queen's Conjuror – The Life and Magic of Dr Dee, Benjamin Woolley
(Flamingo, 2002)

John Dee – The World of an Elizabethan Magus, Peter J. French
(Routledge & Kegan Paul, 1972)

*Medicine and Magic in Elizabethan London: Simon Forman, Astrologer,
Alchemist, and Physician*, Lauren Kassell (Oxford University Press,
2005)

*The Notorious Astrological Physician of London: Works and Days of Simon
Forman*, Barbara Howard Traister (University of Chicago Press,
2001)

Robert Fludd: Hermetic Philosopher and Surveyor of Two Worlds, Joscelyn
Godwin (Thames and Hudson, 1979)

Sir Francis Bacon: A Biography, Jean Overton Fuller (George Mann
Books, 1994)

Francis Bacon: from Magic to Science, Paolo Rossi (University of Chicago
Press, 1968)

The Magus of Freemasonry – The Mysterious Life of Elias Ashmole, Tobias
Churton (Inner Traditions, 2004)

William Stukeley – an Eighteenth-Century Antiquary, Stuart Piggott
(Thames & Hudson, 1985)

The Janus Faces of Genius: The Role of Alchemy in Newton's Thought,
Betty Dobbs (Cambridge University Press, 1991)

*The Flying Sorcerer – Being the magical and aeronautical adventures of
Francis Barrett, author of 'The Magus'*, Francis X. King (Mandrake,
1992)

Annie Besant: A Biography, Anne Taylor (Oxford University Press, 1991)

Women of the Golden Dawn: Rebels and Priestesses, Mary K. Greer (Park Street Press, 1996)

Magicians of the Golden Dawn: A Documentary History of a Magical Order, 1887–1923, Ellic Howe (Red Wheel/Weiser, 1972)

The Magicians of the Golden Dawn, Susan Roberts (Contemporary Books, 1978)

The Sword of Wisdom: MacGregor Mathers and The Golden Dawn, Ithel Colquhoun (Putnam, 1975)

Starlight Man: The Extraordinary Life of Algernon Blackwood, Mike Ashley (Constable & Robinson, 2001)

Cyril Scott: Composer, Poet and Philosopher, Arthur Eaglefield Hull (Library of Music and Musicians Best Books, 2001)

Cyril Scott and a Hidden School: Towards the Peeling of an Onion, Jean Overton Fuller, Theosophical History Occasional Papers, Vol VII

A Magick Life: The Life of Aleister Crowley, Martin Booth (Coronet, 2000)

Aleister Crowley: The Nature of the Beast, Colin Wilson (Aeon, 2005)

The Confessions of Aleister Crowley – An Autohagiography, edited by John Symonds and Kenneth Grant (Routledge & Kegan Paul, 1979)

The History of British Magick After Crowley, Dave Evans (Hidden Publishing, 2007)

My Rosicrucian Adventure, Israel Regardie (Israel Aries Press, 1936)

The Magical Dilemma of Victor Neuburg, Jean Overton Fuller (Mandrake, 2005)

Austin Osman Spare: Artist – Occultist – Sensualist, Keith Richmond (Beskin Press, 1999)

Borough Satyr: The Life and Art of Austin Osman Spare, Robert Ansell (Fulgur, 2005)

'Universal Majesty, Verity and Love Infinite – A Life of George Watson Macgregor Reid', Adam Stout, in *The Mount Haemus Lectures Volume One* (Oak Tree Press/Order of Bards Ovates & Druids, 2008)

Priestess: The Life and Magic of Dion Fortune, Alan Richardson
    (Aquarian, 1987)

The Quest for Dion Fortune, Janine Chapman (Weiser, 1993)

*20th Century Magic and the Old Religion: Dion Fortune, Christine Hartley,
    Charles Seymour*, Alan Richardson (Llewellyn, 1996)

The Avalonians [Dion Fortune, Fiona Macleod, Frederick Bligh Bond,
    Alice Buckton, Wellesley Tudor Pole, John Arthur Goodchild],
    Patrick Benham (Gothic Image, 2008)

*Showmen or Charlatans? The Stories of 'Dr' Walford Bodie and
    'Sir' Alexander Cannon*, Roger Woods and Brian Lead (Brian
    Lead, 2005)

Gerald Gardner: Witch, Jack Bracelin (Octagon, 1960) [Ghost-written by
    the prominent Sufi author Idries Shah]

Wiccan Roots: Gerald Gardner and the Modern Witchcraft Revival, Philip
    Heselton (Capall Bann, 2000)

Gerald Gardner and the Cauldron of Inspiration, Philip Heselton (Capall
    Bann, 2003)

Ithell Colquhoun: Pioneer Surrealist Artist, Occultist, Writer, and Poet, Eric
    Ratcliffe (Mandrake, 2007)

The Magical Writings of Ithell Colquhoun, Steve Nichols (Lulu, 2007)

Journeys of the Soul – The Life & Legacy of a Druid Chief [Ross Nichols],
    Philip Carr-Gomm (Thoth, 2009)

Diary of a Witch, Sybil Leek (Prentice Hall, 1968)

Writer on a Broomstick [Stewart Farrar], Elizabeth Guerra with Janet
    Farrar (R.J. Stewart Books, 2008)

Fire Child: The Life and Magick of Maxine Sanders, 'Witch Queen',
    Maxine Sanders (Mandrake, 2007)

The Old Sod – The Odd Life & Inner Work of William G. Gray, Alan
    Richardson & Marcus Claridge (Ignotus Press, 2003)

Painful but Fabulous: The Lives and Art of Genesis P. Orridge, ed. Genesis
    P. Orridge (Soft Skull, 2002)

An English Figure – Two Essays on the Work of John Michell, Laurel
    Schreiber and John Nicholson (Bozo, 1987)

✍ Occult London ✎

> *... he who cannot find wonder, mystery, awe, the sense*
> *of a new world and an undiscovered realm in the places*
> *by the Gray's Inn Road will never find those secrets*
> *elsewhere, not in the heart of Africa, not in the fabled*
> *hidden cities of Tibet.*

ARTHUR MACHEN, *THINGS NEAR AND FAR*

Of all the locations relevant to a study of the history of English magic, there is one that continually recurs as a place of importance: the capital city, London. Within a few square miles in the heart of London you can travel vast distances in time. By walking just over a mile from the British Museum to Treadwell's Bookshop in Covent Garden you can travel through over half a millennium of England's magical history, visiting sites frequented by over a dozen famous magicians of the past, and potentially encountering several living magicians too, browsing the shelves of bookshops or scrying in John Dee's obsidian mirror.

Start in the Enlightenment Gallery of the British Museum to marvel at the Dee artefacts, visit the Anglo-Saxon treasures and the Egyptian section that so inspired the founders of the Golden Dawn, and the Reading Room where they, along with Madame Blavatsky and scholars of Enochian magic, have pored over faded manuscripts and the diaries of John Dee. Then walk the few hundred yards to the Atlantis Bookshop in Museum Street, which first opened in 1922. Since that time, every magician of any importance has walked through its doors. It was here that the Order of the Hidden Masters gathered in the 1940s, here that Gerald Gardner's first novel on witchcraft was published, here that the old Chief Druid Ross Nichols helped to edit *The Occult Observer*, and here that an ex-lover of Aleister Crowley narrowly avoided an encounter with his nemesis the Great Beast.

Walking down Drury Lane leads you to Freemasons' Hall where

you can take a guided tour of the temple, visit the Masonic shop and go upstairs to visit the museum and library. In addition to the permanent exhibition, the museum features new exhibits: in 2008 on Women and Freemasonry, in 2009 on the Hermetic Order of the Golden Dawn. As you walk on, you soon come to Treadwell's, close to the site of William Stukeley's Masonic initiation and of John Denley's magical bookshop that inspired a generation of occultists in the eighteenth and nineteenth centuries, supplying Francis Barrett with the source texts for his 1801 *magnum opus The Magus*. You could then continue on to Watkin's, in Cecil Court off Charing Cross Road, which claims to be the world's oldest occult bookstore, founded in 1897.

Further afield sites of esoteric interest abound, such as Temple in the City and Primose Hill, site of Druid ceremonies to this day. And even further afield – all over the country – lie sites of magical significance awaiting exploration and discovery. To help you discover these places see:

Occult London, Merlin Coverley (Pocket Essentials, 2008)
Earthstars: London, City of Revelation, C.E. Street (Hermitage, 2001)
A Guide to Occult Britain, John Wilcock (Sphere, 1977)
The Traveller's Guide to Sacred England, John Michell (Gothic Image, 2003)
Mysterious Britain, Janet and Colin Bord (Granada, 1974)
The Secret Country – More Mysterious Britain, Janet and Colin Bord (Granada, 1978)
www.crossbones.org.uk to explore the mysteries of Southwark.

❧ On the Uses of Enchantment ❧

It is not less absurd, then strange, to see how some
Men . . . wil not forbeare to rank True Magicians with
Conjurors Necromancers, and Witches . . . who insolently
intrude themselves into Magick, as if Swine should enter
into a faire and delicate Garden, and, (being in league
with the Devill) make use of his assistance in their workes,
to counterfeit and corrupt the admirall wisdome of the
Magi betweene whom there is as large a difference as
between Angels and Devils.

ELIAS ASHMOLE, *THEATRUM CHEMICUM BRITANNICUM*

In this book we have surveyed the history of magic in England, but of what possible use is magic in this modern age? A poet or artist might say it is supremely necessary to give inspiration to the soul, a psychologist or philosopher might say that magic can provide meaning in a world that can try us all at times. Like Hermes, who is both messenger of the gods and patron of thieves, magic can be used to dazzle and seduce, to curse and summon demons, or it can be used to heal, to inspire, to acquire knowledge and to effect personal transformation.

Magic defies simple definition – for some it offers a means for changing consciousness, for others a way of accessing the spirit-world, to others still it offers ways of manipulating the circumstances of their lives or of opening themselves to a sense of awe and wonder. Though a concise definition may evade us, we can still list some of its most important uses:

For transforming the Self – which is the ultimate aim of High Magic and
   of Spiritual Alchemy.
For discovering one's true purpose in life – known in some magical systems
   as gaining the Knowledge and Conversation of one's Holy Guardian
   Angel, or one's Higher Self.
For the development of supercognition or Extra-Sensory Perception – in

other words the development of clairvoyance, clairaudience, and clairsentience through such methods as psychometry, dowsing, scrying, divination, or astral travel into the future, past or present.

For enhancing 'normal' cognitive functions – such as imagination, memory, intuition and perception.

For achieving altered states of consciousness – that engender feelings of bliss, ecstasy, joy and heightened powers of cognition.

For the development of virtues – such as wisdom and compassion.

For living longer, improving health, and enduring hardship, pain or illness – through developing equanimity cultivating the life-force, and enhancing perception and body awareness through methods such as meditation.

For engaging in scientific/Gnostic inquiry – to 'penetrate the Mysteries', to discover the nature of reality.

For learning how to 'fly/travel' – in astral travel with out-of-the-body journeys, through levitation, shamanic journeying, or lucid dreaming.

For finding things that are hidden – such as treasure, or the hidden causes of disease or misfortune (or anything) through dowsing, divination or ESP.

For communicating at a distance – in space or time and with those who have left this earth, through mediumship or ESP.

For Time Travel – through perfecting the ability to travel in the Otherworld.

For influencing events – through spellmaking, sympathetic magic or summoning spirits, often with the aim of engendering wealth, love or success.

For protection against misfortune – to repel the enemies of disease, ill-will, poverty, and war.

For inducing 'miracles' – since magicians claim that their practices increase the incidence of the fortunate and remarkable coincidences known as synchronicities.

For controlling and utilising the forces of nature – to help the magician or an entire community.

✿ General Resources ✿

The Book of English Magic web community at www.bookofenglishmagic.
com offers discussions, networking, news of events and courses,
videos and photo galleries.

The Society for the Academic Study of Magic is run by Dr Dave Green,
Deputy Director of the Unit for the Study of Religion and Spirituality
at the University of the West of England in Bristol. See www.sasm.
co.uk. The society's *Journal for the Academic Study of Magic* is
available from www.amazon.co.uk

The Exeter Centre for the Study of Esotericism led by Professor Nicholas
Goodrick-Clarke at Exeter University offers a part-time two-year
distance-learning MA course in Western esotericism. See www. huss.
exeter.ac.uk/research/exeseso

The Far Away Centre in the Lake District, run by graduate of the Exeter
Centre, Marcus Katz (MA in Western Esotericism) offers courses
in magic, ritual and witchcraft. Marcus also offers the 'Crucible
Programme' – a comprehensive distance-learning course in Western
esotericism and magic, and courses in the Kabbalah and Tarot, plus
individualised apprenticeships in magic that include regular contact
using skype video meetings. See www.farawaycentre.com and www.
tarotprofessionals.com

A training in psychology or psychotherapy that includes an
understanding of the human being from a spiritual perspective
can be invaluable when engaging in a study of magic. See The
Institute of Psychosynthesis at www.psychosynthesis.org, The
Psychosynthesis & Education Trust at www.psychosynthesis.edu,
Re-Vision Centre for Integrative Psychosynthesis at www.re-vision.
co.uk, and The Centre for Transpersonal Psychology at www.
transpersonalcentre.co.uk.

A magical training developed by Philip Carr-Gomm, grounded in both
psychological and esoteric understanding, with thousands of members
in England and around the world is offered by the Order of Bards,
Ovates and Druids. Lessons are sent as booklets or CDs monthly and
a team of fifty tutors, internet forums, a monthly journal, camps and

meetings are available as support. See www.druidry.org and www. philipcarrgomm.druidry.org

The Arcanorium College offers online training in magic. The college is divided into different departments, such as Magic, Design and Communication, Sorcery and Alternative Science, or Magical Literature and Arcane Arts. Tutored by Peter Carroll, Lionel Snell, Dave Lee and others. See www.arcanoriumcollege.com

The Cambridge Centre for Western Esotericism encourages dialogue between scholars and practitioners in the field of Western esotericism, and organises an annual conference in Cambridge. See www.ccwe.wordpress.com

The University of Kent offers an MA course in the Cultural Study of Cosmology and Divination. See www.kent.ac.uk/secl/thrs/postgraduate/cosmology

The European Society for the Study of Western Esotericism organises conferences and publishes books and monographs. See www.esswe.org

The Esoteric Conference & Occult Book Fair is held annually in the Assembly Rooms, Ludlow, Shropshire. Details from Verdelet @ P.O. Box 82, Craven Arms, Shropshire, SY7 8JW

The Ogdoadic Journal of the Western Mysteries is available online at www. astrumsophia.org

To explore the connections between stage magic and spiritual magic, see the work of Mark Townsend, author of *The Wizard's Gift* and *The Magician's Tale* (O Books, 2008). Mark is a magician who combines mind-bending stage magic with story-telling, mythology and a deep appreciation of the spiritual and magical. See www.magicofsoul.com

◉ *Bookshops*

Atlantis, 49a Museum Street, London WC1 www.theatlantisbookshop.com

Treadwell's, 34 Tavistock Street, Covent Garden, London WC2 www. treadwells-london.com

Watkins, 19 Cecil Court, Charing Cross Road, London, WC2 www. watkinsbooks.com

⊙ *Specialist Publishers and Online Bookshops*

Capall Bann Publishing www.capallbann.co.uk
Fulgur Limited www.fulgur.co.uk
Heart of Albion Press www.hoap.co.uk
Madragora www.mandrake-press.co.uk
Mandrake of Oxford www.mandrake.uk.net
Magis Books www.magisbooks.com
Rite Magic www.ritemagic.co.uk
Scarletimprint www.scarletimprint.com
Thoth Books www.thoth.co.uk
Wooden Books www.woodenbooks.com

~ Notes ~

CHAPTER ONE: ANCIENT ROOTS AND MAGIC WANDS

1. Paul Bahn, Francisco Muñoz, Paul Pettitt and Sergio Ripoll, 'New Discoveries of Cave Art in Church Hole (Creswell Crags, England)', *Antiquity*, Vol. 78, No. 300, June 2004.
2. See references to Stukeley in Ronald Hutton, *The Druids* (Hambledon Continuum, 2007).
3. See Stuart Piggott, *Ancient Britons and the Antiquarian Imagination* (Thames & Hudson, 1989) and *William Stukeley: An Eighteenth-Century Antiquary* (Thames & Hudson, 1985).
4. In the twelfth century, Geoffrey of Monmouth wrote that the stones of Stonehenge had healing properties and originated in Africa. Giants brought them to Ireland, and Merlin conveyed them magically from there to Salisbury Plain (see *History of the Kings of Britain*).
5. From 'Becoming a Ley Hunter' at www.leyhunter.com.

CHAPTER TWO: THE MAGICIANS ORGANISE THEMSELVES

1. This quotation and all other significant statements on the Druids by classical authors can be found in translation in John Matthews, *The Druid Source Book* (Blandford Press, 1996), pp. 15–25.
2. Albion is the oldest name for Britain, and although the Romans thought it referred to the white cliffs of Dover, believing the word originated from 'albus', the Latin for white, the name actually comes from a Celtic word meaning 'earth' or 'world', and referred to the whole island of Britain.
3. For a detailed discussion of the role of Bards, Ovates and Druids see Philip Carr-Gomm, *Druid Mysteries* (Rider, 2002), ch. 6.
4. Philip Carr-Gomm, *What Do Druids Believe?* (Granta, 2006), ch. 1.

CHAPTER THREE: STAR-CUNNING AND WYRD-CRAFT

1. Stephen Pollington, *An Introduction to the Old English Language and Its Literature* (Anglo-Saxon Books, 1996).

2. Brian Bates, *The Real Middle-Earth: Magic & Mystery in the Dark Ages* (Sidgwick & Jackson, 2002).

3. Bill Griffiths, *Aspects of Anglo-Saxon Magic* (Anglo-Saxon Books, 1996), p. 180.

4. Bates, *The Real Middle-Earth.*

5. For an orthodox translation and description of the Land Ceremonies Charm, see Griffiths, *Aspects of Anglo-Saxon Magic*; for a shamanic interpretation, see Bates, *The Real Middle-Earth.*

6. Ibid.

7. BL Royal MS 12 D.xvii, quoted in Griffiths, *Aspects of Anglo-Saxon Magic.*

8. Ibid.

9. From Alfred's translation of Boethius, quoted in Brian Branston, *The Lost Gods of England* (Thames & Hudson, 1957), p. 59.

10. Bob Oswald, *Discovering Runes* (Bookmart, 2008).

CHAPTER FOUR: THE MATTER OF BRITAIN

1. For the prophecies and a full discussion of their potential meanings, see R.J. Stewart, *The Prophetic Vision of Merlin* (Thoth, 1991).

2. Gerry Fenge, 'Tudor Pole's Grail: The True Story of the Cup and the Quest' (2006) at www.wellesleytudorpole.com.

3. Peter Dawkins, 'The Grail Land of Europe' at www.zoence.co.uk.

4. Janet and Stewart Farrar, *The Witches' Way: Principles, Rituals and Beliefs of Modern Witchcraft* (Robert Hale, 1984).

5. Ross Nichols, *The Book of Druidry* (Thorsons, 1992), p. 302.

6. Quoted in Trevor Ravenscroft, *The Spear of Destiny* (Red Wheel/ Weiser, 1983), p. 9.

CHAPTER FIVE: SKIN-TURNING AND SPELLCRAFT

1. Wayne Shumaker, *The Occult Sciences in the Renaissance: A Study in Intellectual Patterns* (University of California Press, 1972), p. 61.

2. See Swain's contribution in Robert Poole, ed., *The Lancashire Witches: Histories and Stories* (Manchester University Press, 2002).

3. See Geoffrey Scarre and John Callow, *Witchcraft and Magic in Sixteenth and Seventeenth Century Europe* (Palgrave Macmillan, 2001).

4. See Malcom Gaskill, *Witchfinders: A Seventeenth-century English Tragedy* (John Murray, 2006).

5. Ronald Hutton, *A Brief History of Britain 1483–1660* (Constable & Robinson, 2009); see also James Sharpe, *Instruments of Darkness: Witchcraft in England 1550–1750* (Hamish Hamilton, 1996).

6. Quoted in Shumaker, *The Occult Sciences in the Renaissance*.

7. See Hutton, *A Brief History of Britain*.

8. Justine Glass, *Witchcraft, the Sixth Sense and Us* (Neville Spearman, 1965).

9. *The Witch's Ballad* by Doreen Valiente, copyright John Belham-Payne; see also www.doreenvaliente.com.

10. Griffiths, *Aspects of Anglo-Saxon Magic*, p. 197.

11. Ibid., p. 200.

12. Ralph Merrifield, *The Archaeology of Ritual and Magic* (Batsford, 1987).

13. Robin Skelton, *Spellcraft* (Phoenix, 1998).

14. These two spells come from Robin Skelton, *The Practice of Witchcraft Today* (Citadel, 1994).

15. The most likely influence being Henri Gamache's *The Master Book of Candle Burning*, published in the USA in 1942. For comprehensive information on Hoodo see www.luckymojo.com.

16. The Builders of the Adytum was founded by the American author Paul Foster Case in the early twentieth century and offers distance learning in the Western Mystery Tradition focusing, in particular, on the Qabalah and Tarot. See www.bota.org.

CHAPTER SIX: TRANSMUTATION AND TRANSFORMATION

1. Cherry Gilchrist, *The Elements of Alchemy* (Element, 1991), p. 37.

2. Ripley's '*The Compound of Alchymy; or, the Twelve Gates leading to the Discovery of the Philosopher's Stone*' was dedicated to King Edward IV.

3. Eric John Holmyard, *Alchemy* (Penguin, 1968), p. 170.

4. Both quotations can be found in Dan Merkur, 'The Angelic Stone in English Alchemy', www.danmerkur.com/onlinewritings/Stone. PDF.

5. Ashmole's note reads: 'My [spiritual] father Backhouse lying sick

in Flettestreete over against St: Dunstans Church, and not knowing whether he should live or dye, about eleven a clock, told me in Silables the True Matter of the Philosophers Stone: which he bequeathed to me as a Legacy.' Quoted in Tobias Churton, *The Magus of Freemasonry: The Mysterious Life of Elias Ashmole – Scientist, Alchemist, and Founder of the Royal Society* (Inner Traditions, 2006), p. 162.

6. Hans Andréa, lists more similarities on his website www.harrypotterforseekers.com, writing that in the fifth Harry Potter book, *Harry Potter and the Order of the Phoenix*, 'there are even more similarities than in the other parts. For example both Harry and CRC (Christian Rosenkreutz) struggle with a dream of a door they can't open, and in both stories a dream is mentioned in which scissors play a role. Harry dreams of his two friends, Hermione and Ronald, wearing crowns. CRC sees the young king and queen, who are later reborn after the alchemical process, with a crown hanging over their heads. But the most remarkable coincidence of all is a secret room. In both stories there is a room that is always locked. In *The Alchemical Wedding*, CRC is told that this is the sepulchre of (sleeping) Venus. In *Harry Potter and the Order of the Phoenix* we are told that "There is a room . . . that . . . contains a force that is at once more wonderful and more terrible than death, than human intelligence, than the forces of nature . . . It is the power held within that room that you possess in such quantities and which Voldemort has not at all." This force is love, which is called Venus in *The Alchemical Wedding*.'

7. From Philip Pullman's website at www.philip-pullman.com.

8. From an interview with Jennie Renton, *Textualities*, 2005, at www.textualities.net/jennie-renton/philip-pullman-interview.

9. Ibid.

10. See 'Dear Soul, the Nature of Daemons: A Druid's Viewpoint' by Juliet Marillier, in *The World of the Golden Compass: The Otherworldly Ride Continues*, ed. Scott Westerfeld (Borders, 2007).

CHAPTER SEVEN: THE QUEEN'S ASTROLOGER

1. John Dee, 'Compendious Rehearsal' in Thomas Hearne, ed., *Johannis confratris & monarchi Glastoniensis, chronica, sive historia rebus Glastoniensis* (Oxford, 1726), p. 5.

2. *Acts of the Privy Council*, 1554–1556, n.s., V, 137. See also Peter J. French, *John Dee: The World of an Elizabethan Magus* (Routledge & Kegan Paul, 1972).

3. Suggested by Richard Deacon in *John Dee: Scientist, Geographer, Astrologer and Secret Agent to Elizabeth I* (Muller, 1968).

4. Benjamin Woolley, *The Queen's Conjuror: The Science and Magic of Dr Dee* (HarperCollins, 2001), p. 190.

5. For an account of Bruno's visit to England, see Frances A. Yates, *Giordano Bruno and the Hermetic Tradition* (Routledge & Kegan Paul, 1964).

6. Quoted in Woolley, *The Queen's Conjuror*, p. 291. Dee's wife gave birth to a boy in 1588, forty weeks almost to the day that she slept with Kelley.

7. Ibid., p. 306.

8. Stephen Skinner and David Rankine, *The Goetia of Dr Rudd: The Angels and Demons of Liber Malorum Spirituum Seu Goetia Lemegeton Clavicula Salomonis with a study of the techniques of evocation* (Golden Hoard Press, 2007).

9. Frances Yates, *The Rosicrucian Enlightenment* (Routledge, 2001).

10. The origin of the language remains a mystery. Dr Donald Laycock, a professor of linguistics at Canberra University, analysed Enochian and used it magically. His book *The Complete Enochian Dictionary* (Weiser, 2001) is the standard work on the language. In it he writes: 'I think that real angels would speak a more euphonious and more consistent tongue than Enochian.' Of the angels he once said that 'their limitations are those of Kelley; their occasional sublimities, those of Dee'. Stephen Skinner comments: 'His conclusion was that Enochian had the structure of a real language, its phonology and grammar are that of English, but the translation was so free that there was "not much to build a grammar on", so on balance it has the structure of a language, but there are not enough words to convincingly argue that it was a consistent language. However Laycock thought it unlikely that Kelley was smart enough to have made it up, and Dee certainly did not' (email to authors, 12 November 2008).

CHAPTER EIGHT: THE SHAG-HAIR'D WIZARD OF PEPPER ALLEY

1. John Gough Nichols, ed., *Narratives of the Days of the Reformation* (Camden Society, 1859), p. 334.

2. Marion Gibson, *Witchcraft and Society in England and America, 1550–1750* (Continuum, 2006), p. 195.

3. Melton, *Astrologaster*, pp. 21 and 47, quoted in Owen Davies *Cunning-Folk: Popular Magic in English History* (Hambledon & London, 2003), p. 68.

4. Ibid., p. vii.

5. This is presumed, since the wizard is noted for his shock of hair. We do know, however, that cunning-folk often made use of their appearance to impress their clients. Owen Davies in *Cunning-Folk*, p. 113, notes that 'One nineteenth-century Yorkshire wise-woman was described as having "some eye to stage effect, and possessed some stage properties". These included a stuffed and dried lizard, while papers and herbs were strung from the ceiling.'

6. From 'A Briefe Description of the Notorious Life of John Lambe', in C. L'Estrange Ewen, *Witchcraft and Demonism* (Kessinger, 2003), p. 203.

7. Keith Thomas, *Religion and the Decline of Magic* (Peregrine, 1973), p. 217.

8. Minor White Latham, *The Elizabethan Fairies* (Columbia University Press, 1930).

9. Emma Wilby, *Cunning Folk and Familiar Spirits: Shamanistic Visionary Traditions in Early Modern British Witchcraft and Magic* (Sussex Academic Press, 2005), p. 19.

10. Katharine Briggs, *The Vanishing People: A Study of Traditional Fairy Beliefs* (Batsford, 1978).

11. Barbara Rosen, *Witchcraft in England, 1558–1618* (University of Massachusetts Press, 1991), p. 43.

12. Wilby, *Cunning Folk and Familiar Spirits*, p. 247.

13. See Andy Letcher, *Shroom* (Faber & Faber, 2006).

14. Wilby, *Cunning Folk and Familiar Spirits*, p. 200.

15. Davies, *Cunning-Folk*, p. 195.

16. Ibid., p. 62.

17. Wilby, *Cunning Folk and Familiar Spirits*.

18. Keith Thomas, *Religion and the Decline of Magic* (Peregrine, 1973), p. 275.

19. Davies, *Cunning-Folk*, p. 103.

CHAPTER NINE: 'THE ENGLISH MERCURY LOVER'

1. In addition, according to Prof. Roland Rotherham, Dr Erasmus Darwin referred to Lichfield as the 'spiritual natal point of England', and more recently the magician Dion Fortune, the historian Geoffrey Ashe and the writer Alby Stone have all referred to Lichfield as spiritually significant (personal communication).

2. Venerable Bede, *An Ecclesiastical History of the English People*, p. 731.

3. Robert Plot, *The Natural History of Staffordshire*, 1686, ch. 8.

4. John Evelyn, BL MS.173f9.

5. Quoted in Churton, *The Magus of Freemasonry*, p. 108.

6. Anon. (personal communication to authors).

7. Valiente, *Charge of the Goddess*, p. 54.

8. Quoted in Churton, *The Magus of Freemasonry*, p. 147.

9. A poem on numbers sent to Noah Bridges, ibid., p. 162.

10. See Frances A. Yates, *The Art of Memory* (Pimlico, 1992). Delmonico created a 'Memory Theatre' – a wooden model which acted as a mnemonic device. Yates writes: 'Giulio Camillo, or Giulio Camillo Delminio to give him his full name, was one of the most famous men of the sixteenth century. He was one of those people whom their contemporaries regard with awe as having vast personalities. His Theatre was talked of in all Italy and France; its mysterious fame seemed to grow with the years.'

CHAPTER TEN: THE SPIRITS OF DEAD MAGICIANS

1. Ronald Hutton, *The Triumph of the Moon* (Oxford University Press, 1999), p. 59.

2. Ibid., p. 60.

3. 'It is true that the Prophet Joseph Smith was visited by many heavenly messengers who helped inaugurate this final dispensation. Heavenly beings came to Joseph Smith to bestow

priesthood keys, to unfold the majesty and glory of future events, and to warn or to admonish the maturing Prophet. Certainly to a remarkable degree the Prophet Joseph Smith received communication from an array of angels who helped prepare him to carry out his foreordained mission.' LDS Church Publication, *Ensign*, October 1994, p. 62.

4. See John L. Brooke, *The Refiner's Fire: The Making of Mormon Cosmology, 1644–1844* (Cambridge University Press, 1994); D. Michael Quinn, *Early Mormonism and the Magic World View* (Signature Books, 1998); Michael W. Homer, ' "Similarity of Priesthood in Masonry": The Relationship between Freemasonry and Mormonism', *Dialogue: A Journal of Mormon Thought*, 27, Fall 1994, 1–113.

5. Hutton, *The Triumph of the Moon*, p. 82.

6. The *Fama* can be read online at www.levity.com/alchemy/fama.html.

7. For a deeper exploration of the history of Rosicrucianism see Christopher McIntosh, *The Rosicrucians: The History, Mythology, and Rituals of an Occult Order* (Red Wheel/Weiser, 1997).

8. From 'Beyond our Ken: a review of "Against the Light: A Nightside Narrative" ' by Alan Moore, at www.fulgur.co.uk/authors/grant/articles/beyond-our-ken.

9. Frances Yates, in the *The Rosicrucian Enlightenment* (Routledge, 2001) believes Dee was influential, but more recent scholars, such as Carlos Gilly, working on the Early Rosicrucians Project at the Library of Hermetic Philosophy in Amsterdam, have challenged this theory. See www.ritmanlibrary.nl. see also Ron Heisler, *The Forgotten English Roots of Rosicrucianism*, The Hermetic Journal, 1992 and at www.levity.com/alchemy/h_ros.html.

10. De Quincey was not the only one to hold this view. Members of the Golden and Rosy Cross founded in Prague in the early eighteenth century taught that Rosicriucianism originated in Egypt, from whence it moved to Scotland, until it was resurrected as Freemasonry by Oliver Cromwell.

11. From the privately published rituals of the Fellowship of the Rosy Cross, printed by G. White, 396 King's Road, Chelsea, 1916. At the temple you were likely to have been amongst a preponderance of

women, and a smattering of Russian aristocrats. In a list of members
of the Fellowship, out of a total of 88, 63 were women; of 5 doctors
listed all were female; and 3 members of the Russian aristocracy
were noted: Count Alex Bobrinskoy, and the Princes Constantine
and Andrew Lubanoff-Rostovsky. (Philip Carr-Gomm. Private
Collection.)

12. A letter, dated 3 July 1870, to Hargrave Jennings, author of *The
Rosicrucians, Their Rites and Mysteries*, quoted in Lytton, *The Life of
Edward Bulwer, First Lord Lytton* (Macmillan, 1913), Vol. II, p. 42.

13. James Webb, *The Occult Underground* (Library Press, 1974), p. 83.

14. Ibid., p. 84.

15. Ibid., p. 7.

16. Francis X. King, *The Flying Sorcerer: Being the Magical and
Aeronautical Adventures of Francis Barrett, author of 'The Magus'*
(Mandrake Press, 1992).

17. Francis Barrett, *The Magus* (Helios Books, 1964).

18. King, *The Flying Sorcerer*, p. 41. For more on *The Magus* see Davies,
Cunning-Folk, pp. 142–3.

19. Quoted in Hutton, *The Triumph of the Moon*, p. 73.

20. C. Nelson Stewart, *Bulwer-Lytton as Occultist* (Kessinger, 1996), p. 36.

CHAPTER ELEVEN: OPENING PANDORA'S BOX

1. Aleister Crowley, *The Rites of Eleusis* (Mandrake Press, 1990), p. 26.

2. Since Crowley was subject to one of the first smear campaigns of the
British press, stories attributed to him need to be approached with
caution. However, even sympathetic biographies, such as Martin
Booth's *A Magick Life*, accept that he invoked demons, cursed his
lover Victor Neuberg and the magazine editor Horatio Bottomley,
showed no compunction in passing on venereal diseases, executed
and ate a frog, slit a goat's throat in a magical act of bestiality,
probably sacrificed a cat and ordered its blood to be drunk by an
initiate who died soon after, and wrote pro-German propaganda
from New York during the First World War that included justifying
the execution of the humanitarian nurse Edith Cavell and the
sinking of the *Lusitania*. Defenders of Crowley believe he may have
been a British spy, mocking the Germans by writing obviously

absurd articles; that the animal incidents were few and may have been exaggerated; that the initiate who died after supposedly drinking the cat's blood may have been infected from another source; and that in Crowley's day there was less knowledge about the dangers of drugs and sexually transmitted diseases. They also stress the fact that he acted like a scientist – diligently recording his experiments and experiences in the sincere desire to contribute to greater understanding.

3. In the first half of the twentieth century psychology influenced magic primarily through the work of Freud, Jung, and Reich. Freud's influence is explained in this chapter. Jung's influence lay in his theory of the Collective Unconscious and the power of the archetypes which helped magicians understand and explain many of the processes of magic. Reich's theory of Orgone energy appealed to those magicians interested in the life-force. In the second half of the century, the development of Transpersonal psychology effected a merging of much magical and psychological understanding. Pioneers in this field included Roberto Assagioli, founder of Psychosynthesis, who worked with the ideas of Alice Bailey, author of *A Treatise on White Magic* (Lucis, 1970) and Ian Gordon-Brown and Barbara Somers, founders of the Centre for Transpersonal Psychology in London in 1973.

4. The idea that the magician should seek to develop self-knowledge, strictly speaking, lies at the heart of 'High Magic', while in 'Low Magic' self-knowledge is not considered a prerequisite to the casting of spells or the attempt to effect change in the world, including healing.

5. See Letcher, *Shroom*.

6. Moriarty was always referred to as Dr Moriarty, but it seems he had no doctorate. Dion Fortune's biographer Alan Richardson, in *Priestess: The Life and Magic of Dion Fortune*, explains it thus: 'It is a common conceit of the magus to claim academic distinctions. He sees himself – and accurately – as far more intelligent than peers who have gained degrees by more orthodox means. He is aware that because of his own karmic propulsion through life the scholarly prizes were denied him. Sometimes, because of this, he feels that he

with his infinitely wider and more original knowledge, entirely self-taught, *should* be so distinguished. The line between *should* and *as if* becomes blurred; doctorates appear like invoked spirits.'

7. This quote is so vied for, three knights clash for the honour of saying it: Arnold Bax, Malcolm Sargent, and Thomas Beecham.

8. Magicians who incorporate an understanding of psychology into their work include Vivianne Crowley, Rufus Harrington and Marcus Katz. Those with a more traditional view include Alan Richardson, who in his biography of Dion Fortune suggests she made an awful mistake in studying psychology, and Emma Restall-Orr who writes in *Living Druidry: Magical Spirituality for the Wild Soul* (Piatkus, 2004), p. 55, that 'It could be said that psychiatry and psychology . . . have been more damaging to Paganism than any monotheism over the past century.'

9. Stephen Fry blog entry 6 December 2008 at www.stephenfry.com.

10. Ramsey Dukes, *What I Did in My Holidays: Essays on Black Magic, Satanism, Devil Worship and Other Niceties* (Mandrake, 1998), p. 409.

11. See 'Fictitious Tibet: The Origin and Persistence of Rampaism, Agehananda Bharati', Tibet Society Bulletin, Vol. 7, 1974, and at www.dc-international.org. Enthusiasts of Lobsang Rampa will prefer to explore *T. Lobsang Rampa – New Age Trailblazer*, Karen Mutton (TGS, 2006) and www.lobsangrampa.net.

12. Credit for first bringing the teachings of Tantrism to the West, through his translations, must go to Sir John Woodroffe (1865–1936), who wrote under the name of Arthur Avalon. Crowley, Fortune and Gardner are most likely to have studied his work, including *The Serpent Power: The Secrets of Tantric and Shaktic Yoga*, published in 1918.

13. See www.time.com/time/magazine/article/0,9171,847772,00.html. For the full story of Cannon, see Roger Woods and Brian Lead, *Showmen or Charlatans? The Stories of Dr Walford Bodie and Sir Alexander Cannon* (Brian Lead, 2005).

14. All the cards shown in this section are from *The Sharman-Caselli Tarot Deck* by Juliet Sharman-Burke, published by Connections Book Publishing, www.connections-publishing.com. Card images copyright © Giovanni Caselli.

15. The Tarot may have been influenced by early traditions of magic and philosophy coming from ancient Egypt and Greece, but it only emerged historically in fifteenth-century Renaissance Italy.

CHAPTER 12: THE WIZARDS' RETURN

1. See www.spielplatzoasis.co.uk. Later both Gardner and Nichols transferred their allegiances to the nearby Five Acres resort (see www.fiveacrescountryclub.com). Naturism was an idea that evolved in the 1920s as part of the process of the freeing of individuals from outmoded social restrictions that had started to occur following the First World War. It was all part of the move 'back to nature', in which people sought to escape from the horrors of war, the alienation of city life and rampant industrialisation. They did not want anything, not even clothes, between them and the elemental forces of nature – water, air and sunlight.

2. Ross Nichols and James Kirkup, *The Cosmic Shape* (Forge Press, 1946).

3. In 1977 *Gay News* published Kirkup's poem 'The Love that Dares to Speak its Name', about a Roman centurion's supposed love for Christ on the cross. Kirkup and the newspaper's editor were successfully prosecuted for blasphemy by Mary Whitehouse, then secretary of the National Viewers' and Listeners' Association. In speaking of the case, Lord Scarman said: 'The offence [of blasphemy] belongs to a group of criminal offences designed to safeguard the internal tranquillity of the kingdom.'

4. Tolkien also wanted to create such a mythology. 'The Land of the White Bull' was never published and the manuscript has been lost. Portions found their way into Ross Nichols' book *The Book of Druidry* (Aquarian, 1990). See Philip Carr-Gomm, *Journeys of the Soul: The Life and Legacy of a Druid Chief* (Thoth, 2009).

5. See Joscelyn Godwin, *The Theosophical Enlightenment* (State University of New York Press, 1994).

6. For the most thorough historical treatment of this subject, see Ronald Hutton, *Stations of the Sun: A History of the Ritual Year in Britain* (Oxford Paperbacks, 2001).

7. Nichols, along with fellow naturist George Bernard Shaw, admired

the doctrines of the ascetic Jains, and believed that Druidism may have shared a common origin. Gardner made use of the Jain term 'skyclad' for his version of witchcraft, Wicca.

8. In fact it was not until the 1980s that either tradition began to be considered as forms of 'Earth religion' or 'Nature spirituality' – as they are today.

9. Speech to the North American Conference on Religion and Ecology in Washington, 18 May 1990.

10. This view, although prevalent, is now considered by most historians as simplistic, belying the complex set of issues that led to the triumph of the Roman Church in Britain.

11. Sarah Whittaker, 'The Whitby Conclave' in *The Philosopher's Stone*, 1994, at www.the-philosophers-stone.com/articles/whitby/whitby.htm.

12. The author probably means 'junk metal sculptor' rather than a junkie who is a sculptor, but who knows when anything goes? From http://www.ain23.com/topy.net/ultimate_weapon.html.

13. The motto is known as 'The Four Powers of the Sphinx' and is first mentioned in Eliphas Lévi's *Transcendental Magic* (Red Wheel/Weiser, 1968). In his final work, *The Great Secret* (Red Wheel/Weiser, 2000), Lévi says: 'The great secret of magic, the unique and incommunicable Arcana, has for its purpose the placing of supernatural power at the service of the human will in some way. To attain such an achievement it is necessary to KNOW what has to be done, to WILL what is required, to DARE what must be attempted and to KEEP SILENT with discernment.'

14. Paul Geheimnis, *Chaos International*, No. 15.

15. *Chaos International*, No.17, quoted at www.thebaptistshead.co.uk.

16. This quote is attributed to Hassan-i Sabbah and was used by Friedrich Nietzsche in his *Thus Spoke Zarathustra*.

17. Extending this gross generalisation, we could add that New Agers particularly like synthesiser music. A similar generalisation could be suggested in terms of visual aesthetics, expressed negatively as most Thelemites, magicians and pagans finding New Age art worryingly flaccid, New Agers finding pagan art coarse and kitsch, while pagans and New Agers alike find Thelemite and Chaos imagery vulgar and slightly sinister.

18. Whether Freemasonry originated in England or Scotland is a
    remarkably complex question. David Stevenson's book *The
    Origins of Freemasonry: Scotland's Century, 1590–1710* (Cambridge
    University Press, 1990) makes a good case for the theory that the
    first steps of the process that turned stonemasons' guilds into the
    speculative Craft took place in Scotland, but this is challenged in
    Tobias Churton's *Freemasonry: The Reality* (Lewis Masonic, 2007).
    'Whether or not the initial steps occurred in Scotland, the rest of the
    process that gave birth to the speculative Craft unquestionably took
    place in England; the Craft as it exists today has been powerfully
    shaped by English culture; and England was the centre from which
    Masonry spread to the rest of the world' (J.M. Greer, personal
    communication to authors).

19. Luke Rhinehart, *The Dice Man* (HarperCollins, 1999) and *The
    Search for the Dice Man* (HarperCollins, 1999); see also www.
    lukerhinehart.net.

ᴗᴥ Acknowledgements ᴥᴗ

To survey such a wide spectrum of beliefs, practice and history the authors consulted and interviewed numerous friends, colleagues and specialists. Heartfelt thanks for their contributions go to Professor Ronald Hutton, Marcus Katz, Dr Christopher MacIntosh, John Michael Greer, Dr Christina Oakley-Harrington, Geraldine Baskin, Louise Hodgson, Lionel Snell, Mike Howard, Phil and Carol Rickman, Philip Heselton, L.R. Fredericks, John Michell, Peter Taylor, Ivan McBeth, Patrick MacManaway, Hamish and Ba Miller, Caitlin Matthews, Adrian Rooke, Peter Aziz, Dr Andrew Stirling, Dr Brian Bates, Bob Oswald, Bob Ronald, Lord Northampton, Michael Poynder, Nigel Pennick, John Matthews, Prof. Roland Rotherham, Dr Vivianne Crowley, Maxine Sanders, Marina Baker, Julian Vayne, Patrick Harpur, Dr Geo Trevarthen, Hans Andrea, Gary Nottingham, Sarah Fuhro, Rufus Harrington, Stephen Skinner, Robin Cousins, Cassandra Latham, Phil Kane, Rufus Harrington, David Conway, Jake Stratton-Kent and Mischa, Terence Duquesne, Mark Townsend, Alan Richardson, Jon Sandifer, the Custodian of the Steyning Museum, Sir John Scudamore, Phil Kane, Lyn Guest De Swarte, Cathy Gibb, John, Keith and Liz from Wolfshead Vixen Morris, Keith Hall from the Spiritualist Association of Great Britain, Lorrie and Eugene O'Connor, Mike Crowson, Julia Phillips, Alfred Douglas, Rick Hayward, Peregrin Wildoak, 'A Golden Dawner', 'An Anonymous Alchemist', 'Garry' who was haunted by John Dee, Anne, the 'Monkey Lady' and her partner, Mike, with a Demon on his shoulder. In addition, we would like to thank all the English magicians in the 'other reality' who have helped us resolve points of difference between the authors, identify true adepts and recognise real magic. As is the way with such folk, they prefer to keep their names secret.

Our grateful thanks also go to Kate Parkin, Amanda Jones, Celia Levett, Victoria Murray-Browne, Caro Westmore, and the rest of

the team at John Murray. We would also like to thank in particular
Penny Billington, who compiled most of the fiction recommenda-
tions and wrote many of the descriptions of those books, as well
as compiling much of the list of biographical and autobiographical
works listed in the Appendix.

✎ Picture Acknowledgments ✎

Most of the pictures are from the authors' collections.

Additional sources: Arthur Findlay College 423. The Barge Inn
45. Corbis 55, 90. Cresswell Heritage Trust 12. Kim Dent-Brown
205. Jeanette Ellis 184. Mary Evans Picture Library 409. Fortean
Picture Library 60, 61. Getty Images 314. John Goodall 209. John
Hooper/Hoopix™ 201. John Michell 23. Museum of Witchcraft
327. Courtesy of the President, Fellows and Scholars of Queens'
College, Cambridge 137. Private Collection/Bridgeman Art
Library 211. V&A Images, Victoria and Albert Museum 344,
349. Wellcome Library London 405. Will Worthington 231.
Zéfiro 169.

~ Index ~

Numerals in italics denote illustrations.